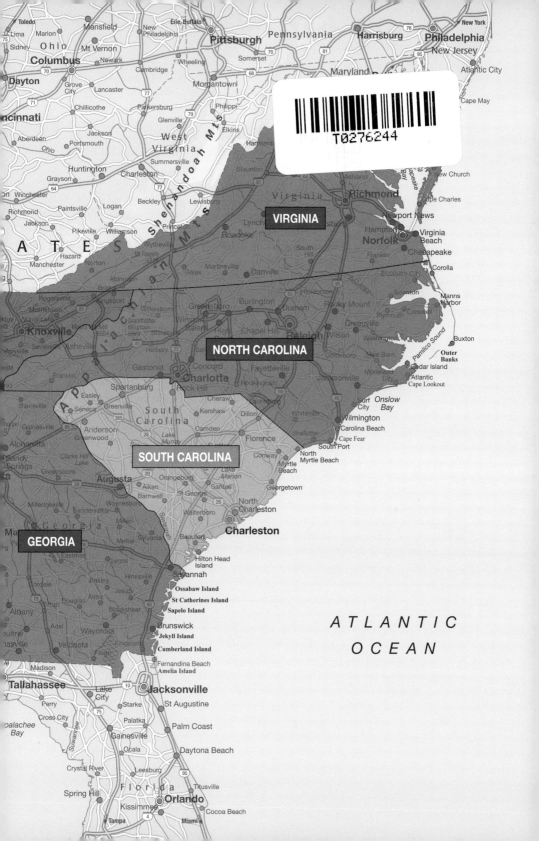

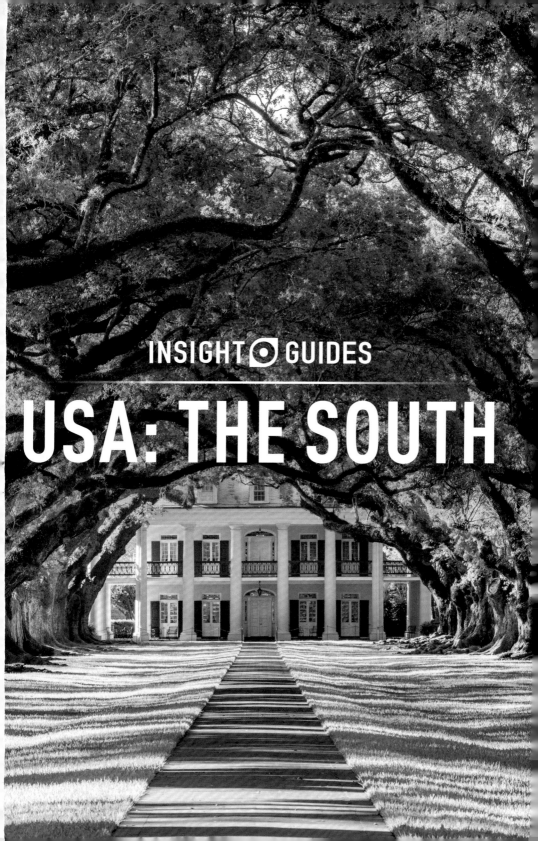

INSIGHT ⦿ GUIDES

USA: THE SOUTH

PLAN & BOOK
YOUR TAILOR-MADE TRIP

BRAZIL

CHILE

ECUADOR

TAILOR-MADE TRIPS & UNIQUE EXPERIENCES CREATED BY LOCAL TRAVEL EXPERTS AT INSIGHTGUIDES.COM/HOLIDAYS

Insight Guides has been inspiring travellers with high-quality travel content for over 45 years. As well as our popular guidebooks, we now offer the opportunity to book tailor-made private trips completely personalised to your needs and interests. By connecting with one of our local experts, you will directly benefit from their expertise and local know-how, helping you create memories that will last a lifetime.

HOW INSIGHTGUIDES.COM/HOLIDAYS WORKS

STEP 1

Pick your dream destination and submit an enquiry, or modify an existing itinerary if you prefer.

STEP 2

Fill in a short form, sharing details of your travel plans and preferences with a local expert.

STEP 3

Your local expert will create your personalised itinerary, which you can amend until you are completely satisfied.

STEP 4

Book securely online. Pack your bags and enjoy your holiday! Your local expert will be available to answer questions during your trip.

BENEFITS OF PLANNING & BOOKING AT INSIGHTGUIDES.COM/HOLIDAYS

PLANNED BY LOCAL EXPERTS

The Insight Guides local experts are hand-picked, based on their experience in the travel industry and their impeccable standards of customer service.

SAVE TIME & MONEY

When a local expert plans your trip, you save time and money when you book, even during high season. You won't be charged for using a credit card either.

TAILOR-MADE TRIPS

Book with Insight Guides, and you will be in complete control of the planning process, from the initial selections to amending your final itinerary.

BOOK & TRAVEL STRESS-FREE

Enjoy stress-free travel when you use the Insight Guides secure online booking platform. All bookings come with a money-back guarantee.

WHAT OTHER TRAVELLERS THINK ABOUT TRIPS BOOKED AT INSIGHTGUIDES.COM/HOLIDAYS

Trip to Portugal

Every step of the planning process and the trip itself was effortless and exceptional. Our special interests, preferences and requests were accommodated resulting in a trip that exceeded our expectations.

Corinne, USA   ★★★★★

Trip to Vietnam

The organization was superb, the drivers professional, and accommodation quite comfortable. I was well taken care of! My thanks to your colleagues who helped make my trip to Vietnam such a great experience. My only regret is that I couldn't spend more time in the country.

Heather   ★★★★★

DON'T MISS OUT
BOOK NOW AT
INSIGHTGUIDES.COM/HOLIDAYS

CONTENTS

Travel tips

TRANSPORTATION

A – Z

FURTHER READING

Maps

Inside front cover USA: The South
Inside back cover National Parks, Reserves
  and Monuments

LEGEND

🔍 Insight on
📷 Photo story

THE BEST OF THE SOUTHERN STATES: TOP ATTRACTIONS

△ **US Space and Rocket Center Museum**. With one of the largest collections of space rockets on planet earth, this Huntsville museum is a guaranteed hit for science enthusiasts and kids who want to grow up to be astronauts. See page 143.

△ **World of Coca-Cola**. It's the world's most popular and successful soft drink, so it stands to reason Coca-Cola is celebrated in its home city of Atlanta, with 20 acres (8 hectares) of exhibits, and taste tests. See page 115.

▽ **The Sixteenth Street Baptist Church**. The 1963 bombing of this church in Birmingham Alabama, was a pivotal moment in the Civil Rights Movement. Travelers from the world over pay their respects here. See page 138.

△ **The Robert Johnson Crossroads**. Legend has it that superstar of blues Robert Johnson owes his success to a deal he made with the devil at these very crossroads in Clarksdale, Mississippi. See page 169.

△ **New Orleans's French Quarter**. It's the heart of New Orleans and the epicenter of the now infamous Mardi Gras. Bourbon Street is the backbone of the quarter with 24/7 jazz clubs, Cajun culinary fare, and drinks so strong they'll knock your socks off. See page 188.

△ **Central High School**. It was here at this unsuspecting high school in Little Rock, Arkansas, that forced school desegregation happened in 1957, pitting federal and state troops against each other in the process. See page 213.

△ **Beale Street**. For a real taste of Memphis music and lifestyle, head to the world famous Beale Street. The annual music festival in May spans three days and is worth every cent. See page 224.

△ **The Spoleto Festival**. The best introduction to Charleston, South Carolina is the city's annual performing arts festival, when many of the city's most beautiful venues throw open their doors to host the 17-day extravaganza. See page 243.

△ **The Great Smoky Mountains Railroad**. The best way to see the Great Smoky Mountains of North Carolina is in style with a cocktail in hand, on board America's answer to the Orient Express. See page 279.

▽ **Shenandoah Caverns**. One of Virginia's lesser-known natural wonders, these caverns have to be seen to be believed, with rock formations that naturally resemble bacon, right down to the trim of fat. See page 294.

THE BEST OF THE SOUTHERN STATES: EDITOR'S CHOICE

Picnic area in the Great Smoky Mountains National Park in Tennessee.

BEST FOR FAMILIES

Georgia Aquarium. Home to thousands of animals, this huge aquarium is an all-round family treat, teaching conservation and preservation. See page 115.

US Space& Rocket Center. Home to one of the largest collections of rockets that have been put into orbit, including the Space Shuttle Pathfinder, this showcase of space travel is educational for all ages. See page 143.

National Museum of Naval Aviation. It's the world's largest naval aviation museum and certainly the most impressive, featuring 3700 aircraft, including a selection of today's most advanced fighter jets. See page 178.

Graceland. No visit to Tennessee would be complete without a trip to Elvis's palace, not to mention his collection of private jets and Cadillac cars. See page 226.

Chattanooga Choo Choo Train Station. Not just the subject of the famous song, the Chattanooga Choo Choo is a fun family treat, plus you can stay in the railcars of yesteryear, now converted into hotel rooms. See page 229.

Graceland, Memphis.

BEST SCENERY

Bankhead National Forest. Considered to be the jewel in Alabama's crown, the forest spans almost 200,000 acres (80,937 hectares) and is a much-cherished conservation area. See page 142

Tishomingo State Park. There aren't many places that are as visually stunning as the Tishomingo State Park, found in the foothills of Mississippi's Appalachian Mountains. See page 163.

Eureka Springs. Hidden away in the Ozark Mountains of northern Arkansas, the Eureka Springs mix healing waters with views reminiscent of Italy's Lake Como. See page 218.

Rock City Gardens. From this mountaintop lookout, a short drive from Chattanooga in Tennessee, you can see seven different states and a good deal of wildlife too. See page 228.

Great Smoky Mountains. Separating North Carolina from Tennessee, this mountain range is famous the world over for spectacular sunsets, complete with Hollywood movie style mist. See page 228.

Table Rock State Park. One of South Carolina's most picturesque landmarks, the park gets its name from the distinctive round dome of Table Rock Mountain. See page 254.

The Big South Fork.

BEST HISTORIC SITES

The Sixteenth St Baptist Church. This flashpoint in the Civil Rights Movement is where the bomb detonated in 1963, killed four young girls and ignited national outrage. See page 138.

The Windsor Plantation Ruins. All that's left of the plantation today is an eerie collection of 23 Corinthian columns, highlighting the huge scale of slavery in Mississippi's past. See page 161.

St Louis Cemetery No. 1. The most famous cemetery in New Orleans is home to the tomb of voodoo legend, Marie Laveau among many others. See page 196.

Crater of Diamonds State Park. The only place in the world where the public can sift through volcanic remains in search of diamonds. Better yet, you get to keep what you find. See page 216.

National Civil Rights Museum. Built around the motel where Martin Luther King was assassinated, the museum is a poignant but important reminder of the human cost in the Civil Rights Movement. See page 225.

USS North Carolina. Permanently moored in her namesake state, this World War II Battleship is now a fascinating museum, detailing the history of the US Navy's most decorated vessel. See page 271.

Windsor Plantation.

BEST MUSEUMS AND GALLERIES

The Margaret Mitchell House and Museum. The author of *Gone with the Wind* deemed this home to be a dump, but it's certainly worth a stop if you're in Atlanta. See page 118.

The Birmingham Civil Rights Institute. As one of the largest museums of its kind, the Birmingham Civil Rights Museum thoughtfully conveys the struggles of the Civil Rights Movement in Alabama. See page 138.

The John C. Stennis Space Center. Better known as NASA's rocket testing center, the tours here are a wonder to behold, as is the scale of this extra-terrestrial travel research facility. See page 183.

Voodoo Museum. You'll find this intricate catalogue of all things Voodoo in the French Quarter of New Orleans, sandwiched between Bourbon and Royal Streets. See page 195.

Clinton Presidential Center. This presidential center, library, and park honors the 42nd US President in his hometown of Little Rock, Arkansas. See page 212.

Levine Museum of the New South. Profiling life in the South after the end of the Civil War, the Levine Museum is unmatched in its breadth of content – thoughtfully and interactively laid out. See page 267.

Virginia Museum of Fine Arts. No trip to Richmond, Virginia would be complete without a visit to the wonderful, and free, exhibits contained within the walls of the Virginia Museum of Fine Arts. See page 287.

BEST WILDLIFE VIEWING

The Chattahoochee River National Recreation Area. The variety of wildlife here is astounding, and you're likely to see the famed Bald Eagle. See page 122.

Oak Mountain State Park. Renowned for its many waterfalls, this park due south of Birmingham, Alabama, has a vast variety of flora and fauna. See page 138.

Lake Ouachita. This lake was created when the US Army Corps built the nearby Blakely Mountain Dam. A prime directive in the dam's creation was wildlife conservation, and to create new habitats. See page 215.

Big South Fork. Spanning a massive stretch of the Cumberland River, the Big South Fork National River and Recreation Area is a haven for wildlife. See page 231.

Myrtle Beach. This area of the South Carolina coast is one of the few safe places left for the endangered sea turtles, which arrive en masse each spring to lay their eggs. See page 261.

Cotton fields near Clarksdale, Mississippi.

American alligator in Georgia.

River barge on the water near
Little Rock, Arkansas.

Neon signs and clubs along Broadway Street, Nashville, Tennessee.

SOUTHERN ASPIRATIONS

The romance of the South has not gone with the wind – instead, there's a fresh breeze of creativity blowing.

Gulf coast sunset

The South may be the last undiscovered place in the United States. Established images of the South, romantic as they are Gothic, are out of date. Estate homes, riverboat gambling and gator-filled swamps are still there, of course, but there is an air of optimism, a very American spirit of reinvention.

Research and technology thrive in North Carolina's Raleigh-Durham Triangle, and the medical community at Birmingham, Alabama, is recognized worldwide for its contributions to healthcare. The Right Stuff pumps hard around the jet-jockeys of the world's biggest air force base at Eglin in Florida, as well as the space and rocket centers at Huntsville, Alabama, and Stennis in Mississippi.

The South has always been a hothouse of creativity. Many of the rhythms and syncopations of the 20th century came from the South; the blues, rock'n'roll, country & western, and jazz were all born under Southern stars. Musicians like Blake Shelton and Taylor Swift carry that light aloft today. Writers like John Grisham and Donna Tartt follow literary paths mapped out by William Faulkner and Eudora Welty.

Southern sporting meccas range from the world's oldest baseball stadium at Rickwood Field in Birmingham, Alabama, across the fairwways of some of *Golf Digest's* best "Little Golf Towns in the US" on the Gulf Coast, to the Masters Tournament course in Augusta, Georgia. The Atlanta Braves are a team to beat – if anyone can.

The most coveted homebases for the well-to-do movers and shakers in Washington, DC are all in Virginia, and places like Savannah, Georgia and Hot Springs, Arkansas, and the Azalea coast of Alabama feature regularly on lists of America's most desirable places to live. The history and the heritage, the culture and the celebrations, the achievements and the aspirations, are all reasons to visit the South.

⊘ A NOTE TO READERS

At Insight Guides, we always strive to bring you the most up-to-date information. This book was produced during a period of continuing uncertainty caused by the Covid-19 pandemic, so please note that content is more subject to change than usual. We recommend checking the latest restrictions and official guidance.

The Cotton Wagon, painted by William Aiken Walker in 1888.

DECISIVE DATES

600–1500 AD
Ancestors of Native Americans settle at what is now Toltec Mounds State Park, 10 miles (16km) east of Little Rock, Arkansas.

1541
Spanish explorer Hernando de Soto, traveling cross-country from present-day Florida, becomes the first European to see the Mississippi River.

1587
Nearly 150 pioneers sent from England by Sir Walter Raleigh settle on Roanoke Island, Virginia, but are never seen again.

1607
Establishment of Jamestown, Virginia, by British explorers and settlers.

Jamestown, Virginia, c.1615.

1619
The first enslaved people arrive in Jamestown, Virginia.

1670
A prosperous city south of Virginia in the Carolinas is established, called Charles Towne (present-day Charleston).

1702
Two French-Canadian brothers establish Fort Louis de la Mobile (present-day Mobile).

1733
James Oglethorpe receives a royal charter to establish the colony of Georgia near present-day Savannah.

1763
The first Acadians move from Nova Scotia to the swamps of Louisiana.

Surrender of Cornwallis at Yorktown, October 1781.

1768
Charlotte, North Carolina, is named after the wife of King George Ill, the British monarch.

1781
The Revolutionary War with Britain ends on the Yorktown Peninsula in Virginia.

1789–1825
Four of the first five elected presidents are from Virginia: George Washington, Thomas Jefferson, James Madison, and James Monroe.

1793
Eli Whitney invents the cotton gin, vastly increasing profits and productivity.

1803
President Thomas Jefferson concludes the Louisiana Purchase with France's Napoleon, which doubles the size of the nation.

1815
Americans fight the British in the Battle of New Orleans in the War of 1812.

1817
Mississippi becomes the 20th US state.

1819
Congress creates the Arkansas Territory.

1820
The combined population of the lands known as "the South" is 4.3 million; 1.5 million are enslaved people. The Missouri Compromise raises the political profile of the issue of slavery.

The siege and capture of Vicksburg in 1863.

1836
Arkansas becomes a US state.

1837
Atlanta (then called Terminus) is established at an intersection of three Georgia roads.

1846
Baton Rogue is named the state capital of Louisiana.

1852
Harriet Beecher Stowe publishes the influential but inflammatory novel Uncle Tom's Cabin.

1857
The Dred Scott court case decides that Mr Scott, a Black man, is not a citizen and cannot sue for his freedom.

1860
Abraham Lincoln is elected president; South Carolina secedes from the union.

1861
The Confederate States of America is formed with Jefferson Davis as president; the opening shots of the Civil War are fired at Fort Sumter, South Carolina.

The first reading of the Emancipation Proclamation in 1863.

1862
Lincoln's Emancipation Proclamation is a symbolic landmark for Southern Black people.

1863
Vicksburg, Mississippi falls to the Union after a 47-day siege, giving them access to the river.

1864
Rebel victory over Richmond, Virginia, but General William T. Sherman's siege of Atlanta is followed by a march across Georgia, plundering everything.

1865
General Robert E. Lee surrenders to Ulysses S. Grant at Appomatox, Virginia. A few days later, Lincoln is assassinated in Washington, DC.

1865–1879
The Reconstruction era.

1886
Coca-Cola is brewed by an Atlanta druggist.

1895
Booker T. Washington becomes a major spokesman for Black Southerners.

Booker T. Washington.

1915
McKinley Morganfield (Muddy Waters) is born in the small town of Rolling Fork, Mississippi.

1925
40,000 robed KKK members march on Washington, DC. The Grand Ole Opry starts broadcasting in Nashville, Tennessee. The "Scopes Monkey Trial" begins, originally as a test case against Tennessee state law forbidding the teaching of the theory of evolution in public schools.

1925–35
Southern literature garners high acclaim with writers like Eudora Welty, Robert Penn Warren, and Katherine Anne Porter.

1933
President Franklin D. Roosevelt signs the TVA Act, helping to transform a poverty-stricken Tennessee area into a forward-looking community.

1934
Great Smoky Mountains National Park is created, straddling Tennessee and North Carolina.

1935
Elvis Presley is born in Tupelo, Mississippi; his family later moves to Memphis, Tennessee.

1936
Publication of the book *Gone with the Wind*; three years later the movie wins eight Academy Awards.

1941
Delta Air Lines moves to Atlanta.

1948
Tennessee Williams is awarded the Pulitzer Prize for A Streetcar Named Desire.

1950
Author William Faulkner is awarded the Nobel Prize for Literature.

1955
The Montgomery, Alabama, bus boycott serves as a model for Black protest movements around the South.

1957
Attempts to integrate a Little Rock high school are met by a jeering mob and the Arkansas National Guard, requiring the intervention of troops acting on orders given by the US president.

1960
A sit-in by four Black college students at a Woolworths lunch counter in Greensboro, North Carolina, is a significant turning point in the Civil Rights movement.

1961
"Freedom Rides" throughout the South organized by Northern activists highlight segregated transportation facilities.

1963
Protests in Birmingham, Alabama, and other Southern cities result in a massive march on Washington, DC, where the Rev. Martin Luther King, Jr gives his "I Have a Dream" speech.

1964
President John F. Kennedy passes the Civil Rights Act.

1965
The Alabama Selma-to-Montgomery march is one of the decisive demonstrations in the Southern struggle for civil rights.

1968
Martin Luther King, Jr is assassinated at the Lorraine Motel in Memphis, Tennessee.

Martin Luther King Jr on the march to Washington, August 1963.

Bill Clinton and Al Gore on their successful election night in 1992.

1976
James Earl Carter, governor of Georgia, is elected president of the United States.

1980
Ted Turner establishes Cable Network News, based out of Atlanta.

1986
The King Biscuit Blues Festival begins in Helena, Arkansas.

1991
The Louisiana state legislature legalizes riverboat gambling on the Mississippi River; a year later the state of Mississippi does the same.

1992
Bill Clinton, the governor of Arkansas, is elected to the presidency, with Al Gore, a senator from Tennessee, as vice-president, the first "double-South" ticket since 1860.

1996
The Olympic Games are held in Atlanta. A bomb explodes in Centennial Olympic Park, killing one bystander and injuring 111 others.

2003
Hurricane Isobel hits the Outer Banks, NC.

2005
Hurricane Katrina devastates New Orleans, killing nearly 1,500 people.

2008
Barrack Obama wins the swing state of Florida and is elected the 44th President of the United States.

2010
The Deepwater Horizon oil rig explodes in the Gulf of Mexico, causing the largest environmental disaster in US history.

2011
The final Space Shuttle mission launches from NASA's Kennedy Space Center.

2015
Gay marriage is legalized across the Southern states and all of America in a US Supreme Court ruling.

2017
White supremacists march in Charlottesville.

2018
Hurricane Michael brings destruction to the Florida Panhandle and carves a devastating path through the South.

2019
Atlanta hosts the Super Bowl for the first time since 2000.

2020
Covid-19 spreads throughout the Southern states.

2021
In Florida, a 12-story condominium partially collapses, killing 98 of its residents.

2022
International African American Museum opens in Charleston.

The devastation wreaked by Hurricane Katrina in 2005.

I.
Bon der Ankunfft der Engelländer
in Virginia.

SECOTAN

Pasquenoke

Dasamonquepeuc

WEAPEMEOC

Roanoac

Trinety harbor

Hatorasck

T. B.   2

Je Port oder Meerhafen der Landschaffte Virginia ist voll Inseln/ die da verursachen/ daß man gar beschwerlichen in dieselben kommen kan. Daß wiewol sie an vielen orten weit von einander gescheiden sind/ vnd sich ansehen lässet/ als solte man dadurch leichtlich können hinein kommen/ so haben wir dannoch mit vnserm grossen Schaden erfahren/ daß dieselben offne Plätz voll Sandes sind. Deßwegen haben wir niemals können hinein kommen/ biß so lang wir an vielen vnd mancherley örtern mit einem kleinen Schiff die Sach versucht haben. Zuletzt haben wir einen Paß gefunden/ auff einem sonderlichen ort/ der vnsern Engelländern wol bekañt ist. Als wir nun hinein kommen/ vnnd eine zeitlang darinn ohn vnterlaß geschifft hatten/ sind wir eines grossen fliessenden Wassers gewar worden/ dessen Außgang gegen den Inseln/ von welcher wir gesagt haben/ sich erstrecket. Dieweil aber der Inngang zu demselbigen Wasser deß Sandes halben zu klein war/ haben wir denselben verlassen/ vnd seyn weiter fort geschifft/ biß daß wir an eine grosse Inseln kommen sind/ deren Eynwohner/ nach dem sie vnser gewar worden/ haben alsbald mit lauter vnd schrecklicher Stimm zu ruffen angefangen/ dieweil sie zuvor keine Menschen/ die vns gleich weren/ beschauwet hatten. Deßwegen sie sich auch auff die Flucht begeben haben/ vnd nicht anders dann als Wölffe vnd vnsinnige Leut/ alles mit ihrem Heulen erfült. Da wir ihnen aber freundlich nachgeruffen/ vnd sie widerumb zu vns gelocket/ auch ihnen vnsere Wahr/ als da sind Spiegel/ Messer/ Puppen/ vnd ander geringe Krämerey (an welchen wir vermeyneten sie einen Lust haben solten) fürgestelt hatten/ sind sie stehen blieben. Vnd nach dem sie vnsern guten Willen vnd Freundschafft gespürt/ haben sie vns gute Wort geben/ vnd zu vnser Ankunfft Glück gewündschet. Darnach haben sie vns in ire Statt/ Roanoae genannt/ ja das noch mehr ist/ zu irem Weroans oder Oberherrn geführet/ der vns freundlich empfangen hat/ wiewol er erstlich sich ab vns entsetzte. Also ist es vns ergangen in vnser ersten Ankunfft der newen Welt/ so wir Virginiam nennen. Was nun für Leiber/ Kleydung/ Art zu leben/ Feste vñ Gastereyen die Eynwohner daselbst haben/ das wil ich stück für stück nach ein ander einem jeden vor die Augen stellen/ wie nachfolget.

BEGINNINGS TO THE GOLDEN AGE

From rude beginnings as a mosquito-infested colony to a haunting, romantic land of myths where cotton was king, the South has always been a place apart.

More than any other part of America, the South stands apart. Some say it's the climate – the thick, oppressive subtropical atmosphere that for eight or nine months every year gives life a unique quality: men and beasts move slower when it's 90 degrees in the shade. Today, however, the South has – and has in abundance – air-conditioning, interstate highways, franchise fast-food restaurants, and all the other paraphernalia of American consumerist culture. And still, it is undeniably the South. Thousands of Northerners and foreigners have migrated to it and work happily in its prosperous cities and beguiling countryside, but Southerners they will never be. For this is still a place where you must either have been born, or have 'people' who were born here, to feel that it is your native ground.

Locals will tell you this. They are proud to be Americans, but they are also proud to be Virginians, South Carolinians, Tennesseans, and Alabamians. But they are conscious of the pull of another loyalty too, one that transcends the usual ties of national patriotism or of state and local pride. It is a loyalty to a place where life has always been lived in unique ways, a place where habits are strong and memories are long-lasting. If those memories could speak, they would tell the stories of a region powerfully shaped by its history and determined to pass some of it along to future generations of the South.

Warm winters, a robust infrastructure and a booming economy make the southern states a popular place to live, work, retire, and play.

Settlers landing on the site of Jamestown, 1607.

SWAMPY BEGINNINGS

The permanent settlement of what would later become British North America began on the swampy shores of the Chesapeake Bay region in 1607, just four years after the death of England's first Queen Elizabeth and nine years before the death of William Shakespeare. After having known of this continent's existence for more than 100 years, northern Europeans, and in particular Englishmen, undertook what over centuries was to become one of the greatest cultural transplants in recorded history. The region that would evolve into the American South was one of its first and most long-lasting results. Unlike some of its neighbors to the north, such as Massachusetts and Pennsylvania, the land halfway down the eastern seaboard that would become Virginia was not settled according to some grandiose scheme. Its history witnesses no effort to rule men by the power of a single grand, inspiring, or fearful idea. On the contrary, Virginia and the civilization that was developed and passed on to the larger South can be understood only if it is seen as a thoroughly earthly effort to transplant the institutions and the general style of living of old England to the soil of a new wilderness world.

If the Pilgrims and the Puritans clung to the rocky shores of Massachusetts Bay in an heroic

Powerbrokers of the new colony.

English settlement in Virginia and explore the region. Members of the first team of settlers returned to England disgruntled, but Raleigh remained determined to establish an outpost, and in 1587 he sent 150 settlers to the New World once again. Although their original destination was Chesapeake Bay, these settlers landed first at Roanoke Island, on a narrow strip of land off the coast of what is now North Carolina, and remained there.

As the settlers struggled to carve out a niche of civilization, Spain cast its acquisitive eyes toward England, and the British government was forced to divert most of its efforts into defeating the Armada.

LOST COLONY

When matters in Europe settled down, Raleigh dispatched another expedition carrying supplies and new settlers to the Roanoke colony. What these settlers found when they arrived in 1590 was not a thriving community. All the original settlers had vanished, and the only clue to their demise was the word 'Croatoan,' the name of a group of Native Americans carved in the bark of a tree. Despite the mysterious and frightening end of the 1587 lost colony, Englishmen continued to devise new methods of financing settlements in the New World. Joint-stock companies, such as the London Company and the Plymouth Company, were formed with an eye toward maximum profits and minimum risks.

To that workaday end, the London Company secured from King James I a royal charter to

effort to flee from the Old World's vices, the Virginia colonists hoped to celebrate and fulfill there the Old World's virtues – an Old World with which the majority of them had no serious religious, ideological, or philosophical complaints. Except in one important respect, these were satisfied men.

What drew them across a wild ocean to the edge of a wilder continent was ambition of a largely economic sort, which could find no adequate outlet in Europe. For decades, the Spanish had been extracting fortunes in gold and silver from their southern American preserves – perhaps Englishmen could do the same.

In March 1584, Sir Walter Raleigh obtained a charter from Queen Elizabeth I to establish an

⊘ ROANAKE COLONISTS

Myths and legends abound when it comes to the fate of the missing colonists at Roanoke. The more popular tales include accounts of slaughter at the hands of Native Americans, fatal diseases not encountered by the English until their arrival, supernatural curses cast by powerful witches, and even assassination at the hands of rival colonial powers.

The missing remains of the colonists perpetuate the mystery of their disappearance to this very day and popular TV shows such as *American Horror Story* and *Sleepy Hollow*, sensationalise their suspected ill fate.

found a colony in the southern part of 'Virginia,' as the entire region claimed by England was called. Not quite sure of what they would find, the company bosses sold shares and set about recruiting settlers. They paid each settler's passage, and the latter agreed to work for the company for seven years before striking out for himself.

In 1606, 120 men set sail toward Virginia in three ships under the command of Captain Christopher Newport. Their instructions were to establish a fortified post from which they were to trade with the natives and search for a passage to the Pacific Ocean. The ships reached Chesapeake Bay in April 1607, after a fourmonth voyage that claimed the lives of 16 members of the party. The group sailed 30 miles (48 km) up the James River and selected as their site a densely wooded area bordering a mosquito-ridden swamp. The settlers then split into three groups, each with a specific task: constructing a fort, planting crops, and exploring the region further.

By August, mosquitoes brought an epidemic of malaria, and eight months after their landing, only 38 of the original settlers were still alive. Their salvation was due in part to the efforts of Captain John Smith, who negotiated with the Native Americans and persuaded them to trade with the settlers for maize.

The Native American people in the region were loosely bound in a confederacy headed by a powerful chief called Powhatan. A shrewd leader who mistrusted the English objectives, Powhatan resisted efforts by the British to force the native Indigenous people into a tributary status. In later years, under the leadership of Governor Edwin, peace was finally achieved between the English and the Native Americans. However, it was not just due to the Crown's grand scheme to form a partnership; instead, it was furthered by a marriage in 1614 between John Rolphe, an English settler, and Pocahontas, Powhatan's brave and stylish daughter.

WOMEN, CHILDREN AND ENSLAVED PEOPLE

In 1609, the first women and children came to Virginia. Their arrival, together with that of the first Black enslaved people in 1619, marked its transition from trading post to colony. As settlers got control of their own parcels of land, they turned to a new crop that was to be their salvation: a broad-leaved plant, grown by the Natives and refined with West Indian stock that the world came to know, love and revile, as tobacco. Thanks to tobacco, Virginia attracted labor and capital and became a viable commercial colony.

The labor required for the cultivation of tobacco came at first from indentured servants – men and women willing to sell themselves into personal service in return for the price of a passage to Virginia. The problem was that such laborers were white Englishmen who, after a fixed period of time,

Pocahontas.

would have to be paid and would change overnight from cheap bound labor to expensive free labor.

The importation of enslaved Black people ultimately resolved this difficulty. Yet the purchase price of a good African laborer remained substantially higher than the lease price of a good English servant. The relative price of enslaved people fell only by the end of the 17th century, because the European slave traders and their African suppliers were growing more efficient at their unsavory business. For now, rising life expectancy in the American colonies made it likely that a planter would in fact get a full lifetime's labor out of an enslaved person who had cost him approximately twice as much up front as an indentured servant.

In 1618, the London Company concluded that the most practical way to govern Virginia was to let the colonists govern themselves. Under the leadership of Governor Edwin Sandys, the company allowed the planters to elect representatives to an assembly, which, together with the governor's council, was empowered to legislate for the colony.

The first such assembly, the House of Burgesses, met in Jamestown in August 1619. Free white males over the age of 17 elected two representatives from each of Virginia's 11 towns. It

They promised prospective settlers from England freedom from customs duties on wine, silk, capers, wax, and other goods shipped from the colony back to Britain. Then in 1669, the proprietors each agreed to contribute £500 to a proposed settlement at Port Royal. Three ships had set off from England in August 1660, landing first in Virginia to purchase supplies and then in Barbados to recruit more colonists.

That fall, the ships sailed for the Carolinas, but one was wrecked in a gale in the Bahamas. The other two ships took refuge from the storm

Tobacco, the colony's first successful crop, made for prosperous beginnings.

is remembered today as the first colonial legislature to be set up in the New World.

THE CAROLINAS

Settlement in the Carolinas got its start in 1653 when colonists from Virginia pushed southward into the area around Albemarle Sound. Eager to escape the taxes and all the trappings of civilization taking hold in Virginia, these settlers found to their dismay that life in the Carolinas was no better: 10 years later, Charles II granted large tracts of land in the region to eight men who had supported the restoration of the English monarchy.

These eight new proprietors were determined to increase the population of their colony and not to depend alone on refugees from Virginia.

in Bermuda and after repairs took to the seas again in February 1670. Led by William Sayle, a Puritan settler in the Bahamas and former governor of Bermuda, the group abandoned plans to land at Port Royal and selected instead a site on the Ashley River. They named their new home Charles Towne in honor of the king.

GLITTERING CITY

Shortly after landing, the settlers began constructing another town, which they also called Charles Towne, having renamed their original town Kiawah. By the beginning of the 1680s, the new city was home to around 1,200 people. Despite the intention of the proprietors to speed growth in both Upper and Lower Carolina, they generally directed most of their attention to the southern region of the colony, and settlers in the north became dissatisfied. Governors were deposed, and direct appeals were made to the Crown in England. In 1719, the Carolinas' petition to be made a royal colony was at last granted; a few years later Parliament divided the region and made North Carolina yet another royal colony.

The differences between the two colonies ran deep. North Carolina had been settled as early as 1653, 10 years before Charles II granted land to the proprietors. Many of these settlers had completed terms as indentured servants and were eager to grab bits of land for themselves. In addition, ever-increasing numbers of new settlers were attracted by laws that forbade suits over earlier debts, and also by laws that exempted them from taxes for one year.

TOBACCO ROAD

Tobacco became the primary crop of North Carolinians, but because of the area's treacherous shoreline, the settlers found it difficult to move their produce to the marketplace. Generally, they were forced to haul their crops overland to Virginia where government agents imposed importation taxes. As a result, for a long time North Carolina remained a region of small farms, where subsistence rather than trade was the main rule.

South Carolina, on the other hand, became a region of great estates growing easily marketed crops such as rice and indigo. By the 1730s, the commercial possibilities of the rice culture were being realized on a large scale along the length of the tidal and inland swamplands of the Low Country. Indigo, a plant grown for its rich blue dye, thrived on the drier soils unsuitable for rice, ideally complementing it. Neither did indigo require attention in the winter, leaving the enslaved labor force available for other tasks.

Within a few years of the establishment of the first rice plantations in South Carolina at the end of the 17th century, the Black population was

greater than the white. Laborers died quickly in the malarial conditions of the swamplands, but planters grew rich and replaced their dead and sick workers with an ever-increasing number of Black enslaved people. Owners of the sprawling estates often lived in Charleston (formerly Charles Towne) and left the management of their land and workforce in the hands of overseers. Cruel punishments were inflicted on many South Carolina enslaved people for minor infractions, and overseers were generally more concerned over the commissions they received

Charleston, South Carolina, 1673.

for harvests than over the health and welfare of the workforce.

Between 1740 and the Revolution – the golden age of colonial South Carolina – prices rose and planters increased production. Rice exports tripled, those of indigo quadrupled, and the annual value of these crops soared five times over. Everywhere planters prospered, many to a degree that would never be experienced again in the South. Both of South Carolina's great crops were much better suited to large-scale farming than tobacco, which meant that, even though South Carolina was a much younger colony than Virginia, its plantation system, totally dependent on enslaved labor, established roots fast and deep.

With so many farmers focused solely on cotton, smaller operators found diversifying their crops to include tobacco, rice and indigo, was a more lucrative alternative.

FROM SALZBURG TO SAVANNAH

The last English colony in America, Georgia was also the only colony that formed the focus of a political and social experiment. General James Oglethorpe was concerned with protecting his interests in a rice company in South Carolina where attacks by the Spanish from Florida were common. He was perhaps no less concerned over the insidious conditions in English debtors' prisons. His two interests coalesced in a scheme to establish a new colony that would serve as a buffer between South Carolina and Florida and would be settled by former debtors' prison inmates who would repay their debts through military service.

Parliament approved the plan and granted to a group of philanthropists the right to establish the colony of Georgia. These proprietors were to govern and supervise the colony for 21 years and then return it to the hands of the Crown. The first group of settlers (130 men, women, and children) arrived at the mouth of the Savannah River in 1733. General Oglethorpe laid out the city of Savannah almost immediately, and over the next six years, nearly 5,000 immigrants from Salzburg, Scotland and Moravia joined the original group. The proprietors allotted 50-acre (20-hectare) tracts of land to settlers in exchange for military service.

From the colony's founding, Parliament had banned the importation or use of enslaved people in the region because of fears that they would aid the Spanish in any hostilities that occurred. To help the settlers in farming, the proprietors encouraged indentured servitude, but the costs were too high for many settlers. They envied the large estates and slave holdings of their neighbors in South Carolina, and only seven years after Georgia's founding, they began to ignore the law banning slavery. By the end of the 1740s, the law was repealed, and the plantation system gained a stronghold in the colony.

Sieur de Bienville, founder of New Orleans.

⊘ A NEW START FOR CONVICTS

The opportunity of freedom for debtor's prison inmates in Georgia, in exchange for military service, was part of a growing trend at the time and something that helped British colonies in North America, and indeed around the world, grow at a pace greater than their European rivals. Similar colonial population growth and security strategies were applied to missions dispatched to Australia, New Zealand, Africa and beyond, helping to cement Britain's position as a global power, albeit a precarious and thinly stretched one. In the annals of history, Georgia is one of the last examples of this empirical expansion.

GO WEST

Interest in western lands began as early as 1650 when Captain Abraham Wood led an expedition through the Blue Ridge Mountains to the falls of the Roanoke River. Over the next 50 years, many Virginians made fortunes in the fur trade in the west, reaching as far as the fertile Tennessee Valley. In 1716, Virginia's governor Alexander Spotswood led a group of explorers into the Valley of Virginia, returned to Williamsburg, and petitioned the Crown for grants of land in the western territory.

Joining these explorers were settlers from Pennsylvania, whose colonial government encouraged individuals who had completed terms as indentured servants to move south. They moved to areas around Martinsburg and Shepherdstown in what is now West Virginia and to the region around Winchester, Virginia, in 1726. Within just eight years, the Virginian colonial government had organized Orange County to impose a governmental system on the new western settlements, and four years after that the districts of Frederick and Augusta were established. Further west, the area that contains the present-day states of West Virginia, Kentucky, Ohio, Indiana, Illinois, Michigan, and Wisconsin was named West Augusta.

North Carolina's western region filled up with Scots-Irish and Germans from Virginia, and six counties were formed between 1743 and 1762. South Carolina's western lands were parcelled out to prospective settlers who also received livestock and supplies from the colonial government. The western settlers were of a different temperament to the Tidewater settlers, and their surroundings imposed a contrasting lifestyle. Because of the ongoing difficulty of moving their produce to markets, the western settlers generally operated small farms not dependent on enslaved labor.

REVOLUTION

In 1763, the year generally regarded as the end of the Colonial period and the beginning of the Revolutionary, the South was inhabited by 700,000 people, not counting Native Americans. Basically of English descent, the white population carried on their cultural traditions in the face of the more recent arrivals of Germans, Roman Catholic Irish, Scots-Irish, and French Huguenots. The population included about 300,000 Black enslaved people. A large number of those people were American-born, but the slave trade with Africa continued. Virginia had more enslaved people than any other colony, about 100,000 in 1763, whereas about 50,000 enslaved people lived in North Carolina and 70,000 lived in South Carolina. These people manned the plantations, raising tobacco, rice, and indigo.

As an economic institution and as a system of racial control, slavery defined relations between Black and white. Racial prejudice came to these shores with the Europeans, and in the 18th century abstract questions about the morality of slavery were, in the face of that institution's indisputable economic utility, kept muffled and largely private.

On the eve of the Revolution, slavery was practiced in the Northern colonies as well. However, nowhere north of the Potomac River did Black people constitute anything approaching 40 percent of the population, as they did in Virginia and in most other Southern colonies, to say nothing of the 66 percent currently living in South Carolina.

The war by which America became one united nation was fought between 1775 and 1781 throughout the English colonies, from New England to Georgia. Southerners and Northerners alike shed blood in the attempt to throw off the British yoke. The leader of their armies, George Washington, was a brave Virginian, and a slaveholder. The war began on Northern soil at Lexington and Concord in Massachusetts. It ended

Thomas Jefferson.

on Southern soil, on the Yorktown Peninsula in Virginia, not far from the original colonies of Jamestown and Williamsburg.

In the wake of independence, all the states drew up constitutions, reducing the powers of the Crown-appointed governors, but none granted universal male suffrage. The Church of England was disestablished everywhere, but efforts to create public schools failed. Most Southern states began to abolish the slave trade, but not slavery itself. Many planters felt that the existing order depended on the continuation of a massive Black labor force and thus, necessarily, of slavery, and while there was genuine moral aversion to it within the South, it was usually coupled with the conviction that emancipation was unthinkable without 'coloni-zation' of Black people back to Africa.

As the states emerged from war with a great world power, there was much to bind them together despite themselves. They had a common enemy and felt a healthy fear of further British aggression that lasted long into the post-war period. The war had enlisted men in a common army, but could the more populous North, progressively turning toward commerce and manufacturing, coexist contentedly with a staunchly agricultural South?

Battle of New Orleans, 1815.

⊘ LOUISIANA – A CAUSE FOR WAR?

When Jefferson began his negotiations with France for the purchase of Louisiana, international tensions were high. France had surrendered much of its land in America after the French and Indian War, and so it became a point of nationalist pride for Napoleon to restore his country's territory in America. This event made war between France and America a very real possibility, and so Jefferson opened his negotiations for the land purchase with aplomb, and veiled threats 'This little event of France possessing herself of Louisiana is the embryo of a Tornado which will burst on the countries on both shores of the Atlantic and involve in its effects their highest destinies.'

Virginian George Washington was 57 when he was inaugurated the first president of the United States under the new Constitution in 1789; he was also one of the richest men in America. Washington was succeeded in office by John Adams, but it was the presidency of Thomas Jefferson (1801–09), architect, gentleman, and author of the Declaration of Independence, that ushered in the palmy days of what came to be known as the 'Virginia dynasty.' For the next 25 years, Virginian planters occupied the White House and presided over a young nation generally enjoying a flush of nationalism and optimism about its prospects.

THE LOUISIANA PURCHASE

Jefferson 'the nationalist' bought the vast Louisiana Territory – reaching from the Mississippi River to the crest of the Rocky Mountains that doubled the size of the nation – from Napoleon in 1803, although there was nothing in the Constitution that gave the president the right to acquire new lands. In 1805, he asked Congress for money to buy the territory of Florida from Spain.

At the time of Louisiana's transfer to the US from France, New Orleans was a small, provencial town of just over 8,000, with Black people accounting for slightly more than half of the population. More than 50 percent were enslaved people, but the number of free Black people was also substantial. Creoles of French, African, and Spanish descent were in the majority, but there was also a significant element with other origins. Physically, the town consisted of about 1,300 structures situated almost entirely in the area that is today called the *Vieux Carre* or, more commonly, the French Quarter.

The South itself was undergoing change. As the price of staple crops tumbled 75 percent and the Industrial Revolution took hold in the North, old sectional realities, based since colonial times on very subtle but profound cultural differences, re-emerged now heightened by economic grievances. When this was combined, from the 1830s onwards, with the emergence of the slavery issue as the most powerful agent of sectionalism, one era in Southern history gave way to another.

The nationalist South, which had won independence in concert with the North, written the Constitution, and forged the federal republic, gave way to the sectional South, which, due to the burden of slavery and its own understandings of the American polity and the good life, finally forsook that republic for a nation of its own imaginings.

ANTEBELLUM ERA

There is something about the history of the South between the Revolution and the Civil War that makes it, in the popular imagination, loom larger and more vividly than any other moment. That period is strewn with durable images of masters and enslaved people and Southern belles, the divisiveness of sectionalism took hold, and then to observe the political flashpoints that marked the South's increasing self-awareness as a place apart, with a destiny all its own.

On the eve of the antebellum era, the South had ample reason to be satisfied with America's national affairs. The Republican Party – then the only political party worthy of the name, and not to be confused with the antislavery party of Abraham Lincoln, which was not founded until the 1850s – was strongly influenced by Southerners.

James Monroe, a Southerner and the last of

Idealized depiction of a cotton farm on the Mississippi River

of plantation houses with white pillars and broad fields of cotton. This is the South immortalized in Margaret Mitchell's *Gone with the Wind* and trivialized in countless subsequent volumes of historical romance. It is a South that seems both content and sure of itself as being a place apart from, and superior to, the rest of America, even as it headed for disaster. It is a picture that only truly characterizes the South of the late antebellum period and then only unevenly, and it is a South that was the product of a gradual evolution.

A PLACE APART

To understand that point of arrival, it helps first to consider the texture of Southern life before the 'Virginia dynasty,' was still president; William Crawford of Georgia, John C. Calhoun of South Carolina and William Wirt of Virginia constituted half of Monroe's cabinet.

The flush of nationalism from the Revolution itself and from the second war with Britain in 1812 – culminating in the successful Battle of New Orleans – still wanned the land. Five signatories of the Declaration of Independence were still alive. Thomas Jefferson, its author, was still master of his magnificent house, Monticello, in Virginia, and was also still a reminder of the boldness of the American national experiment, and of America's genius for a new kind of politics.

But if the South was politically still at peace with the rest of America, there were palpable differences in its cultural and economic life from which political particularism, aggravated by the debate over slavery and western expansion, would grow. At the time the Constitution was written, and for some years into the early history of the young republic, it appeared that the population of the Southern states would at least equal, and perhaps even exceed, that of the North. The national census in 1820 still mirrored the old colonial demographics. One in every four Southerners was a Virginian, yet not even one in 25 people lived in Louisiana.

However, despite these statistics, it was only in the states of Tennessee and Kentucky that Black people accounted for less than one-third of the population.

KING COTTON

In the 18th century, the South's great crops had been those of seaboard Virginia and South Carolina: tobacco and rice. In the 19th century, sugar was the chief crop in Louisiana, which required great investment in both land and enslaved people. Sugar was unique among Southern staple

Loading cotton on the Mississippi, 1870.

Maryland, Virginia, and North Carolina boasted half of the entire Southern population, while the three most southwestern states of Mississippi, Alabama, and Louisiana were home to less than one-tenth of the population.

But these were the areas that were growing most quickly. Between 1810 and 1820, the white population of Tennessee, Alabama, Mississippi, and Louisiana increased by as much as 50 percent, while that of Maryland, Virginia and the Carolinas rose just 12 percent. There were also significant variations with regards to slavery. At one extreme, enslaved people constituted nearly 53 percent of the population of South Carolina and were also in the majority in Louisiana; in Tennessee they accounted for just 19 percent of the total.

crops in its dependence on tariff protection. But short-staple cotton, which could be grown anywhere, either by gangs of enslaved people or by white yeomen, on rough land as well as fertile, was becoming more popular.

The Deep South states of Louisiana and Mississippi especially thrived on the new crop's popularity, but cotton fields also expanded westward across Alabama and Mississippi into Arkansas and Texas.

The introduction of Eli Whitney's cotton gin in 1793 had made possible the rapid combing of the plant and vastly increased the South's cotton output and its profitability. By 1820, cotton had already surpassed all other Southern produce, and three-quarters of the crop of 353,000 bales went for export. Over the next 30 years, the price declined steadily but yields increased, almost doubling in every decade leading up to the Civil War.

For many people, cotton represented their big chance, not just of making a living but of achieving real success, and the legendary path from dogtrot cabin to white-columned splendor was genuinely trodden by countless Southerners who started with little, but who, by the 1850s, took their proud place as grandees of 'The Cotton Kingdom.'

back to Africa. Slavery was obviously a Southern problem and one that involved both the moral problem of holding other humans in perpetual bondage and the practical problem of what to do with an alien race should it be emancipated. The American Colonization Society was founded in 1816 and was headed by Southerners James Madison, James Monroe, and John Marshall from Virginia. In 1826, of the 143 emancipation societies in existence in the country, 103 had been founded in the South, many of them by Quaker Benjamin Lundy, who spread the abolition mes-

Duels were fought in New Orleans City Park.

STEAMBOAT'S A COMIN'

Before the railroad era, which did not reach much of the South until the 1840s and 1850s, the need to transport bulky 500-lb (230-kg) bales of cotton to market put a premium on water transportation and briefly sustained the fleets of steamboats that had plied the Mississippi River from 1811. Slavery, which had attached itself to the South in colonial times, proved well adapted to the cotton trade and helped fuel its expansion. However, much of the enlightened opinion of the age, both in the North and the South, had doubts about the morality of the institution.

In the 1770s, Thomas Jefferson, a slaveholder until the day he died, proposed repatriating ('colonizing' as it came to be known) Black people

sage through the mountainous regions of Tennessee and North Carolina. In addition, there were several anti-slavery newspapers in the South, including the *Emancipator* in Tennessee.

Some Black people were in fact 'colonized' back to Africa, and the West African nation of Liberia owes its existence to the movement; its capital city, Monrovia, was named for President James Monroe. But the numbers were simply too daunting – and the economic stakes too high – for 'colonization' ever to be tried widely.

Besides, there was the pull of cotton, which was so compatible with slavery, and which not only profited the Southern planters but also represented the bulk of United States exports and fueled the entire national economy. For a new country trying to establish itself, Southern cotton, whether or not it was grown by enslaved people, constituted a tremendous economic resource that no one, not even Northerners, were prepared to put at risk.

TRIANGULAR TRADE ROUTE

The South's increasing reliance on staple-crop agriculture had consequences both inside and outside the region that no one could fully foresee. Indeed then, with cotton constituting the lion's share of American exports, that reliance

Enslaved people made for a prosperous economy.

did not seem excessive. But Southerners relied heavily on others to transport their precious staples to faraway markets, as they themselves sailed few ships and built almost none.

Thus, like it or not, they found themselves locked into a sort of triangular trade, in which cotton from the South went to England, and manufactured goods from England and Europe came to New York, and then sold to the South. It was a far-flung economic system, which in general relied on the factories of the Old World, the commercial and transportation services of the American Northeast, and the staple agricultural products of the American South.

As a key player in such an international system, Southerners came early and strongly

to believe in free trade as a cornerstone for prosperity. Potential for abuse existed, but the pattern usually fitted the region's needs, and Southerners generally felt well served by it. With their exports exceeding $30 million a year, some Southerners enjoyed great credit far and wide, displaying it splendidly.

Insofar as Southerners manufactured things for themselves, they made relatively simple items necessary to service the needs of their agricultural society. They worked with wood, iron, and hides, and they ground grain into meal, grits, and flour. In most of the South, the white artisan class, which also had to compete with trained plantation and urban enslaved people, were too few in number and too dependent on agriculture to become as important as they would be in the North. Such trades were all small-time, with usually only two or three men to a shop, and they served largely local markets.

By contrast, tobacco and iron were sometimes worked in establishments of considerable size. Virginia, which was the nation's largest coal producer, turned out pig iron, castings, nails, firearms, and farm implements. Tobacco factories transformed half the tobacco crop into plugs and twists for chewing, snuff, pipe tobacco, and cigars. And yet, there were probably more field hands in some single counties of the South Carolina Low Country in 1820 than there were factory workers in the whole of the South.

It would be a mistake to regard the South, at this point still 40 years before the Civil War, as a place powerfully united by either character or conviction. Two types of internal tension in particular strained the unity of Southern life, creating political ramifications as the antebellum years wore on. The conflict between Low Country and Up Country reached back to colonial times, when the coastal regions of South Carolina and Virginia had boasted more advanced social institutions, more ample material possessions (including more enslaved people), and larger towns than the remoter regions.

In Tennessee, it was the fertile central and western regions that corresponded to 'Low Country,' while the mountainous eastern sections played the role of 'the backwoods.' Obviously much could depend on which of these groups controlled the state governments, and the unity of the South would depend in part on whether the same type of groups were in power in each of the states.

The second source of internal division was between the upper South and the cotton, or Deep, South. Agriculture in Virginia was more diversified, and much produce was sold domestically; it boasted more commerce and manufacturing and enjoyed greater proximity to the outside world. In most of the Deep South, cotton was the predominant money crop, with rice and sugar at the edges, and it sold abroad on the world market. The upper South had more free Black people; the Deep South had the heaviest concentration of enslaved people. Of all the Southern states, South Carolina probably shared the least with anybody else. Virginia still enjoyed the most revered heritage but seemed somehow to be losing its economic and political grip. And the transmontane states such as Tennessee were assuming new vigor and importance every year.

CIVIL UNREST

With 'colonization' providing an outlet for moral frustrations about slavery, and with cotton constituting a key to national prosperity, it would seem that the matter of slavery might not necessarily have led, as it did, to the dissolution of the Union and civil war. Indeed, slavery was basically left as something to be regulated by the states as they themselves saw fit. So it might have remained, at least for a much longer time, had the new American nation been a fixed, static place, as most older nations were by then. But America in the early 19th century was a land on the verge of both economic growth and geographical expansion, the likes of which the world had not seen before, and it is in this context that slavery – localized in the South but linked to the growth of the cotton trade – became the explosive issue of the later antebellum era. It invited the resurgence of sectionalism, which increasingly came to mean the slavery question, and finally provoked the constitutional crisis that nearly ended the American experiment.

Thomas Jefferson called this forging 'an empire for liberty' – the process of statemaking outlined in the Northwest Ordinance of 1787, which became the manual for the orderly growth of the American republic westward across the continent. Slavery ceased to be merely a local

Southern matter, and Southern sectionalism, which was increasingly aggravated by both anti- and pro-slavery arguments, pushed the nation toward disunion. In 1819 there were 22 states, 11 slave and 11 free, the careful result of admitting first one type and then the other so as to maintain equal representation in the Senate. The problem came in the House of Representatives when the slave states, falling behind their Northern sisters, filled 81 seats compared with the North's 105.

At this early stage, it is foolish to dwell too

Slave market in the United States in the 1850s.

closely on purely sectional divisions in the halls of the national government. The Republican Party was a national organization with major constituents, united by class and interest, on both sides of the Mason-Dixon Line – the state boundary between Maryland and Pennsylvania considered to be the dividing line between North and South.

THE MISSOURI COMPROMISE

In 1820, what focused attention so sharply on the matter of Congressional balance was the imminent admission to the Union of the state of Missouri. It was an occasion without precedent: if Missouri went 'free', Southerners had reason to fear that so might the whole of the trans-Mississippi West. If that happened, the South, with its 'peculiar institution' comprising hordes of Black enslaved people, would find itself in a permanent minority in the government. Should that government then ever choose to amend the Constitution so as to attack slavery, the whole South would be at its mercy.

On March 3, 1820, a government compromise was reached in which Missouri would be admitted as a slave state but was to be paired with the admission of Maine as a free state. That much seemed fair to everyone and portended no ill for the future admission of other states. What did set off alarm bells and a new precedent was Congress's extension of the 36/30 latitude straight west across the whole Louisiana Purchase, for the purpose of dividing future free from future slave territory.

On the surface and in retrospect, this would seem a plausible enough thing to have done, but that is not to take into account the expansive spirit of nationalism that was then suffusing American life and whose compelling symbol was the Great West. Congress, now boldly legislating with regard to slavery in the new territories acquired in the west since the Revolution, banned it from some of that territory not yet even organized into states. The 36/30 line cut across the boundless spirit of the age and left a livid scar that said the west was now split. Thomas Jefferson most memorably captured the long-range meaning of what had happened. The compromise struck him, he said, as a fire bell in the night, and he warned the nation that any such fixed geographical line that divided the North and the South and was identified with political and moral principles could never be erased peacefully. In the compromise, the Southern nationalists heard a distant death knell for the Union.

FREE TRADE

The South's marriage to both staple-crop agriculture and the system of enslaved labor that made this possible continued to set the region apart from the rest of the country, even as cotton became an ever more valuable national asset. Cotton's value was tied to conditions in the world market, and the more the trade expanded

Mardi Gras during the 1800s.

⊘ MARDI GRAS MYSTERY

Although the South may present itself to outsiders as a gracious, united land, rivalries between states and cities have been known to occur. Nowhere is this more apparent than in the American origin of Carnival, or Mardi Gras. Traditionally associated with New Orleans, Mobile in Alabama lays claim to having hosted the first celebration. Certainly, the French in New Orleans were attending masked balls and parties as early as 1718, which continued until the Spanish authorities banned them. But Mobile dates its first celebration to 1703, when the Cowbellion de Rakin Society took loudly to the streets armed with rakes, hoes, and cowbells. Although they marched on New Year's Eve and not Fat Tuesday, Mobilians claim they were a true antecedent of Mardi Gras. Later, some of the Mobile members of the Cowbellion de Rakin Society traveled to New Orleans and were instrumental in the formation of the Mystick Krewe of Camus which, all agree, was New Orleans' first and most prestigious Mardi Gras society, established in 1857. It was then that the event gained status and momentum.

Carnival was suspended during and after the Civil War, but from around 1866 onward, both cities resumed the parades, floats, masking, and general merriment that makes Mardi Gras so memorable.

and prospered, the more Southern agricultural interests became convinced that everything depended on free trade. So it was that, at the end of the 1820s, the issue of the tariff became as sectionally divisive as the issue of slavery expansion. The problem for a staple-crop producer was a classic dilemma of selling cheap, if the world price happened to be low, and buying expensively, for the manufactured goods that Southern planters had to buy came at prices that were artificially inflated by tariff protection.

As far as Northern factory owners were concerned, protective duties encouraged growth in the early stages of industrialization; as far as the South was concerned, the duty imposed by the tariff was robbing them of valuable profit.

UNHAPPY WITH THE UNION

As the nation expanded to the west and as the North's growth and vigor began to outdistance the South's, support would grow for secession from the Union. Even as the tariff declined as a divisive issue, that of slavery, infinitely more complex and emotional, took its place. To the very large extent that no Northerner was being asked to bear the burden of emancipation, it seemed to many Southerners that the North's allegedly noble convictions about the universal rights of man were actually very cheap convictions to hold. Like no other issue before it, anti-slavery laid bare the critical rifts inherent in the American nation, even as that nation was striving to reproduce itself in the west. To oppose slavery was, to Southerners, to oppose the way the South lived and prospered.

In a sense, either side could claim that it was the other side that threatened the Union. Northern anti-slavery voices argued that no nation founded on liberty could live up to those first principles as long as it tolerated slavery.

Southern pro-slavery voices argued that when the Union was put together in the 1780s, it was done in the complete knowledge of the existence of slavery in the Southern states, for whose economic concern alone slavery must remain. To attack it, therefore, was to attack the contract that had been established between the states that constituted the Union, putting something else – a 'higher law' – above the Union. This was, of course, exactly what Northerners would accuse Southerners of when the latter spoke of nullification and the right of a state to secede: of putting something else – states' rights – above the Union.

As the anti-slavery movement and the abolitionists shouted about a 'higher law,' Southerners responded by erecting an elaborate structure of arguments defending it. They warned of abolition's dire consequences, which would mean economic ruin for the South and the nation, destitution for the Black people, and extermination of the white people. They argued that the Old and the New Testaments were strewn with references to masters and servants.

Enslaved people using a cotton gin.

Immutable laws of nature, pro-slavery apologists argued, ordained a 'mudsill class,' on whose crude labors a higher culture could be built by those of superior knowledge and power. In the South, so the argument went, this meant a cultured and leisured white planter class at the top and, at the bottom, Black enslaved people whose natural burden it was to hew the wood and haul the water, but whose inestimable benefit it also was to have been redeemed from African savagery and converted to Christianity.

And so, as the end of the 1850s approached and as the threats to slavery multiplied, even moderate Southerners raised radical doubts about the wisdom of union with the American nation.

📷 PLANTATIONS – A LEGACY OF THE SOUTH

Present in almost every Southern state, these vast estates and their equally vast mansions are a bittersweet reminder of just how prevalent slavery was in the South.

From the Antebellum Plantation, now called Historic Square, in Georgia and the Charleston Tea Garden of South Carolina, to the Laura Plantation of Louisiana and Monmouth in Mississippi, the old agriculture and slave master mansions are grand in scale and legacy. Behind these wealthy facades, many of which are now museums or bed and breakfasts, are tales of oppression, inhumanity, the fight for freedom, and a slave trade that would propel the United States into a bloody and divisive civil war.

Nowhere is this scar of the South's past more apparent than the Windsor Ruins, in Claiborne County, Mississippi. Just South of Port Gibson, all that remains of the main house are 23 standing Corinthian columns, in the center of what was once a 2,600-acre (1,052-hectare) plantation. Owned by Smith Daniell, the mansion was short lived and stood from 1861 to 1890, when an alleged stray cigarette started a fire that ravaged the mansion, and everything in it. After the blaze all that was left of the grand estate were the Corinthian columns. Local legend however stands firm that the fate of the estate was a deliberate and fitting end to a mansion built on the backs of enslaved people, who in stark contrast, were forced to live in squalor, working every conceivable minute of the day.

Majestic oak tree canopy leading to Rosedown Plantation in Louisiana.

The Old Slave Mart Museum, Charleston.

The Corinthian columns at the Windsor Ruins.

Statues of enslaved children at the Whitney Plantation, Louisiana.

Louisiana's Darkest Chapter: The Whitney Plantation

A 30-minute drive from New Orleans is the **Whitney Plantation Museum**, where the past is conveyed to visitors, through more than 2,000 first-hand accounts, collected from former enslaved people during the Federal Writers' Project. Every museum visitor is handed a card containing the memories and experience of a former enslaved person, in the hope that if the scale of slavery is too much to process, the human experience of one individual who survived it is not. Volunteers here also explain that it is their hope these cards will be carried out into the world and shared, perpetuating the horrific memories.

This former sugar cane plantation was home to more than 350 African enslaved people at any one time, but the scale of the industry isn't the focus for the tour guides here. Instead, they stress the importance of education and information, not romanticism of the past or shaming those ignorant of history. The emotional spectrum of this educational experience is almost impossible to adequately put into words, but if you would like a real account of the plantations of the past, and not a walking tour led by a guide in period costume ending in a gift shop, the Whitney Plantation tour is for you (tel: 225-265 3300; www. whitneyplantation.com).

Slave cabins at Boone Hall Plantation in Mount Pleasant, Charleston.

Laura Plantation House.

Slave cage at Whitney Plantation, Louisiana.

Storming Fort Wagner, 1863.

FROM THE WAR BETWEEN THE STATES TO WORLD WAR II

The first modern war devastated a land that saw itself prosperous and powerful. It would be many, many years before the South would rise again

At the time, the American Civil War was a war like no other. It was the first real war of the industrial age; it was the first war in which armies were supplied by railway; it was the first war to be conducted by telegraph and so able to be reported quickly to civilian populations. It saw the introduction of the observation balloon, the repeating rifle (an early form of machine gun) and, at sea, the iron-clad, steam-powered warship. When it first began in the spring of 1861, there was much talk on both sides of a quick and neat conflict with the soldiers being home in time for Christmas.

Naive Northerners saw it merely as a police action to curb the seemingly ungovernable South; naive Southerners boasted that one dashing young Southern cavalier could whip ten cowardly abolitionists. More thoughtful men on both sides, including Abraham Lincoln and Jefferson Davis, understood that the sectional controversies of four decades had aroused deep passions and that in all likelihood, once the war began, blood would flow until some final settlement was achieved.

Confederate General Robert E. Lee.

The American Civil War is considered the first modern war in history. Never before had a conflict been fed by railways, machine guns and steel sided battleships.

SEEDS OF SECESSION

The intemperate economic arguments over tariffs that strained the Union in the 1850s, and the South's reputation as the 'wealth producing' section of the country, giving reason to believe it could go it alone, went hand in hand with perceived moral and cultural rifts. Demand rose in the South for Southern textbooks and Southern teachers and for the South to emancipate itself from literary dependency on Northern and European writers.

The most tangible cultural bond had already snapped in 1845 when the two largest Protestant denominations in America, the Methodists and the Baptists, had divided over the slavery question into Northern and Southern groupings. In each case, the stigma of immorality was placed on the slaveholding South. But it was the publication of one particular book in 1852 – *Uncle Tom's Cabin* or *Life Among the Lowly* that contributed to the course of disunion more than any other single cultural event. Author Harriet Beecher Stowe's experience of the South's peculiar institution was limited, to say the least, but the impact of her novel was not. Stowe, a member of a Northern anti-slavery family, drew heavily on the highly negative reports of conditions in the South to be found in Theodore Dwight Weld's propagandistic *Slavery As It Is*, and she reflected all its simplicities: overseers (Simon Legree) were universally sadistic; the enslaved people (Uncle Tom) were angels. Slavery was worse in the Deep South.

Illustration from Beecher Stowe's Uncle Tom's Cabin.

EXPLOSIVE LITERATURE

While Stowe shared all the white racist attitudes of her time, slavery and not racial equality was her point, and she made it brilliantly. In the South, reaction to Stowe's book was vehement. Attacking the author and the book equally, newspaper editors claimed that Stowe had no knowledge whatsoever of the conditions of enslaved people in the South, possessed no 'moral sense,' and had plagiarized Charles Dickens. The book achieved a permanent place in American literary history, but at that particular time it also added the explosive element of moral self-righteousness to the slavery debate by strengthening the stereotype of slavery as a malevolent institution that stood, literally and

morally, in the path of national progress. Thousands of Northerners, having previously held themselves aloof from the moral question, were swayed by the book to join the abolition cause. Self-righteousness settled on both sides, as the South counterattacked the libel on its character with no less than 15 novels of its own and with sweeping arguments that Northern wage earners were actually worse off than enslaved people. For in the late 1850s, as troubled as the political landscape had become, the South's actual landscape of estates and farms enjoyed enormous prosperity. For this reason, the myth that cotton was indeed king grew strong. This myth lent acceptability to the momentous decision to leave the Union by many Southerners who reasoned that a cotton-hungry Great Britain would have to give support to the South if that country itself were to survive. But places other than the South grew cotton, and the only calculation that went into Britain's decision about whom to support in the American Civil War was the cool calculation of which side it was that was most likely to win.

DRED SCOTT

Each of the remaining three years of the decade had brought grim omens. In 1857, the Supreme Court, five of whose nine justices were Southerners, waded into the slavery controversy with the Dred Scott Decision. The case involved the migrations of a Black enslaved person, Dred Scott, who during the 1830s had been carried by his master, John Emerson, an army surgeon,

⊘ HARRIET BEECHER STOWE

A fact often lost in the tales of Beecher Stowe's visceral novels is the heart-breaking true-life tragedy that spurred the author to put pen to paper. At just 18-months-old, Stowe's son unexpectedly died and it was this loss that led her to speak to, and subsequently empathise with, the enslaved mothers who had their children unjustly stolen away to be sold.

Stowe was further horrified by the passing of the Fugitive Slave Law, making it legal for runaway enslaved people to be hunted and returned to their owners, even if they had run away to a state where slavery wasn't lawful.

from the slave state of Missouri to Illinois, where the Northwest Ordinance of 1787 forbade slavery, and then to Wisconsin Territory, where the Missouri Compromise also forbade slavery. Scott finally returned to Missouri and sued for his freedom on the grounds that his stay in free territory made him a free man.

In a broad decision, the court seemed determined to vindicate the South and inflame the anti-slavery North. As a Black person and as an enslaved person, the court decided, Dred Scott – and therefore all other Black enslaved people and their descendants – was not a citizen and could not sue for his freedom. John Brown's raid on the federal arsenal at Harpers Ferry, Virginia, in October 1859, also had an irrational impact on the course of events. John Brown, destined to become a mythical figure in American history, may well have been a madman. Certainly his scheme to liberate a number of enslaved people, whom he would then turn into guerrilla bands in the Virginia mountains, had a bizarre quality about it, while his tactics in trying to carry it off suggest greater theatrical than military genius.

His band of 21 included his own sons and several Black people, and no local enslaved people came to their aid, as had been anticipated they might. When a passing train alerted the outside world to their attack, Brown's raiders proved no match for the contingent of Marines, commanded by Robert E. Lee, who were sent to quell them.

Most Northerners, while disapproving the raid's methods, lauded its aims. Moderate Southerners responded slowly at first but hardened their attitudes when it was revealed that Brown had been financed by a secret cadre of wealthy Northern abolitionists. As extreme reactions set in on both sides, the raid became a turning point in the fast-developing secession crisis. Southerners who came to identify John Brown with the North – an oversimplification certainly, but a compelling one – concluded that they must secede to be safe, and that the fear that moved them was real and immediate.

South Carolina, predictably, responded first and, in December 1860, set in motion the train of secession. By February 6, 1861, all five of the other Deep South states – Mississippi, Florida, Alabama, Georgia, Louisiana – had followed,

along with Texas. The states of the Upper South – Virginia, North Carolina, and Tennessee – hesitated, as did Arkansas, but warned that they would resist any attempt by the federal government to coerce any state that left the Union. President Abraham Lincoln, in his inaugural address on March 4, attempted to walk a fine line aiming to preserve what was left of the Union and to reassure the South: 'I have no purpose directly or indirectly to interfere with the institution of slavery in the states where it exists.' He also asserted that secession

Dred Scott (1795–1858).

was legally not possible: 'No state upon its own mere action, can lawfully get out of the Union.' Both sides hesitated to make a move toward violence, and while the first shot was fired by the South, it was said to have been in response to overt Northern aggression.

Coercion, or at least the appearance of it in the South's eyes, came in April 1861 when Lincoln, after much delay, attempted to resupply Fort Sumter in Charleston harbor, one of the few federal military installations in the Deep South that had not surrendered to state authority. The garrison commander, Major Robert Anderson, refused South Carolina's ultimatum, and at 4:30am on April 12, South Carolina forces commenced a bloodless bombardment of the island fortress. The national colors came down 34 hours later.

A SOUTHERN NATION

The confrontation instantly galvanized the North in defense of the Union, and Lincoln issued a call for 75,000 three-month volunteers to put down the, as he put it, 'insurrection.' Lincoln's call for troops at last forced the hand of the states of the moderate border South: Virginia seceded on April 17, Arkansas on May 6, Tennessee on May 7, and North Carolina on May 20.

The Confederate States of America first came into being in 1861 in an attempt to achieve a state of independence without leaving the greater American Union. The object of doing so was to avoid an all-out war.

marine. The 11 states of the Confederacy had a population of some 9 million, a third of whom were Black enslaved people. Its manufactur-

The fall of Richmond, 2 April 1865.

Slaveholding Kentucky, Maryland, and Missouri did not leave the Union but with their Southern sisters, they joined to declare the independence of a new Southern nation, the Confederate States of America.

While neither side ever lacked the resolution to see the fight through to the bitter end, the North had the clear advantage in numbers and economic strength. The 23 Northern states contained a population of 22 million, augmented by heavy foreign immigration. The North could, even in a long conflict, replace its losses. Though heavily agricultural like the South, it had a more balanced economy with an advanced industrial establishment, strong financial institutions, an excellent railroad grid, a navy, and a merchant

ing was undeveloped and tied to agriculture; it had no substantial iron industry and it made no heavy armaments. Its railroad network was still rudimentary and utterly unprepared for the massive load soon to be placed upon it. Yet the discrepancy in resources, which Southerners recognized, was not initially compelling, for the South was taking a calculated risk on several counts. These were that the North would not actually fight to save the Union; that Great Britain and France, hungry for Southern cotton, would intervene on the South's behalf; and that the South's control of the Mississippi River would weaken western support for the Northern war effort. In each case, the South guessed wrong.

The government of the new Confederacy got its start on February 4, 1861, in Montgomery, Alabama, where representatives of the six states that had by then seceded met at a convention. The representatives adopted a provisional constitution, modeled faithfully after the Constitution but specifically clarifying issues of states' rights that had become muddled over the past 70 years. They elected Jefferson Davis of Mississippi as president and Alexander H. Stephens of Georgia as vice-president. In military preparations, the Confederacy had some genuine advantages. Davis issued a call for 100,000 volunteers, and most who answered were well armed and clothed. In its officer corps, the Confederacy had Robert E. Lee, who had served as the superintendent of the crack military academy West Point and was attached to a western command at the time of secession. Lee had been offered command of the Northern armies but had turned it down, resigned from the US Army, and returned to his home state of Virginia, where he was named major-general of the Virginia Confederate troops. Almost immediately upon hearing this news, more than 380 other officers resigned their commissions and took new positions in the Confederate forces.

While Davis was engaged in fielding his new armies, dissension grew in the southern Allegheny region of western Virginia and east Tennessee. The western counties of Virginia had not been represented at the convention that had approved the state's secession. On June 11, 1861, western delegates met to denounce secession and form a new government. The delegates elected Francis H. Pierpont governor, selected senators, and adopted a new state constitution for West Virginia, which was admitted to the Union in April 1863. In east Tennessee, only the establishment of martial law kept Unionists from following West Virginia's lead.

The opening shots of the war were fired on Fort Sumter, South Carolina, in April 1861. Exactly four mind-numbingly tragic years later, in April 1865, General Robert E. Lee surrendered to Ulysses S. Grant in Appomattox. (For

Battle of Five Forks, Virginia, April 1, 1865.

⊙ CIVIL WAR FACTS AND IRONIES

The Civil War goes by many names. Some of these include: the War of Northern Aggression; the War of Rebellion; the Brothers' War; and the Late Unpleasantness.

Four of Abraham Lincoln's brothers-in-law fought on the side of the Confederates. Winchester, Virginia, changed hands 72 times. Missouri sent 39 regiments to fight in Vicksburg, Mississippi: 17 to the Confederacy and 22 to the Union.

April 14, 1865, the date of Lincoln's assassination, was also the fourth anniversary of the surrender of Fort Sumter in South Carolina. It has been said Lincoln was invited to the ceremony but declined in order to go to the theater.

Some 10,500 armed conflicts occurred during the war. According to a study done by the Civil War Sites Advisory Commission, 384 of these were principal battles that took place in 26 different states. The Southern States that were engaged in 15 or more major conflicts include:

Virginia   123 battles
Tennessee   38 battles
Georgia   28 battles
Louisiana   23 battles
North Carolina   20 battles
Arkansas   17 battles
Mississippi 16 battles

more on the major conflicts and battlefields, see Civil War Sites on page 91).

The physical costs of the Civil War were huge on both sides. The war killed between 600,000 and 700,000 young men in a nation totaling only 33 million: a fatality rate around double that suffered by American forces in both world wars. The nation, both North and South, lost not only these men, however, but the children, the grandchildren and the greatgrandchildren who never were, a cultural loss that is beyond calculation.

The South suffered the most physically, for its

General Lee surrenders to General Grant at Appomattox.

cities, towns, and farms were devastated and its economy ruined. During its brief and turbulent existence, the Confederacy, which had failed to stay the run and establish Southern nationhood, had at least crystallized Southern distinctiveness.

RECONSTRUCTION ERA

As the Confederacy crumbled and the Union took control of region after region in the South, President Lincoln was determined not to direct malice toward the conquered people. Despite heavy opposition in his party, the president devised a 'Proclamation on Amnesty and Reconstruction.' This plan called for the restoration of civil rights to all Southerners, except highly

ranked civil and military officials, after they took an oath of allegiance to the Constitution. The plan also specified that when 10 percent of the state's voters had taken the oath, the state could then re-establish a government. The president's plan had not been signed when, on April 14, 1865, John Wilkes Booth assassinated Lincoln at Ford's Theatre. With Lincoln's death, the Reconstruction debate fell to President Andrew Johnson.

Johnson, a former tailor from North Carolina and then Tennessee, was a self-educated man who had slowly risen through the ranks of political office from alderman to US Senator. He had retained his seat in the Senate after Tennessee seceded – the only Southern senator to do so – and after the fall of Nashville, President Lincoln had appointed him military governor of Tennessee. Johnson's plan for Reconstruction was announced on May 29. It included all the provisions of Lincoln's plan but added that individuals with property valued at $20,000 or more were exempt from amnesty.

CARPETBAGGERS

In this way, Johnson attempted to alter Southern society. No lover of the wealthy, white, planter class, Johnson wanted to make room for small farmers and poor whites in the Southern political scene. There were also wide-reaching reforms for Black people. But these same reforms opened up the doors to scalawags (unscrupulous white Southerners who supported Republican policy) and carpetbaggers

⊙ ABRAHAM LINCOLN

President Abraham Lincoln was shot in the head by John Wilkes Booth on April 14, 1865 whilst he was watching the play *Our American Cousin* at Ford's Theatre in Washington, D.C. Lincoln survived through the night but died the next morning. The immediate aftermath was not only a scene of nationwide despair but also one of recrimination. The ensuing manhunt for Booth and his accomplices was the largest in the nation's history. A $100,000 reward bolstered the nationwide hunt and on April 26, Booth was discovered on a tobacco farm where he had been hiding and was promptly shot dead on the porch of the farm in Virginia.

(Northerners who came South to take advantage of the conditions for personal gain). For years afterward, most white Southerners couldn't say enough bad things about these times, and it became a sacred part of Southern myth that Reconstruction constituted the 'blackout of honest government' and the unforgivable insult to the white race. Others – literate Black people and radical partisans – recalled it as a noble and well-intentioned experiment in which the native virtue and sterling performance of Black people was matched only by the unadulterated malice of their Southern white adversaries.

For all their ineptitude, the Republican governments in the South did more than take bribes and swindle the taxpayers. Even though the presence of Black people in public office would soon pass away, these regimes made marks that would last longer than they did themselves. The state constitutions on which they rested were superior to, or at least more modern than, their antebellum predecessors. Participation in politics was broadened to universal white manhood suffrage. Even Black people, now guaranteed the vote by the Fifteenth Amendment, usually favored the vote for all whites regardless of the latters' past association with the Confederacy and the defense of slavery.

The first Black man to sit in the United States Senate was Hiram Revels, an ordained minister and a schoolteacher from Mississippi. Revels was the first Black person to fill the chair once occupied by Jefferson Davis, and he was followed soon after by another Black man, Blanche K. Bruce, who had been born an enslaved person in Virginia, escaped bondage to become a teacher, and then returned to the South in 1869 to settle in Mississippi. Black people from Florida, Louisiana, Mississippi, Georgia, North and South Carolina, and Alabama served in the United States House of Representatives, and while not all of their careers in public life were especially memorable, neither were they any less remarkable nor any more prone to corruption than those of many of their white counterparts.

The new constitutions asserted the right of children to schooling, and the new state governments backed this up with appropriations that at least began to support such institutions. These administrations also began to give some tentative legal

protection to women, who in much of the region had until this time to rely pretty much on their wits and their gender to get along in a man's world.

The government also did what it could to promote the economic rebuilding of the South, though in this it was severely limited by powerful prevailing notions about the limited role the state itself should play in the economy. The constitutions established both agencies to promote immigration into the South and, especially important, programs to promote industrialization. And, of course, these were the govern-

Civil War cemetery in Tennessee.

ments that for the first time gave Black people a real, though limited, chance to show what they could do in positions of power, trust, and responsibility.

But Reconstruction is only part of the story, for better or worse, of the Republican regimes in the state capitals. The South was not just a place being acted upon, but it was also a place filled with people acting on their own behalf to maintain their values and assert their influence on the nation.

SABOTAGE

From today's perspective, in the wake of the Civil Rights movements of the 1950s and 1960s, it is easy to look back on the white Southerners of the Reconstruction era with contempt for a people so morally dulled as to sabotage such a noble experiment in racial justice. But viewed by the standards of that age, it was they and not their reformist antagonists who represented the American mainstream. These were men convinced of the absolute impossibility of the Black and white races coexisting in one place, except in a relationship of complete white control and, therefore, complete Black submission.

Their commitment to white supremacy sprang from tradition, and in the 1870s and

Black people line up to vote at a state election in the South during Reconstruction in 1867.

1880s, it was also bolstered by scientific opinion. Herbert Spencer and William Graham Stunner pioneered a fierce brand of social Darwinism that dovetailed rather effectively with the practice of white supremacy at home and abroad. White Southerners were no longer alone; they were not an isolated, embattled minority of evil people who never outgrew the subjugation and brutality inflicted on Black enslaved people.

Nevertheless, the idea of the Ku Klux Klan was conceived at Pulaski, Tennessee, in 1865. It began as an organization of unemployed Confederates and, by the late 1860s, had become a popular and ever-growing extralegal paramilitary brotherhood, wrapped in legendary

bedsheets and shrouded in exotic secretive ceremonies and rituals.

Large themes such as 'racial adjustment' always take up prominent places in the history books, but there is a danger in this. For thousands of Southerners, the years after the Civil War were not judged by some far-off national reference points. They were a time neither of the perceived disaster of Black alien rule, nor of the sparkling dawn of brotherhood and ultimately, racial equality. Rather, they were years without very much, if any, extraordinary moral dimension at all, when Southerners were not as preoccupied as we are commonly led to believe with either momentous political choices or intractable racial dilemmas.

These were years spent trying to make as much money as they could, and trying to solve the immediate, local, concrete problems that come with trying to stay alive in changed and constantly changing circumstances. The South then was a world of harvest yields, of the weather, of freight rates to market, of prices in that market, of technological change, and of social resistance to change.

The 1870s were hard times in the South, as elsewhere, and it was the limits of the Southern economy as much as anything else that determined that the radical reforms of Reconstruction would not succeed. In a poor region, concern for prosperity far outweighed concern for civil rights and would continue to do so until that far distant day when the South finally got to its feet.

⊙ THE KU KLUX KLAN

This first era of the Ku Klux Klan stretched from its inception in 1865 through to 1871, when the group's objective to overthrow pro-reconstruction governments in the South through violence against Black leaders, failed.

The Klan however didn't simply cease to exist. The seeds sown in this first phase went on to help give rise to a disturbingly mainstream second era, from 1915 until 1944. Marketed as a social group that well-to-do Americans should aspire to be a part of, the group tried and failed to target Catholicism and Judaism during a time of religious mass exodus from Europe in World War II.

SHARECROPPERS

Slavery had been replaced by sharecropping, and all of those alleged new farms were not in fact worked by happy yeomen but by dour, overworked tenants, poor as ever and far from independent. Sharecropping was a simple arrangement whereby the landowner decided what crops were grown and then arranged for their marketing.

The proceeds were split into thirds: one for the labor, one for the land, one for the seeds and implements. Or put another way: one-third for the cropper, two-thirds for the owner. The plantations once worked by enslaved people were divided into plots worked by tenant families, and it was each of these new units that was counted in the census as a 'farm.' Thus the general structure of the Old South's estates– land held in parcels and worked by cheap labor with no other options – persisted.

Thousands of Northerners had come to realize that the underdeveloped South presented vast opportunities. It offered ingredients of early-stage industrial development in abundance: land, timber, coal, water power, and cheap labor. 'How to get rich in the South' propaganda streamed out of the North, and countless afterdinner speeches to eager groups of Northern businessmen and investors began with ringing admonitions to 'Go South, young man ...'

Many Southerners, eager to put away the rancor of the war and its after-years, seemed keen to embrace their share of the nation's new industrial destiny. In a spirit of sectional reconciliation undergirded by a common desire for profits and prosperity, they welcomed the Yankee investors and industrialists, and not just with words.

With expanding railroads, by far the most magical technology of the age, the way was opened for the development of the South's vast iron ore and coal deposits and for the growth of cities such as Birmingham, Alabama, which Southerners John T. Milner and Daniel Pratt did their best, quite successfully, to turn into the Pittsburgh of the South. By 1898, Birmingham had become the largest source of pig iron in the United States and the third largest source in the whole world, yet in 1860 there had been nothing there at all.

Beginning in the middle and late 1880s, the South's oldest cash crop, tobacco, proved that it too offered new market opportunities. But the greatest substance and the greatest symbolism of the new industrializing South grew from the crop most closely identified with the region: cotton. More than anything else, the cotton mill came to typify the effort of the South to be more like its former enemy, the North. Between 1880 and 1900, the number of Southern mills rose from 161 to some 400, which far outstripped the rest of the country.

Workers pick cotton on a farm.

Viewed on the surface, the South's industrial progress seemed impressive, and yet it was still tarnished not far below. The region had induced capital and manufacturing to come to it by offering everything at its command more cheaply – taxes, power, land, raw materials, and especially labor. But once the initial processing had been done in the South, the final, more valuable (and infinitely more lucrative) work was done somewhere else, imprisoning the South in a self-defeating 'colonial economy' of Southern enterprises controlled from Northern boardrooms and Southern factories feeding the profits of Northern shareholders.

This newer South fitted comfortably within this mainstream. The South had to start from a lower point than the rest of America, and it seemed that Southerners always had to run harder just to keep up. But about the worthiness of the race itself, prophets of this newer South had no doubts. So spacious was their faith that there was even room in it for the South's most forgotten man – the Black man.

BOOKER T. WASHINGTON

Booker T. Washington, born an enslaved person in the Virginia backcountry, became the greatest Black spokesman that the New South produced. He concluded that no sane white man, who truly

Booker T. Washington.

hoped for the progress of his section, could profit by keeping millions of Black people in a condition of perpetual serfdom. It went against the grain of practicality not to allow everyone on the bandwagon, even though it went without saying that Black Southerners would only ride at the rear.

But riding at the rear was better than not at all, and it was, Washington understood, about the best that could be expected. It was more essential for a Black person to be able to earn a dollar at a good job than to be able to spend a dollar in the same opera house as a white man. So, he put forward his famous program for the vocational education of Black people both in skills, to enable them to support themselves and their families in modest comfort, and in

trades, to give them some claim to the prosperity brought about by wider economic changes.

Booker T. Washington's enduring monument is Tuskegee Institute in Alabama (see page 145), an industrial training center where he hoped to educate Black people in the most practical ways of being useful to their own community. Today, Washington's measures seem mild, halfhearted, and to some even 'Uncle Tom-ish.' Then, however, they appeared prudent and not without a genuine vision for Black people. But the United States Supreme Court effectively scotched any notions of Black social equality with its famous doctrine of 'separate but equal.' Racial segregation in public accommodations and education, the court said, could not be construed as 'unequal' or as 'discriminatory'' so long as the facilities available to both races were comparable in quality.

Even though things in the South were, in fact, almost always separate but unequal, 'separate but equal' remained the law of the land for race relations in all of the United States until as late as the 1950s. And in the South, which was where the vast majority of Black people still lived, a rigorous pattern of social segregation, known as the era of Jim Crow, clamped down on the many Black people with unrelenting discipline. (The name Jim Crow comes from a song in a minstrel show.)

WORLD WAR I

With the outbreak of hostilities in Europe in 1914, key cotton exchanges did not open, and prices initially tumbled. But due both to its congressional influence and its felicitous climate, making year-round training possible, military camps and bases proliferated, and many cities continued on in peacetime. Southern ports became important embarkation points and home to an ever more immense American fleet. The wartime boom – once the initial cotton panic had passed – gave fresh substance to the New South's not so new boasts that industrialization was the path to a prosperous future. Munitions factories in Tennessee and Virginia, chemical plants in Alabama, and textile mills everywhere pulled Southerners out of the fields and, in what was a new experience for many, gave them a taste of earning real money.

The whole nation dashed toward the 1920s with pent-up energy. The industrial boom triggered by the war expanded and, in the water-power rich South, was driven by electricity. The chemical and textile industries especially profited, and the region of the Carolina Piedmont overtook New England as the nation's primary consumer of the South's raw cotton.

The fashion for cigarettes and an increasing number of female smokers gave new life to the South's oldest source of wealth, tobacco, and it was at this time that names such as Camel and Lucky Strike entered the American vernacular. But none of these could match the Southern beverage that had first been brewed by an Atlanta druggist in 1886 and then made famous by Robert Woodruff in the 1920s: Coca-Cola. Everywhere there were new roads, automobiles, movie palaces, and real estate subdivisions. But by 1920, the 11 American states with the lowest per capita income were all Southern, with Alabama at the bottom and Louisiana at the top. Thus, poverty joined with race, religion, and the memory of defeat to set the South apart as America's most sectional of sections.

THE KKK

The Ku Klux Klan, which was reborn on Stone Mountain in Georgia on Thanksgiving night, 1915, still skulks about the South today, representing the anachronistic voice of white supremacy. Then, it was the authentic voice not only of the South's unrelenting race prejudice but also of the more general fear among a rural people that change was making a mess of old moral certainties. In this respect, the Klan did not mirror only Southern anxiety, and indeed some of its greatest 'successes' came from places as far afield as Indiana, where it actually operated a successful political machine. But the Klan's general lack of a well-articulated program bespoke its truer nature – that of the defense mechanism, and death rattle, of a dying America and a more slowly dying South. For such ill-educated people, whose daily lives were an endless (and for many hopeless) routine of planting cotton and waiting for it to grow, the rituals and mystique of the exotic hooded order fostered a sense of camaraderie and belonging amid the distress of an otherwise grim agricultural existence. The price of admission was $10, and it bought a knighthood in the Invisible Empire of the Ku Klux Klan, where there were wizards and cyclopses – and always someone else to blame.

Although the Klan became an influence in state politics, it never had a platform and could never boast the powerful political leadership needed for long-term success. Most of the major urban newspapers of the day vociferously opposed it, and the KKK ultimately fell victim to its own excesses.

THE 1930S

It was President Franklin Roosevelt, not the KKK, who had the greater impact on Southerners' lives during the 1930s. Roosevelt, a New York blue blood with a house in Warm Springs, Georgia, always claimed to know the South well – indeed to

Ku Klux Klan initiation at Stone Mountain in 1949.

love it and understand its problems. Among many other projects, he was instrumental in furthering the Tennessee Valley Authority (TVA), one of the largest public works projects ever attempted.

The TVA's genesis reached back to 1916 to the federal authorization, for reasons of national defense, of power and nitrate plants on the Tennessee River at Muscle Shoals in Alabama and to a belief that there should be a public yardstick for measuring the cost of private utilities. At stake was water power, the generation of electricity, the production of fertilizer, flood control, navigation, conservation, and other facets of regional planning. The project encompassed an area touching on parts of seven states and nearly as large as England.

The TVA became a powerful ally of the New South once recovery came, adding immensely to the region's attractiveness for industrial development. The orchestration of resources by the TVA helped attract Northern capital anew. Along with the continued growth of textile and garment manufacturing, paper milling and furniture manufacturing, and increasingly chemical and petroleum industries, the TVA proved that, despite the drawbacks of outside investment – and thus of outside control – if there were enough of it to go around, there would also be

Huey P. Long.

sufficient profits for the South.

HUEY P. LONG

Louisiana's Huey P. Long posed the only serious threat to Roosevelt in the early 1930s. By then a senator, Long provided crucial help in securing the Democratic Party nomination for Roosevelt in 1932 and at first pledged support. Two years after the election, that support evaporated as Long issued diatribes against the president's economic and labor policies. Long's dreams were not bounded by state lines. In 1932, he announced his 'Share-Our-Wealth' program, through which he proposed the liquidation of large personal fortunes; guarantees of $2,500 in annual wages to

every worker; adequate pensions; and college educations for all qualified students.

Two years later, Long took his program nationwide and soon claimed that 7.5 million members belonged to his 27,000 clubs. His popularity soared to the point that poll-watchers estimated Long could win 6 million votes as a third-party presidential candidate in the 1936 election. That prediction was never proved. In September 1935, Long was assassinated by Dr Carl Austin Weiss in the Louisiana State Capitol. The presumed motive was that Weiss was infuriated over Long's attempts to oust Weiss's father-in-law from his judgeship. That, too, was never proved. After firing the shot that killed Long, Weiss was gunned down by the senator's bodyguards, and the mystery remains.

Frivolous, but no less meaningful events, also took place in the 1930s. Atlantan Margaret Mitchell's book, *Gone with the Wind*, set the imagination of the nation alight, prompting a glamorous ascent that culminated in a starry premiere of the MGM movie three years later. World War II was shorter and less traumatic for the United States than for most of the other participating nations, but for a country that still clung tenaciously to old notions of innocence and isolation, it brought the cares – and the challenges – of the world crashing down on American shoulders with resounding finality. Both the goal and the means employed to achieve victory were loaded with important implications for the South, whose people once again eagerly flocked to their country's colors. Those implications meant change.

⊘ CIVILIAN CONSERVATION CORPS

Anyone camping near the Skyline Drive or Blue Ridge Parkway in Virginia's Shenandoah Valley, or picnicking in Tennessee's Great Smoky Mountains National Park, is probably reaping the rewards of one of Franklin D. Roosevelt's most successful 1930s relief programs, the Civilian Conservation Corps (CCC). Enrollees were generally underprivileged young men who were assigned outdoor work in national parks near where they lived. At the same time, they were given educational opportunities to improve their social and occupational skills. Projects included building campgrounds and picnic areas, hiking trails, cabins, and other lodging amenities, many of which are still in use.

JEFFERSON DAVIS

One of many disparaging remarks the 'Sphinx of the Confederacy' endured during, and after, the Civil War was that he was 'overmatched and outplayed.' Scholars have even suggested that if their roles had been reversed, and Lincoln had been president of the Confederacy, the Union might well have lost the war. Jefferson Davis, the only president of the Confederacy, was a complicated and enigmatic personality who never sought, and didn't want, the job.

In 1824, Davis attended the United States Military Academy at West Point. Love for Sara Knox Taylor, daughter of his commanding officer, Colonel Zachary Taylor, caused Davis to resign from the army in 1835 because the colonel opposed the match. They married anyway and moved to Mississippi where Davis bought a plantation. But Sara died from malaria within three months. Davis spent the ensuing 10 years working his farm, and by all accounts his manner towards the enslaved people was patriarchal rather than brutal. He was a well-regarded local figure.

Davis married Varina Howard in 1845, the same year he was elected to the US Congress as representative for Mississippi. When war against Mexico was declared, he fought and returned a hero. A seat in the US Senate soon followed.

Henry Clay's 1850 Compromise Slave Act was anathema to Davis who, as a strong supporter of states' rights, felt Clay's bill violated the terms of the US Constitution. Davis resigned and went home to Mississippi. In 1853, President Franklin Pierce made Davis Secretary of War. He served with distinction until he was re-elected to the Senate.

The election of Abraham Lincoln in 1860, and his declaration that there would be no additional slave-owning states admitted to the Union, broadened the schism between North and South. In January 1861, Mississippi seceded. Davis resigned his Senate seat

and was appointed major-general of the state's troops. The deadlocked Confederate Congress, meeting in Montgomery, Alabama, found in Davis a compromise presidential candidate, and elected him to the Confederacy's highest office. Davis received the news with something less than joy: 'I thought myself better adapted to command in the field.'

In the beginning, he was a popular choice. His cabinet included men of ability, and he listened to the advice of his generals. But 1863 saw a turn in Davis's fortunes. Becoming autocratic, he meddled in army matters, countermanding orders and promoting favorite officers. Many felt he had usurped powers

Jefferson Davis.

not granted by the electorate. Until the war's last days, Davis insisted it would be won by the Confederacy, and refused to consider any peace proposals except those that left the South independent.

When Lee surrendered at Appomattox in April 1865, Davis attempted to flee with his family to Mexico, but was caught and imprisoned. After his release, Davis settled on a plantation near Biloxi, Mississippi, where he wrote his version of the Confederacy's history, *The Rise and Fall of the Confederate Government*. Mississippians wanted to return Davis to the US Senate, but he refused to ask for a federal pardon.

Jefferson Davis died peacefully on December 6, 1889, in New Orleans, Louisiana. His body now rests in Richmond, Virginia.

Martin Luther King Jr, and his wife, Coretta, lead a five-day march to the Alabama State Capitol in Montgomery in 1965.

MODERN TIMES

Racial conflict in the 1950s and '60s seared the air, but the emergence of 'the Sun Belt' as an economic force foreshadowed the South.

The changes of the past 100 years had been profound ones for the South. From a profitable, self-sufficient land of plantations and Old World values, it had been transformed into a place of small farms and light industry, dominated by Yankee know-how and dependent on Northern investment. The years following 1945 saw the development of the much vaunted 'affluent society' in America, and Southerners made it known once and for all that they intended to be full partners in it.

Southern boosters proclaimed afresh all the region's advantages: abundant natural resources and sources of energy, congenial state legislatures at the ready with favorable tax laws and additional incentives, a cheap and plentiful supply of labor, and long-deprived markets for durable and consumer goods. The conversion of wartime plants helped start the boom, which soon became self-sustaining as factories multiplied, producing air conditioners, washing machines, farm implements, and in time even automobiles, in addition to the old standbys such as textiles and chemicals.

SOUTHERN ZEAL

Exhibiting a zeal that matched the bonanza-sized opportunities, Southern leaders in both public and private life ceaselessly put the South's case as the undoubted site of America's next industrial revolution.

The affluence of the South in the 1950s and 1960s, was lauded by many as akin to the golden age of New York in the 1920s. The architecture was just as grand as the social scene.

A Black student is jeered as he tries to enter school in Clinton, Tennessee in 1956.

Southerners thus kept alive the old scalawag tradition of enticing Northern investment, using the lures of relatively low expenses and high prospective profits. Large Northern-based corporations did enter the South to build plants and factories and hired Southern workers to staff them. Management, while commonly non-Southern at first, was eventually recruited from the native work force.

Industrialization wrought extremely visible changes in the South's economic life. These ranged from the complete domination of the economies of small towns such as Camden, South Carolina, and Waynesboro, Virginia, by Northern-based corporate giants such as Du

Pont and General Electric, to the complete remaking of regional landscapes. This is what happened in the Tennessee Valley where, by the early 1970s, the dams and power plants of the Roosevelt-era Tennessee Valley Authority were turning out 10 percent of the United States' electricity needs.

Along the Mississippi River, oil refineries and petrochemical plants lined the shore all the way from Baton Rouge to New Orleans. Defense contracts provided an artificial, though highly tangible, boost to industrial growth, and as Cold

South's original admonition to farmers to diversify, diversify, diversify. By the 1960s, tree farms were as common as cotton fields and produced approximately a third of the nation's lumber. Southern pastures, which likewise profited from the region's generous growing season, fed beef cattle that produced an income for Southern farmers three times that earned by 'the great white staple' of yore.

Commercial poultry production soared, and from the long, low-roofed sheds that became a fixture on thousands of Southern farms there

Farm workers harvest tobacco plants in North Carolina.

War military budgets swelled, the South's share of them grew disproportionately. America's space race was run from Southern headquarters whose names became famous throughout the world in the 1960s and '70s: Cape Canaveral in Florida, the Marshall Space Flight Center in Alabama, and the Mission Control Center in Houston, Texas.

Change also came to the land itself, which remained for many Southerners, however they made their living, at the core of their identity. Once the 'land of cotton' whose 'kingdom' stretched from Virginia's Tidewater to Texas, Southern agriculture of the post-World War II years turned decisively to other more profitable commodities, and at long last it lived up to the

⊙ WHY NASA CHOSE FLORIDA

NASA first came to Florida in 1968 when the NASA Launch Operations Center (better known today as the John F. Kennedy Space Center) opened its doors. Charged with the mission of outpacing the Russians in the Space Race to put humans in orbit and then on the moon, this facility soon became NASA's primary launch hub.

This location was chosen specifically because the atmospheric pressure here is statistically much lower than any other landmass location in the United States, making it much easier and faster for rockets to escape the earth's gravity and enter planetary orbit.

came millions of chickens and eggs. Almost all of America's tobacco continued to be grown in Virginia, Kentucky, and North Carolina, and the South still produced the lion's share of America's cotton, though most of it came from regions west of the Mississippi.

THE SUN BELT

Whatever the ancestral and economic pull of the land, however, the demographics of the post-1945 South told a different story. It was a story of the seemingly ineluctable migration of South-

well as privately. This, coupled with the enduring lure of a mild climate and a generally lower cost of living, gave birth to the lucrative Sun Belt phenomenon.

Southern cities grew out, not up, and they grew in a hurry. There was no time for, and little interest in, the agglomeration of dense innercity neighborhoods; the Sun Belt cities sprouted in the middle-class, white-collar era, and because of an ethnic homogeneity utterly unlike the older industrial cities of the North, their residents tended to sort themselves along simple

A Delta Air Lines passenger jet is loaded with cargo containers at Hartsfield-Jackson Airport.

erners from the countryside and small towns to the cities. Industrialization speeded urbanization and breathed new life into oldfashioned towns such as Augusta, Georgia; Nashville, Tennessee; Montgomery, Alabama; and Richmond, Virginia.

The South's premier city, Atlanta, Georgia, which had always made much of rising from the ashes left by William Tecumseh Sherman's Federal Army in 1864, set the pace, establishing itself as the commercial and transportation hub (first in the era of the railroad and later in the airline age) of the entire Southeast. Less than half a million people were living there in 1940; 30 years later the figure was as great as 1.2 million. Such growth was fueled publicly as

⊘ DELTA AIR LINES

Delta is a household name and one of the world's largest (and subsequently one of the busiest) international airlines, with its hub in Atlanta. However its origins are somewhat more modest: founded almost 100 years ago in Macon, Georgia, the airline was originally a crop-dusting business known as Huff Daland Dusters. As it grew, the airline moved to Louisiana and then finally to Atlanta in 1941, a city chosen because it was the most central point between the numerous regional airlines Delta had acquired over the years. Today, Delta operates almost 4,500 flights a day and employs upwards of 75,000 people.

lines of income and, even after segregation was made unlawful, of race. In this sense, the cities' growth conformed to old Southern characteristics. But in their renewed promise of an utterly transformed physical and social land scape, the cities clashed sharply with the region's fundamental conservatism.

The single change in the South that very few lamented, and that no one would admit to lamenting anyway, involved the issue that most visibly went to the heart of Southern distinctiveness: race.

and the next years witnessed much talk among Southern governors of 'state interposition' and 'massive resistance' to hold back the tide. They were not alone, and thousands of ordinary white Southerners rallied to their cry.

But the times had changed decisively, and there were now thousands of native Northerners who had come to the South in the post-war economic boom and who were at best indifferent to the system of segregation. States' rights held little allure for them, and in the years of the 'sit-in' and the 'freedom march,' the old racial

A cemetery and chemical plant in Louisiana.

In 1954, the landmark Supreme Court decision of Brown v. Board of Education set aside 'separate but equal' and opened the door on a tense period during which the forces of state and nation faced off as they had not done since the secession crisis of 1860 and 1861. This time no one talked of leaving the Union, but segregationist Southerners did make a series of last stands in a not altogether unsuccessful attempt to slow the steamroller of federally mandated racial equality.

CIVIL RIGHTS ACTS

In 1957, Republican President Dwight D. Eisenhower sent federal troops to Little Rock, Arkansas, to protect Black students at the newly integrated Central High School (see page 212),

arrangements of the South crumbled because of two factors: outside pressures and internal weariness.

Federal force was used again in the early 1960s against recalcitrant state governors such as Ross Barnett of Mississippi and George Wallace of Alabama. But it was the nonviolence of Black leaders in the South – best exemplified by Martin Luther King, Jr, who had come to prominence during the Montgomery Bus Boycott of 1955 and was brutally assassinated in Memphis 13 years later (see pages 140 and 225) that eventually triumphed. The spectacle of peaceful Black demonstrators being met with the clubs and dogs and water cannon of white police departments, brought instantly into people's homes by television, revolted the moral conscience of the nation and moved moderate-minded people everywhere to the judgment that the South's racial prejudices no longer had a place in modern America.

That consensus was reflected in the passage of the Civil Rights Act of 1964 and of the Voting Rights Act of 1965, which finally completed the work begun in the Reconstruction era following the Civil War. That the pattern of racial arrangements changed so quickly, and with so little social disruption, is testimony both to how truly

BIBLE BELT

But it was not in politics but in religion – in the unadulterated orthodox faith of their fathers – that Southerners continued to find the solace of continuity amid rapid social and economic change. Almost half of Southern church members are Southern Baptists, a denomination so all-embracing and so influential that it has fairly been called the folk church of the South. The secular impact of such religious identification, and of the faith it reflects, is notoriously hard to judge, but there's no doubt

One of Georgia's most famous presidents, Jimmy Carter, who was president from 1977–81.

outdated it had become and to the salient fact that white Southerners, who were in a majority in most parts of the region, no longer needed to fear the tyranny of a vengeful Black majority.

In the absence of the bogy of race, and despite the persistent populism that boiled to the surface in the third-party presidential bids of Alabama Governor George Wallace and, finally, in November 1976, in the election of Georgian Jimmy Carter to the presidency on an anti-Washington platform, a sturdy new sense of self was developing among the prosperous citizens of this newest South.

It was helped, of course, by the election of another Southerner, Bill Clinton from Arkansas, to the presidency in the early 1990s.

⊙ SOUTHERN BAPTIST CHURCH

The Southern Baptist Church was founded in Augusta Georgia in 1845. Today, it is one of the largest Christian denomination in the world, with just over 14 million registered members. Its origins can be traced back to a split with the northern Baptist Church over the issue of whether Southern slave owners should be eligible to serve as missionaries. Further divisions developed in the aftermath of the American Civil War, when freed enslaved people began establishing independent Black congregations. At the last count, more than 4 million Americans attend a weekly service at a Southern Baptist Church.

that it contributes mightily to the conservative cultural cast of the region. The Black church, which provided so much of the nurturing ground and leadership for the great victories of the 1950s and 1960s Civil Rights movement, remains today still predominantly populated by Black people. On both sides of the color line, it seems, the church doors are open, but no one chooses to pass through of his own free will. Nor is it something that troubles most Southern Christians, Black or white.

Louisiana State Police.

SMALL-TOWN VALUES

By contrast, another main theme of Southern history seems to have rather less of a future today, at least in the form that most Southerners once knew it. Ruralism is on the wane, and whatever parallels might be drawn between the small farms idealized in the 1920s, and the 'green revolution' of the 1960s and 1970s, the fact remains that, by 1970, 65 percent of Southerners were classified by the census as urban. Yet this was urbanism Southern-style, and in most cases, it was on a smaller scale than elsewhere. Only 25 percent lived in cities with populations over 100,000; 40 percent lived in suburbs or in the 4,500 'cities' of less than 100,000 people. It is frequently remarked that

most Southern cities, even the big ones, retain the quality of overgrown country towns. Indeed, many urban residents have only recently come from the country and still have familial ties there. And, in the 1970 census, there was that hefty 35 percent who were still officially 'rural.' These were not the rural folk of myth: four out of five earned a living 'in town,' commuting by car to an office or factory while remaining very much country people in outlook. And while the truly rural population was relatively small, it remained divided much as it had been throughout its long history into planters, yeomen, and landless laborers, with all the different social distinctions to match.

Finally, poverty and a perceived powerlessness will cease to shape the South's future as they once shaped its past. The new prosperity of the Sun Belt boom is not imaginary; this is the South in the flesh at last, after all those years of blustery talk. It is no coincidence that the world-wide headquarters of the courier company Federal Express are located in Memphis, Tennessee; that North Carolina, home of the vastly profitable R. J. Reynolds tobacco company, boasts both the headquarters of the airline US Airways and a highly recognized 'Silicon Valley' computer corridor near Raleigh-Durham; or that the soaring architectural towers of Atlanta, inspired by local son and internationally respected architect John Portman, house many corporate headquarters mentioned in the Fortune 500.

There is no reason to suppose that the new prosperity of the South will not grow even greater in the future. It should not be surprising that the region should at last have opted for a newer South. Backwardness, after all, is picturesque only in fiction and old movies. Like Americans in colder climates, Southerners perceive the good life through a lens that is largely materialistic. They are subject to the same economic pressures and temptations as other people and, in general, they make their choices from the same broad set of options.

And yet there remains an almost imperceptible difference that is impossible to quantify and that has nothing at all to do with colonial economies, textile mills, high-tech industries, or per capita income. Rather, to use the Southern idiom, it is a matter of accent, and to talk about it means having to deal with matters of taste and personal standards.

Consider the following: it is a cliché that any real Southerner will remain polite until he gets mad enough to kill. Not that many kill (although deer hunting and the stalking of small animals remain popular outdoor pursuits, and the prevalence of gun stores takes many a foreign visitor by surprise), but it's true that most Southerners remain polite even in this age of 'candor' and enlightened free expression. In sophisticated Southern cities and on urbane university cam-

RELATIVE VALUES

Consciousness of kin – the saints and the sinners alike – remains powerful and, in a much-attenuated form, so does consciousness of class. Despite the great movement of people and wealth into the South from outside, a select gentry survives comprising descendants of antebellum planters who owe their existence more to the power of tradition than to money or influence, which have long since passed to others. There is a distinction in the South between 'good family' and 'good people' that is not often made in Iowa

Members of the Little Rock Nine are joined by Bill Clinton at a ceremony.

puses, one can still witness a certain charming deference of man to woman, of youth to age, of student to teacher.

It's difficult not to notice the still pervasive 'no, ma'ams' and 'yes, sirs' that punctuate ordinary everyday conversation – leftovers for sure of a more class-conscious age but showing few signs of retreat even in these rigorously egalitarian times. Many of the rituals and restraints of etiquette that seem to have fallen out of use elsewhere in the world still thrive in the South, perhaps less in their more outlandish Sir Walter Scott forms than simply as traditions of courtesy and good manners. Church, home, and family still serve as a prime source of social conventions and of cultural and moral values.

or Pennsylvania. Admittedly, it is only the shade of an aristocratic tradition, but one that, shorn of its less lovely trappings, has been redeemed.

Its heirs can be stuffy and pretentious at their worst – undistinguished in either abilities or assets. But at their best, they can be a happy exception to the boredom and tastelessness of modern mass culture, through which every person is automatically accorded equality with every other person to achieve a uniformity of low regard. Besides this, character traits such as personal integrity, honor, understated graciousness, and the cultivation of 'good living' (as distinct from simply making a good living) are praiseworthy wherever they are found. In this case, all over the New South.

At the Ground Zero Blues Club in Clarksdale, Mississippi.

At the Mighty Mississippi Music
Festival, in Greenville.

SOUTHERNERS

From good ole boys and Southern belles to Internet start-up millionaires and international bankers – Dixie charms 'em all.

Southerners divide the world into two parts: the South, and everywhere else. The authority for this view is unassailable. Dixie, the South's anthem, declares that 'the world was made in just six days/ And finished off in various ways/ Look away! Look away! Look away, Dixie Land! God made Dixie trim and nice/ But Adam called it Paradise/ Look away! Look away! Look away, Dixie Land.' By this logic then, to be a non-Southerner, is to be excluded from Paradise.

INFINITE VARIETY

Those unfortunate enough to be outsiders generally base much of their knowledge of Southerners on one novel and its movie version: Margaret Mitchell's 1936 bestseller *Gone with the Wind*, immortalized three years later by MGM. What the entire world has imagined – many as they read the novel in translation, and later had confirmed while watching the movie on Ted Turner's TV station – was Scarlett O'Hara with skirts billowing as she floated over Tara's sweeping lawns under blossoming magnolias.

This was a limited view of the South even in the 1860s. Trying to fit all Southerners into the mould of Mitchell's main characters is to deny the infinite variety of human beings. Yet Southern types as distinct and recognisable as their world-renowned accents do exist, you just need to know what to look for.

The past in the South defines the present. Once you cross the Mason-Dixon line – that imaginary border between North and South – the past ceases to be the past. It just won't lie down. Knowing who did what, and when, in history is just as important as knowing what year Elton John bought his lavish apartment in Atlanta, or which restaurant in Birmingham, Alabama, made Gourmet's Top Five list.

A New Orleanian.

You might easily find, for example, on a summer afternoon, heated discussions taking place on the porches of numerous homes in Rutherford County, Tennessee, about the details of daring cavalry raids under the command of General Nathan Bedford Forrest in 1864. The men who rode with him were known as Forrest's Escort and most came from the immediate vicinity. The discussion is as animated as if the raid had occurred this morning and news of it had just arrived. Who participated. Who did what. The outcome – as if it were still in doubt and still mattered. But it does matter, to them. If it were known that yo' great-grandpappy did not ride with Forrest's Escort, you would be permitted no part in the conversation.

The 'living in Paradise' attitude dates back even farther in Southern consciousness. Settlers bound for Virginia were assured in an ode by Michael Drayton (1563–1631) that Virginia is 'Earth's only Paradise.' The Cavalier/ planter/ Christian gentleman figure appeared hauntingly in the novels of antebellum writers long before he actually trod the soil of Virginia as that ultimate Southern icon, General Robert E. Lee.

Today's descendants may still own the same land or may be two generations away from it, engaged in a high-tech business in the city. But

Old friends chatting in Mississippi.

⊘ NATHAN BEDFORD FORREST

Born and raised in Tennessee, General Nathan Bedford Forrest is one of the most controversial figures from the American Civil War, and indeed throughout wider American history. Elected as the first Grand Wizard of the Ku Klux Klan from 1867 to 1869, Forrest was known to deliberately target and massacre Black Union troops. However, his successes on the battlefield saw him labeled in many quarters as a military genius. His primary tactic and phrase 'Get there the firstest with the mostest' is still quoted by tacticians to this day. He died in 1877 and upwards of 20,000 were said to join his funeral procession.

Edgar Allan Poe's tale The Gold Bug popularized Sullivan's Island, located in South Carolina, and was an example of detective fiction cryptography, a popular fiction genre in the 1840s.

there will still be an historical recollection, a family group memory. The land confers a sense of place on an individual. It's a rootedness rare in other Americans, whose historical continuity is more fragmented.

Contemporaries who have broken with the past, however, point out problems faced by those held in its thrall. 'There's nothing wrong with Mr S,' they might say, 'except that he's got ancestors.' There's an almost Asian strength to ancestor worship in the South, the Virginia variety being especially intense, with the Carolinas not far behind.

The semi-tropical landscape of South Carolina's Low Country, with its weirdness and melancholy, was the setting for Edgar Allan Poe's story *The Gold Bug*, specifically Sullivan's Island at the entrance to Charleston Harbor.

Today, dank tarns and funereal, coastal woodlands still abound in legends and superstitions. One of the most celebrated tales of the Low Country started in the back alleys of Charleston and graduated to successful productions in New York and major European cities, including a performance at Milan's La Scala. The odyssey of a work about South Carolina Gullah African-Americans began with the publication in 1925 of DuBose Heyward's novella *Porgy*. The author, an admirer of the poetry and pathos in the lives of those in Charleston's dilapidated quarter, turned his novella into a play two years later. In 1935, George Gershwin's music joined Heyward's libretto to become the folk opera *Porgy and Bess*. Hollywood followed in 1959.

Catfish Row is no minstrel world of stereotypes, though. There's Porgy, crippled but a true hero; Bess, a genuinely seductive heroine; Crown, embodiment of erotic primitive brutality; the bootlegger Sporting Life; the matriarch Maria. No clowns, no Uncle Toms, no Mr Interlocutor. It made a refreshing change.

In pinning down the appeal of these characters, the punchline in an apocryphal Southern anecdote may prove as illuminating as critical analysis. As the story goes, a well-meaning white employer suggests that if his employee's conduct over the weekend had not been so improvident, he would be feeling much better and more like working on Monday morning. The employee replies: 'Yessir, boss, that's true, but you ain't never been a Black man on a Saturday night.' Heyward appreciated what he called this 'unique characteristic' in the lives of Black people. He saw the person of African descent as the 'inheritor of a source of delight' that he would have given much to possess.

SOUTHERN BELLES

A bestselling country song once advised unwary males that 'there's girls, there's women, and there's ladies.' The first and last terms are references to Southern belles and Southern ladies, Scarlett O'Hara and Melanie Wilkes being the two best known in their respective categories. Matriarchs and spinsters are a sub-class of Southern ladies. 'Women' includes all other females from independent female tycoons to Appalachian mountain beauties. The code word for Southern belle among those who are and do not have to concern themselves with definitions is 'real cute girl.' For a divine example of the 'real cute girl' syndrome, read Rebecca Wells' *The Divine Secrets of the Ya-Ya Sisterhood* (with a movie adaptation starring Sandra Bullock in 2002), about a daughter, her mother and her mother's highstepping society pals in Louisiana. Never refer in public to a young woman as a Southern belle. No one with pretensions to a high social intelligence quotient would prattle in such a manner. Southern belle is a term of convenience applied by outsiders in their attempts to understand an inexplicable life form. Over time, the persona of the Southern belle has changed. The definitive description was penned in 1959 by Frances Gray Patton for *Holiday* magazine. The modern belle, Patton found, sees her 'essentially passive role at odds with a society increasingly with hazards of coarseness and strident ambitions.' But then did the 'gently nurtured Southern girl' ever really exist outside the Gothic Southern imagination? Her personal aura comprises equal parts of purity and passion. And, no matter what she has been doing all day, she can dance all night in high heels to the melodies generated by juke box, rock band, or full orchestra. Her smile makes the old feel young and the poor feel rich.

In her presence any male – be he nine or 90 – feels alternately soothed and energized, gallant, competent, invincible. She does exist, and she confirms his expectations by always doing what is expected of her.

STEEL MAGNOLIAS

The Southern female – now typically called a 'steel magnolia' – was originally categorized

A graduation ceremony at the College of Charleston.

as a Southern lady who, if she survived multiple childbirths, became a matriarch. In Virginia, there's a saying that it takes three generations to make a gentleman, four to make a lady. Ladies had the responsibility of formulating and ritualizing the social conventions that well-bred girls from Little Rock, Mobile, and all over the South would be taught from their cradles. Such a lady referred to her husband only by his title and his surname, a custom that has not entirely disappeared. Forced by circumstances to manage and oversee huge plantations while their husbands and other male relatives were away from 1861 to 1865, the ladies were loath to return to 'china doll' status after the Confederacy's collapse. Today they can be found staffing charity auctions in Atlanta, or as trustees of art institutes in New Orleans.

RURAL REALITIES

The contrast between rural past and urban present is fresher in the Southern consciousness than in other regions because the change from one to the other is so recent. It wasn't so long ago that 85 percent of Southerners made their living from the land, and the number remains high. These are ordinary folks, yeoman farmers, working class and lower middle class, many of

Hiker on the Appalachian Trail.

German and Scots-Irish descent.

In the Carolinas they are textile workers and tenant farmers who raise tobacco; in the Mountain South they are coal miners, loggers, and hardscrabble farmers, tilling rocky, unforgiving soil called 'creek farms' in eastern Tennessee, where 'bottom land,' rich loamy soil is scarce and very precious.

These people live a few miles 'out from town' in a house trailer on county-maintained roads that were once wagon ruts and loggers' roads. The Mountain South, especially around Tennessee and Virginia, has long been home to small groups whose occupation has excited inordinate interest. In the mountain idiom, they are moonshiners. Like farming, moonshining – the illegal

distilling of whiskey – was a family business. Producing mountain dew or white lightnin', two other terms for home-distilled whiskey, was a cash crop in a region where a diligent farmer could end the growing season with a lot of corn and not a single penny in his coveralls.

The generations-old family activity was criminalized when a remote federal government decided to collect a tax on the making of such whiskey. The change led to years of violence in the Appalachian hills and, curiously enough, to the development of the South's favorite sport after football. Stock-car racing grew out of the ability of the bootleg runner's high-performance car (carrying his 'stock') to outrun the cars of agents.

BUBBAS AND GOOD OLE BOYS

Three terms used to describe white Southern males – bubba, redneck, and good ole boy – are not synonyms. Bubba is a fellow whose reactions are constrained by his limited intelligence. Two of a bubba's three standard reactions involve shooting: (1) shoot it and have it stuffed for a wall trophy; (2) shoot it and cook and eat it; and (3) marry it. Today's bubba can be rural or urban, and may even be the overindulged, spoiled-brat son of a small-town lawyer.

A redneck is rural. The term, not originally derogatory, referred to those who labored in the field (today on the construction site) under the South's hot sun. As a result, their neck acquired a red, ridged appearance. The original rednecks were from humble, but honorable, beginnings.

⊘ STEEL MAGNOLIAS

The 1989 movie *Steel Magnolias* is lauded by many as a particularly accurate portrayal of matriarchal society in the South during the late 20th century. With an all-star cast including Sally Field, Julia Roberts, Shirley MacLaine, and Dolly Parton, the plot is a true to life tale from the mind of author Robert Harling based on a play he wrote in 1987. The title conveys that women of the South could be both tough as steel and delicate as a magnolia flower. Many in the South have a soft spot for the movie, making this the perfect conversation starter for solo travelers in their exploration of the Southern states.

Moonshine might be a key component in craft cocktails of the 21st century, but its speckled history includes unlawful production, smuggling, and distribution throughout the South.

Andrew Jackson, seventh president of the United States, came from such folk.

Today's rowdy redneck often has a fairly hefty income, which he spends on camping equipment, fishing, and weekends at stock-car races. Away from the racetrack, the redneck can still be recognized. All drive pick-up trucks. All have profoundly conservative politics.

A good ole boy exemplifies all the masculine virtues esteemed by his region. His life is equally devoted to guns, hunting, fishing, drinking, football and women, seasoned with a dash of nostalgia for trains. He is affable, amiable, likeable, and stubborn beyond belief – 'sot [set] in his ways.' One of his main activities is swapping anecdotes with his buddies ('stories' would be his word) in some social group variously called a gun, rifle, or hunting club. Typically, the group owns a number of acres in an isolated rural area on which members hunt or target practice on a regular basis.

For the good ole boy, hunting acquires mythical proportions. Good ole boys can be found at both the high and low ends of the economic scale. The ones whose fathers never got any farther from home than raccoon hunting in the next county or one trip to the state capital will today casually mention just having returned from a month in Kenya or Tanzania. Many a lawyer, politician or CEO, who could pose for the cover of *Gentleman's Quarterly*, calls himself a 'good ole boy' when interviewed.

NEW SOUTHERNERS

New Southerners also come in three varieties. The first are distinctly rural, escapees from the city, who live in the green hills of the Blue Ridge Mountains, or lovely Victorian villages like Eureka Springs, Arkansas. Educated, literate, and longing for a simpler life, these are modern-day hippies, but with cable TV, superfast internet and interesting jobs or unusual hobbies. In the more remote areas, though, conflict can arise. 'Those damn hippies, they don't want to change a thang,' grumbled one elderly storekeeper in Virginia, whose five-and-dime was now outfitted for tourists who want to experience an old-timey past. 'They just don't understand progress.'

Escape is also the game plan for thousands of rural youngsters who flock to the cities, dreaming of becoming tycoons, tech business owners, and computer software designers. And in the South this is feasible, something their grand-

A bicycle shop in Greenville, South Carolina.

parents would never really understand. Joining them at Delta Airways and other corporations are transplanted Yankees who work in John Portman-designed Atlanta towers and sweat it out in the gym after dining on shrimp and grits in a wood-and-chrome, awardwinning wine bar. Although this last category can never be considered truly Southern, parents up North are apt to comment on their child's slower way of talking, and how that frenetic New York jog has transformed into an amiable, ambling gait.

Given the fact that there are so many different types of Southerners, don't let anyone tell you, in Southern phraseology, that 'there's no such of a thing left.' They do exist – in all shapes and accents – all over the South.

Savannah Film Festival at one of the SCAD Theaters.

THE NEW SOUTH

A strong Southern spirit of reinvention gave the world Coca-Cola, CNN, Walmart, the Sweet Potato Queens and America's second-largest bookstore Books-A-Million.

When Atlanta newspaperman Henry W. Grady delivered an address entitled 'The New South' on December 21, 1886, in New York City, he began a movement that long outlived him and that future generations each in their turn and in their own way would call 'new.' Twenty years after the Civil War, as the South was still faltering, Grady had in mind the economic rejuvenation of his region. The time had come, he said, to put away animosity and to forget the rancour of war and its aftermath. It was now time for the South to reinvent itself.

This spirit of reinvention is probably the single most defining quality of the New South. From Little Rock to Richmond, the warehouses that once were stacked with bales of cotton or crates of produce have been reborn as art galleries, dining areas, and loft accommodations for the young singles who flock to clatter the keyboards of today's digital economy.

CHANGE AND REJUVENATION

Change and rejuvenation doesn't stop there. Savannah has reinvented itself as a party town and, courtesy of the Savannah College of Art and Design (SCAD), has renovated fine and distinguished buildings all around town as classrooms and student accommodations. Now the school attracts students from all around the world. The Raleigh-Durham area of North Carolina has become a humming center of hightech innovation and excellence.

Birmingham, Alabama, has a world-famous medical center that specializes in open-heart surgery, diabetes treatment, and AIDS research. Memphis, Tennessee, has transformed its downtown area into a world capital of blues, rock'n'roll and soul music, as well as an international freight-forwarding hub based around the Federal Express headquarters.

Coca-Cola art in Atlanta.

Jackson, Mississippi, integrated itself into the new economy, and along the way spawned a social phenomenon: the Sweet Potato Queens. In 1999, Jill Conner Browne wrote a book, The Sweet Potato Queens' Book of Love (Crown Publishing) that kicked the dust right out of any clichés of simpering Southern belles. Miz Browne and a group of girlfriends, women of indeterminate age with a fondness for dressing up in garish red wigs and green sequinned ball gowns, began dancing on a float in the annual St Patrick's Day parade.

Such was their *gutsy élan*, that other women in Jackson wanted to be queens, too, flinging ladylike decorum to the wind, and surrendering to the charms of their number one consort,

Lance Romance. The phenomena swept out of the flat Mississippi countryside and into the hearts of American women from coast to coast, and in no time at all the Queens' cookbooks, calendars, and alumni chapters were dancing and sashaying around the nation.

Birmingham, Alabama, is one of the towns free from Old South baggage, having made its mark six years after the end of the war. The town's Vulcan Statue a tribute to the industrial heroism of steelmaking, not a Confederate hero or a founding father. Undefined by their histo-other, the companies built in succession several skyscrapers, each one taller than the last. In 1992, when the Bank of America building was completed, it was taller than Wells Fargo (then known as Wachovia and before that First Union). Locals tell the tale that Bank of America kept its design secret until the rival design was shown to the world. Bank of America architects took one look and threw a crown on top of their tower in order to walk off with the title 'tallest in the city.'

The uncontested 'capital of the New South' is Atlanta. From John Portman-designed skyscrap-

Krispy Kreme Doughnuts in Nashville.

ries, these cities have been free to do things their way, time and time again.

SKYLINE CITIES

Two Southern cities virtually unrecognizable from the dusty settlements they were when cotton was King are Charlotte, North Carolina, and Atlanta, Georgia. Perhaps it's no coincidence that these cities, lacking the seaports or navigable rivers that could have guaranteed an easy living from shipping and cargo, made their ways with creative entrepreneurism right from the very start.

Charlotte's skyline has been transformed in the past 30 years, principally by the efforts of two of the nation's largest banks, Wells Fargo and Bank of America. In an effort to outdo each ers with dizzying atriums spring a staggering array of high earning, high-profile company headquarters. Metro Atlanta's Fortune 1,000 companies generate more than $429 billion in sales revenues, with three-quarters of all the Fortune 1,000 companies having a presence in the city. The names of Atlanta-based companies ring loud and proud: CNN, Home Depot, UPS, Delta.

It is a fact that some Southern corporations are Yankee transplants, lured from the chilly North by good weather, cheap rents, and proximity to mountains and the sea. But homegrown talent fares well, too. Top of the list is Coca-Cola (see below), while coming up behind are a trio of well-established locally born corporations with businesses and reputations to be reckoned with.

The architecture of downtown Atlanta has been described as 'roco-cola.'

Sam Walton and his wife Helen opened their first variety store in 1945. They were joined by Sam's brother, J.L. (Bud) Walton and together they had nine stores by 1959. The first store bearing the Walmart name was in Rogers, Arkansas, in July, 1962. The dynamic company that evolved from those modest beginnings has been called the retailing phenomenon of the 20th century.

Krispy Kreme began as a family business in 1933. Four years later, Vernon Rudolph moved to Winston-Salem, North Carolina, and with $25 he rented the front of a store and talked the owner into loaning him the ingredients to make doughnuts. By 2001, Krispy Kreme had gained such a reputation that, rumor has it, sales rose dramatically in the aftermath of the World Trade Center attacks as Americans sought relief and comfort in a homegrown brand that was tasty and safe.

Founded in 1917 as a street corner newsstand in Florence, Alabama, Books-A-Million, Inc. has grown to become the premier book chain in the Southeast, and the second-largest book retailer in the US. Based in Birmingham, the company currently operates more than 260 stores in 32 states and in the District of Columbia.

These dynamic companies of the South invariably owe their success in some part to traditional Southern values like loyalty and consistency, values harking back to the Old South. The past is never too far away here; it wafts on the air like a sweet, haunting perfume, giving a keynote to the present, drifting in the direction of the future.

OLD AND NEW MOTIF

The logo for Charlotte's Levine Museum of the New South, created by a local firm, Crescent PR, pays tribute to both. Three converging horizontal lines suggest the plowed fields of the rural past, while, rising from the horizon, three vertical lines symbolize the factory stacks, or skyscrapers, of a new, glittering future.

Cityscape of Charlotte, North Carolina.

⊘ PUTTING THE FIX IN COCA-COLA

Coca-Cola is the most ubiquitous consumer product in the world, and it all began in Georgia. In 1886, a pharmacist by the name of John 'Doc' Pemberton invented a thick, sweet syrup as a soda fountain drink. His partner was a Yankee named Frank Robinson, and his flowing Victorian handwriting is still embodied in the company's logo. When Pemberton died in 1888, never having tasted the sweet success of his invention, the product was sold to Asa Candler.

A marketing genius, Candler handed out free coupons for people throughout the South to sample the novel drink and produced high-quality calendars and posters to keep the name in the public eye. In 1916, to thwart rival cola drinks, the distinctive waist-shaped bottle was introduced. Seven years later, Atlantan Robert Woodruff took charge and steered the company for more than five decades. Under his helm came the radio jingles recorded in the 1960s by Aretha Franklin, Ray Charles, and Roy Orbison.

During World War II, Woodruff ensured than every G.I. overseas got a Coke for 5¢, a plan that paid off handsomely later. Norman Rockwell was hired to draw illustrations, as was Haddon Sundblom. Supposedly it was Sundblom's Yuletide ads that got Americans thinking of Santa Claus as the tubby, white-bearded man in a red tunic who graces contemporary Christmas cards.

Hard Rock Hotel and Casino.

LAS VEGAS BY THE SEA

Across formerly sleepy resorts and barren cotton fields, the jangle of slot machines drifts on the moist night air.

On the lovely Bay of Biloxi, out of a sleepy resort town of the 1980s, a little tinsel town has burst like a firework display. Biloxi's mayor A. J. Holloway said, 'We don't want to be the Las Vegas of the South. We want to be – and we are – the playground of the South,' and there is truth in that. Behind the waterfront neon extravaganza, there is still a pretty coastal Mississippi town with cafés, art galleries, and as musty a rare bookstore as any quiet community could nurture. But what hits the eye is the massive sea-wall of casinos.

Along the coast road, there are beautiful antebellum homes on stilts, across the street from Gulf Coast silver-white sands by the water, followed by a crescendo of towering hotels, sparkling with brash neon and with large annexes poking out over the bay.

The 1,800-room Beaux Rivage is a glittering fantasy of Steve Wynn's in the image of his Las Vegas landmark, Bellagio, complete with a private marina, an enormous showroom, and a bar wild enough to draw recruiters for reality TV shows. Mississippi actively casts its net for casino operators by making one of the lowest tax-takes in the country, less than half that of its Louisiana neighbors. The gaming license fees are also about a quarter of those charged in Louisiana, but there is still a local undercurrent of moral disquiet about the business.

NO LIMITS

America's love-hate affair with gambling has made a massive turn-around in the past 15 years. In 1988, gaming was legal in only two states, Nevada and New Jersey. In 2022 there are only two states – Utah and Hawaii – where it is illegal. Mississippi, one of the leading enthusiasts for the revenue spilling off the green baize

The Margaritaville Casino in Biloxi.

tables, probably has the most schizophrenic legal position.

There are no restrictions on the number of gaming licenses that a county or district may issue, nor on the amount of gaming space that a casino can use, but dealer schools are prohibited.

Biloxi, being by the sea, pioneered the toleration of wagering sports as early as the 1980s when 'cruises to nowhere' were permitted by the state legislature, taking guests out into international waters and then immediately opening up the tables, slot, and craps pits.

Bobby Mahoney of Mary Mahoney's Biloxi restaurant said: 'The statute in Mississippi preventing dealer schools from operating just means all the best (casino) jobs go to folks from out-of-state.' On the other hand, Nonnie DeBardeleben, a former politician from the nearby town of Pass Christian, once said: 'My supervisor's only complaint is that he can't get a wheelbarrow big enough to carry the money across the street to the bank.'

The anomalies began with the original dockside casino legislation, passed in Congress in 1990. Eight conservative senators were pledged to vote against the bill, but all suffered mysterious stomach upsets on the day of the vote. One may wonder if they lacked the gastro-intestinal fortitude to vote against such a spew of revenue.

The Ameristar Casino, built to look like a riverboat.

CASH FLOATS

With the exception of the Gulf Coast, Mississippi state law requires all casinos to be sited on the waterfront, ostensibly on the site of a comparable structure. What kind of a 'comparable structure' preceded the eye-popping six-story brick-built replica galleon of Treasure Bay casino, one can only wonder.

The 'dockside' rule is that the gaming house itself has to be a separate structure, wholly over the water, meaning that the money-making part of Beaux Rivage, for instance, float on vast pontoons, but are connected internally to their landside hotels. From inside, it's quite difficult to ascertain where one structure ends and the other begins.

Gambling and casinos are a multi-billion-dollar industry in the South. Unlike Hawaii and Utah where the practice is totally banned, gambling is encouraged here with many tax break incentives offered to prospective casino operators.

In Tunica County, it seems that although a previous dockside development had to exist, somehow the water didn't have to be there. An entirely new canal was dug for Horseshoe and other casinos to perch over, raising a landscaped fantasy of resort hotels in what were flat, empty cotton fields a few years before. Tunica County had only 20 hotel rooms in 1992. Six years later there were more than 6,000, and almost as many more to come. Residents in the nearby town of Clarksdale tell of how Tunica County had so little infrastructure, there wasn't even a chief of police, and they had to lure away Clarksdale's, leaving the larger town without a senior lawman for many worrying months.

Tunica has positioned itself, literally, as a centerpoint, accessible from Memphis, and also from Arkansas, Alabama and the rest of southern Tennessee. This has enabled Mississippi to achieve what might have seemed impossible – it has enticed gaming business away from Nevada. To this end, operations like the Gold Strike and Biloxi's Beau Rivage market themselves not just as gambling houses, but as resort destinations. Spas, large showrooms, and entertainments like Legends at Tunica Horseshoe are all part of the 'complete entertainment package.' So far, though, there is no sign of the trumpeted 'family friendliness' that Las Vegas was so keen on, up until recently. Neither has Biloxi given in too overtly to the sleazier end of 'adult' recreation which is so often a feature of gambling destinations.

However, the reborn riverboats have certainly brought their share of woes along with them. After the Lady Luck Riverboat Century Casino Caruthersville opened in Natchez, Adams County judge Charles Vess said, 'Our civil cases ballooned – auto repossessions, furniture repossessions, a big influx of bad checks.' There is also evidence that, if anything, poor people have gotten poorer since the arrival of the dealers.

LOUISIANA

If Mississippi has had an uneasy relationship with the slots and tables, Louisiana has been positively struggling. The only land-based casino in New Orleans, Harrah's, has distinguished itself by teetering on the verge of bankruptcy since opening in 1992. Infighting between local and state government, as well as the high rates of Louisiana gambling taxes are blamed. Presumably none of Louisiana's legendary political murky dealings were involved. There are also Mississippi-style waterfront casinos on Lake Pontchartrain. Otherwise, Louisiana has a bizzare complex of laws that permit closed off gaming rooms in some bars and gas stations, mostly featuring slot machines, and the isolated and frankly alarming 'truck-stop' casinos.

The other major change on the betting landscape has been the rise of Native American casinos. After a case brought by the Seminole Natives in Florida, a decision by Congress in 1988 conceded that a reservation in a state where gaming was legal could conduct games of their own, without state interference. Native councils have taken this opportunity, and unemployment among Native Americans has dropped from around 30 percent to almost nothing as a result. Nearly all states that allow gambling now have reservation gaming. At first, the traditional casino operators forcefully resisted the trend, but in a pragmatic, 'if you can't beat them, join them,' spirit, they are increasingly partnering up with the Native Americans.

Even with the partnerships, reservation casinos are not usually as lavish as their resort counterparts, and this is in part because banks are unwilling to lend money for development. The reason given is that they cannot seize property if a loan is defaulted. There are reservation casinos in all the states of the South.

The Bible Belt is adapting to the congregations of Mamon, streaming into temples of chance with their devotion to numbers, dice, and dollars, but for many it isn't an easy relationship. Still, the jangle of slots, the snap of the cards, and the clatter of a silver ball in a wheel are accompaniments to 21st-century Southern life that look set to stay.

The Beau Rivage's post-Hurricane Katrina re-opening.

⊘ HURRICANE KATRINA AND MISSISSIPPI'S FLOATING CASINOS

Casinos have been floating in the Mississippi river since the early nineteenth century. According to Mississippi law, all casinos must be built on water to keep them physically separate from nearby communities, with the exception of the Gulf Coast. Translated into reality this means the construction of vast barges able to bear the weight of hefty multistory buildings, designed ostensibly to resemble their land-based casino counterparts. Weight over water is of course an issue when it comes to buoyancy and stability; therefore, many of these venues were built using lightweight, plywood materials with hollow walls. To many, this seemed to be a somewhat ingenious idea

– that was until the force of nature known today as Hurricane Katrina arrived. When this category-five hurricane made landfall in Mississippi, it quickly became apparent that these frail buildings were no match for 150mph (241kmh) winds. When Katrina hit in 2005, it all but wiped out Biloxi's waterside venues. Since then, however, many have been rebuilt using more resistant materials. The widespread destruction caused by Katrina prompted many legal petitions for casinos to be built on land, due to safety reasons. The state has since ammended the law to allow casinos to be built on land but they have to be within 800 feet of the water.

Cajun food is served at Café Reconcile, New Orleans.

WHAT'S COOKING

The styles of Southern cuisine are as melodic as the accents and as varied as the landscape from Virginia to Louisiana

Southern cooking arrives like the embrace of Southern hospitality, courteously warm and comforting, but varied, spicy, and elegantly unfussed. Like everything in the South, dining is familiar, but the accent is softer, and proceedings are a good deal less hurried.

CAJUN AND CREOLE

Cajun cooking is based on simple traditions and ingredients, but with herbs that the Atchafalaya settlers learned from the Native Americans and the red peppers used by the Spanish. Like everything Cajun, the food is cooked in no kind of a hurry. It features the crawfish, catfish, shrimp, crab, and alligator the bayous offered in abundance, mixed in with rice, peas, and yams.

Authentic Cajun fare is a rarity in New Orleans restaurants, whatever it may say on the menu. Although tasty, this food in its native form is not appealing to the eye, and most establishments tend to dress it up. To sample Cajun for real, try to get to a private house or a party in rural Louisiana. The culinary artistry of the Cajun's French heritage shines through in bisques, boullions, and boudins. Solidly French dishes like rack of lamb en croute are almost as likely as the ever-tasty gumbo soups, made with chicken, shrimp, or smoked duck. The name 'gumbo' comes from an African word meaning okra, invariably mixed into the pot. Except in regional Louisiana, Creole

Spicy Cajun crawfish boil with an Asian twist.

and Cajun dishes are almost intertwined now, but Creole dishes tend to be based on rich and creamy roux sauces, and spicier than the Cajun, clinging to the three essential ingredients; black pepper, white pepper, and red pepper.

SOUL FOOD

Soul food means chitterlings (deep-fried small pigs' intestines known in the South as chitlins), collard greens, pork neck bone, and pigs' feet. It's country. If there's meat other than chitlins or pigs' feet, it'll be pork or chicken. There will probably be potatoes, rice, and peas, or maybe corn to accompany. This all harks back to the simple meals using the cheapest ingredients that sustained the poor, mostly Black,

> *If you only try one classic Southern dish on your visit, make it chitlins. These boiled-down intestines, served with hot sauce and apple cider vinegar, are a lot tastier than they sound.*

sharecroppers and urbanites. Now, like much food once eaten by the poor, soul food can be found in fashionable restaurants. The town of Salley in South Carolina holds an annual chitlins festival, feeding as many white folks as Black.

ESTATE-STYLE DINING

Sweltering in large kitchens, usually detached from the farm mansions, cooks blended the richness of fresh ingredients with oysters and rabbit, catfish or tasty pecans. In the melting pot of Louisiana, sauces were derived from Creole recipes, adding a dash of spice.

Elsewhere, presentation leaned more toward traditional French cuisine, picked up from plantation owners' frequent trips to Europe and given a Southern twist. Poached capons and stuffed game hens featured along with classic stews, Kentucky Bourbon grilled steaks and – like most Southern dining – ham and corn.

NOUVELLE SOUTHERN

Louis Osteen, while at Louis's Charleston Grill in South Carolina, aimed to keep these traditions alive, believing the plantation was 'where the finest food in the South was made.' During his career and restaurants to date, Louis became a minor celebrity and leading exponent of what is called 'New Southern,' or sometimes even, 'Nouvelle Southern' cuisine. Its creations are inspired by traditional American cooking techniques but combining the signature ingredients of the South. These might include collard-green egg rolls with tasso (Cajun-style ham), red pepper puree and peach chutney. Local fish may be grilled and served with a hoisin and ginger or Szechwan peanut sauce. Foie gras could even be served with a hush puppy.

BARBECUE

Anywhere else, barbecue simply means cooking outdoors on an open grill. In the South, it's a sacred art, more likely to involve a whole pig than any kind of a fiddling-ribs affair. Virginia barbecue sauce is tomato-based, with a dash

Barbecued pork spare ribs.

⊙ SOUTHERN FOOD TERMS

Boudin: a red-hot Cajun sausage made with rice, herbs, and onions. Pronounced *boo-dan*.

Chitlins: yummy deep-fried small pigs' intestines.

Collards: a large, green-leaf vegetable traditionally served on New Year's Day with pork and black-eyed peas.

Green tomatoes: sliced thin green tomatoes rolled in white cornmeal and fried in hot fat.

Grits: coarsely ground hulled corn, boiled and eaten for breakfast or served at night with shrimp or catfish.

Hush puppies: round puffs of cornmeal mixed with minced onion, and sometimes beer, then deep fried.

Jambalaya: served on top of yellow rice, the best contains anything in the kitchen: sausages, seafood, vegetables.

Moonshine: also called 'white lightning,' the legal corn whiskey is best taken straight; the illegal kind can kill you.

Okra: a long pod vegetable with seeds, okra came to the New World with enslaved people, who hid the seeds in their hair.

Spoon bread: made from corn and baked like a custard, the bread is so soft it must be eaten with a spoon.

Tomato pudding: cubed old bread softened in tomatoes, covered with crumbs and baked. Popular in Appalachia.

Yams: similar to sweet potatoes, but usually served 'candied,' or sliced and flavored with syrup and spices.

of vinegar and pepper. South Carolina has a unique barbecue with mustard. 'That's for hot dogs,' was all a Georgia gourmet would say. North Carolinians pack the pork with coleslaw. Tennessee-style barbecue, called 'dry rub barbecue,' has a blend of spices rubbed dry onto the pork skin. Memphis plays host to the World Barbecue Championship, a major highlight in the Memphis in May festival. Down a dark, unpromising alley near the Peabody Hotel, Charlie Vergos' Rendezvous is the Memphis shrine of barbecue. A popular local tale is that

promotes a trailer-trash recipe for ham cooked in cherry Coca-Cola. It's delicious, too.

CATFISH

Catfish are plentiful in the South – so much so in Louisiana that they are often scooped into sacks right off the shore, and in Mississippi catfish farms are taking over from cotton plantations. The soft, white fish shows up in jambalaya and étouffée, but all over the South it is most likely to arrive at the table deep-fried in a cornmeal and cayenne pepper breading and lemon

North Carolina barbecue, cornbread, slaw, potatoes, and all the country fixings.

one of the early owners was charged with murder. He said he'd caught the man in bed with his wife and shot him. The judge said that was no excuse for murder. The chef pleaded, 'But she'd told him my secret barbecue recipe.' 'In that case,' said the judge, 'you should have shot her, too. Case dismissed.'

CULINARY ARTFORM

The curing, smoking, hanging and preparation of rich, succulent hams is another devotional Southern art form. Virginia hams are prized the world over and sent by Virginians to friends and relatives unfortunate enough to be out of state for any length of time. In another 'poorfood chic' twist, the British TV chef Nigella Lawson

wedges. Other fish like trout and mullet show up for supper and, around the coasts, redfish and snappers.

GRITS

The South's own breakfast treat is the recipe that settlers probably learned from the Native Americans, hominy grits – sometimes strange to the foreign palate but a delicacy when the taste is acquired. Corn is treated with lye water (potash water, as it was known in the old days) to make it swell and produce hominy. This is then dried and ground to produce grits. The best grits are smooth and creamy, served hot with butter, salt and pepper, and with a fried egg on the side.

DANCING IN THE STREETS

From blues and soul to country, from jazz to rock'n'roll, many of the rhythms that swept the world originated in the South

There is music everywhere in the South. Walk around the French Quarter in New Orleans, Beale Street in Memphis or just about anywhere in Clarksdale, Mississippi, and in no time your feet will be syncopating. Most of all, there's music and poetry in the droll, sparkling Southern talk. From this cultural richness, the Southern United States became the most fertile musical lands of the 20th century. Country, gospel, jazz, the blues, soul, and rock'n'roll were all conceived in the South. So too, were their many offspring such as Cajun, Zydeco, country & western, and rhythm & blues.

James Brown and Ray Charles came from Georgia, Jerry Lee Lewis from Ferriday, Louisiana, blues legends Robert Johnson, Muddy Waters, Willie Dixon, and John Lee Hooker hailed from the Mississippi Delta, as did rock & roll and soul innovators Ike Turner and Sam Cooke. Jazz giants Louis Armstrong and the Marsalis family, and the Neville Brothers all came from New Orleans. The father of country music, Jimmie Rodgers, was a Mississippian from Meridian, and Hank Williams was born in Olive Hill near Georgiana, Alabama. Then there was Sam Phillips in Memphis. Most of the great artists that his Sun Studio produced came from the South, including a boy from Tupelo, Mississippi, name of Elvis Aaron Presley.

European folk music began the musical seeding. Settlers from Scotland and Ireland brought their fiddles and harmoniums, and a hearty tradition of jigs and reels to dance to. They blended in with folk styles from Holland, Spain, and Germany. Church music and the rhythms of Africa were also key ingredients.

Added to the mix in Louisiana, a French influence came by way of Canada with the Acadians and developed into the jubilant Cajun music. Nearly all the vocals are sung in French,

Wilson Pickett recording at Muscle Shoals in 1969.

⊘ TENNESSEE'S GREAT STUDIOS

Any visit to the great state of Tennessee should involve a trip to the legendary Sun Studio, where you can indulge yourself in all things Elvis Presley. However also in Memphis is the equally iconic Stax Records, which is not to be overlooked. Not only did this label have major acts on their books including Otis Redding and The Staple Singers, but the owners were also trailblazers in championing civil rights and multicultural music arts. Today the Stax Records studios is a museum, remembering the progress made toward equality in mainstream 1960s music, and paying tribute to the lives lost along the way.

showing the fierce independence of Cajun spirit as the language was banned from Louisiana schools in the 1930s. Around Mardi Gras time in Eunice, Lafayette and all over bayou country, there are Cajun and Zydeco bands getting the dancers up from the crawfish étouffée and jambalaya. Hank Williams took a Cajun tune to fame with his country classic Jambalaya.

SOUL

Soul music was an evolution of rhythm & blues, a more solidly Black dance beat than the slightly

Louis Armstrong.

sanitized rock'n'roll making white radio play. Often with a heavy, rhythmic brass section, soul was more raw and emotional, more an amplification of the spirit of its blues roots.

The two Southern cauldrons of soul, Stax Records in Memphis and the FAME Recording Studios in Muscle Shoals, Alabama, both started at the beginning of the 1960s. Stax was formed by the white brother and sister team of Jim Stewart and Estelle Axton. They took the label name from the first letters of their surnames: STewart, AXton. Stax recorded in an old movie theater, under a marquee proclaiming it 'Soulville USA.' Here they recorded Rufus and Carla Thomas, Otis Redding, Sam and Dave, Wilson Pickett, and Isaac Hayes, most of them over the

house band which was basically Booker T and the MGs, recording stars in their own right.

In Muscle Shoals, Rick Hall owned the FAME Recording Studios and label, and produced Arthur Alexander's You Better Move On, later covered by the Rolling Stones, and Etta James' hugely successful Tell Mama album, both in 1961. There was a crossover with Stax when Otis Redding brought Arthur Conley to Muscle Shoals to record the classic When a Man Loves a Woman. FAME was the studio where a Memphis girl named Aretha Franklin cut some of her early hits, while the Muscle Shoals Rhythm Section went on to back big-name rock bands in the late 1960s and '70s.

JAZZ

Jazz may be America's greatest contribution to the music world, and it all started in the South. New Orleans, to be exact, although the word itself may come from the name of Charles 'Chas' Washington, a drummer from Vicksburg, Mississippi. Jelly Roll Morton claimed to have coined the term in 1902 to distinguish it from ragtime, but researchers have pointed out that he was only 12 years old at the time.

Around the turn of the 20th century, a new kind of sound began to develop in the form of African rhythms, marching bands, Creole and gospel sounds, and the parlor piano. The emerging motifs of the blues, some syncopation, and the cultural mix of New Orleans contributed. The city's talent pool provided extraordinary musicians to define the new form, players like pianist Jelly Roll Morton, then later, trumpeter Louis Armstrong. Many of them traveled north, or even to Europe, to achieve recognition and popularity for themselves and for the new art, and from Chicago to New York, to Paris, London, and Helsinki, it caught on pretty fast.

The first jazz records were made, paradoxically it seems now, by a white ensemble, The Original Dixieland Jazz Band. They weren't original, they were covering Black music, and they recorded for the Victor Company in New York,

Not only did the Southern states give the world jazz, they also nurtured Louis Armstrong and many other acts who would go on to achieve global acclaim.

but they were formed in New Orleans. Every spring the greatest names in jazz make pilgrimage to New Orleans, as they have since 1959, to listen and play at the spectacular JazzFest.

GOSPEL

European church music was an influence for two distinct strands of what is now called gospel music. White gospel comes from Protestant roots, and ranges from small vocal harmony groups, through choirs with bands, to massed choirs in assembly rooms. Before the Civil War, revival

stations, the music and its message are flourishing. Mahalia Jackson, a major gospel star, spurned all offers of secular engagements, but she did record Come Sunday with Duke Ellington, and sang at the inauguration of President Kennedy, as well as Martin Luther King, Jr's funeral.

BLUES

Archaeologist Charles Peabody first documented the working songs of the Black laborers on a dig in 1903 at Stovall, Mississippi. He later described it in the influential Journal of Ameri-

Mural of renowned blues singer B.B. King in his adopted hometown of Indianola, Mississippi.

and campfire meetings were accompanied by the hymn-like singing of songs, later collected into songbooks like Gospel Hymns and Sacred Tunes (1875) and The Christian Harp (1877).

Black gospel music traces its roots back to the late 19th and early 20th centuries. Rhythms and harmonies from the working songs, spirituals, the blues, and ragtime all came to church, and mixed with the cadences of the revival hymns. In turn, some of the choirs and preachers took their music back out to the secular world. James Brown and blues legend Son House were both preachers, and B.B. King learned his early musical lessons in the church choir.

With the recent popularity of Christian music in America spawning record labels and radio

can Folklore as 'weird in interval and strange in rhythm; peculiarly beautiful.' That same year, musician W.C. Handy heard the sound of a guitar played with a knife-blade as a slide and set about popularizing it in his repertoire.

Robert Johnson, the undisputed king of Delta bluesmen, lived from 1911 to 1938. The influence of the 29 songs recorded in the last two years of his life inspired artists from Muddy Waters to Robert Cray and Eric Clapton. The Mississippi Delta was the stomping ground of the early blues, and nowhere more than in Clarksdale (for more on Clarksdale, Johnson, and Handy, see pages 169). In the 1920s and 1930s Delta blues musicians started migrating; electric players followed Muddy Waters to Chicago; others were drawn to the studios in Memphis. Beale Street was crackling with musicians playing on street corners. B.B. King was among them, and his skills eventually bought him one of the corners for his Beale Street restaurant.

A very influential outlet for the blues was radio's 'King Biscuit Time,' which still airs each day at 12:15pm out of KFFA in Helena, Arkansas.

THE BLUES HAD A BABY

Sam Phillips worked as a disc jockey in Muscle Shoals, Alabama, but when he decided to set up man coming in to record a song for his mother's birthday in 1953. In fact, Phillips turned Elvis away at least once, but when he sang Arthur Cruddup's That's All Right, Mama, Sam heard what he had been searching for – a white kid who could bring rhythm & blues to a white audience. After 10 record releases, Phillips sold his contract with Elvis to RCA for just $35,000, a tiny sum by modern standards. Sam died aged 80 on July 30, 2003.

Phillips aimed to synthesize something between the dark, exciting rhythm & blues and vibrant, electric country. The results, including

Jazzman Terry 'Harmonica' Bean performs at Clarksdale's Club Red Jazz Club.

shop with a recording studio in 1945, his enthusiasm for country music and the blues drew him to Memphis. His 706 Union Avenue studio has been available for rent by the hour ever since. The Memphis Recording Service's first customer was Ike Turner, who later cut Rocket 88 in the modest studio in 1951. This track is one of the true contenders for the title of 'the first rock'n'roll record,' and was part of Phillips' motivation to open his own record label. Charlie Rich, Carl Perkins, Jerry Lee Lewis, Roy Orbison, and Johnny Cash all reached the ears and dancing feet of the world through Phillips' label, along with the man he described as 'My greatest discovery. When he sings, you can hear clear down to his soul' – the legendary Howlin' Wolf. Then there is the story of a shy young Elvis's early records, were called 'rockabilly.' Another Phillips discovery, Arkansan Johnny Cash's outlaw, hard-life image, honed in prison gigs, bridged the rock'n'roll and country styles perfectly until his death in 2003.

COUNTRY

The history of modern country music dates back to 1927, when Ralph Peer set up recording equipment in Bristol, Tennessee, while scouting for the New York Victor label. Near the border with Virginia, the Bristol sessions attracted both the Carter Family and Jimmie Rodgers. The Carter family popularized traditional songs of England and the rural South with strong and distinctive harmonies, and Maybelle Carter developed a style of melodic rhythm guitar picking that is still a country mainstay. Rodgers returned to Victor to record Blue Yodel, a white blues that set a standard for songs of the working man's struggles.

At a young age, Earl Scruggs instinctively developed the three-finger picking banjo style that became the emblem of bluegrass. Bill Munroe coined the term 'bluegrass' for his band the Bluegrass Boys, where Scruggs and Lester Flatt first played together.

The biggest star of the Grand Ole Opry, though, was Alabamian Hank Williams. He learned from

and made the transition from a hillbilly dancehall image to a lush, intimate sound drenched in sentiment. Owen Bradley produced Brenda Lee singing I'm Sorry in the same style and sold 15 million records.

The tamed, suburban Nashville sound of the 1960s was born. Nashville had moved from the songs of working peoples' troubles and blues to a smooth, marketable product. That left the raw, sincere heart of country out to be stolen.

It was picked up by non-Southerners like Willie Nelson, Merle Haggard and Gram Parsons,

Country artist Jason Aldean performs at Jason Aldean's Kitchen and Rooftop Bar in Nashville.

the age of eight to play the blues on the guitar from a mentor, Rufus Teetot Payne, and his vocal style drew on Roy Acuff's Gremel Ole Opry broadcasts. Williams's song Move It On Over anticipated Bill Haley's hit Rock Around the Clock by 10 years. A tough childhood and a stormy love life with his wife Audrey inspired poetry that still reaches out. Cold, Cold Heart, which he first recorded in 1951, is still regularly covered, recently on a Grammy-winning album by Norah Jones.

Chet Atkins and Owen Bradley were leading producers in Nashville, and in the mid-1950s, when the American audience was deserting for Elvis and rock'n'roll, they developed a smoother, more commercial country style to recapture the market. Chet produced Jim Reeves's Four Walls

who brought a liberal viewpoint and synthesized country with rock. Now, Garth Brooks and K.D. Lang may be a long lost highway from Hank Williams, but the country roads still run either to or from Nashville, Tennessee.

To this day, from North Carolina's innovative lyrical son Ryan Adams to one of Georgia's newer voices, Lauren Alaina, the South still has a whole lot of shakin' going on.

'The blues had a baby and they named it rock'n'roll', sang Muddy Waters, asserting his parental claim on the blossoming genre.

Cannon at Kennesaw Battlefield Park, Georgia.

CIVIL WAR SITES

The Civil War killed more than 600,000 young men and changed the South forever. Its sites are moving and poignant reminders

In his famous address at Gettysburg, Abraham Lincoln spoke movingly of hallowed ground. Many of the most important battlefields of the Civil War are part of the National Park Service, and for Americans none of the other land that the nation has set aside for preservation bears the emotional force of these consecrated places. Brutal battles were fought here, pitting kinsmen against kinsmen in an awful conflict that scarred the national psyche. Fighting raged across most of the eastern states for four years, killing more than 600,000 men and nearly destroying the young republic.

The sites administered by the Park Service include battlefields, cemeteries and memorials. Some are clustered together and can easily be visited in a day or two. Others require long-distance driving and a serious investment of time. Almost all are open every day except major holidays, but it's best to call ahead to check; to find the location of each historic site, see the individual state maps.

Reenactment on Cedar Creek Battlefield, Virginia.

THE OPENING SHOT

In 1860, Lincoln was elected president, and momentous events came in a rush. On December 20, an angry South Carolina convention voted to secede from the Union, followed quickly by Alabama, Florida, Georgia, Louisiana and Mississippi. The Confederate States of America formed in February 1861, electing Jefferson Davis as president (see page 55), and nearly all Federal forts in the South were seized by Confederate forces.

In South Carolina, Major Robert Anderson realized that the building at what is now **Fort Sumter National Monument** (tel: 843-883 3123) was the only defensible fort of the four Federal installations in Charleston, and he consolidated troops there. When Lincoln took office on March 4, 1861, he made clear that he would hold the fort. At 4:30am on April 12, Confederate batteries opened fire on Fort Sumter, and the Civil War had begun.

Anderson surrendered late the next day. The Union Army laid siege to the fort for 22 months, but never retook it; Confederate troops remained until 1865. Today, boats licensed by the National Park Service carry visitors to Fort Sumter, which is located on an island in Charleston harbor.

Just west of Washington, DC, **Manassas National Battlefield Park** (tel: 703-361 1339; www.nps.gov/mana; daily sunrise to sunset; free) in Virginia was the site of two major clashes.

General Irvin McDowell led 35,000 Union troops toward a key railroad junction at Manassas on July 18, 1861, expecting to take Richmond, the Confederate capital, easily and end the war quickly. But waiting there, near the Stone Bridge on Bull Run Creek, was General Pierre G.T. Beauregard and 22,000 Confederate troops. Another 10,000 Confederates arrived later in the day. Confederate soldiers rallied behind General Thomas J. Jackson's fresh Virginia brigade. Jackson 'stood there like a stone wall' – earning his nickname, 'Stonewall' Jackson. Union forces

Manassas, where over 4,200 people died in two battles.

fled in disarray, hindered by the carriages of sightseers who had come to watch the fighting. Some 900 soldiers died on the first day alone.

A mile-long self-guided walking tour follows the course of the battle. A second walk covers the area of the Stone Bridge; Union troops who were wounded here received aid and medicine in an effort organized by Clara Barton. At the age of 40 she had quit her US Patent Office job and would later found the American Red Cross. Visitors can tour the **Ben Lomond Manor House**, which was possibly used as a hospital, and watch the battle depicted in a film shown in the visitor center.

The second Battle of Manassas (Bull Run) came more than a year later, this time involving not raw recruits but veteran soldiers. Robert E. Lee, the new commander of the Confederate Army of Northern Virginia, dispatched Stonewall Jackson's force to engage General John Pope's Union troops. After several battles and tactical mistakes by Pope during the engagement, Jackson sent Union forces fleeing once again. The confrontation killed 3,300 men. A 12-mile (19km) driving tour covers much of the large area of the second battle of Bull Run. General George B. McClellan rebuilt the fleeing Federals into the 100,000-man Army of the Potomac and in May 1862 marched on the heavily fortified Confederate capital at Richmond, Virginia. On May 15, Confederate fire drove off five Union ironclad ships that had been moving up the James River toward Richmond. June 26 was the start of seven days of fierce battles on Richmond's eastern outskirts. Lee's forces repulsed McClellan's Union troops, with casualties on both sides numbering 35,000.

Richmond was not safe for the Confederates, however. Battles in regions north of the city continued through the coming months and years. In March 1864, Ulysses S. Grant became commander of the Union field forces, and immediately proclaimed as his chief objective the capture of Richmond.

The battlefield at **Cold Harbor** sits midway between two roadside taverns. When Grant's soldiers attacked there on June 3, they suffered 7,000 casualties in 30 minutes, forcing him to change to a siege strategy. Union soldiers, including several regiments of

⊘ THE COST OF THE CIVIL WAR

The first shots, fired on April 12, 1861, marked the beginning of a war that would eventually claim the lives of more than 600,000 soldiers and come close to destroying the entire American republic. President Lincoln in the North marched against President Davis in the South, in a war that lasted for four years and decimated an entire generation of young men. When a peace was finally reached, around two percent of the nation's population had been killed. The wartime destruction of the agricultural and transportation infrastructure opened the door to famine and disease, claiming hundreds of thousands of civilian lives, during and after the war.

African-American troops, took Fort Harrison on September 29. Richmond held on until April 1865, falling only after Lee's forces withdrew. It's possible to trace the whole of the encounter at the 10 units of **Richmond National Battlefield Park** (tel: 804-226 1981; www.nps.gov/rich; daily 9am–5pm; free). A complete tour requires an 80-mile (130km) -long drive.

WAR FOR THE WEST

Far to the west, both sides coveted the state of Missouri, with its strategic position on both the Missouri and Mississippi rivers. The battle for Missouri moved to a climax at the beginning of 1862, when Union Brigadier General Samuel R. Curtis launched a drive to push Confederate forces from the state. Rebel troops regrouped south of Fayetteville in Arkansas under Major General Earl Van Dorn. Van Dorn's forces marched toward Missouri but met Curtis's troops at what is now **Pea Ridge National Military Park** (tel: 479-451 8122; www.nps.gov/peri; daily 6am–sunset), 10 miles (16km) northeast of Rogers, Arkansas, which ultimately saved the state of Missouri for the Union.

Until 1862, the Union military had seemed unable to gain an important victory. Confederate defensive lines had few weak points, but Union commanders decided to test the line in western Tennessee, where **Fort Henry** on the Tennessee River and Fort Donelson on the Cumberland River sat just 12 miles (19km) apart. Union iron-clad gunboats commenced fire on Fort Henry on February 6, 1862, while the virtually unknown Brigadier General Ulysses S. Grant led a ground assault. Grant was slow in reaching the fort, and by the time he arrived, the ironclads had destroyed it, and almost the entire garrison had left, fleeing for Fort Donelson.

When Union forces attacked on February 14, gunboats could not duplicate their feat against Donelson's heavier guns. Changing tactics, Grant encircled the fort and laid siege. The Confederates surrendered on February 16. These were the Union's first big victories, and the newly tested General Grant had made a name for himself. Driving and walking tours are available at **Fort Donelson National Battlefield** (tel: 931-232 5706; www.nps.gov/fodo; daily 8am–4.30pm; free), a mile west of Dover in Tennessee. Visitors can also see the **Dover Hotel**

(Surrender House), which has been restored to its Civil War appearance.

ARMY OF THE TENNESSEE

After the losses at Fort Henry and Fort Donelson, Confederate forces withdrew. In Mississippi, General A. S. Johnston consolidated a force of 44,000 troops at Corinth, planning to overwhelm Grant. Grant, in turn, moved his own 40,000-man Army of the Tennessee to an encampment around **Shiloh Church**, 22 miles (35km) northeast of Corinth. Grant drilled his

Fort Pulaski National Monument

new recruits but set up almost no defenses. Johnston's attack on April 6, 1862, caught Union forces by surprise. Grant's troops spent the entire day in fierce, retreating battles at locations such as **Hornet's Nest**.

Confederates used a barrage of 62 cannons – the largest artillery assault of its day – to inflict huge losses on a Union division. Johnston was killed in action and P.G.T. Beauregard assumed command. By the end of the day, Grant's remaining forces reached **Pittsburgh Landing** and set up a position fortified by gunboats and thousands of men.

By the morning of April 7, Grant's forces numbered 55,000, but, unaware of the reinforcements, Beauregard attacked. By the time

Beauregard retreated, his troops were low on ammunition, and Confederate casualties swelled to 15,000. **Shiloh National Military Park** (tel: 731-689 5696; www.nps.gov/shil; daily sunrise–sunset; free) includes a visitor center and a self-guided driving tour.

Even before the battle at Shiloh, Union forces were preparing to attack Fort Pulaski, a newly completed fort, now in Confederate hands, which guarded the river approaches to Savannah in Georgia. After taking Hilton Head Island, Union forces moved 10 experimental rifled can-

McLean House, site of the Confederate surrender.

nons into position on Tybee Island, a mile away from the fort. On April 10, 1862, the Union's new cannons opened up on Pulaski's brick walls, which ranged in thickness from 7 to 15ft (2–5 meters), Confederate Colonel Charles H. Olmstead and his troops held on through 30 long and brutal hours of devastating high-technology barrage.

By noon on April 11, explosive shells opened an outer wall and exposed the fort's main powder magazine. Fearing that an explosion might destroy not only the fort but also the men inside, Olmstead surrendered. **Fort Pulaski National Monument** (tel: 912 786-8182; www.nps.gov/fopu; daily 9am–5pm) is reached via Highway 80 from Savannah.

> *The bloodiest battle of the war was fought July 1–3, 1863 at Gettysburg, Pennsylvania. The Confederates lost 28,000 men; the Union army 23,000.*

As 1862 drew to a close, Major General William Rosecrans took command of the Union Army of the Cumberland, charged with driving Confederate forces under General Braxton Bragg out of Tennessee. Rosecrans found Bragg waiting for him in a grove of cedars near the Stones River in **Murfreesboro**, Tennessee, 27 miles (46 km) southeast of Nashville.

Troops on both sides acted out one of the heartbreaking ironies of warfare as they camped within sight of one another on December 30, 1863, singing rousing songs well into the evening. Then, at dawn on December 31, in a day that went badly for Union forces, they were driven back nearly a mile before establishing a new line. There was neither music nor fighting on New Year's Day. On January 2, Bragg's forces drove Union soldiers back to Stones River, where Rosecrans's superior artillery was waiting. Bragg lost 1,800 soldiers at the river, and the battle ended as his forces retreated. The Confederates had lost Tennessee. The casualties after two days of pitched fighting were 13,000 Union soldiers and 10,000 Confederate soldiers. **Stones River National Battlefield** (tel: 615-893 9501; www.nps.gov/stri; daily 8am–5pm; free) lies in the northwest corner of Murfreesboro and includes a very informative driving tour.

Only 30 miles (48km) west of Jackson, the Mississippi state capital, is **Vicksburg National Military Park** (tel: 601-636 0583; www.nps.gov/vick; daily 8:30am–5pm), the site of the last Confederate stronghold on the Mississippi River (see page 158). After a crippling 47-day siege, on July 4, 1863, Confederate Lieutenant General John C. Pemberton surrendered to Grant. When Port Hudson fell five days later, the Mississippi belonged to the Union.

EMANCIPATION PROCLAMATION

Tragic as Vicksburg was, it was only one example of the horrors of this war. Autumn of 1862 brought the costliest battle of the Civil War

– the Battle of Antietam, fought on both sides of Antietam Creek in Maryland, where more than 23,000 men fell.

Although the Confederates had not lost, its army had taken a step toward losing the war. On September 22, President Lincoln issued the Emancipation Proclamation, which on January 1, 1863, freed enslaved people in states 'in rebellion against the United States.' Only then did emancipation become a formal objective of the war.

It was possible to 'take the pulse' of the war

Fredericksburg, Jackson handily won the battle, inflicting big losses on the Federal troops. More than 15,000 Union soldiers are buried at **Fredericksburg National Cemetery**, while **Chatham Manor**, a Georgian mansion used as a field hospital, is where volunteer Clara Barton and poet Walt Whitman tended to injured soldiers.

DEATH OF A REBEL HERO

A drive west leads to the **Chancellorsville Battlefield**, where in May 1863 Jackson's forces again won a victory against Federal troops. Here

Mural depicting the burning of Fort Sumter at the National Civil War Museum.

at **Fredericksburg** in Virginia. The city's proximity to Washington, DC, and Richmond – it lies halfway between – had been a blessing before the war, but after secession its strategic location became a curse. One hundred thousand men died near Fredericksburg in four major battles. **Fredericksburg and Spotsylvania National Military Park** (tel: 540-693 3200; www.nps.gov/frsp; daily sunrise–sunset; free) encompasses 7,775 acres (3,146 hectares) of land that includes four battlefields and three historic buildings. **Fredericksburg Battlefield** is where General Ambrose E. Burnside's Union troops crossed the Rappahannock River in December 1862 to attack Lee's forces, commanded by Stonewall Jackson. Heavily defended on hills west of

Jackson was shot by 'friendly fire.' Following the amputation of his left arm on May 4, General Lee wrote to him, 'You are better off than I am, for while you have lost your left, I have lost my right arm.' Jackson died of pneumonia on May 10 at **Guinea Station**, 15 miles (24km) south of Fredericksburg, where the **Stonewall Jackson Death Site** now stands.

To the west is **Wilderness Battlefield**, where, a year later, on May 5–6, 1864, Lee and Grant first faced each other in an indecisive battle. Grant broke away to march toward the Spotsylvania Court House. Lee's army actually reached Spotsylvania first, and he fended off several small Union attacks. When more Union troops arrived, along with a thick fog, the fighting grew more savage.

After 20 hours of hand-to-hand combat and several days of a staunch Confederate defense, Grant pulled his troops out and called the fight at 'Bloody Angle' a Union victory, a key to winning the war.

Lee lost his right-hand man in Stonewall Jackson, but not his fighting spirit. On June 3, he began a march west into Pennsylvania. This was to lead to the fateful Battle of Gettysburg, where his 70,000 soldiers would clash with General George G. Meade's 93,000 Union troops. In three days, the two armies suffered 51,000 casualties

> *Hiring a personal guide to a Southern Civil War site, especially in one of the smaller parks, is a great idea. Guides are very often local people who not only grew up playing in the parks but can recount family stories about the war.*

– the greatest losses incurred in any battle ever fought in North America.

STRUGGLE FOR THE SOUTH

A visit to **Chickamauga and Chattanooga National Military Park** (tel: 706-866 9241; www.nps.gov/chch; daily sunrise–sunset) in Georgia, just miles outside Chattanooga in Tennessee, stirs the imagination and provides insight into the four-year struggle for the South. Hiking over its fields, hills, and hardwood forests, picture two battles – one an empty Confederate victory on September 18–19, 1863, at **Chickamauga Battlefield**; the next, a Union triumph in the Battle of Chattanooga on November 23–25. The best way to imagine this battle is by hiking up to **Point Park** on **Lookout Mountain**. From here all of Chattanooga can be seen.

After Ulysses S. Grant was named supreme commander on March 9, 1864, the Union Army traveled south from Chattanooga toward **Atlanta** – 'too important a place in the hands of the enemy to be left undisturbed,' as General Sherman put it. The Federal Army wanted to get its hands on the weaponry, the foundries

The USS Cairo, an ironclad gunboat, at Vicksburg.

⊘ SAVE OUR CIVIL WAR SITES

More than one-third of all principal Civil War battlefields have either vanished or are hanging on by the slenderest of threads. According to a study conducted by the Civil War Sites Advisory Commission, around 10,500 armed conflicts occurred and of these 384 have been identified as of historical significance. The National Park Service is in a position to maintain only the most important of these battlefields, while 43 percent of the other major sites remain solely in private hands, subject to the whim of their owners. The report does not even include the countless smaller sites, such as cemeteries, forts, prisons, and other buildings that are at risk.

One of the problems is the changing nature of the South, as it moves from a rural to a more urban economy. As long as the battlefields were agricultural land, they were relatively safe. But along with the building of superhighways, especially around Washington, DC, came increasing residential and commercial development, especially in the verdant green hills of Virginia, the site of more than 50 percent of all battles. The South is again under siege, but this time the enemy is as likely to be a greedy Southerner as any damn Yankee. For information, contact American Battlefield Protection Program or go to www.nps.gov/abpp.

'and especially its railroads, which converged there from the four great cardinal points,' Sherman said.

Kennesaw Mountain National Battlefield Park (tel: 770-427 4686; www.nps.gov/kemo; daily sunrise–sunset; free) memorializes the 1864 Atlanta campaign, which began when Sherman led 100,000 troops out of Chattanooga in early May, only to confront 65,000 Confederate troops in the mountains of northwest Georgia. For months the two armies battled for key points along the Western & Atlantic Railroad, which

week later, Sherman began his ruthless March to the Sea – still recounted by Southerners today – destroying or stealing nearly everything in his path: crops, buildings, railroads, horses. He promised to 'make Georgia howl.'

Hiking trails from 2 to 10 miles (3–16km) lead to the most important sites. These are Kennesaw Mountain, with a vista of northern Georgia, and where the armies clashed; **Pigeon Hill**, where a foot trail leads to Confederate entrenchments; **Cheatham Hill**, site of the most savage fighting; and **Kolb's Farm** (not open to the public), head-

Confederate troops stand at attention during a Civil War battle reenactment at Brattonsville.

ran from Chattanooga to Atlanta. A climax was reached on June 22 at **Kennesaw Mountain**, just northwest of Atlanta. Hand-to-hand combat killed more than 2,000 of Sherman's men at Kennesaw, while the Confederates lost several hundred men in winning the battle.

MARCH TO THE SEA

Still, Sherman pushed General Johnston's Confederate troops south into Atlanta by July 9. After several attacks, Sherman placed the city under siege, concentrating on the railroads. He won the last one, the Macon & Western, on August 31, and telegraphed the fall of Atlanta to Washington on September 2. Riding the victory, Lincoln was re-elected on November 8. A

quarters of General Joseph Hooker.

Two small parks in Mississippi mark strategic points in the ongoing conflict between North and South. Sherman's army needed to defend the Nashville–Chattanooga Railroad, a critical Union supply line. In June 1864, the Confederates, under General Nathan Bedford Forrest, an unschooled farm boy who had become a millionaire, routed Union soldiers at Brices Cross Roads, displaying brilliant military tactics and taking advantage of torrential downpours that mired Union troops in mud. Victory in battle, however, didn't help the Confederate position, as Sherman was still able to defend the railroad. It is possible to see the battlefield and markers at the small

"I have fought against the people of the North because I believed they were seeking to wrest from the South its dearest rights. But I have never cherished toward them bitter or vindictive feelings, and I have never seen the day when I did not pray for them." Robert E. Lee

Brices Cross Roads National Battlefield Site (tel: 662-680 4027; www.nps.gov/brcr; daily 9am-

limits, about a mile east of the **Natchez Trace Parkway**.

Grant's army was everywhere during the spring of 1864. Even while Sherman waged the Atlanta campaign and smaller forces defended the Nashville and Chattanooga Railroad, Federal troops were focused on Richmond. The Union Army reached Petersburg, Virginia, which Grant called 'the key to taking Richmond,' in mid-June 1864. For 10 gruelling months, Grant kept Petersburg under siege. He cut Lee's supply lines from the south, diminishing troop strength

Confederate reenactors stand on the ramparts of Fort Moultrie to mark the 150th anniversary of the Civil War.

4:30pm; free).

Only a month later, arid, hot weather created as many difficulties as did the earlier rain, tiring soldiers on both sides. Again, Federal troops battled Confederate men to protect their southern supply line. On July 14, the two sides met at **Tupelo**, Mississippi, with exhausted, ill-fed Union troops winning a close victory. For two months, the two sides skirmished. Finally, in September, Confederate troops pushed north past Federal soldiers into Tennessee. But Sherman's forces no longer needed to protect the railroad; they had already won Atlanta and were on their way to the sea. **Tupelo National Battlefield** (tel: 662-680 4025; www.nps.gov/tupe; daily 9am-4:30pm; free) is located within Tupelo city

through direct attack, hunger, and demoralization. Petersburg finally surrendered on April 2, 1865. On the same day, the proud capital of Richmond fell.

One of the most tragic sites at **Petersburg National Battlefield** (tel: 804-732 3531; www.nps.gov/pete; daily 9am–5pm) is the **Crater**. Here, the 48th Pennsylvania Infantry, which included many former coal miners, dug a tunnel toward a Confederate fort at Pegram's Salient. In this tunnel they blew up 4 tons of gunpowder, planning to send Union troops through the gap it would create, with the intention of shortening the siege. The explosion, which blew up Confederate artillery, created a crater 170ft (52 meters) long, 60ft (18 meters) wide and 30ft (9 meters) deep.

The Union Army went directly into the crater but were unable to go farther and lost 4,000 men when Confederate troops attacked. The battlefield is within Petersburg city limits.

THE FINAL DAY

From here, it is possible to visit the 27 historic structures lying 20 miles (32km) east of Lynchburg within the restored village of **Appomattox Court House National Historical Park** (tel: 434-352 8987; www.nps.gov/apco; daily 9am–5pm; free), where Robert E. Lee, with

built in 1864, most people thought the war would soon be over. The Confederate government had built the prison to hold 10,000 captives, but soon there were 32,000 men suffering in the filthy, unsanitary conditions of the prison camp. Prisoners died from disease, poor sanitation, malnutrition, overcrowding, or even exposure to the elements.

Following the war, the prison commander, Captain Henry Wirz, was hanged as a war criminal, although his crimes were simply those of the ailing Confederate government, which had

Vicksburg National Cemetery.

a soldier's dignity, surrendered to Ulysses S. Grant only one week after Richmond fell. The national park site encompasses nearly 1,800 acres (730 hectares) of rolling hills in rural Virginia, which include the **McLean House** (where the surrender took place) and the **Appomattox Court House**.

A LASTING LEGACY

One of the saddest sites of the Civil War is to be seen at **Andersonville National Historic Site** (tel: 229-924 0343; www.nps.gov/ande; daily 9:30am–4:30pm; free) in Georgia. Andersonville was the largest encampment housing Federal prisoners, and a third of those confined here, almost 13,000 Union soldiers, died. When it was

no money or resources with which to feed and house its own troops, much less its prisoners. Andersonville's life as a prison ended abruptly in early 1865.

While at Andersonville, visit the **National Cemetery**, the atmospheric prison, and **Providence Spring House**, which the Women's Relief Corps built in 1901 as a tribute to the site where, during a downpour on August 9, 1864, a spring began to flow. Prisoners thanked 'Divine Providence' for the fresh water. Today, this historic site is a memorial not only to the men who were imprisoned and who died at Andersonville, but also to all Americans ever confined as prisoners of war – the only such national park in the country.

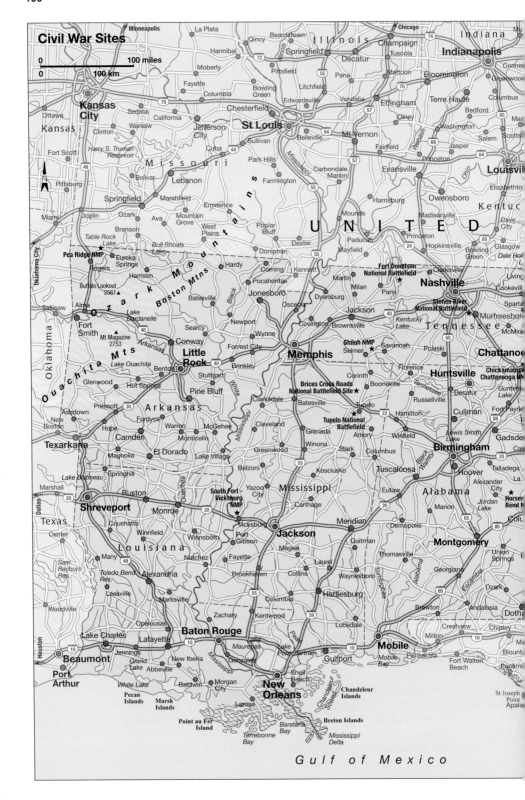

Civil War Sites

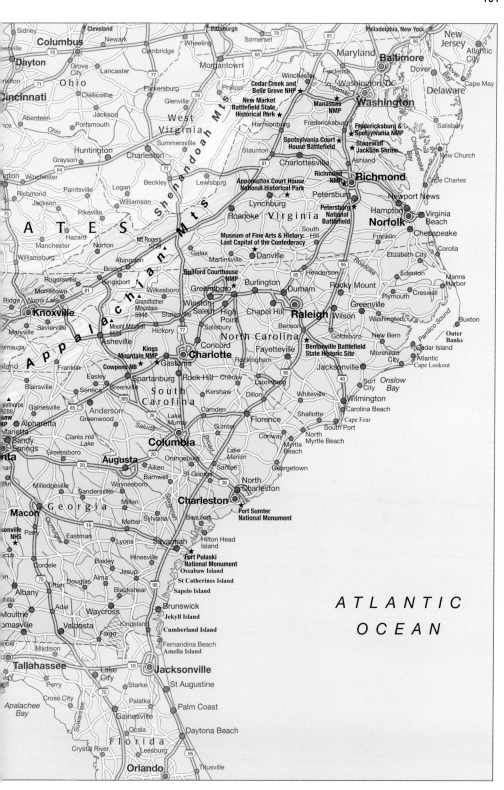

Mural about Highway 61, better known as the Blues Highway, in Mississippi.

Shrimp boats on the bayou at
Pointe-aux-Chênes, Louisiana.

Arched oak branches on an estate in Yemassee, South Carolina.

Hikers at Lindy Point in
Blackwater Falls State Park,
West Virginia.

INTRODUCTION

A detailed guide to the South, with principal sites clearly cross-referenced by number to the maps

Abe's Bar-B-Q restaurant in Clarksdale, Mississippi

Shiny-new cities like Charlotte in North Carolina, Birmingham in Alabama, and Atlanta are emblems of transformation in the cultural landscape. Savannah, Memphis and Biloxi bid for the coveted title of best vacation playground, vying with New Orleans for the party crowd, although little can compete with the Big Easy's annual Jazz Festival or Mardi Gras.

From the Atlantic shores of Virginia and the Carolinas to the silver sands and emerald sea of the Gulf Coast, and from the Great Smoky Mountains to the swamps and bayous of Louisiana, the country is lush and epic. The Art Deco panache of Hot Springs, Arkansas and Alabama's tranquil, wooded Azalea Coast offer bijoux bed and breakfasts, and sumptuous places for pampering, all served up with a uniquely Southern welcome.

Plantations and antebellum mansions drape the hills throughout the South. Graceful places to visit, and often to stay, since many offer overnight hospitality, they keep alive a picture of how the South was. In the South, the other side of that currency has found expression. The Martin Luther King National Historic Site in Atlanta and the National Civil Rights Museum in Memphis, along with countless museums and sites of heritage across the land where cotton was King, attest to the struggles of the more recent past.

Anywhere in the South is worth visiting for the food alone. Creole and Cajun spice, along with variations on traditional French sauces whet and satisfy appetites across Louisiana. The abundance of seafood in coastal regions is matched only by the varieties of culinary heritage that go into its preparation. Regional barbecue specialties set lips smacking from North Carolina to Nashville, and Southern-style dining is still a rich and elegant affair.

The Southern beaches from South Walton to Pass Christian attract travelers of all kinds – the family-fun crowds flock to Panama City beach and anglers love the bayous and coastal waters at the edge of the Gulf, while golfers lug their woods and irons to the world-famous links at Augusta and South Carolina near the Atlantic coast. The wild, unspoiled shorelines offer hikers, birdwatchers, and campers a natural nirvana. The haunting wilderness around the Natchez Trace and the spectacular Skyline Drive in the Blue Ridge Mountains make for driving trips that linger and echo in the memory. The history and the heritage, the culture and the celebrations, the aspirations and the achievements are all reasons to visit the South.

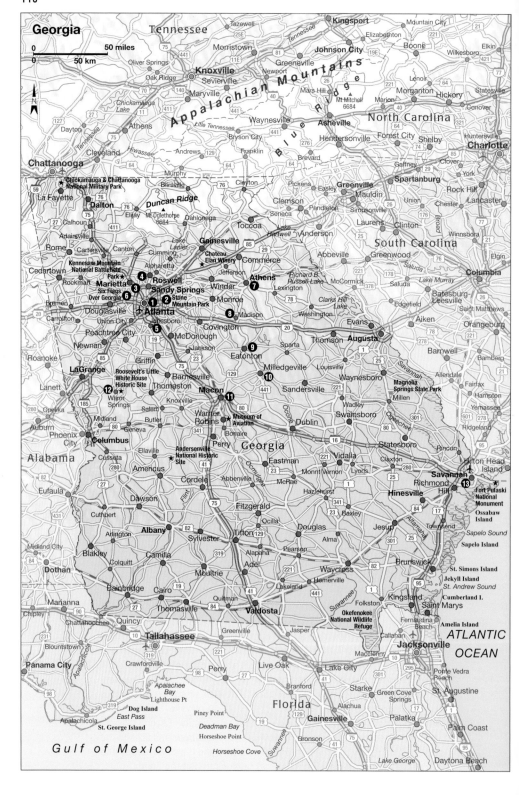

Georgia

0 _____ 50 miles
0 _____ 50 km

GEORGIA

The song *Georgia on My Mind*, sung by native son Ray Charles, is as poignant and elegant as the state itself.

From the green forests of the northern hills to the moss-draped streets of 'Slowvannah,' as the colonial town of Savannah is called, Georgia treads a fragrant path through the past and the future. Savannah was created by royal charter in 1733 by James Oglethorpe, the first settlement in 'the colony of Georgia in America.' He designed the town on a grid of broad thoroughfares, interspersed with public squares. Today Savannah is as design-conscious as it was then, for the highly successful Savannah College of Art and Design (SCAD) not only renovates buildings all around town, but attracts a hard-working, fun-loving group of international students.

Ray Charles himself is immortalized in Macon, a quintessential town with an upbeat lilt, which bills itself as 'the song and soul of the South.' Celebrated along with Charles in the Georgia Music Hall of Fame are fellow musicians Alabamian Little Richard, Otis Redding, Lena Horne, R.E.M., Brenda Lee, and Johnny Mercer.

Macon is just one town along what has become known as the 'Antebellum Trail,' a series of towns – Athens, Madison, Eatonton, Milledgeville – where tree-lined streets shade 1860s Italian and Greek Revival mansions. The trail, ambling through rolling countryside, is so relaxed that it's difficult to

Estate homes in Madison.

make even the one and only decision: whether to stroll a while or sit a spell.

The future is Atlanta, the undisputed capital of the South. Atlanta leads the ranks in new jobs, new businesses and new opportunities. As early as 1859, Greene B. Haywood was writing in Sketch of Atlanta: 'the population of the city is remarkable for its activity and enterprise. Most of the inhabitants came here for the purpose of bettering their fortunes.' And come they did.

Henry W. Grady, editor of the Atlanta Constitution and originator of the phrase

 Main attractions
World of Coca-Cola
SkyView Ferris
Georgia Aquarium
Bank of America Plaza
The Margaret Mitchell House and Museum
Piedmont Park
The Apex Museum
Stone Mountain Park
The Chattahoochee River National Recreation Area

Maps on pages 110, 112

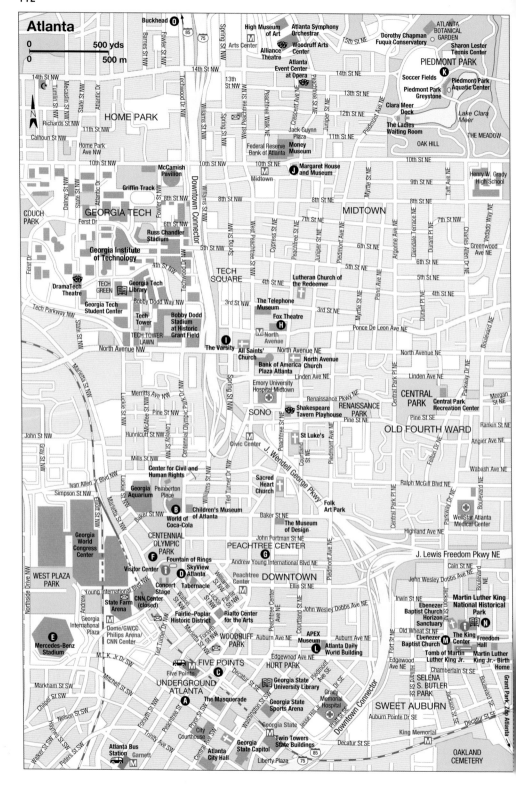

'the New South,' in 1886 wrote: 'I want to say to General Sherman ... that from the ashes he left us in 1864 we have raised a brave and beautiful city; that somehow or other we have caught the sunshine in the bricks and mortar of our homes.' Today, this 'sunshine in the bricks and mortar' is reflected in the Victorian mansions of neighborhoods like Druid Hills and Inman Park, and bounces, bright as a new penny, off the steel and chrome skyscrapers of Downtown, designed by internationally known Atlantan John Portman. The buildings are brash and audacious, as is the manner that has contributed to the city's success. Portman himself remarked after the successful bid for the 1996 Olympics: 'Clearly we don't just let things happen – we make them happen.'

ATLANTA

Called 'the capital of the new South' by Henry Grady, the bold skyscraper city of **Atlanta ❶** has CNN, Coca-Cola, history, and ambition to go.

Atlanta's Chamber of Commerce likes to call Downtown, ringed by tree-lined suburbs, 'the sweetest part of the peach.' But Downtown is a brash place, an urban maze where canyons of towers are relieved by softer relics like the Flatiron Building, a smaller version of New York's landmark. There's an international bustle, people of all races, colors, and creeds, young and old, mingling in cafés, bars, and restaurants. In 'the town that's too busy to hate,' some bemoan Downtown's almost sterile environment, but a short MARTA ride soon reaches the airier surroundings of older homes, supermalls and parks.

The entertainment and historic shopping neighborhood of **Underground Atlanta ❹** (a four block radius around Peachtree and Alabama streets) is the ideal place to begin a tour, as this is where Atlanta was born. With no navigable river or seaport, Atlanta's birth was a coincidence of favorable topography and the expansion of the railroads. Today, the train tracks just north follow the same route as these original beds, laid down over 150 years ago.

The Varsity, thought to be the world's largest drive-in restaurant.

The Atlanta skyline, seen from Piedmont Park.

⊘ GO UNDERGROUND

Underground Atlanta first opened as a shopping hub back in 1969. The location was chosen because of the busy roads nearby, bringing traffic and with it customers The original mall had two main halls, both of which were sold in 2017 to a developer with plans to reopen the site in 2020, as a revitalized hub of restaurants, bars, boutique stores, and high-end apartments. The original success of this entertainment hotspot can be traced back to a state-wide law during the 1960s that forbade the serving of mixed alcoholic drinks everywhere in Georgia except Fulton County, in which Atlanta resides. Even then such drinks could only be sold to men wearing suits and ties. Thanks to this law, Underground Atlanta quickly became the go-to party spot (for men in suits and ties drinking mixed drinks) during the 1960s and 70s.

The Georgia Aquarium.

DOWNTOWN ATLANTA

Under renovation until 2020, the architects of Atlanta have vowed to breathe new life into this historic neighborhood with new stores, bars, and cafés encompassing four city blocks above and below ground. Just as in the late 19th century, **Kenny's Alley** will once again become Downtown Atlanta's center for nightlife and entertainment.

A major attraction near the Underground complex is the **World of Coca-Cola ⓑ** (tel: 404-676-5151; www.worldofcoca-cola.com; Mon–Fri 10am–7pm, Sat–Sun 10am–9pm). One of Atlanta's most visited attractions, its exhibits feature both rare and familiar Coke memorabilia, a theater showing a film celebrating life's moments, a pleasantly reproduced soda fountain from the past, and brightly colored displays of the Coke advertising art that has made so many generations reach for the famous 'pause that refreshes.'

At the end of a visit, top off your tour with free samples of more than a dozen soft drink flavors.

Across the street from Coca-Cola is the Gothic-style **Shrine of the Immaculate Conception**. On the crest of the hill, east of the church, is the gold-domed **State Capitol Building**. Follow Peachtree Street northward, past the MARTA Five Points Transit Station to arrive at **Five Points ⓒ**, the symbolic heart of Atlanta. Here, north of the railroad tracks, at the intersection of Marietta, Peachtree, and Decatur Atlanta's bustling business district grew in the early 1840s. Following Marietta Street west, stop off at the **Bank of America Plaza**, 35 Broad Street, built in 1901 and redesigned in 1929 by noted architect Philip Trammell Shutze, and admire the main banking floor.

While London has its famed London Eye, Downtown Atlanta has **SkyView ⓓ**. (tel: 678-949 9023; www.skyviewatlanta.com; hours vary depending on the season) Although it's not as stately and doesn't afford the waterside views of its UK counterpart, folks of all ages can enjoy a ride on the Ferris wheel that gives riders a spectacular view of Atlanta. The ride towers 20 stories high, and takes about 10 minutes to

complete its circular journey. One highlight is the VIP gondola, which has Ferrari-style seats and a glass floor for those who want to ride in style.

Downtown also houses the **Mercedes-Benz Stadium** ⓔ, home of the Atlanta Falcons and Atlanta United. The stadium replaced the Georgiso bank a Dome in 2017, which was the venue for the 1996 Olympics. Next door is the **Georgia World Congress Center**, one of the largest conference facilities in the nation.

PARKS, POP, AND PEACHTREE

Bordered by Marietta Street and Techwood Drive is the 21-acre (9-hectare) **Centennial Olympic Park** ⓕ. This urban parkland features an outdoor space where visitors can walk and solace in the middle of bustling Atlanta. More infamously, it was the site of a fatal bombing during the 1996 summer Olympics. The **Atlanta Visitor Information Center** dispenses information and recounts a history of the games; there's also a coffee shop attached.

At the corner of Baker and Centennial Olympic Park Drive is the

Children's Museum of Atlanta (tel: 404-659-5437; www.childrensmuseumatlanta.org; Thur-Tue 9:30am–4:30pm). Aimed at two- to eight-year-olds, this interactive museum is one of the city's most fun educational experiences. Nearby you will find the **Georgia Aquarium** (tel: 404-581-4000; www.georgiaaquarium.org; Mon–Thur 9am–9pm, Fri-Sun 8am–9pm), which is entertaining, interactive (bring a poncho), and educational.

Sharing the 20-acre (8-hectare) site is the **World of Coca-Cola entertainment complex**, designed by the Jerde Partnership. Just like the partnership's previous enterprises – CityWalk in Los Angeles and the Fremont Street Experience in Las Vegas – the World of Coca-Cola is dazzling and innovative.

Capping a string of Atlanta's finest skyscrapers, at the summit of a ridge is the **Westin Peachtree Plaza Hotel** at 210 Peachtree Street. This soaring 70-story cylinder of glass and steel, built in 1976, was for many years the tallest hotel in the world. At the top of the building is the Sun Dial

Children play at the Centennial Olympic Park.

COCA-COLA

Atlanta's most famous creation and export was originally created as a remedy for morphine addiction.

Coca-Cola is the most famous soft drink on the planet. However, the reason for its very existence isn't anything to do with thirst-quenching or global domination. The drink was originally concocted for soldiers wounded in war as an alternative to the painkiller morphine, a drug to which many became addicted, including John Pemberton, the inventor of Coca-Cola. Pemberton served as a colonel in the Confederate army during the American Civil War and felt strongly that there needed to be a non-habit-forming alternative to morphine, following his own struggles.

It was at Pemberton's Eagle Drug and Chemical house that the very first Coca-Cola prototype was created, containing both coca leaves and cola nuts. It was modeled on a medicinal French wine and

Coca-Cola advert from 1906.

called Pemberton's French Wine Coca nerve tonic. However, when prohibition legislation gained significant momentum across the South, Pemberton removed the alcohol and rebranded his creation as Coca-Cola. Initially, Coca-Cola was sold at pharmacies only and the product initially enjoyed a successful partnership with the then-popular soda fountain business. This was during an era when carbonated drinks were considered to be good for your health. Riding this wave of positivity, Pemberton took Coca-Cola to the market not only as a cure for morphine addiction, but as treatment for migraines, impotence, and nerve disorders.

As the years rolled on, investors were brought to the table to help grow the company. Shareholder Asa Candler sought to gain full control of the brand after Dr Pemberton's death, but Pemberton's son Charley stood in his way. However, after Charley's death in 1894, Candler went on to assume full control in 1888, and thus began a new chapter in the company's history.

In 1919 the Coca-Cola Company was valued at, and subsequently purchased for, $25 million, and then floated on the stock market. The 500,000 shares available were valued at the handsome sum of $40 each – a small fortune in itself at the time. In late 2021, the company was valued at close to $88 billion.

The Coca-Cola brand has grown exponentially throughout the 19th, 20th and 21st centuries. Today its advertising campaigns are synonymous with national and international holidays. Among the most recognized is the 'Holidays are coming' jingle, accompanied by the fairy light adorned Coca-Cola delivery truck, making its way through snow-capped villages to deliver its Christmas bounty. The firm's Diet Coke television ad featuring Etta James' *I Just Wanna Make Love to You* is also famous.

Atlantans are understandably proud of Coca-Cola's global success, given that it was originally brewed in their backyard. They also appreciate the company's position within the city's economy. It is the fourth-largest employer in Atlanta, behind The Home Depot and UPS, and is renowned for going above and beyond when it comes to looking after its employees.

Restaurant, voted as having the best views in Atlanta.

The **Peachtree Center ⑥** complex is architect and developer John Portman's vision of a Southern-style Rockefeller Center, which has been a work in progress for more than 45 years. Portman, who also designed the Westin, has redefined the Downtown business district and parlayed his experience here into prestigious commissions around the world. Possibly the most recognizable building in the center is the 1967 **Hyatt Regency Hotel** with its soaring 22-story atrium lobby featuring a bar and market area. An evolution of this theme is the 48-story open, curving atrium lobby of the nearby **Atlanta Marriott Marquis Hotel**. Described by some as 'Jonah's view of the belly of the whale,' a glance downward from the upper floors of the hotel is not recommended for the faint of heart.

The elaborate **Peachtree Center** is located beneath the corporate towers at 231 Peachtree Street. A feature more commonly found in northern cities than in the sunny South are the climate-controlled pedestrian walkways that connect all the Peachtree Center buildings. These walkways also provide a respite from Downtown's more unsavory urban aspects.

MIDTOWN

If Downtown is the business and historic heart of Atlanta, Midtown is where the city's cultural lifeblood flows strongest. While Midtown may be more a state of mind than a district measured by rigid boundaries, its center is the busy area around the intersection of Peachtree and 14th streets. Proximity to four MARTA Transit Stations – Civic Center, North Avenue, Midtown, and Arts Center – makes access to all points fairly easy.

The highlight of a visit to Midtown's southern region is one of America's great movie palaces, the Moorish-style **Fox Theatre ⑪** at 660 Peachtree Street, built in 1929 and with an interior reminiscent of an Arabian courtyard. It's a lavish setting in which to enjoy a Hollywood blockbuster and, thanks to a recent restoration, it's

> **⊘ Fact**
>
> John Portman, Atlanta architect extraordinaire, started out with just two employees and grew his business to have influence worldwide.

Atlanta's historic Fox Theatre.

⊘ GETTING AROUND

The Metropolitan Atlanta Rapid Transit Authority (MARTA) is one of largest and most efficient public transit systems in all of America. With 48 miles (76km) of tracks, 38 stations, and a connecting bus network to cover where the trains can't go, MARTA is used by just over half a million passengers every weekday. The most cost-effective travel option is a Breeze Card, which you can purchase from the machines in almost any station. Simply load it with a seven-day unlimited travel pass, a set amount of credit, or a 20-trip ticket, which is a good deal cheaper than paying the standard $2.50 per journey. Then you're set to go! Breeze Cards work like London's Oyster card system: simply tap your card on the barrier when entering and exiting the system.

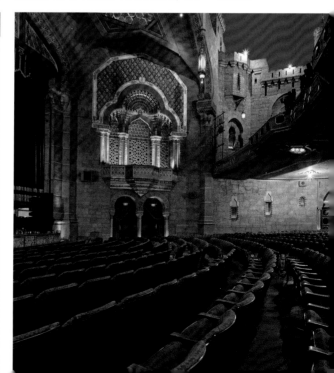

never looked better (tel: 855-285-8499; www.foxtheatre.org; Mon–Fri 10am–5pm, Sat 10am–3pm).

Two buildings dominate the area's skyline. One is the 52-story **Tower Square**, at 675 West Peachtree Street; the other, to the south, is the **Bank of America Plaza**. Still one of the world's tallest buildings, the Bank of America is topped with an open pyramidal structure sometimes called Atlanta's Eiffel Tower.

A few blocks west is a landmark of a completely different kind. At Spring Street and North Avenue is **The Varsity** ❶, an Atlanta culinary tradition since 1928. The current Art Moderne building, erected in 1940, has long been a gathering place for Georgia Tech students and an essential stop for locals showing out-of-town guests the best chili-dogs, onion rings, and hamburgers.

GEORGIA TECH

Across Interstate 75/85 on North Avenue, residential facilities built as part of the Olympic village for the 1996

High Museum of Art.

games mark the entrance to the campus of the Georgia Institute of Technology, or **Georgia Tech**. Established only two decades after Atlanta was devastated in the Civil War, Georgia Tech was a tangible outcome of journalist Henry Grady's call for a 'new South' combining business, industry, and agriculture.

Architectural highlights include the Tech Tower (1888), the Aaron French Building (1899) and the Carnegie Building, which was the school's first library and a 1907 gift from Andrew Carnegie.

A few blocks northeast, the **Margaret Mitchell House and Museum** ❶ (tel: 404-249-7015; www.atlantahistorycenter.com; hours vary), erstwhile home of the author of *Gone with the Wind*, sits at the corner of 10th and Peachtree streets. Though the house, which Mitchell ingloriously referred to as 'the Dump,' is sometimes rented out for parties, tours normally take place daily. A short film describes the struggle to restore the building; the tour then continues to the apartment in which Mitchell penned her celebrated novel. A museum honors the 70th anniversary of the premiere of 'GWTW,' as aficionados call the movie. The museum contains everything you could wish to know about one of the South's defining movies and displays include the original Tara doorway from the film set; fans will surely swoon.

At 1280 Peachtree Street is the **Woodruff Arts Center** (tel: 404-733-4200; www.woodruffcenter.org; Mon–Fri 9:30am–5:30pm and 9:30pm–12am, Sat 12am–5:30pm), which hosts concerts of the Atlanta Symphony, performances by the Alliance Theatre and the Atlanta Symphony Orchestra). Adjacent to the Arts Center is the striking, modern **High Museum of Art** (tel: 404-733-4400; www.high.org; Tue–Sat 10am–5pm, Sun 12pm–5pm), designed by the architect Richard Meier. The name has nothing to do with the museum's exalted position but reflects the generosity of art patron Harriet High who, in 1926, donated her home for use as an art museum. The pre sent bui!ding is of white porcelain-enameled steel, and the permanent collection includes Sub-Saharan African Art.

The upscale neighbourhood of **Ansley Park** has fine old homes, and the elegant Beaux Arts-style **First Church of Christ, Scientist** (1914). But its enduring popularity is, in part, for its convenience to both Peachtree Street and Atlanta's largest public park, **Piedmont Park** . Since its days as a mustering ground for Confederate veterans' reunions, Piedmont Park has been a gathering place for Atlantans from all walks of life. The largest event takes place every 4th of July, when 55,000 runners sweat it out in the Peachtree Road Race. A place to cool off again in the north of the park is the **Atlanta Botanical Garden**, featuring one of the world's largest permanent displays of tropical orchids. For a closer look at Ansley Park or Piedmont Park, join a volunteer from the Atlanta Preservation Center on one of their guided walking tours.

SWEET AUBURN AVENUE

Auburn Avenue, east of Downtown beyond Interstate 85, is best known for its associations with Dr Martin Luther King, Jr. The street's nickname 'Sweet Auburn Avenue' was earned through its prosperity. Between 1890 and 1960, the avenue was always jumpin'. By day, Black men and women thronged the Blackowned businesses like banks and insurance companies, beauty salons, retail stores, barber shops, and grocery stores. Nights were even livelier, with people strolling in the street, and jiving in the nightspots. The **Preservation District** is the western portion of the street that leads to the Martin Luther King, Jr National Historic Site. Both are overseen by the National Park Service. Poised at the 'gateway' to Auburn Avenue, at the corner of Courtland Street, is the **Auburn Avenue Research Library on African American Culture and History**. Next to the library heading east is the African American Panoramic Experience, more commonly known as the **APEX Museum** (tel: 404-523-2739; www.

Runners in the Peachtree Road Race.

⊙ PIEDMONT PARK

Fondly referred to as Atlanta's Central Park, this 190-acre (77-hectare) green space is where city dwellers and tourists come to relax. Designed by Frederick Law Olmstead, the same architect behind New York's Central Park, this oasis hosts a myriad of events at the baseball field, tennis courts, visitor center, and lakeside. Every Saturday morning, come rain or shine, the Green Market is a must-see if you're a fan of supporting local farmers and small businesses, or just a good brunch. The park also hosts trivia nights and guided history tours in addition to classes, such as gardening and fishing in season.There's even an Aquatic Center originally built in 1911 which features an outdoor pool that puts on movie nights on a giant inflatable screen. Check online for details (www.piedmontpark.org)

apexmuseum.org; Tue–Sat 11am–3pm). It features traveling exhibits from all over the world. The APEX is the perfect part to start a walking tour of Auburn Avenue. Along the walk important sites are identified by informative National Park Service plaques.

The music you hear from the moment you set foot on Auburn Avenue usually comes from the **Royal Peacock Lounge**. In the 1950s, the Peacock was the hottest of nightspots. On weekends, Black people from all over town would pack the Peacock to hear the Four Tops, B.B. King, or Gladys Knight and to dance on the polished dance floor. **Big Bethel A.M.E. Church** grew out of a church organized before the Civil War. The freedmen who founded Big Bethel established Atlanta's first school for Black children.

MARTIN LUTHER KING NATIONAL HISTORIC SITE

At 407 Auburn is the most famous church in the South, **Ebenezer Baptist Church **. It is the family church of the late Dr King, with a legacy that dates back to Dr King's maternal grandmother. Martin Luther served as co-pastor of the church with his father.

Today, Sunday services are held in the large Horizon Sanctuary across the street. Tours of the original church are given throughout the week and on Saturday afternoons. There's the added possibility of hearing one of Dr King's sermons, which are regularly piped into the sanctuary. Just past the church is the complex that attracts many more visitors than any other in the Atlanta area, the **Martin Luther King National Historical Park** (tel: 404-331-5190; www.nps.gov/malu; daily 9am–5pm; free). The **Visitor Center** has a video program and can help with questions, while the **Plaza** contains a rose garden, amphitheater, and a poignant statue called *Behold*. Based on the MLK Center for Nonviolent Social Change founded in 1968 by King's widow Coretta and others, headed by the King's younger son, Dexter Scott King, is the **King Center**. The organization continues to work for economic and social equality. The centerpiece of the memorial is the great man's resting place. His **gravesite**, a white marble tomb, tops a circular red brick base, at the foot of a long blue-watered pool.

Preserved homes dot the avenue all the way to Boulevard Street, but for many visitors Auburn's Freedom Walk ends with a beginning – at the steps of a modest, two-story, yellow and brown house at 501 Auburn Avenue – the **Martin Luther King, Jr Birth Home**. The Queen Anne-style house has been restored to its appearance from 1929, when King was born, to 1941, when his family moved to another house nearby.

BUCKHEAD

Buckhead, about 4 miles (6.5km) north of the city's central Downtown area, is Atlanta's best address. If Atlanta were a super-highway, Buckhead would be the fast lane. All the best, brightest, and most marketable projects the city has up its sleeve are

The birthplace and boyhood home of Dr Martin Luther King Jr.

based in Buckhead. All Atlantans want to live here, and on weekends it often seems that all Atlantans, and every university student in Georgia, do. The area is served by three MARTA stations: Lenox, Buckhead, and Lindbergh. The perfect place to learn about Buckhead – and indeed, Atlanta itself – is at the **Atlanta History Center** (130 West Paces Ferry Road; tel: 404-814-4000; www.atlantahistorycenter. com; Tue–Sun 9am–4pm). This attractive, tree-shaded campus occupies more than 30 acres (12 hectares) and includes the **Atlanta History Museum**. It's advisable to spend the best part of a day here, since the cool, flower-filled grounds and tranquil atmosphere are a perfect antidote to the urban bustle that swirls around so much of the city.

In a compact area along Buckhead's Roswell Road, Peachtree, and adjacent side streets such as Pharr Road, Buckhead Avenue, Irby Avenue, and East Andrews Drive, is an eclectic mix of cafés, clubs, restaurants, stores, and theaters that draws shoppers during the day, diners in the evening, and partygoers into the night. There's always something to do here; little wonder that the governor of Georgia has a house in the neighborhood.

If Buckhead is Atlanta's shopping mecca, then Phipps Plaza and Lenox Square are the ultimate destinations for millions of plastic-wielding pilgrims. At the corner of Lenox and Peachtree roads, **Phipps Plaza**, a monument in polished brass and marble, is the Taj Mahal of malls. Tiffany's, Louis Vitton, Gucci, Versace, and Saks are here, as well as a movie theater complex. Built in 1959, **Lenox Square**, on East Paces Ferry Road, was Atlanta's first mall and, with continual expansion, is the largest in the Southeast. The four-level mall is home to almost 200 stores, many of them unique to Atlanta. An **Atlanta Visitors Center** information booth offers brochures and maps of the city, and pointers to the highlights of Buckhead's varied and often notorious nightlife.

AROUND GEORGIA

Elegant wineries, a relaxed college town and a fine park are just miles away from Atlanta, while nestled deep in the countryside are homes so beautiful even Sherman couldn't bear to burn them.

From Atlanta outward, the hills and history of Georgia have an Antebellum Trail, Athens, famous for its music and football, and the controversial Stone Mountain. This massive hunk of almost-bare granite poking high out of the earth has a carving of Confederate generals Robert E. Lee and Stonewall Jackson riding alongside the Southern president Jefferson Davis. The carvings are under intense scrutiny from protesters calling for them to be removed and arguing against the parks upkeep. Today this confronting historical landmark still attracts tourists with an interest in Georgia's dark history as well as the natural beauty of the **Stone Mountain Park** ❷ (tel: 800-401-2407; www.stonemountainpark.com;

Swan House at the Atlanta History Center.

daily 5am–midnight). Known to the Creek Natives as 'Therrethlofkee,' or 'the mountain on the side of the river (Chattahoochee) where there are no other mountains,' Stone Mountain is the world's largest outcrop of granite and commands the horizon 16 miles (26km) east of **Atlanta**.

Stone Mountain Village is a throng of vintage buildings and quaint shops. The 1857 **Stone Mountain Railroad Depot** survived the Civil War and is now the village's town hall. The **Stone Mountain Country Store** at Main and Manor streets offers a wide selection of crafts and antiques. Just east of the depot is **Memorial Hall** featuring geological and human history displays of the mountain, photographs, and artifacts, plus a museum of Civil War weapons.

TOURING STONE MOUNTAIN

Most tours start with a ride on the **Stone Mountain Scenic Railroad**. From the depot on Robert E. Lee Boulevard, the vintage steam engine rocks and sways along a 5-mile (8-km) loop around the mountain's base, providing a pleasant

overview of the park's attractions and the area's landscape. If you want to stretch your legs, hike to the top along the **Stone Mountain Walk-Up Trail** which ascends nearly 800ft (240 meters) meandering through several climate zones, from the Appalachian Forest at the base to the harsh environment of the summit. The **Stone Mountain Skyride** offers a breathtaking, five-minute gondola ride from the base to the summit and provides the park's best close-up view of the disputed carving.

Antebellum Plantation, on John B. Gordon Drive, re-creates a working plantation. The centerpiece of this exhibit is the **Charles M. Davis House**, a beautifully proportioned neoclassical structure built in 1850 as the main residence of a 1,000-acre (400-hectare) plantation near Albany, Georgia. There are also two 150-year-old **Slave Cabins**. These primitive structures stand in stark contrast to the elegant homes of the plantation owner and overseer. If the undeniably lovely plantation has whetted your appetite for a taste of the 'Old South,' travel east on Lee Boulevard to the shores of **Stone Mountain Lake**. On the lake, listen out for the soft musical tones of the **Stone Mountain Carillon** (consisting of 732 bells) on the western bank of the lake.

At the western base of the mountain, near the Memorial Drive entrance, **Confederate Hall** features a three-dimensional map of Georgia that depicts General Sherman's 1864 invasion. More adventurous folks will enjoy time at Geyser Towers, an adventure park filled with high platforms, suspended bridges, and rope tunnels. Throughout this high-up attraction, geysers spray sporadically to cool off guests. Little ones can enjoy playing in a trickling creek if they are too young to enjoy the active park.

NEAR ATLANTA

The **Chattahoochee River National Recreation Area** (CRNRA) stretches like a 'strand of pearls' from Atlanta's western

The Southeastern Railway Museum.

suburbs to Lake Lanier. Its woodlands and shoreline make for great fishing and water sports. To the northwest and simmering with small-town Southern charm is **Marietta ❸**, founded in 1833.

The town square is ringed by historic buildings, cafes, restaurants, and antiques shops. The **Marietta Welcome Center** (tel: 770-429-1115; Error! Hyperlink reference not valid.; Tue–Fri 10am–5pm, Sat 10am–4pm, Sun 1–4pm) is in the 1898 railroad depot at 4 Depot Street. Just across the street, **Kennesaw House** was built in 1855 as the Fletcher House Hotel. James J. Andrews' Federal raiders met here on April 11, 1862, to iron out their plan to steal a locomotive and head north toward Union lines, and destroy the railroad behind them. It now houses the **Marietta Museum of History** (tel: 770-794-5710; www.mariettahistory. org; Tue–Sat 10am–4pm).

For a racier time, hit the indoor go-karts at the **Andretti Speed Lab** (www. andrettikarting.com; tel: 678-712-4972, open daily), an entertainment complex devoted to Formula One racing located ❹, 20 miles (32km) north of Atlanta. The town of Roswell has a wealth of historic buildings. The fine 1845 Archibald **Smith Plantation House** (935 Alpharetta Street; tel: 770-641-3978; www.roswellgov. com/smithplantation; Tues–Sat 10am–4pm, Sun 1–4pm) is one of the city's best preserved landmarks. In 1853, town founder James Bulloch's daughter Martha married Theodore Roosevelt in the dining room of **Bulloch Hall** at 180 Bulloch Avenue. Their son, Theodore junior, would lead the 'Rough Riders' in the Spanish-American War, and later served as the 26th president of the United States.

East of Roswell, in the town of **Duluth**, the entertaining **Southeastern Railway Museum** (tel: 770-476-2013; www.train-museum.org; Thur–Sat 10am–5pm, Sun 1pm-5pm) houses an extensive collection of antique railroad cars and artifacts.

The **Chateau Elan Winery** (tel: 678-425-0900; call for opening times) on Georgia 211 at Interstate 85 includes a visitor center, wine shop, restaurant, and rotating art exhibits. There is also an elegant inn, tennis center, golf course, European-style spa, and nature trails. Continue through the green rolling hills of Henry County to **Panola Mountain State Conservation Park** (tel: 770-389-7801; www.gastateparks. org/panolamountain; daily 8am–7pm) a 600-acre (242-hectare) park that is a smaller version of its neighbor, Stone Mountain.

Margaret Mitchell drew inspiration for her epic, *Gone with the Wind* at **Jonesboro ❺**, 16 miles (25 km) south of Atlanta via I-75 and Georgia Highway 54. As a child, Margaret visited ageing relatives here and heard their stories of the Civil War. Several lavish manor homes still remain in the town. **Stately Oaks** (tel: 770-473-0197; www.historical-jonesboro.org; Mon–Sat 11am–4pm), a 1830s Greek Revival mansion is the site of the annual 'Tara Ball.' Go to the **gift shop** for *Gone with the Wind* souvenirs. Just south of Jonesboro on Talmadge Road is **Lovejoy Plantation**. The visits

> **Tip**
>
> The Chattahoochee River National Recreation Area stretches from Atlanta to Lake Lanier, alongside a 48-mile (77km) section of the Chattahoochee River. It was officially opened over 40 years ago on August 15, 1978, by then-President Jimmy Carter.

University of Georgia.

Rollercoaster at Six Flags Over Georgia.

The Georgia Bulldogs, who play at Athens' Sanford Stadium.

young Margaret Mitchell made to her great-grandfather Philip Fitzgerald's house, now on these grounds, was the model for Twelve Oaks in her book.

Finally, any visit to Atlanta would be incomplete without spending a day at **Six Flags Over Georgia** ❻ (tel: 770-739-3400; www.sixflags.com/overgeorgia; call for opening times). Located on Six Flags Parkway and I-20, Six Flags features over 100 rides, including wild roller coasters and the exhilarating Dare Devil Dive.

ATHENS

For many Georgians, **Athens** ❼ means one thing and one thing alone – football, and the 90,000 rabid, red-and-black-clad University of Georgia fans who descend for Saturday afternoon games. Out-of-state visitors are more likely to think of the home of REM and other successful American rock bands. Either way the city's enormous university is the focus of life here.

Chartered in 1785, the **University of Georgia** was the first state university established in the new United States.

The fine wrought-iron gateway to the campus – **The Arch** – is on Broad Street, at College Avenue. Just to the south is **Old College**, the school's first permanent structure, erected in 1806. The bell in the magnificent Greek Revival-style 1832 **Chapel** once summoned students to compulsory religious services; now it tolls to celebrate athletic triumphs. The Main Library, with a collection of over 3 million documents, includes the original Confederate Constitution, which was handwritten in 1861.

The **Georgia Museum of Art** (tel: 706-542-4662; www.georgiamuseum.org; Tue–Sat 10am–5pm, until 9pm Thu, Sun 1–5pm; free) has various works, including the Kress Collection of Italian Renaissance Art and African-American art. The Historic **Athens Welcome Center** (280 East Dougherty Street; tel: 706-353-1820; www.athenswelcomecenter.com; daily 10am–5pm) is in the restored 1820 **Church-WaddelBrumby House**, the oldest standing residence in Athens. Atop the hill across Hancock Street is **City Hall** and the celebrated

☉ A FAILED INVENTION

The experimental weapon, the double-barreled cannon, can be traced back to the American Civil War and an overly ambitious mechanic named John Gilleland. Sensing the opportunity to make a considerable sum of money selling advanced new weaponry to the Confederate Army, Gilleland talked up the destructive merits of his double-barrelled cannon. In theory, firing two cannonballs connected by a chain would mow through the enemy ranks like a hot knife cutting though butter. In reality however, the test firings were only affective against targets that the cannon was not aimed at, including an unsuspecting dairy cow. Somewhat unsurprisingly, Gilleland never became rich from his failed invention, but he did become notorious.

Double-Barreled Cannon (see box) cast for the Confederate Army at the nearby Athens Foundry in 1863. The gun, designed by John Gilleland, was supposed to fire two balls tethered by a chain to 'mow down Yankees like a scythe cuts wheat.' Tried only once, the cannon was never used in combat. South on College Avenue toward Broad Street is where Athens' students and business people meet and mingle. Behind the facades of 19th-century commercial buildings are popular eateries and clubs where the beer is cold and refreshing, the music loud, and the fun fast-paced.

Local landmarks to look for include the fabled **40 Watt Club**, at 285 West Washington Street, where Athens-based bands such as the B-52's and REM started out in the 1970s. Walk north to Prince Avenue and follow it west to some of the finest antebellum houses in Georgia. The **Joseph H. Lumpkin House**, at 248 Prince Street, was built in 1841. Just south, at 279 Meigs Street, is the 1833 **Joseph Camak House**, an early Federal-style brick house with beautiful wrought-iron details. At 489 Prince Street is **Fire Hall No. 2**, a triangular, single-bay Victorian brick station constructed for horse-drawn engines in 1901. Across Prince, at 698 Pope Street, the 1835 **Howell Cobb House** was home to a notable figure in Georgian history: Cobb served as Governor, Secretary of the US Treasury under President James Buchanan (1856–60), president of Georgia's 1861 Secession Convention, and as a general in the Confederate Army.

Three miles (5 km) south of Athens, at 2450 South Milledge Avenue, is The **State Botanical Garden of Georgia** (tel: 706-542-1244; www.botgarden.uga.edu; daily 8am–7pm; free) set above the Middle Oconee River on 313 forested acres (127 hectares). Visitors come to enjoy the gardens, hike the miles of nature trails, and take classes in various aspects of gardening.

ANTEBELLUM TRAIL

The Antebellum Trail isn't really a trail, in the romantic, magnolia-laned way the name suggests, but it does take in middle and east Georgian historic towns, and Civil War battle sites. Much of the quintessential – and mythical – Old South romanticized by *Gone with the Wind* is here to explore; the type of territory foreigners think Atlanta should be but isn't. It even includes Br'er Rabbit, the South's most famous critter.

From Atlanta, pick up the Antebellum Trail by driving I-20 for 30 miles east (48km) through Social Circle, Rutledge and then into **Madison ❽**, renowned as the town so beautiful even General Sherman couldn't bear to burn it. There are dozens of palatial Greek Revival mansions built in the 1830s that survived the ravages of war, the Great Depression, and Progress. At the **Madison County Welcome Center** (East Jeffferson Street; tel: 706-342-4454; www.visitmadisonga.com; Mon–Fri 9am–5pm, Sat 10am–4pm, Sun 11:30–3:30pm), pick up brochures to the town's historic buildings. The **Morgan**

SkyView Atlanta ferris wheel.

County Court House is listed on the National Register of Historic Places.

Two well-known authors were born in **Eatonton** . Stories from antebellum plantations inspired Joel Chandler Harris (1848–1908) to write the folksy Tales of Uncle Remus. Later on, Alice Walker turned her early experiences here into the Pulitzer Prize-winning *The Color Purple*. Harris's tales of Br'er Rabbit, Br'er Fox, The Tar Baby and other 'critters' are commemorated at the **Uncle Remus Museum** (tel: 706-485-6856; www.uncleremusmuseum.org; Mon–Sat 10am–4pm, Sun 1–4pm). A walking/driving tour guide is easily available at the Chamber of Commerce on the courthouse square and takes visitors past landmarks in the life of Alice Walker.

Until 1868, when Atlanta was given the honor, **Milledgeville**  served as Georgia's capital. Stop at the **Milledgeville-Baldwin County Convention and Visitors Bureau** (200 West Hancock Street; tel: 478-452-4687; www.visitmilledgeville.org; Mon–Fri 9am–5pm, Sat 10am–4pm) for tour maps and information. One of Georgia's most cherished historic landmarks, the lovely **Old Governors' Mansion**, built in Palladian Greek Revival style between 1835 and 1838, has a prized ticket to the 1825 ball commemorating the Marquis de Lafayette's farewell tour of America. The well-known novelist and short-story writer **Flannery O'Connor** found Milledgeville's traditions and Old South Gothic paradoxes an ideal foil for her Irish Catholic wit. In the library at **Georgia College** – her alma mater, across from the Old Governors' Mansion – the **Flannery O'Connor Room** displays manuscripts and mementoes from her career.

MACON

At the exact center of the state, **Macon**  is the largest city on the Antebellum Trail. A bridge over the **Ocmulgee River** honors Macon-born soulman Otis Redding. 'Little Richard' Penniman (Tutti Frutti) hailed from here, as did the Allman Brothers Band. The **Visit Macon Tourist Information Center** (200 Cherry Street; tel: 478-743-3401; www.visitmacon.org; Mon–Fri 9am–4pm, Sat 10am–4pm) is in the old Terminal Station, Downtown. The University of Georgia's **Special Collection Libraries** (tel: 706-542-3251; www5.galib.uga.edu; call for hours and ticket information) showcases the above musicians and also other talented home-grown stars who found fame on the world stage. The **Hay House** (tel: 478-742-8155; www.hayhousemacon.org; Wed–Sun 10am–4pm) is the must-see house-museum. Completed in 1859, the grand Italian Renaissance *palazzo* is visually stunning inside and out. The **Tubman Museum** (310 Cherry Street; tel: 478-743-8544; www.tubmanmuseum.com; Tue–Sat 9am–5pm) celebrates local and national African-American achievements.

Warm Springs  is forever associated with former President Franklin Delano Roosevelt. The future four-time president first came in 1924 to soak his polio-afflicted legs in Warm Springs'

The Br'er Rabbit statue at the Uncle Remus Museum.

mineral waters. He built his six-room cottage, The Little White House, in a heavily wooded site (tel: 706-655-5870; www.gastateparks.org/LittleWhiteHouse; daily 9am–4:45pm). Some of the strategic legislation of his 'New Deal' was formed in these pinepaneled rooms. On April 12, 1945, Roosevelt suffered a fatal stroke while posing for a portrait in the dining room. His unfinished portrait is still on the easel.

SAVANNAH

Author and local resident Rosemary Daniell once observed: 'Savannah is the kind of town where drunken, irreverent fun, and thumbing one's nose at propriety are still permissible, even popular. It is said the first thing one is asked in Atlanta is, "What do you do?"; in Charleston, "Who were your ancestors?" and in Savannah: "What would you like to drink?"'

Only a 40-minute plane ride away from the gleaming skyscrapers of Atlanta, **Savannah** £ is the oldest city in Georgia. People are attracted here by the leisurely pace and because, although there are fine houses and museums, the jewel is the town itself; there are few absolutely 'must see' attractions. Some outsiders call the city 'Slow-vannah' for this reason. Perhaps it's the high humidity that makes locals move that way. They speak slowly, drive slowly, and eat slowly. So take your time: there's no reason to hurry here.

In 1733, James Oglethorpe received a royal charter to establish 'the colony of Georgia in America.' Two of the many reasons for this were to protect the lands from Spanish Florida, and to produce wine and silk for the British Empire.

Oglethorpe designed the town on a grid of broad thoroughfares, punctuated at regular intervals with spacious public squares. Today, 21 of the 24 squares have been refurbished, forming the nucleus of Savannah's **Historic District** – one of the largest, loveliest urban, National Historic Landmark districts in the country, covering a 2.5-mile (4km) radius.

DISTINCTIVE SQUARES

Each square has a distinctive character, defined by the structures that encompass it, whether a towering cathedral, a Confederacy statue, or an ornate fountain. **Bull Street**, running the length of the district north to south, links the most beautiful squares to each other. These excel in Savannah's most characteristic details: fancy ironwork and Spanish moss. The ironwork, scrolled and lacy enough to rival New Orleans' finest, decorates fountains and monuments or balconies suspended from Greek Revival mansions. Sometimes the metal is in the shape of animals and put to use as water spouts or foot scrapers.

A walking tour allows visitors to set their own pace, but it is difficult to cover the entire Historic District in one afternoon, especially when the heat is at its most oppressive. There's a selection of transportation options, however, including horse-drawn carriage tours and free shuttle buses.

River Street, Savannah.

A good place to start is the **Savannah Visitors' Center** (301 Martin Luther King Jr Boulevard; tel: 912-644-6400; www.visitsavannah.com; daily 9am–4pm), 14 blocks south of the river and just to the west of the Historic District. Sharing premises with the **Savannah History Museum**, where the exhibits include the Oscar earned by local son and nationally known composer Johnny Mercer for the song Moon River; the center is in the former Civil War-era Central Georgia Railway depot. The visitors' center is the place to check for elegant accommodations. A handful of the houses in the Historic District have been turned into bed-and-breakfast inns, which are luxurious, and luxuriously expensive. The main area for more modest accommodations is the motel strip near the Visitors' Center, a 30-minute walk away from the restaurants, stores, and attractions Downtown.

SAVANNAH COLLEGE OF ART AND DESIGN

Opposite the center is the campus of the **Savannah College of Art and Design** (SCAD). The college has restored 56 buildings around town – including a couple of funky 1950s movie houses – many of which are used as classrooms or student accommodations. SCAD's little white vans and colorfully-clad international residents are ubiquitous, and the college's influence on making Savannah such a vital, fun town cannot be overestimated.

A few blocks east on **Telfair Square** is the **Telfair Academy** (tel: 912-790-8800; www.telfair.org; daily 10am–5pm,), one of the oldest art museums in the South. It is housed in a Regency mansion designed by British-born William Jay. The museum has a fine permanent collection of paintings and furniture. Another opulent division of the Telfair Museum is through Wright Square to **Oglethorpe Square**, the **Owens-Thomas House & Slave Quarters**. A splash of distinctive architectural details, like a side porch supported by four Corinthian columns, were the first American work by William Jay; he designed it when he was only 20 years old and then he came to Savannah to supervise the building's construction. The house shows a major

Leopold's Ice Cream parlor and a SCAD cinema in downtown Savannah.

portion of the Telfair's decorative arts collection. Also featured on the grounds are rare intact examples of urban slave quarters with objects on long-term loan from the Acacia Collection of African Americana. The **Jepson Center for the Arts** is the most recent addition to the Telfair Estate and is home to rotating exhibits of 20th- and 21st-century art collections.

All of Savannah's squares are dotted with daily activity, as well as vendors of art, hot-dog stands, and freelance musicians. Summer brings festive free jazz concerts to Johnson Square, near the river, while impromptu weddings are performed in the gazebo at Wright Square. A spring visit is the most opportune time to savor the myriad colors when the landscape is in full bloom. At night, fountains and monuments are lit by street lanterns, and although the squares may be tempting they also provide a breeding ground for purse snatchers and pan-handlers: it's best to enjoy their attractions before the sun goes down.

Wright Square is a gorgeous example of Savannah landscaping. A huge boulder marks the grave of Torno-Chi-Chi, the Yamacraw Native chief who welcomed General Oglethorpe and the other early settlers. On the east side is the Lutheran Church of the Ascension, a celebrated landmark dating back to 1772, which has a beautiful Ascension window in the main sanctuary.

Between Wright Square and **Chippawa Square** is the **Juliette Gordon Low Birthplace** (tel: 912-233-4501; www.juliettegordonlowbirthplace.org; Mon, Tue, Thurs–Sat 10am–4pm). While living in Britain, Low was introduced to a scouting program and, on her return to Georgia in 1912, founded the Girl Scouts of America, a movement that rapidly spread throughout the country. The house, built between 1818 and 1821 and richly furnished, can be enjoyed in a 30-minute tour guided by a local in period dress. Be prepared

to share the tour with girl scouts, as the house is now a national scouting headquarters.

AROUND MIDNIGHT

The most talked about residence in recent memory is the lovely **Mercer House** on **Monterey Square**, built by composer Johnny Mercer's grandfather. The residence was the home of the late antique dealer Jim Williams, the subject of John Berendt's book *Midnight in the Garden of Good and Evil* and the 1997 movie directed by Clint Eastwood.

In 1981, the eccentric but debonair millionaire Williams shot his 22-year-old male companion. The victim had a reputation for wildness and excess, and Williams claimed self-defense. Convicted twice of murder, jailed and released and tried a third time to a hung jury, the fourth time he was tried and successfully acquitted.

Williams died of a heart attack the year he was freed. His sister occupied the house, a magnificent structure filled with antiques, for many years. Popular local rumor has it that the late

Juliette Gordon Low, founder of the Girl Scouts of America.

Mercer Williams House Museum.

Jacqueline Onassis once tried to buy the house herself. The shutters are nearly always drawn tight, and the house is definitely not open to the public.

The Historic District's procession of squares ends at beautiful **Forsyth Park**, a 31-acre (13-hectare) setting for constant outdoor activity: jogging, frisbee tournaments, walking, and football. The centerpiece of the park is an elaborate fountain similar to the one in the Place de la Concorde in Paris.

RIVER CITY

The development in Savannah of Eli Whitney's cotton gin (see page 34) in 1793 kick-started the American Industrial Revolution. In turn, it also heralded a massive boom in shipping, and by 1795, US exports were 40 times greater than in previous years. Savannah, positioned neatly on the Atlantic Ocean and looking out toward Europe, quickly became the largest port in the Southeast. In the early 19th century, Savannah's commerce thrived, and the launch of the steamship SS *Savannah* opened up new shipping routes.

Factors Row, a cobblestoned walkway near the river, is lined with 19thcentury buildings, and the lovely 1852 **US Customs House**. The **Old Cotton Exchange** was constructed in 1887 when Savannah was the leading cotton exporter in the world.

The five-story brick warehouses and former shipping offices have now become a meeting point for tourists, reached by a series of steep steps. The buildings provide a nostalgic setting for thriving businesses, lavish inns, rustic restaurants, and novelty gift shops the length of **River Street**, where the ramps and walkways are covered with attractive stones imported from Europe. If you plan an evening on the town here, it might be wise to forgo the high heels.

The riverfront air is always filled with music, from South American natives playing soothing pan pipes to jazz saxophonists and threesomes picking banjos and guitars. This all makes for a wonderful stretch of waterfront to eat, drink, shop, and generally to while away some pleasant time.

Slow-moving ships hauling everything from melons, bananas and pineapples, to kaolin clay, pass at a leisurely pace just yards away. The *Georgia Queen* and the *River Queen* replicate the paddlesteamers that plied the waters during the city's heyday, and both offer sightseeing cruises.

A signature Savannah sight is the touching riverside statue of *The Waving Girl*, erected in 1971 in remembrance to Florence Martus. Florence lived with her brother, the lighthouse-keeper, at the Elba Island Lighthouse in the mouth of the Savannah River. Every day for 44 years she waved a white handkerchief in welcome to each incoming ship. She had begun by hoping that any one of the ships might bring home the sailor she loved. Once she had started, it just didn't seem right to stop.

If the port evokes a yearning for food, River Street merchants offer an

Tybee Island lighthouse.

eclectic range of cuisine from fresh seafood to honey-dipped chicken fingers to fried onion rings. The area really comes to life at night and on St Patrick's Day, when the city plays host to one of the largest celebrations in the country – not a party for the faint-hearted.

The riverfront skyline, dominated by the 185-ft (56-meter) tall great **Savannah Bridge**, was long known locally as 'the bridge with no name.' More revelry, restaurants and nightlife can be found in **City Market**, four blocks of restored buildings within walking distance at Jefferson and West Saint Julian Street near **Franklin Square**. In the daytime, City Market is the place to climb aboard for a horse-drawn carriage tour of the town, or to shop for upscale souvenirs and gifts.

Leaving Downtown and heading east on **Victory Drive** – known for its palm trees, handsome houses, and flowering azaleas – in the direction of the coastal islands, it's possible to catch a glimpse of old wealth in **Ardsley Park**. The stately, columned homes grace middle-to-upper class neighborhoods shaded by giant trees, and driving around at random provides a visual treat.

BY THE SEA

Nearby is **Bonaventure Cemetery**, a luxurious final resting place for Savannah's most distinguished citizens. A former plantation, Bonaventure is wistfully beautiful, dripping with moss, and overflowing with azaleas, jasmine, magnolias, and live oak trees.

Fifteen miles (24km) east of Savannah, on Highway 80 heading toward Tybee Island, is **Fort Pulaski National Monument** Civil War site (see page 94). **Tybee Island**, 18 miles (29km) east of Downtown is known as 'Savannah's beach.' The small barrier island has a 3-mile (4.8km) long beach that's backed by sand dunes covered with sea oats. It's a low-key resort with a well-known landmark, the **Tybee Island Light Station**. The **lighthouse** offered mariners safe entrance into the Savannah River for more than 270 years and is open to the public every day except Tuesday.

Bonaventure Cemetery.

Riverboat at City Hall landing.

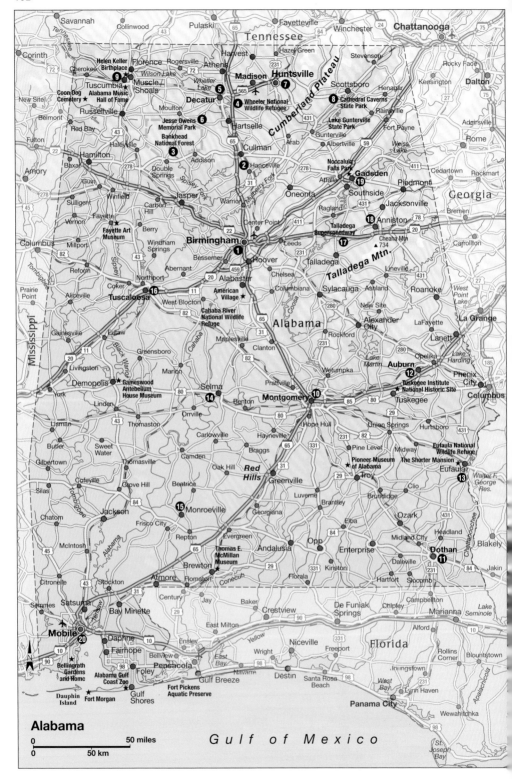

Alabama

0   50 miles

0   50 km

G u l f o f M e x i c o

ALABAMA

A woman, it is said, is a candidate for Mobile's Mardi Gras queen only if she was conceived under an azalea bush, the azalea being a trademark flower of the state.

Family roots matter in Alabama, and most of the people who were born here tend to stay here. Four singers who formed a band called – funnily enough – Alabama, created an anthem titled *My Home's in Alabama*. They might well be singing about a number of notables whose houses across the state are open for tours. Hank Williams's frame boyhood home is in Georgiana. Martin Luther King, Jr lived in a parsonage within walking distance of where Jefferson Davis resided during the early months of the Confederacy. The novelist F. Scott Fitzgerald wrote *Tender is the Night* in his home a few blocks away. W.C. Handy, 'the father of the blues,' grew up near Helen Keller, the deaf and blind woman famous from the play and the movie, *The Miracle Worker*.

In Alabama, food is almost as important as family. The state has landscape from haze-covered mountains to sandy beaches, and its culinary choices are equally wide-ranging. In north Alabama, barbecued pork is smothered with a unique vinegar sauce; in the south a tomatobased sauce is the popular choice. Award-winning restaurants in Birmingham honor grits, tomatoes, and black-eyed peas. German automakers at the Mercedes plant and locals alike crave the dripping barbecued ribs at Dreamland in Tuscaloosa, while Alabama shrimp

Trumpeter at Mobile's Mardi Gras.

and oysters netted on the Gulf Coast are served up 'fried, stewed, and nude.' It's not surprising, then, that Birmingham's Highlands Bar & Grill restaurant is among the nation's top eateries.

What can be surprising, though, is the diversity of Alabama's attractions – sports, space, and civil rights sites, for instance. Golfers discover that some of the nation's best-value golfing can be enjoyed along 100 miles (160 km) of public courses that Robert Trent Jones, Sr designed for the state pension fund. Others learn that

Main attractions

The Alabama Theatre
The Birmingham Museum of Art
The Alabama Sports Hall of Fame
The Birmingham Civil Rights Institute
The Sixteenth Street Baptist Church
Oak Mountain State Park
The Barber Motorsports Park

Maps on pages 132, 134

the first rockets that sent American astronauts into space came from a facility in Huntsville. Alabama was the scene of many Civil Rights battles, and heritage museums show how non-violent protests successfully overturned a system of discrimination and became a source of inspiration to oppressed minorities.

Huge expanses of forests, rivers, and mountains give credence to the nickname 'Alabama the Beautiful.' Birmingham has two sprawling wildlife areas within minutes of Downtown, and more than two dozen state parks are scattered statewide.

Family, food, and fantastic scenery – no wonder everyone calls it Sweet Home Alabama.

BIRMINGHAM

With a smart, affluent workforce of medical and engineering professionals, great food, and a creative arts scene, **Birmingham** ❶ is a major player in the South

Aloft on the foothills of the **Appalachian Mountains**, a massive statue of Vulcan is a proud tribute to the industrial heroism of steelmaking. The 56-ft (17-meter) high Roman god of fire and the forge was Birmingham's signature representative at the 1904 World's Fair in Saint Louis, and just as much today, proclaims Birmingham as one of the pioneering capitals of the South. Named after the industrial powerhouse town in England, Birmingham achieved prominence in 1871, shortly after the

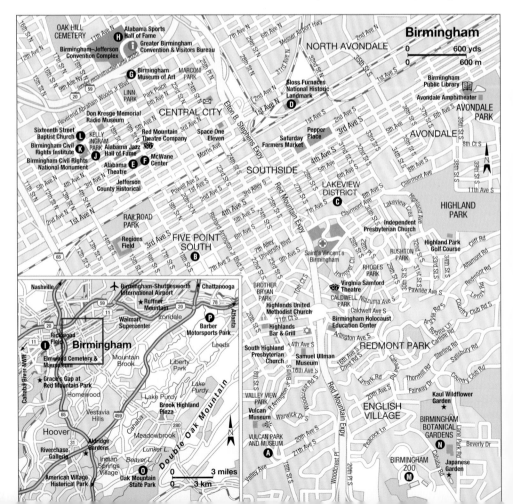

Civil War, as a commercial hub at the crossing of two major railroads. Carrying none of the antebellum baggage or Old South history that its neighbors were steeped in, the 'Magic City' was forged in the very beginnings of the New South, and grew through commerce and industry, rather than agriculture.

Long known as 'the South's capital of football,' Birmingham even took that reputation out onto the international soccer field at the 1996 Olympic Games, when the soccer championships were held at Legion Field. Sports of all kinds play a healthy role in the life in the city, not least at the Alabama Sports Hall of Fame museum.

DYNAMIC METROPOLIS

Vulcan Park Ⓐ (151 Vulcan Park Drive; tel: 205-933-1409; www.visitvulcan.com; daily 10am–10pm) is a good place for an overview of Birmingham and its evolution. The statue of Vulcan, restored for its centennial, now presides over an entirely different kind of city. Born in the smelting pots and hammered during the civil rights clashes in the 1960s, Birmingham survived the nation's 20thcentury downturn in steel production to become a dynamic and integrated metropolis of a million people. Now, they are more likely to be working in modern service industries like health care, education, or banking than to be sweltering in manufacturing. After seeing the cityscape from this high vantage point by the second-largest statue in America, head down the mountain to the city. **Five Points South** Ⓑ, the business district along Highland Avenue at 20th Street, is home to several of Birmingham's four-star restaurants. Many of the city's younger generation like to hang out around the fountain near Frank Fleming's *The Storyteller* sculpture of a goat reading to turtles and other animals.

Barbecue and 'country cooking' like fried green tomatoes remain permanently popular choices, but the city has earned a reputation for a new type of food. Chef Frank Stitt III opened **Highlands Bar & Grill** (2011 11th Avenue South, tel: 205-939-1400; www.highlandsbarandgrill.com; Tue–Sat 5.30–10pm) in 1982, and its success has led him to open two more, Bottega and Chez FonFon. In these high-powered kitchens, Frank perfects his trademark dishes, using Southern staples like grits and bacon to prepare gourmet creations. *Gourmet* magazine has ranked Highlands as one of America's top restaurants, and the New York Times equates Stitt's popularity with that of athletic superstars.

LAKEVIEW DINING

Go north on 20th Street and turn east on University Boulevard (8th Avenue) to 29th Street for the **Lakeview District** Ⓒ, a cluster of popular restaurants and bars. Dining choices here range from local pork barbecue topped with tomato sauce to beef and good Southern seafood. Five blocks north is the **Pepper Place** design and antiques district, named for the Southern classic soda, Dr Pepper, which was once bottled here. In summer, Second Avenue South between

Stained-glass window at the Sixteenth Street Baptist Church, depicting a crucified Black Jesus Christ, next to the words 'You do it unto me'.

The Vulcan Statue, Vulcan Park.

⊘ Fact

The Birmingham Museum of Art is the largest public art museum in the South, with more than 27,000 sculptures, installations, paintings, prints, and drawings.

28th and 29th streets is transformed into a lively Saturday market for organic produce, chef demonstrations, and entertainment. A member of one of the city's steel families used her wealth to enable some of the restoration projects.

THE SPIRIT OF REINVENTION

Return to 20th Street and head north to leave Southside for Downtown. Turn east on First Avenue North to 34th Street, then left on Second at 32nd to tour **Sloss Furnaces National Historic Landmark** (tel: 205-254-2025; www.slossfurnaces.com; Tue–Sat 10am–4pm; free). This monument to early 20th-century industry is the largest preserved steel plant in the world, and a festival site. Kids or even adults who aren't interested in learning how to make steel are usually intrigued by ghost stories, including one of a furnace worker who died a particularly grisly death in a cauldron of molten steel.

Two other urban landmarks are neighbors on Third Avenue. Each has a proud history and has had a new lease on life in recent years. The marquee

Sloss Furnaces National Historic Landmark.

outside the **Alabama Theatre** (1817 Third Avenue North, tel: 205-252-2262; http://www.alabamatheatre.com) has offered entertainment choices since it opened on Christmas Day, 1927. On the sidewalk are metal stars honoring Alabama-born entertainers like actress Tallulah Bankhead (born in Huntsville) and Disney star Dean Jones (from Decatur).

The opulent 3,000-seat theater reigned like a dowager for more than a half century. When demolition loomed, fans of the theater's Wurlitzer organ raised money to buy the building. Now a delightful venue for classic movies and concerts, it's worth the price of admission just to see the lobby's gold-leafed hexagonal ceiling, and the auditorium's sumptuous Moorish spiral terra-cotta columns.

A nearby former department store also has a new purpose. The old Loveman's of Alabama, next to the theater, now houses the **McWane Science Center** , one of the South's largest children's hands-on science centers. Financed by one of the city's steel families, it encourages children to romp through subtle science lessons. One floor hosts touring museum exhibits that appeal to adults, while the domed IMAX theater is a particular treat.

A few blocks north is the **Birmingham Museum of Art** (2000 Reverend Abraham Woods Jr Boulevard, tel: 205-254-2565; www.artsbma.org; Tue–Sat 10am–5pm, Sun noon–5pm; free), the South's largest public art museum. There are works from a wealth of 17th-century Dutch and Flemish painters, plus 18th-century English and 19th-century French artists; these include Monet, Rodin, Sargent, and Gainsborough. The Wedgwood collection is the largest in the United States.

A public park facing the art museum is named **Linn Park** for a prominent family. A century ago, when boosters coined the nickname 'Magic City,' it was named Capitol Park in anticipation of Birmingham becoming the state capital. (That

didn't happen; Alabama's state capital is Montgomery.) The Downtown park is the hub of the state's largest music festival, held annually on the third weekend of June. City Stages attracts hundreds of thousands of fans, and acts range from church choirs to superstar headliners. The festival is a fine time to meet people from Birmingham at their best.

Just north of the elevated interstate highway near the **Birmingham Jefferson Civic Complex** is a museum that pays tribute to Americans' love of sports. The **Alabama Sports Hall of Fame** ❶ (tel: 205-323-6665; www.ashof.org; Mon–Fri 9am–5pm) celebrates athletes with connections to Alabama. Dioramas highlight the achievements of Olympic track legend Jesse Owens (born near Decatur), football's Bart Starr and Coach Paul Bryant and baseball's Hank Aaron (born in Mobile), not to mention Willie Mays. Boxing heavyweight Joe Louis was born in the east Alabama town of Lafayette.

Another Magic City steel-era legacy is **Rickwood Field** ❶ (1137 Second Avenue), the world's oldest ballpark. Take the Interstate 59 Arkadelphia Road exit south to Second Avenue West. The Coal Barons team was formed in 1885 and steel magnate Rick Wood built the wooden park for his team in 1910. Today's Birmingham Barons play in a newer concrete park in nearby Hoover, but it's worth visiting one of Ted Williams' favorite fields. 'It was a wonderful hitter's park, not because the fences were short ... but the way the ball sounded when it hit the bat,' he said.

HONORING THE PAST

During the first half of the 20th century, in what seems like a parallel universe, African-Americans owned businesses and enjoyed movies in a district just a few blocks from the Alabama Theatre and Loveman's. Black people frequented beauty parlors, barber shops, clothing stores, churches, insurance offices, and banks, all run by people of their race.

With the white community gradually leaving Downtown for the more affluent suburbs of Mountain Brook, Homewood, Hoover, and Vestavia Hills, African-Americans have dominated local governments and boards for several decades. Richard Arrington, the city's first African-American mayor, received active support from both races for his progressive and positive leadership.

To begin healing past race divisions, he encouraged the establishment of shrines from what were formerly civil rights battlefields. Three of these are of particular significance. The indelible images of Birmingham police facing down young demonstrators, with snarling dogs and fire hoses, was played out along a four-block area in 1963 between **Kelly Ingram Park** ❶ (corner of 16th Street and 5th Avenue North) and City Hall. Walk through the now peaceful park to see sculptures of two children through jail bars, a trio of praying ministers, and a particularly gripping image of a German Shepherd dog menacing a Black man. Alabama's largest statue of Dr Martin Luther King, Jr faces the

Exhibit at Birmingham Civil Rights Institute.

The Rickwood Classic, played annually at Rickwood Field.

⊙ Tip

To learn more about the 1963 Sixteenth Street Baptist Church bombing, watch Spike Lee's acclaimed movie, *4 Little Girls*. Nominated for an Academy Award, the film thoughtfully portrays the local and national outcry after the KKK carried out the bombing that killed four young girls, aged 11 to 14.

Sixteenth Street Baptist Church, scene of the grimmest incident in the struggle for civil rights (see below).

CIVIL RIGHTS INSTITUTE

The **Birmingham Civil Rights Institute** Ⓚ (tel: 205-328-9696; www.bcri.org; Tue–Sat 10am–3pm), immediately west of the park, is part history lesson and part audience participation, and proof of how the city has passed the ugly chapter of the 1960s. Moving and evocative photos, videos, audio recordings, and exhibits show just how African-Americans were treated under local segregation laws.

Look for the cell where Dr. King wrote his famous Letter from the Birmingham Jail, galvanizing bystanders to become active in the movement. 'White' and 'colored' drinking fountains, and a 1950s lunch counter symbolize segregation in public places. The danger of the movement hits home in the charred shell of a Greyhound bus, burned by racists near Anniston when Black and white people rode together in a challenge to the state's segregation laws. When the

institute opened in 1992, The New York Times headlined 'Facing Up to Racial Pains of the Past, Birmingham Moves On.' Just north across the street is the **Sixteenth Street Baptist Church** Ⓛ (tel: 205-251-9402; www.16thstreetbaptist.org). Photographs show the aftermath of a bomb planted by white racists in 1963. Near the pulpit are class pictures of the four young girls who were killed while preparing for Sunday school. In the balcony is a stained-glass Black Christ, crucified, with the words 'You do it unto me,' which was a gift from the people of Wales. The congregation of about 500 holds a memorial service on the Sunday closest to the date of the bombing, September 15.

BOTANICALS AND BIKES

First-time visitors to Birmingham are pleasantly surprised by the city's beautiful mountains and lush blankets of trees. This is a city that provides facilities for a wide range of outdoor leisure activities. East on US 280 to Mountain Brook are two of the most popular. The **Birmingham Zoo** Ⓜ (2630 Cahaba Road, tel: 205-879-0409; www.birminghamzoo.com; Wed-Sun 9am–5pm) is home to Siberian tigers, white rhinos, gorillas, and orang-utans. Across the street is the **Birmingham Botanical Gardens** Ⓝ (tel: 205-414-3950; www.bbgardens.org; daily 7am–5pm; free), containing over 30 display gardens. The South's largest clear-span greenhouse shelters tropical plants, camellias, and a cactus collection. Scores of plants native to the South are showcased in a garden sponsored by *Southern Living* magazine, the arbiter of Southern hospitality, design and cooking, based in nearby Homewood.

To get away from urban stress, just 15 minutes south of Downtown take I-65 exit 246 through a tangle of fast-food restaurants and gasoline stations to the tranquillity of **Oak Mountain State Park** Ⓞ, Alabama's largest. Facilities for hiking, swimming, fishing, golf, and horse riding, and a challenging mountain bike

Birmingham Botanical Gardens.

course, are all available. Tranquillity is not, however, on the minds of motorbike enthusiasts, who love to gaze at the world's largest collection of bikes at the **Barber Motorsports Park** ● (tel: 205-699-7275; www.barberracingevents.com; daily), located 20 minutes from Downtown at 1-20 exit 140. When third-generation dairyman George Barber began buying vintage motorcycles in 1988, he probably didn't have it in mind to amass the world's pre-eminent collection, but that's what he's done. He opened a makeshift museum in the old repair shop of the dairy's truck fleet in 1995 and constructed a showplace for his collection. Just for good measure, he built a racetrack to FIA and FIM standards that has come to be known as the 'Augusta National of Racetracks.'

By the time he opened the museum in 2003 he had about 800 bikes, including some dating back to 1904. He selects from his collection and can display about 350 vintage and current models at a time. Barber's bikes aren't only for show, but for racing, too. His race team restores bikes and races the historic

models. The engines are packed with lubricant, but most models can be made race-ready at just an hour's notice.

CHOPPERS

Barber, who lent a gorgeous 1929 Scott Squirrel to the acclaimed Guggenheim Motorcycle exhibition said, 'Nothing annoys me more than when I'm traveling and I tell people where I'm from and they get this blank look on their face. An awful lot of eyeballs watch motor racing on television, and I aim to make their first impression of Birmingham an impressive one.' How many bikes will it take to satisfy him? 'I'll keep collecting until they carry me away in a white jacket.' One of his most recent obsessions is Lotus Formula One race cars. Barber believes he has the largest collection of these, too. Vintage choppers can be seen being restored in the basement of the museum. Coming for a race? Surprisingly, the 2.38-mile (3.8km) racecourse, considered the finest road course in North America, has no bleachers; it's surrounded by a grassy hillside. The Grand Prix-caliber track rises and

The Indy Grand Prix of Alabama at Barber Motorsports Park.

⊘ INDY GRAND PRIX

The racetrack at Barber Motorsports Park is of such a high calibre that the Grand Prix of Alabama IndyCar Series has been held here every year since 2010. Each year, the high-octane 90-lap, 214-mile (344km) race attracts more than 100,000 car-loving spectators from around the world. For the most part, the race is a battle between home-grown US Chevrolet designs and the Japanese car manufacturer, Honda. The event takes place in April each year and is worth an estimated $30 million to the local economy. The Covid-19 pandemic caused various cancellations and disruptions but as of 2022 the event is back on and as busy as ever. Hotels book up well in advance so if you're thinking of attending, it's worth making a reservation as soon as you can.

CIVIL RIGHTS

During the Reconstruction era after the Civil War, amendments to the US Constitution gave freed slaves the right to vote and own property. By the beginning of the 20th century, Southern states had passed segregation laws to limit these rights.

Half a century later, congregations in Black churches – virtually the only institution not controlled by whites – demonstrated to overturn segregation laws. In 1955, seamstress Rosa Parks was arrested for refusing to give her seat on a Montgomery bus to a white person, as required by city ordinance. A young minister, Martin Luther King, Jr, organized the year-long Montgomery Bus Boycott.

Rosa Parks sits at the front of a bus.

Meanwhile, Black people could not vote, drink from the same water fountains as whites, eat in white-owned cafés, or try on clothes in stores before buying them. Complainers in Birmingham were often harassed or beaten by thugs linked to the police. When Black people in Birmingham took their complaints to City Hall in 1963, Police Commissioner Bull Conner turned fire hoses on them, and filled the jail with children who had marched. Within days of Dr King's famous 'I Have a Dream' speech at the March on Washington, Ku Klux Klansmen bombed the Sixteenth Street Baptist Church active in the Civil Rights Movement, killing four young girls. The bombing prompted some white Alabamians to oppose the brutality. Three white men were convicted of the church bombing, one as recently as 2002.

Black people in Selma, frustrated by official tactics preventing them from registering to vote, attempted a 51-mile (82km) march on the state Capitol. Under orders from segregationist Gov. George Wallace, state police attacked them as they left Selma. President Lyndon Johnson pushed the stalled Voting Rights Bill through Congress. In 2000, President Bill Clinton attended a re-enactment of the 1965 Selma-to-Montgomery march. Clinton said that before the Voting Rights Act 'was signed in ink in Washington, it first was signed in blood in Selma.'

As Black people elected public officials and impacted local ordinances, they swept their old foes from office. Voting majorities gave them control of city for the first time in history and county governments in Birmingham and the Black Belt west of Montgomery. A repentant Wallace received their support in 1982, and subsequently appointed many Black people to public office. A Black judge was elected to the Alabama Supreme Court with broad support from both races.

The state tourism office publishes an Alabama Civil Rights Trail brochure showing major sites you can visit, along with the Selma to Montgomery National Voting Rights Trail. The Birmingham Civil Rights Institute is by the Sixteenth Street Baptist Church (see page 138). There are also museums open in Selma and Tuskegee.

falls over 50ft (15 meters), and from any one spot 70 percent of the switchback circuit is visible, eliminating the need for grandstands. Just bring a blanket or folding chairs. The races are televised on the Speed channel.

INTO THE COUNTRYSIDE

The longest free-flowing river east of the Mississippi slices right through the Birmingham Metro area and forms the southern boundary between Jefferson County and its rapidly developing neighbor Shelby County.

The **Cahaba River** is said to have more species per mile than any other river in the continental US and is home to more than 60 rare species of plants and animals. A 4-mile (6.5km) stretch in Bibb County forms the **Cahaba River National Wildlife Refuge** that shelters the largest known stand of rare Cahaba lilies, which bloom in May. Go west on I-59 to exit 97 and turn left on US 11, then west on State Route 5. Turn left on County Route 24 and go 4½ miles (7.2km), then park west of Piper Bridge.

Virginians wandering around south of Birmingham may do a double-take when they might think they've seen George Washington's Mount Vernon home, Williamsburg's Bruton Parish Church, and a 1770 Courthouse. These Colonial landmarks have been meticulously recreated at the **American Village Historical Park** (tel: 205-665-3535; www.americanvillage. org; Mon–Fri 10am–4pm) where visitors can learn more about the theories of liberty and self-government. They can rally with the Sons of Liberty, protest against the imposition of British taxes, and serve as delegates to the Constitutional Convention. Leave I-65 at exit 234.

AROUND ALABAMA

Rugged mountains in the northern part of the state segue gently into the central plains and beyond, revealing a space center, civil rights sites, and a NASCAR Superspeedway.

The first towns settled by English-speaking people in present-day Alabama were around what George Washington called 'the great bend' of the Tennessee River. The mighty bend swoops down through the hills of Chattanooga, crosses Alabama, then winds north to merge with the Ohio River. The river town of Decatur, 77 miles (124km) north of Birmingham, is a good place to stop overnight and think about traveling west to tour the Helen Keller home or heading east to the birthplace of America's space program.

The terrain becomes more mountainous north of **Birmingham** on Interstate 65. A remarkable religious destination – a compound reflecting 13thcentury Romanesque Gothic architecture – lies in the hills 17 miles (27 km) east of the interstate near **Hanceville ❷**. Mother Angelica, whose Eternal Word television channel is broadcast to Catholics around the world, built her **Shrine of the Most Blessed Sacrament** (tel: 256-352-6267; www.olamshrine.com; daily 6am–6pm) for the order of nuns cloistered here. Take exit 291, turn east on State Route 91 for 13 miles (21km), then right onto County

Inside the Shrine of the Most Blessed Sacrament.

747 and right on County 548. The magnificence of the golden chapel interior is worth the pilgrimage detour. Respectful dress is required to enter the chapel, so no shorts or sleeveless shirts.

WILD AND SCENIC RIVER

One of the South's most pristine wilderness areas is west of the interstate at **Cullman**. To reach the sprawling **Bankhead National Forest** ❸ (tel: 205-489-5111; www.fs.usda.gov/detail/alabama; daily), take the I-65 and exit 308 then head west for 30 miles (48km) to **Double Springs**. From here, go 12 miles (19km) north on State Route 33 to County Road 60 and the Sipsey Wilderness. Congress has designated Sipsey a 'wild and scenic river.' Three areas in the forest permit overnight camping, but be sure to make reservations well in advance.

Resume the northern trek to Decatur on Interstate 65 and exit on State Route 67 for 2 miles (3km) to the visitors' center of the **Wheeler National Wildlife Refuge** ❹ (tel: 256-350-6639; www.fws.gov/refuge/wheeler; Tue–Sat 9am–4pm). Migrating waterfowl spend the winter here in the backwaters of the Tennessee River. Raised boardwalks within the refuge are excellent places to photograph the birds and animals.

Turn left on State Route 67 and right on US 31 to reach the commercial and residential areas of **Decatur** ❺ (pop. 55,000). Most of the town, except for an 1833 bank, was destroyed by Union troops in the Civil War. The bank anchors the Old Decatur historic district with a number of Victorian and bungalow houses. Take a side trip west to the community of Oakville, birthplace of track star Jesse Owens. Go west on Old Moulton Road 14 miles (23km) from State Route 67 and follow signs to the **Jesse Owens Memorial Park** ❻ (7019 Co Rd 203, tel: 256-974-3636; www.jesseowensmemorialpark.com; Mon–Sat 10am–4pm, Sun 1pm–4pm with its museum. An Ohio State coach taught the athlete 'to run as if the track is on fire.' In sight is the **Oakville Indian Mounds Park** where a replica of a seven-sided Native American council meeting house contains a museum of Native American artifacts.

Back in Decatur there's a choice to be made; whether first to head west into the Shoals region, where Helen Keller and W.C. Handy were born, or go east to 'the rocket city' of Huntsville and Scottsboro, the home of Unclaimed Baggage. For Huntsville, head north on US 31 and cross the river to Interstate 565. Just past the I-65 interchange, take exit 2 and park in the tiny village of Mooresville (pop. 59). Many of the houses here are occupied by fifth-generation descendants of the builders. If the 'new' post office built in 1840 is open, the 48 wooden call boxes from the 1825 Tavern are still in use. Mooresville played Mark Twain's hometown in a *Tom and Huck* Disney movie.

HUNTSVILLE

Less than 15 minutes from the 19th-century village of Mooresville on Interstate 65 is the birthplace of America's space program. The US Army chose the

Bankhead National Forest.

cotton mill town of **Huntsville** ❼ (pop. 195,000) in 1950 as the research center for German rocket scientists captured during World War II. Dr Wernher von Braun's rockets launched America's first satellite and Mercury astronauts before the Saturn V rocket took Apollo astronauts to the moon. NASA's Marshall Space Flight Center is within the Army's Redstone Arsenal. Test rockets and astronauttraining equipment are on display at the **US Space and Rocket Center Museum** (Interstate 565 exit 15; tel: 800-637-7223; www.rocketcenter.com; daily 9am–5pm). If you're interested in **US Space Camp** and aviation programs, call to check in advance which age groups are scheduled for sessions. Two miles (3km) east of the space museum is the **Huntsville Botanical Garden** (tel: 256-830-4447; www.hsvbg.org; Mon–Sat 9am–6:00pm, Sun 11am–6:30pm), known for its aquatic garden, a butterfly house, and a collection of day lilies. Attendances peak between Thanksgiving and New Year during the holiday lights season. North of the space museum is Cummings Research Park, the nation's second largest technology center.

Take exit 19-C for the **Huntsville Visitor Center** (Church Street; tel: 256-551-2230; www.huntsville.org; Mon–Sat 9am–3pm, Sun 12pm–3pm), not far from the **Historic Huntsville Depot**. Because of the city's space image, its role as the first capital of Alabama is less heralded. Settled at a spring in 1805, the town was the largest in the territory when Alabama's population qualified it for statehood in 1819. Costumed guides demonstrate pioneer chores inside the restored **Alabama Constitution Village** (tel: 256-564-8100; www.earlyworks.com; Mon–Sat 10am–6pm), a block south of the courthouse square. The village, where the state's constitution was first written, is a convenient starting place for a walking tour past the several dozen pre-Civil War homes and churches in the **Twickenham Historic District**. The

oldest is the 1814 mansion of town promoter LeRoy Pope. The 1819 **Weeden House** behind the Episcopal Church is a museum named for a painter-poet. The self-guided tour ends at Harrison Brothers Hardware. Open for a century on the square, it sells more gifts than nails and chains. Screen actress Tallulah Bankhead was born in an apartment facing the courthouse. The **Huntsville Museum of Art** (tel: 256-535-4350; www.hsvmuseum.org; Tue–Sat 10am–5pm, Sun 12pm–5pm), located in Big Spring Park, houses a notable collection of Italian silver Buccellati animals. The ideal time for a visit to Huntsville is in the spring or fall when visitors can experience laid back entertainment at Concerts on the Dock.

Go east for 30 minutes on US 72 to tour the large limestone cavern at the **Cathedral Caverns State Park** ❽ (tel: 256-728-8193; www.alapark.com/cathedral-caverns-state-park; daily 8am–5.30pm), with a stalagmite 'forest' and a massive column 243ft (74 meters) around. The footpaths are smooth and wide enough for wheelchairs. It's worth

Stalagmites at Cathedral Caverns.

bringing a jacket for the guided tour, as it's always 60°F (16°C) inside.

LOST LUGGAGE

Continue east for another 15 minutes to reach the famous Scottsboro **Unclaimed Baggage Center** (509 W. Willow Street, tel: 256-259-1525; www.unclaimedbaggage.com; Mon–Fri 9am–6pm, Sat 8am–7pm; free), described as 'one of the country's best-kept shopping secrets.' Browse through travelers' lost merchandise for potential bargains, or just enjoy wondering, 'who packed those?' For a restful retreat and a mountaintop view of miles of open space, seek out **Gorham's Bluff** (tel: 256-451-8439; www.gorhamsbluff.com), about an hour east of Huntsville. There are spectacular views of the Tennessee River valley below. An inn with a fine restaurant has the perfect view.

To reach **Florence** and the Shoals region from Decatur or Huntsville, go west on State Route 20. In **Tuscumbia** , follow directional signs for 'Ivy Green,' the local name for the **Helen Keller Birthplace** (300 West North Commons,

Montgomery's State Capitol.

tel: 256-383-4066; www.helenkellerbirthplace.org; Mon–Sat 8.30am–4pm). The emotional story of 'The Miracle Worker' unfolded in the 1820s house and a detached cottage. The metal pump where teacher Anne Sullivan spelled w-a-t-e-r in the deaf child's hand is under a shelter behind the house. Local actors perform the play outdoors in summer. A mile south, the **Alabama Music Hall of Fame** (tel: 256-381-4417; www.alamhof.org; Tue–Sat 10am–5pm) celebrates achievements of natives including Hank Williams, Lionel Richie, Jimmy Buffet, and the country band Alabama. This is also the home of the famous **Muscle Shoals FAME Recording Studios** (603 East Avalon Avenue, tel: 256-381-0801; www.fame2.com), where everyone from Aretha Franklin to Bob Dylan made soul music history (see page 86). Seeking Southern oddities? Turn off US 72 onto State Route 247 and go 12 miles (19 km) south to see the graves of legendary hunting dogs in the **Coon Dog Cemetery**.

JEFFERSON DAVIS AND MARTIN LUTHER KING

The distance from Birmingham to the state capital of **Montgomery** ⑩ (pop. 205,000) is 91 miles (146km) to the south via Interstate 65, but architecturally the distance is about a century. Birmingham's rush of building creativity peaked about 1927. Most landmarks in Montgomery predate the Civil War, and many are close enough together to explore on foot. A word of advice: carry a bottle of water in the summer because the city is humid, even by Southern standards. A side benefit of the humidity is the proliferation of gray Spanish moss that drips from the trees.

The **State Capitol**, an 1851 Greek Revival structure, looks down Dexter Avenue. The bronze star under the front portico marks where Jefferson Davis took the oath in 1861 as the president of the Confederate States, and the Old Senate Chamber has been restored to the time when Southern delegates established the Confederacy. Murals painted inside the dome in 1927 romanticize significant periods of the state's history.

Walk a block west of the Capitol for the red brick **Dexter Avenue King Memorial Baptist Church** (tel: 334-263-3970; www.dexterkingmemorial.org; call for opening times) where 25-year-old Martin Luther King, Jr organized the Montgomery Bus Boycott in 1955. A block behind the church is the **Civil Rights Memorial** designed by sculptor Maya Lin. Feel the sheet of water flowing over the names of 40 civil rights martyrs. The houses in which Jefferson and King lived a century apart are only six blocks from each other.

From the south wing of the Capitol, cross the street to the **First White House of the Confederacy** (tel: 334-242-1861; www.firstwhitehouse.org; Mon–Fri 8am–3:30pm,; free). Then drive the few blocks to the **Dexter Avenue Parsonage** (309 South Jackson Street; tel: 334-261-3270; www.dexterkingmemorial.org; Mon–Fri 10am–4pm, Sat 10am–2pm), southwest of the Capitol. A plaque on the porch marks a bomb blast in 1956. The site of Mrs Parks's arrest (see page 140) and the **Rosa Parks Museum** (tel: 334-241-8615; www.troy.edu/rosaparks; Mon–Fri 9am–5pm) is down Dexter Avenue and left on Montgomery Street at the intersection with Commerce Street.

To see more than 40 relocated 19th-century buildings, including the 1818 Lucas Tavern, drive north across Dexter Avenue to **Old Alabama Town** (301 Columbus Street, tel: 334-240-4500; www.oldalabamatown.com; Thur–Sat 10am–3pm). One of the city's most popular destinations has nothing to do with American history, but British theater. Construction magnate Winton (Red) Blount donated the Palladian-influenced building, which houses two impressive theaters at the **Alabama Shakespeare Festival** (tel: 334-271-5300; www.asf.net). Take Interstate 85

exit 6 and follow signs to Woodmere. Even if you don't attend a play, stroll the grounds of the **Blount Cultural Park** and see the art collection Blount gave to the **Montgomery Museum of Fine Arts** (tel: 334-625-4333; www.mmfa.org; Tue–Sun 10am–5pm; free).

Take a 45-minute side trip east on Interstate 85 to reach the **George Washington Carver Museum** (tel: 334-724-6025; www.nps.gov/tuin; call for hours; free) at the famed **Tuskegee Institute**. The Black scientist developed hundreds of by-products from sweet potatoes and peanuts. After a boll weevil infestation in 1915, Carver convinced many South Alabama planters to forsake cotton and plant peanuts. Farmers in the Wiregrass area around **Dothan** ⓫ were so appreciative they invited Carver to visit, which led to the annual National Peanut Festival. Drive south on US 231 or 431 to the southeast corner of the state to see murals painted on sides of commercial buildings.

Football fans and art lovers should continue east on Interstate 85 from Montgomery to the college town of

Mural honoring the peanut industry on Main Street.

The schoolhouse at Old Alabama Town.

Waiter serving ribs at Dreamland Bar-B-Que in Tuscaloosa, Alabama.

Auburn ⑫. The **Jule Collins Smith Museum of Fine Arts** (901 South College Street, tel: 334-844-1484; www.jcsm.auburn.edu; Tue–Sun 10am–4.30pm, Thurs 10am–8pm) has a variety of rotating exhibits, and the permanent collection focuses on 19th and 20th century European and American art. Works also include modern Mexican printmaking, ceramics, pottery, and several examples of American modernism. Sports memorabilia is housed in the **Lovelace Athletic Museum** near Jordan-Hare Stadium on the campus.

To see the state's most spectacular collection of Italianate mansions with wide verandas and overhanging eaves, drive about 90 minutes southeast of Montgomery along US 82 to the river town of **Eufaula** ⑬. North Eufaula Avenue is as pretty as any street in Alabama. The **Shorter Mansion** (tel: 334-687-3793, www.eufaulapilgrimage. com; Mon–Sat 10am–4pm), a neoclassical Revival landmark resembling a wedding cake, was built in 1884. (It featured in the 2002 movie *Sweet Home Alabama*.) West of Montgomery are sleepy Black Belt towns with elaborate mansions built by enslaved people when cotton was king.

SELMA

The 51-mile (82km) route along US 80 to **Selma** ⑭ (pop. 18,000) is best known for the Selma-toMontgomery march of 1965 (see page 140). There's been remarkably little change along the roadway since to disturb the cows grazing in broad rolling pastures. The National Park Service has constructed an interpretive center near Edmund Pettus Bridge.

Cross the Edmund Pettus Bridge and turn left on Water Street to see photos of the protest in the modest **National Voting Rights Museum**.

For an impressive example at the opposite end of the wealth spectrum, turn west off Broad and onto Jeff Davis. Go two blocks and turn left onto Mabry Street for **Sturdivant Hall** (tel: 334-872-5626; Tue–Sat 10am–4pm), built in 1853. Six fluted Corinthian columns support a massive portico that leads to a mansion interior dominated by elaborate plaster friezes. The 1837 **St. James Hotel Selma** (1200 Water Avenue, tel: 334-553-6700), beautifully restored after being shuttered for decades, is the state's oldest. Take a break in the ground floor Sterling Restaurant to hear tales of resident ghosts who don't check out. An hour west of Selma is **Demopolis**, a town founded in 1818 by exiled aristocrats loyal to Napoleon. Leave US 80 for US 43 North to arrive at **Gaineswood** (805 South Cedar Avenue, tel: 334-289-4846; Tue–Sat 10am–4pm) an elegant Greek Revival villa with a ballroom of reflecting mirrors. The house is a National Historic Landmark.

SOUTH TOWARD MOBILE

Monroeville ⑮ (pop. 6,000), about halfway between Montgomery and Mobile, is a treat for fans of the novel or the movie *To Kill a Mockingbird*. The spirits of Scout and brother Jem still pervade the small hometown of reclusive novelist Harper Lee. Take Interstate 65 to exit 96 and head west on County Road 20 for 21 miles (34km). The 1903 courthouse in the town square houses the **Old Courthouse Museum** (tel: 251-575-7433; www.monroecountymuseum.org; Mon–Fri 10am–4pm, Sat 10am–2pm). A movie crew recreated the interior of this very courtroom for the scenes where attorney Atticus Finch (Gregory Peck) defends a handicapped Black man accused of attacking a white girl. You can also see photographs of the novelist and her childhood friend Truman Capote.

The major houses mentioned in the novel are gone, and the Lee family home at 216 South Alabama St (10 doors south of the square) was torn down in the 1960s to make way for a hamburger drive-in. The house next door where Capote (Dill, in the book) visited is gone too, but the rock wall mentioned in the story is still there. A historic marker identifies where Capote visited, but there's none in front of where Miss Lee was born in 1926 because she didn't want one. If you're lucky enough to get a ticket for the play staged in the courthouse each May, ask to be a juror.

MERCEDES AND NASCAR

Interstate 20 that slices through Birmingham has earned the nickname 'wheels alley' because of the Mercedes-Benz plant to the west and the Barber Motorsports Park (see page 139) and 'the world's fastest speedway' to the east.

Some 58 miles (93km) west of Birmingham on Interstate 20/59 is **Tuscaloosa** ⑯ (pop. 100,000), a former state capital and home of the University of Alabama. It's best known now for the **Mercedes-Benz** assembly plant and **visitor center** (tel: 205-507-2252; www.mbusi.com; call for tour schedule). Take exit 86 to see historic vehicles and walk through the clean assembly plant on a guided tour. It's the company's only plant outside of Germany. Football fans follow signs to the university campus and the **Paul Bryant Museum** (tel:

A scene from To Kill a Mockingbird.

⦿ HARPER LEE

Set in Mobile, Alabama, *To Kill a Mockingbird* was the first novel written by author Harper Lee, who was born and died in Monroeville. Published in 1960, the book was an instant bestseller, dealing with the pressing issue of the time: racial inequality. Just one year after the book was published, Lee was awarded the much-coveted Pulitzer Prize for Fiction; in 1966, President Lyndon Johnson appointed Lee to the National Council of the Arts. Lee was also awarded the Presidential Medal of Freedom in 2007 for her contribution to literature.

Lee would write just one other novel in her life, *Go Set a Watchman*, which, although written in the 1950s, was not published until 2015, just one year before she died.

205-348-4668; www.bryantmuseum.com; Tue–Sun 9am–4pm) near Bryant-Denny Stadium. Exhibits and films highlight important victories over Penn State, Notre Dame, Miami, and arch-rival Auburn. Football fans rarely visit T-town without finding time for a plate of barbecued ribs at Dreamland BBQ, the 'roadhouse' restaurant off Jug Factory Road. On two Sundays a year upwards of 180,000 racing fans make a pilgrimage 50 miles (80km) east of Birmingham to the **Talladega Superspeedway** (tel: 877-462-3342; www.talladegasuperspeedway.com) to watch the top NASCAR drivers circle the tri-oval track at speeds approaching 200mph (320kmh). (Not a race fan? Be sure to avoid **Talladega** (pop. 15,000) and Interstate 20 on race days as roads can get crowded pre- and post-race.) Guided tours in a slow van are available on days the track isn't being used for races or testing. You can inspect dozens of famous racecars inside the **International Motorsports Hall of Fame** (tel: 256-362-5002; www. motorsportshalloffame.com; daily 9am–4pm) next to the track. Some of the mangled vehicles may make you wonder how drivers survived the wrecks.

STUFFED ANIMALS

If racing is too hectic, drive east to **Anniston** ⓲ (21,000), where one museum is devoted to stuffed animals, and another to military weapons. Drive east on Interstate 20 and turn north on US 431 for 6 miles (10km) to Lagarde Park and the **Anniston Museum of Natural History** (tel: 256-237-6766, www. exploreamag.org; Tue–Sat 10am–5pm, Sun 1–5pm). Dioramas of birds and animals date from the 19th century. Next door at the **Berman Museum of World History** (tel: 256-237-6261, www.exploreamag.org; Tue–Sat 10am–5pm, Sun 1–5pm) is a remarkable collection of pistols, rifles, bronzes, paintings, and personal objects that belonged to such diverse figures as Hitler, Mussolini, Napoleon, and Jefferson Davis. Farley and Germaine Berman were American spies during World War II who retired to Anniston.

Continue north on US 431 for 30 miles (48km) to **Gadsden** ⓳ (pop. 35,000) to **Noccalula Falls Park** (1500 Noccalula Road, tel: 256-549-4663, open daily 10am–5pm) to view a series of pioneer buildings next to a towering, refreshing waterfall.

MOBILE

Feted by the French, the Spanish, and the British, Mobile retains the unhurried Southern grace of an elegant Grand Dame

Shaded by ancient live oaks dripping in Spanish moss, and bordered with azalea bushes as big as sea-trunks, **Mobile** ⓴ (pop. 190,000) is steeped in 300 years of history. Today, the city displays trophies from her past occupations, and still is every inch a genteel and hospitable Southern belle.

Follow directional signs at Interstate 10 exit 26 (Water Street) to the **Colonial Fort Conde** (150 South Royal Street; tel: 251-208-7569; www.colonialmobile.com; Mon–Sat 9am–4:30pm, Sun

Race at the Talladega Superspeedway.

1pm–4:30pm), a faithful re-creation of a 1724 fort built by the French colonists. The ruins of the original, razed in 1820, were found during excavations for the interstate interchange. Costumed docents recount lively tales of Mobile's founders, and fire off cannons and muskets (minus the ammunition, of course) to demonstrate how the French kept rival Europeans at bay until the English took possession in 1763. The Spanish occupied from 1780 until Mobile joined the US in 1813, 37 years after the Founding Fathers signed the Declaration of Independence, which reinforces the feeling of it being a place apart from the rest of Alabama.

It's a pleasant idea to leave the car in the visitors' lot across the street from Fort Conde, since much of Mobile can be explored on foot. This compact architectural feast for the senses offers museums and historical sites at every turn. One of the South's finest city museums is across Royal Street. The **History Museum of Mobile** (tel: 251-208-7569, www.historymuseumofmobile. com; Mon–Sat 9am–5pm, Sun 1–5pm) is

in the 1857 City Hall. Exhibits describe Jean Baptiste Le Moyne, Sieur de Bienville, founding the outpost in 1702 as the French capital of a vast empire stretching from the Gulf of Mexico into present-day Canada. In 1718, the French moved the seat of power 141 miles (227km) west to New Orleans, but Mobile survived the loss of prestige, and remained an active trading port even through the military conflicts that followed.

THE HOME OF MARDI GRAS

Mobile started something else in the early years, later 'exported' to New Orleans. Mardi Gras (literally 'Fat Tuesday,' the last day before Lent) was first celebrated here in 1703 and became more formally organized in 1830. Two Mobilians who had been members of a mystic society, or krewe, moved to New Orleans and were instrumental in forming that city's first secret society. A man and a woman with deep roots in Old Mobile society reign as King Felix III and his queen over galas and float-filled, family-friendly parades. Don't miss seeing glittering, jewel-encrusted, handmade coronation costumes worn

A majestic Mardi Gras gown and train on display at the Mobile Carnival Museum.

Members of The Order of Myths, Mobile's first and oldest Mardi Gras society.

⊘ MARDI GRAS

The first Mardi Gras celebrations in the United States can be traced back to Mobile in 1702, and a French expedition on behalf of King Louis XIV, led by Pierre Le Moyne d'Iberville. Charged with defending the French claim to American territory, d'Iberville set about establishing not only French settlements, but also French traditions in the area. Thus, the first Mardi Gras (Fat Tuesday) came into being in Mobile, when as Lent approached, all fatty foods (eggs, butter, lard etc) were used up ahead of the 60-day fasting period.

The tradition would later spread along the rivers of the region until it reached New Orleans, a city now world-famous for its iconic and extravagant Mardi Gras celebrations. which go on for around two weeks.

Stained-glass window at the Cathedral of the Immaculate Conception.

Oakleigh House Museum.

by local Mardi Gras royalty at the **Mobile Carnival Museum** (355 Government Street, tel: 251-432-3324; www.mobilecar-nivalmuseum.com; Mon, Wed, Fri and Sat 9am–4pm); the gowns are as regal as in any museum in the nation.

Upstairs is the Civil War section with a replica of the Confederate submarine H.L. Hunley, built in Mobile in 1862, and recently recovered off the South Carolina coast. Mobile's best-known military figure is Admiral Raphael Semmes, the daring Confederate raider who captured 66 ships during the Civil War. A sterling silver presentation sword and his gravestone are presented in the museum. A bronze statue of Semmes, called 'Old Beeswax' by his crew for his flamboyant moustache, faces Mobile Bay from the median in Government Street. Adjoining the museum is the **Exploreum Science Center**, a hands-on science experience with an IMAX theater.

STEAMBOAT CAPTAIN

Mobile has many house museums, and two that definitely should not be missed. Walk to the first museum,

located Downtown, as this is a great way to enjoy the architecture along the way. From the Semmes statue, go four blocks west on tree-lined Government Street to the Radisson Admiral Semmes Hotel (built in 1940), then north seven blocks on Joachim Street (the restored 1927 Saenger Theater is along the way). A steamboat captain built the **Richards-DAR House** (256 North Joachim Street; tel: 215-208-7320; www.richardsdarhouse.com; Mon and Wed–Fri 11am–3.30pm, Sat 10am–4pm, Sun 1–4pm) in 1860. This Italianate home is noteworthy for its ornate, iron-lace trim with a 'four seasons' motif over the brick facade.

Collect the car from Fort Conde via Claiborne, two blocks west of Joachim, to tour the 1835 **Cathedral-Bascilica of Immaculate Conception** on Dauphin Street. The twin towers date from 1890, and the 12 stained-glass windows are richly detailed. A railed entrance descends to the crypt, and to the tombs of bishops. Pope John XXIII designated the cathedral a minor basilica in 1962.

⊘ THE USS ALABAMA

Known affectionately among Alabamans as the 'Mighty A', the USS Alabama, which is now permanently docked in Mobile, is the sixth US Navy ship to bear the name Alabama. After five years of active service, she was decommissioned in 1947 and made a part of the Puget Sound Naval Shipyard Reserve Fleet stationed at Bremerton, Washington. It wasn't until 1964 that she was towed to Alabama, her final resting place.

In 1986, the ship was officially registered as a National Historic Landmark. The USS Alabama was also the primary shooting location for the 1992 Hollywood movie Under Siege, starring Steven Seagal and Colm Meaney. You can also see the battleship in the 2016 movie USS Indianapolis: Men of Courage featuring Nicholas Cage.

To reach the **Oakleigh Mansion** (tel: 251-432-1281; www.historicoakleigh.com; Tue–Sat 10am–4pm) from Royal Street, drive 2 miles (3km) west, under a canopy of live oaks along Government, and turn left on George or Roper streets. The white-raised cottage, commenced in 1833, has period furniture and a Thomas Sully portrait of a Mobile grand dame, Madam Octavia Walton LeVert. The best times to visit are when the azaleas bloom in spring, and Christmas. Sunken gardens outside began when enslaved people dug the clay for the bricks used in the house. Mobile's **Magnolia Cemetery** is one of the state's oldest and largest. To reach Magnolia, turn south on Ann Street at the intersection of Government and continue for 1 mile (1.5km). Some of the most elaborate tombs are near the center, close to the Virginia Street gate. Iron markers and a variety of mausoleum styles are represented. The 1860 Slatter Family Tomb has the finest ornamental cast iron in the cemetery. Some 1,100 Confederate casualties, including the first crew of the H.L. Hunley submarine, are buried near the statue marking the Confederate Rest opposite Ann Street.

THE BATTLESHIP AND THE BAY

Mobile's most popular attraction, **Battlefield Park**, can be seen from any point on the riverfront. The **USS Alabama Battleship** (tel: 251-432-0261; www.ussalabama.com; daily 8am–5pm) is berthed off the causeway in Mobile Bay alongside a World War II submarine. The battleship assisted the British in protecting convoys through the North Sea against German warships and aircraft in occupied Norway. The Alabama saw 37 months of active duty and was never damaged by enemy fire. Several of the battleship's nine battle stars were earned while serving with a strike force in the Battle of Okinawa. The ship sailed with a crew of 2,500 sailors and marines, until she was retired in 1947. The Navy announced that she would be scrapped, and Alabama school children donated

$100,000 in dimes to a $1 million fund to tow her the 5,600 miles (9,000km) from Seattle through the Panama Canal to her berth in Mobile Bay.

Start the self-guided tour with a video of crewmen describing the ship's features. The submarine **USS Drum** also played an important role in the war and became the hero of the western Pacific in 1942, with the highest total of enemy tonnage sunk, including the *Mizuho*, the largest Japanese vessel lost in the war.

ALABAMA'S GOLF TRAIL

Golfers from all over the world are now drawn to Mobile, Birmingham, Huntsville, Opelika, Dothan, and Florence, with green fees not much above those at municipal courses. In all, the **Robert Trent Jones Golf Trail** (tel: 205-942-0444 www.rtjgolf.com) includes 468 holes at 11 locations. Most of the half million golfers who play the trail each year are from out of state, including 6 percent from outside the US. State pension fund chief David Bronner invested retirement funds in golf courses to encourage tourism. Golf Digest magazine readers voted the trail the best value.

USS Alabama.

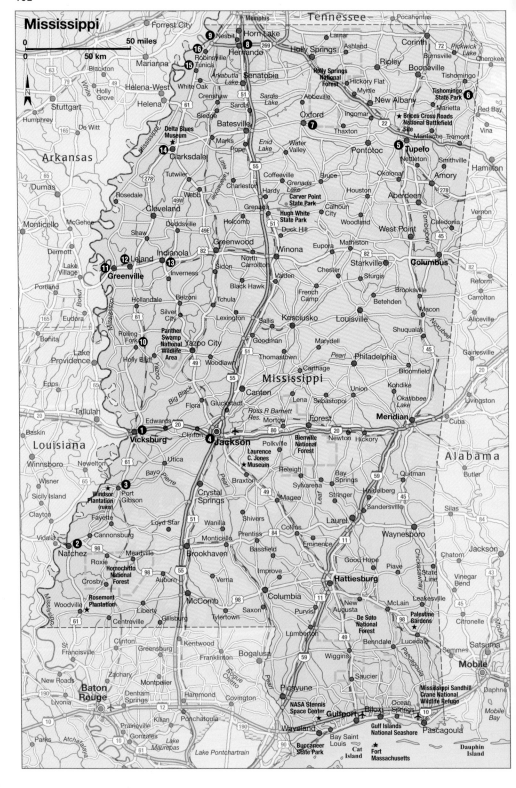

Mississippi

MISSISSIPPI

The Magnolia State offers ancient delights on the Natchez Trace, and Tishomingo Park in the foothills of the Appalachian Mountains.

Named for the river that has been America's great trading route and ranged around the fertile Delta that blazed musical and literary richness, as well as agricultural wealth, Mississippi has an abundant and complex heritage to explore.

The Civil War was writ large across the map of Mississippi. **Vicksburg** ❶ was the site of one of the longest sieges in American history, and the Battlefield Park is a quietening evocation of just how hard and bitter the young country's wrestle with itself was. Jackson has risen from the ashes of the 'Chimneyville' burnings by Sherman, but the scarcity of old buildings can't fail to make a resonant impression. Heartbreakingly beautiful Natchez, paradoxically, still bears the scars of coming through the 'recent unpleasantness' intact.

As bitter, and still in many ways incomplete, as the civil rights struggle was, nowhere was it as raw as it was in Mississippi. From the cotton plantations to the race riots in Oxford, many of the dark milestones on the march to freedom are along the roads of Mississippi. As well as battlefields, there are elegant antebellum mansions to discover, many of which offer the grace of Southern hospitality that the term 'bed-and-breakfast accommodations' can't begin to describe.

Deak Harp's music store in Clarksdale.

The vivid and sometimes stark contrasts may be one explanation for the wonderfully perplexing fountain of literary talent that springs from the Mississippi mud and soil. This state has given the world the words of Eudora Welty, Richard Wright, Tennessee Williams, and John Grisham, to name just a few. William Faulkner, the father of the 20th-century American novel, lived in Oxford, amid lucrative sojourns to Hollywood in its heyday.

Born in the cotton fields from working songs, gospel elevations,

Main attractions
Bieclenharn Coca-Cola Museum
Vicksburg National Military Park
Tishomingo State Park
The Windsor Ruins
The Mississippi Sports Hall of Fame
The Birthplace of Elvis Presley
Natchez Trace

Maps on pages
152, 154

and African rhythms, the blues in turn propagated the seeds for musical innovations that themselves conquered the 20th-century world; jazz, soul and rock'n'roll. Elvis, the King of rock'n'roll, was born in the pretty town of Tupelo. The blues is, or are, still alive and shouting, from its nursery in Clarksdale, through the alma-maters of Greenville and Jackson. Classical education flourishes, too, in the gentle northern slopes of Oxford, where the antebellum campus has a romantic air fit to compare with the 'dreaming spires' of the town's English namesake.

Along with the innumerable senators, scientists, sports stars, and scribes, Ole Miss can claim a prodigious number of former Miss Americas among her august alumni. There's definitely something about Mississippi.

VICKSBURG

Straddling a bluff on a bend in Ole Man River, Vicksburg's Civil War history may be somber, but its attractions are outgoing and popular.

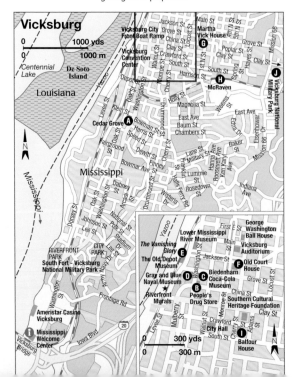

At the southern point of the Mississippi Delta in 1811, the Methodist Reverend Newitt Vick found a bluff 200ft (61 meters) above the great river, overlooking the bend where the Yazoo River joins the Mississippi. He bought 1,220 acres (490 hectares) of land from the government of the territory and planned a town on the 200 acres (80 hectares) north of the river. Reverend Vick never saw it completed, since both he and his wife succumbed to yellow fever less than a year later, but the Vicks left 13 children, and, together with the reverend's executors, they developed the town that carries their name. Known later as 'the Gibraltar of the Confederacy,' Vicksburg has a commanding position on the mighty river. So much so that in the Civil War, Abraham Lincoln called it 'the key.' He and General Ulysses S. Grant were agreed that its capture would cut off Texas, Louisiana, and Arkansas from the Confederacy. The strategy led to a 47-day siege, and one of the two decisive engagements of the war.

The white flag was hoisted on the courthouse on July 3, the same day as Robert E. Lee's defeat at Gettysburg. Grant took the surrender from General John C. Pemberton on the 4th of July 1862. There is a popular belief that Vicksburg did not celebrate Independence Day for another 100 years, but newspapers in the library describe picnics and commemorations.

The festivities, though, did take on a different tone as the town remembered the suffering of the war, and the siege. People from the North also visited on the 4th of July, and still do, to be at the site of their fathers' and forefathers' victory.

VIBRANT VICKSBURG

Modern Vicksburg offers, as well as the solemn tranquillity of the Battlefield Park, a vibrant and ambitious blues museum, riverboat-style casinos, an attractive historic downtown district, and a number of beautiful antebellum mansions, some of which provide gracious B&B accommodations. Vicksburg also has a place in the American history of music. On a visit to the local museum, the city's distinguished and charming Alderwoman Gertrude Anderson Young said, 'You know, jazz got its name from a Vicksburg drummer' (see page 86).

Just south of Vicksburg's Washington Street, on old US 61 by the Ameristar casino, is the attractive and informative **Mississippi State Welcome Center**.

The first of Vicksburg's antebellum mansions is in the historic garden district; it's a short way farther north on Washington, left onto Klein and at the intersection with Oak Street. Offering delightful B&B accommodations and an acclaimed restaurant, **Cedar Grove** 🅐 (2200 Oak Street; tel: 601-636-1000; www.cedargroveinn.com) is a graceful manor house, set near the river among formal gardens, and giving wide sweeping views of the Mississippi from a roof garden. John Alexander Klein built the columned mansion in 1840 as a home for himself and his bride, Elizabeth. On their year-long European honeymoon, they acquired Italian marble fireplaces, French empire gasoliers, and Bohemian glass for the doorway. Elizabeth was related to General Sherman, who personally escorted the family to safety early in the siege, and the house later served as a Union hospital. Although a cannonball remains embedded in the parlor wall, the family's connection with that most hated of Union soldiers didn't endear them to Vicksburg society.

Most of the **Downtown Riverfront** actually fronts onto the Yazoo River, with the waterfront dominated by riverboat-style casinos. Just to the south are the **Isle of Capri** and **Ameristar** casinos. None of the boats actually sail, they merely conform to the letter of Mississippi's idiosyncratic gaming laws (see page 78) but they do give an attractive flavor of the old riverboat style, and are spectacularly illuminated after dark. The Ameristar is popular for its Thursday night events, often with a blues theme.

⊘ WILLIE DIXON

Born in Vicksburg on July 1, 1915, Willie Dixon would go on to become one of the city's most famous and celebrated musicians. There are too many hits of Dixon's to name them all, but his most prolific include *I Just Want to Make Love to You*, *Hoochie Coochie Man*, *You Can't Judge a Book by the Cover*, and *My Babe*. Dixon is considered by many to be the first musician of influence to successfully blend the blues with rock'n'roll. As a result, he went on to work with and write for the likes of Chuck Berry, Jimi Hendrix, Bob Dylan, The Doors, and The Rolling Stones.

Today, Dixon's legacy lives on in the Blues Heaven Foundation in Chicago, providing scholarships and training to the next generation of upcoming Blues musicians.

Riverboats on the Mississippi River receiving cargo and supplies at the Vicksburg landing.

CHESS AND COBRA

Farther north and to the right, about level with where the former Harrah's casino is 'moored,' a short street has been named **Willie Dixon Way** in dedication to Vicksburg's most famous bluesman. The great bass player, producer, and arranger was a mainstay of the Chess and Cobra labels, and supplied Muddy Waters with the diamond-hard riff and brash lyric for Hoochie Coochie Man. The street goes from nowhere to nowhere much else, and nothing happens on the way.

The Downtown historic district is about five blocks around the intersection of Washington and Clay streets, and still has a 19th- and early 20th-century appearance. Less than a block north is the friendly and helpful **Vicksburg Welcome Center**. The cosy, brick-lined office has a wealth of information about attractions, events, and accommodation in town.

Still on Washington, the **People's Drug Store** Ⓑ (1123 Washington Street, tel: 601-636-5214; www.peoples-drugs.com; hours vary) is more than a

useful stop for travelers, providing drugstore requisites like toothpaste, medicines, and shampoo. The store wears its saloon-bar history proudly in the crystal chandeliers still hanging from the ceiling. There are fascinating exhibits of Civil War cures, including jars of angostura bark, some evil-looking potions that might have deterred sickness more than curing it, and a number of bullets bearing deep teeth-marks. There is a display of moonshine whisky with a recipe (still available locally, according to the proprietor), and numerous Civil War weapons, jugs, and surgical instruments. The store also sells more esoteric cures such as St John's wort and natural melatonin.

The place where the sweet, fizzy stuff was bottled for the first time in 1894 is now the **Bieclenharn Coca-Cola Museum** Ⓒ (1107 Washington Street, tel: 601-638-6514; www.biedenharncoca-colamuseum.com; Mon–Sat 9am–5pm, Sun 1:30–4:30pm), a small and friendly museum that could not be more different than its glitzy cousin in Atlanta (see page 115). Inside, it feels like a step into a sepia postcard. The original bottling equipment, which had to be operated in protective clothing because the bottles were given to exploding, is replicated. At the rear, through a red-brick courtyard, is a replica of a 1900s soda fountain with wire-backed chairs and small, round tables.

Upstairs from the Daily Grind Café is the **Attic Gallery**, selling innovative fine art from local artists like the charming Earl Simmonds, as well as art from Southern artists farther afield. Across the street, the **Gray & Blue Naval Museum** Ⓓ has, they claim, the largest collection anywhere of Civil War Naval models and an impressive diorama of the Siege of Vicksburg, with just a trace of bias. The proprietor asserts, 'we're not politically correct, but we are historically accurate.' **The Biscuit Company of Vicksburg** provides great views of the river to go with the food

The Biedenharn Candy Company building in the historic district of Vicksburg.

and drinks. There's often live music in the evenings, too. Back to Clay Street and a block up on the left, the story of the siege is vividly portrayed in **The Vanishing Glory ⓔ** (717 Clay Street), a wide-screen outdoor presentation conjuring the event from eyewitness accounts, letters, and diaries, of soldiers and citizens. The show is hourly on the hour.

Down Levee Street site The Old Depot Museum (tel: 601-638-6500; www.theolddepot.net; Mon–Sat 10am–4pm), which features a tiny replica of one of Vicksburg's battlefields. Visitors can also view railroad memorabilia and explore history. Also of note is the former train depot that houses the museum.

A COURTHOUSE WITH CATS

For one of Vicksburg's most delightful attractions, continue up Clay Street to Cherry Street and make the climb to the top. High on the hill, the **Old Court House Museum ⓕ** (Court Square; tel: 601-636-0741; Mon–Sat 8.30am–4:30pm) was a favorite target for Union artillery during the siege, until someone had the idea of moving in Yankee prisoners. The courthouse survived and now houses a charming museum, guarded by a company of watchful cats. The museum illuminates the lives of the locals more than larger and more distant historical events.

The cosy exhibits evoke the rustic pioneer and dark polished antebellum home life. An engaging Black history display includes a feature on 'Blacks who wore grey.' There is a Confederate flag from Fort McCree which was never surrendered, a post-war 'blacklist' of 'unreconstructed individuals,' newspapers printed on wallpaper during the siege, cannonballs, and shot. The museum is punctuated with stories of the origins of terms like Dixie and Yankee. Tours are advertised as 'selfguided,' but if Gordon Cotton, the curator, catches your eye, you'll likely

be swept along by his twinkling enthusiasm for just about any and every subject of local history and lore. Very little can have happened in Vicksburg in the last two centuries about which Gordon won't gladly enlighten and entertain in his kindly schoolteacher style.

Turn left out of the courthouse and down Grove Street for a couple of blocks to the **Martha Vick House ⓖ** (1300 Grove Street; tel: 601-831-7007; www.visitvicksburg.com/martha-vick-house; daily 11am–5pm), the last surviving home from the founding Vick family. Dating from the 1830s, the house is furnished with English and American antiques of the period.

Take Farmer Street for a few blocks and go left up Harrison Street. In this uncommonly haunted state, the **McRaven Home ⓗ** (1445 Harrison Street, tel: 601-501-1336; www.mcraventourhome.com; hours vary, see website) may be the most haunted house in Mississippi. Furniture moves by itself, footsteps are heard when there's no one else there, and lights go on and off for no obvious reason. Three distinct styles of

One of 32 murals on the Mississippi River floodwall depicting historic scenes and local culture in Vicksburg, Mississippi.

The Old Court House in Vicksburg.

architecture are clearly visible in the house's additions; frontier from 1797, Empire in 1836, and the last, Greek Revival from 1849. On the grounds, barely 100 yds/meters behind the house, the confronting trench lines of the Confederacy and the Union remain, just a few short steps apart.

The elegant **Balfour House** ❶ (1002 Crawford Street) is where Emma Balfour gave Mississippi one of its most treasured first-hand accounts of the siege. She wrote in her journal with description and compassion of seeing 'mortars from the west passing entirely over the house,' and '... our poor soldiers have no rest, as we have few reserves.' The house itself is one of Mississippi's finest examples of the Greek Revival style and features an elliptical spiral staircase.

INDIVIDUAL AND POIGNANT

Follow Clay Street toward US 61 to **Vicksburg National Military Park** ❿ (see page 94). The park covers much of the ground of the 47-day siege, as well as the extensive memorial

gardens. All of the Confederate states and all but six of the US states of the time (20 states in all) have significant memorials to their fallen soldiers here; the siege killed over 19,000 men in total. Each monument is individual and poignant, and it would take a lifetime to tell all the tales. The park is a major draw for visitors from all over America, but it includes no statue or monument to General Sherman. Under a special pavilion is the USS *Cairo*, an ironclad fighting ship sunk in the conflict, raised from the riverbed 100 years later. Much of the ship was so well preserved in the Mississippi mud that a watch found on board was still in working order. The running watch is displayed in an adjacent exhibition.

AROUND MISSISSIPPI

Graceful plantations, a gorgeous college town, a capital where commerce is king, and the ghosts of Elvis and Faulkner – Mississippi beguiles the mind.

Known first for the mighty, misty Mississippi River, this lyrical and

Bridge across the Mississippi River at Vicksburg.

literary state has history, musical and cultural heritage, and beautiful scenery. The verdant hills of northern Mississippi look out over one of the most fertile plains on earth the Mississippi Delta. Having once been America's capital for cotton and rice, the ever-adaptable Mississppians are now raising soybeans and fat catfish under that big, sweltering sky.

Mississippi has fine plantation homes, especially in Natchez and Port Gibson, both of which escaped most of the ravages of the Civil War, or 'the recent unpleasantness,' as it is still sometimes known. Adding in the towering Mississippian giants of musical and literary heritage, plus a few state parks, and great Southern food and hospitality, well, child, what kept you so long? Don't be shy, y'all come now, y'hear?

NATCHEZ

South of **Vicksburg** about 70 miles (112km) on US 61, **Natchez ❷** once was the capital of Mississippi. It was held and governed first by the French, then the English, followed by the Spanish. It shimmers with fading antebellum grace, thanks to the still arguable distinction of surviving the Civil War intact. Natchez surrendered without opposing Grant's occupation, and, because of the awful suffering that Vicksburg endured in its 47-day siege, Natchez citizens still feel a bitterness to their near neighbors. Most Vicksburgers, however, seem to harbor no such feelings, though, believing that since President Jefferson Davis refused to garrison Natchez, the town could never have withstood an invasion.

A good first stop is the visitor center. Follow Highway 61 south of Natchez and join Highway 84. Overlooking the magnificent box girder bridges that carry trains and cars over the steep banks of the Mississippi, the **Natchez Tourism Department** (640 Canal Street; tel: 601-446-6345; www.visit-natchez.org; Mon–Sat 8.30am–5pm, Sun 9am–4pm) offers a great viewing platform. A massive model of the town and the big river illuminates sites of historic and other points of local interest.

Left out of the Visitor Center on Canal Street, take the first left under the bluff by the river. Literally below the town, **Natchez-Under-the-Hill** was once Natchez's dockside area of ill-repute, a strip of bars and brothels. Its act has been cleaned up with restaurants and shops to attract tourists, but it still carries echoes of those rowdy port-of-call days. The **Under-the-Hill Saloon** (tel: 601-446-8023; daily 10am–2am), a former 19th-century bordello, is a romantic, evocative remnant with good food and great views of the river from its decorative balcony. Return to Canal Street and turn left. Just a couple of blocks on, at the corner of State Street, tickets are available for **Natchez Spring and Fall Pilgrimages** (tel: 601-653-0919; www.natchezpilgrimage.com; call or check website for exact dates), a range of tours that take in

Vicksburg National Military Park.

⊙ Tip

Monmouth Historic Inn is set in beautiful, landscaped gardens and has been ranked as one of the top 50 inns in the United States. The best way to experience the inn is with a guided tour (daily at 10am and 2pm), which you should reserve in advance (tel; 601-442-5852; www. monmouthhistoricinn.com).

over 30 plantation and antebellum historic houses. Follow State Street to Commerce Street and into the faded glory, antebellum grace and 20th-century decay of Downtown. **The Historic Natchez Foundation** (109 Commerce Street, tel: 601-442-2500; www.natchez. org) has information about the Historic District, an eight-block area, mostly by the river.

PLANTATION HEAVEN

Lovely **Monmouth Historic Inn** (see picture) is a good introduction to the Natchez plantations, most of which are open every day. From Monmouth, turn right, then right again almost immediately onto Melrose Avenue. On the left is **Linden** (1 Connor Circle, tel: 769-355-2127), an impressive mansion with a long, columned gallery. The house was commenced in 1792 and added to by later owners, though it has remained in the same family for the past 150 years. B&B accommodations are available. The first of Natchez' Greek Revival-style white columned mansions, **Auburn Museum & Historic Home** (400 Duncan Avenue; tel: 601-442-5981; www.auburnmuseum. org) is furnished with antiques, some Regency and some Rococo. The unsupported spiral staircase in the lobby is particularly graceful.

Longwood (140 Lower Woodville Road, tel: 601-442-5193) is an octagonal brick mansion surrounded by columned porches and balconies and topped with a shining, Moorish onion dome. The house is even more remarkable for being externally grand, and internally incomplete. Like a movie set facade, the interior beams and rough brick of the unfinished upper floors remain exposed.

Head across Highway 84 to Homochitto Street for about half a mile, to the stately white columned plantation house of **Dunleith** (tel: 601-897-6300; www.dunleithhistoricinn.com). Sitting among 40 acres (16 hectares) of green pastures and wooded bayous, the house and grounds beautifully curated and offer romantic and secluded B&B accommodations.

NATCHEZ PEOPLE

Described by one French settler as 'one of the most polite and affable nations on the Mississippi,' the attempts of the Natchez Native Americans to coexist with the white newcomers were constantly frustrated. In 1729, the Natchez tried to reclaim their homeland with an attack on Fort Rosalie. The French garrison was wiped out, but the colonists retaliated by killing most of the Natives and driving the rest away. Listed as a National Historic Landmark, the **Grand Village of the Natchez Indians** (400 Jefferson Davis Boulevard; tel: 601-446-6502; www.mdah.ms.gov/new/visit/grand-village-of-natchez-indians; Mon–Sat 9am–5pm, Sun 1.30–5pm) has an authentically re-created hut and three mounds, plus some arts and crafts on show in the friendly visitor center. To get there, return along Homochitto Street, take

Longwood during springtime.

Highway 61 south and turn left onto Jefferson Davis Boulevard to the Grand Village entrance.

About 40 miles (64km) north, Highway 61 leads straight into **Port Gibson** ❸. Grant's decision to spare the town from the torches means that it is one of the few old Mississippi towns to be preserved almost intact.

Three user-friendly self-guided tours are marked by green signs – a Grand Gulf battlefield tour, a Windsor battlefield tour, including the ruins of evocative Windsor Plantation, and the Port Gibson tour covering historic homes and 19thcentury churches.

The Natchez Visitor Center (640 South Canal Street; www.visitnatchez.org; 601-446-6365; Mon–Sat 8:30am–5pm, Sun 9am–4pm) is located by the Mississippi River Bridge. If you head to Church Street, among the chinaberry trees, are a candy-box selection of church architectural styles, from high Victorian Gothic to Romanesque. Most distinctive of all is the **First Presbyterian Church**, a white, stone, plain, Gothic steepled building topped by a huge gold hand, pointing informatively, instructively or as a warning, it's hard to tell. Whichever the message, it points skyward.

Windsor Ruins (tel: 601-576-6952; www.mdah.ms.gov/new/visit/windsor-ruins; 8am–7:30pm daily) on route 552, 10 miles (16km) west of Port Gibson, is well worth a detour. Built in 1861 and held to be the most lavish of Mississippi's Greek Revival expressions, the house was destroyed not by the advancing Union troops, but by an accident in 1890. All that remains are Doric columns, ironwork, and a spectral beauty. Visits near dusk make the most powerful impression.

Just south of Port Gibson, pick up the glorious **Natchez Trace Parkway** (see pages 227 and 227) and take it for about 60 meandering miles (100km) to the town of Jackson. The parkway offers wonderful spots for hiking, walking, picnics, and quiet solitude. Bring your binoculars for spotting unusual birds.

JACKSON

Jackson ❹ was named after Major General Andrew Jackson for his distinction in the War of 1812 and the Battle of New Orleans. In 1822, the Mississippi state capital moved here from Natchez to be more central.

Mississippi was fertile ground for the civil rights movement, spawning activists and events of the era. Jackson is where Medgar Evers was murdered in 1963, and each June the town hosts the Medgar Evers Mississippi Homecoming. Today, Jackson is a clean and green commercial center, humming with pioneers in technology and medical sciences.

The **Old Capitol** (100 South State Street; tel: 601-576-6920; www.mdah.ms.gov/oldcap; call for hours) houses the **State Historical Museum**. The seat of government later moved to the Beaux Arts building, known since 1903 as the **New Capitol** (400 High Street).

Ruins of the Windsor Plantation.

The **Eudora Welty Public Library** (tel: 601-968-5811; Mon–Thu 9am–6pm, Fri and Sat 9am-5pm) is one block north of the Old Capitol, at the intersection with Yazoo Street, with a reading room featuring many of the amazing number of Mississipian literary luminaries, including William Faulkner and Tennessee Williams.

For blues aficionados, Jackson was something of a hotspot, and nowhere more than at **225 North Farish Street**, the site of the Henry C. Spier's original store. Go one block south on State, right on Amite Street to North Farish, then right again. There's not that much to see now, but the footsteps of Spier's pioneering musical discoveries led here, including Charley Patton, Willie Brown, and legendary singer Son House. Spier's well-tuned ear was not infallible, though; he passed on Jimmie Rodgers, the 'father of country music.' A few blocks farther north along Farish Street, on the opposite side, is the former **Trumpet Records Building** (309 North Farish Street) where Lillian McMurry produced Sonny Boy Williamson II and Elmore James, and numerous other blues greats for Trumpet Records in the Diamond Recording Studio in the same building.

Take I-51 north and turn left onto Lakeland Drive for just under a mile to the **Mississippi Museum of Natural Science** (2148 Riverside Drive; tel: 601-576-6000; www.mdwfp.com/museum; Mon–Fri 8am–5pm, Sat 9am–5pm, Sun 1–5pm), which is on the left. It includes a forest area, a large greenhouse and an aquarium forming a swamp exhibit, housing lazy turtles and snappy alligators.

Go north on I-55 to exit 98, and turn onto Lakeland Drive for the **Mississippi Sports Hall of Fame** (1152 Lakeland Drive; tel: 601-982-8264; www.msfame.com; Mon–Sat 10am–4pm). The facility has memorabilia from Mississippi's luminaries of track and field, including baseball heroes Dizzy Dean and Charles 'Pee Wee' Armstrong. Across the parking lot is the **Mississippi AG Museum** (tel: 601-432-4500; www.msagmuseum.org; Mon–Sat 9am–5pm) containing living re-creations of life on a mid-18thcentury farm and a 1920s town. The museum adjoins the **Chimneyville Crafts Gallery** where native traditional and modern members of the Craftsmen's Guild of Mississippi are showcased.

ELVIS SLEPT HERE

The most pleasant way to reach **Tupelo** ❺ is to rejoin the Natchez Trace for the 170-mile (273km) drive. The airy **Natchez Trace Visitor Center** is in Tupelo at parkway milepost 266 (tel: 662-680-4027; daily 9am–4.30pm). There are restrooms, camping amenities, and hiking trails – real Southern hospitality.

Neat little Tupelo draws more than 100,000 visitors annually to the small shotgun shack at 306 Presley Drive, the **birthplace of Elvis Presley** (tel: 662-841-1245; www.elvispresleybirthplace.

Skyline of Jackson, Mississippi, over the Capitol Building.

com; Mon–Thur 11am–4pm, Fri–Sat 9am–5pm, Sun 1–5pm). The 30ft x 15ft (10 meter x 5 meter) singlestory house is restored to the condition it would have been in when the King was, well, a princeling, presumably. With just two square rooms and no indoor plumbing, it resembles the layout and proportions of the sharecroppers' shacks common in the Delta. The house was built in 1934 by his father, Vernon, and his uncle Vester, with $180 that Vernon borrowed from a Mr Bean. Elvis was born in the shack on January 8, 1937. Three years later the family were unable to meet the repayments and Bean repossessed the house.

On his way to stardom in 1957, Elvis was playing at a local fair when he spotted the house and bought it back. The property has been maintained since as a kind of shrine, and it certainly conjures the humble beginnings of the first rock'n'roll megastar. The house is attended by enthusiastic and well-informed guides and makes for a rewarding visit.

Rather less value, information, and courtesy are available from the tiny adjacent **Elvis Museum** although they do keep an appropriately tacky gift shop. At the top of a small hill is a chapel that plays Elvis's spiritual records. The chapel is in great demand for weddings and needs to be booked months ahead. Elvis also left early marks throughout Downtown Tupelo. Head to Tupelo Hardware Co to hear stories about Elvis's first guitar purchase, and head to Relics Antique Marketplace, which was once the garment factory where Elvis's mom worked while pregnant with the future musician.

Tupelo Community Theater at the Lyric (Broadway and Court streets; tel: 601-844 1935; www.tct.ms) is an attractive Art Deco auditorium with a candy-colored lobby. Just south of Main Street, on the outside it's a mild-mannered, unassuming **McDonald's** (519 Gloster Street); inside, it's a temple for the Elvii, with walls lined with framed photographs and memorabilia.

Oxford is just a couple of hours drive west from Tupelo, but first, here is a delightful side trip to a state park in the northern Mississippi hills. Rejoin the Natchez Trace Parkway north to **Tishomingo State Park ⑥** (tel: 662-438-6914; Mile marker 304 from the parkway), named for the famed Chickasaw chief. In the foothills of the Appalachian Mountains, the park is on the National Register of Historic Places, and its 1,530 acres (620 hectares) of unique geology include rock formations dating back to the Paleozoic era, carpeted and canopied by rare ferns and wild flowers in the shade of the ancient woodlands. The park has one of North America's largest white-tail deer populations, as well as many wild turkeys and ducks. Another attraction is the scarce and wonderfully symbolic Bald Eagle, often seen throughout the winter months.

OXFORD

From Tupelo, head west for about 50 miles (80km) into **Oxford ⑦**. Nestling

Elvis Museum in Tupelo.

THE MISSISSIPPI

Ole Man River, as Jerome Kern's lyric christened it, has been a way of life for many civilizations, a source of inspiration, and one of North America's main trading arteries. Writing of his days as a Mississippi river boatman before the Civil War, Mark Twain said, 'It is not a commonplace river, but on the contrary is in all ways remarkable.' Samuel Clemens chose the pen name of Mark Twain from a mark on the side of a cargo freighter by which its load was measured. He aspired to captain a riverboat because he considered the position to be that of a 'king without a keeper.' T.S. Eliot was so moved as to call the mighty waterway 'a great, brown god.'

River traffic on the Mississippi River near New Orleans.

The first European to set sight on the river was Hernando De Soto, in 1542, when the English Queen Elizabeth I was still in her teens, and Michelangelo's paint was wet on the ceiling of the Sistine Chapel in Rome. Hernando stood high on the land, then called 'Quigualtam' by the Native Americans, where the Mississippi town, Hernando, is named after him (see page 165), and saw spread out the alluvial plain now known as the Mississippi Delta; an alluvial plain is a valley filled with sand and silts deposited by water runoff. Because of European indifference, and also perhaps De Soto's demise shortly afterward, it was another 150 years before a white European paid any further attention to the immense river.

Running more than 2,000 miles (3,200km) from its source at Lake Itasca in Minnesota, the Mississippi empties into the Gulf of Mexico at New Orleans. It is the longest river in North America, and the third longest in the world. At its widest, it spans over a mile, and its waters run 198ft (60 meters) deep at Baton Rouge. Providing such a massive navigable trade route, the Mississippi was important, not only in the development of the South, but also to the developing United States, and remains so to this day. It carried cotton through the center of the South, and out to the ocean for export. Its ability to provide the same function for the industrial towns of the North made it a major objective for Lincoln in the Civil War, perhaps even an objective for the war itself.

In the 19th century, paddle steamers were packed outside and in with bales of cotton, and stacked to the gunnels with passengers. As romanticized by countless western tales, they also served as floating casinos, far adrift from tiresome laws and lawmen on land. In the 1990s, riverboat gambling returned to the muddy waters, with static casino boats from Saint Louis to New Orleans.

The battle for control of the Mississippi didn't end in the 19th century; in the 1930s, when Louisiana governor Huey Long oversaw a new bridge at Baton Rouge, it is said that he ensured its span was too low for ocean-going vessels to pass under, compelling freighters to dock in Louisiana.

Great trains of barges still slip through the mist and below the wide spans of box-girder bridges, floating cargo between Missouri and New Orleans, and the Mississippi is still, from any glance, a river of dreams.

in the gentler slopes of northern Mississippi, the town, like its English namesake, has an outstanding university. 'Ole Miss,' as the famed **University of Mississippi** is known, was chartered in 1844. The first university in the South to accept Black students, in October of 1962, the entry of James Meredith was the sparking point for race riots and one of the key moments in the birthing pains of American civil rights.

Among Ole Miss's many garlands of learning, the university has the world's largest archive of blues music in the University Blues Archive. If you can, take a troll around the beautiful campus and faculty houses, which boast venerable names like Faulkner.

Oxford looks and feels like a lovely, elegant, civilized town. The graceful main square is lined with upscale restaurants and stores, including the well stocked **Square Books** (160 Courthouse Square; tel: 662-236-2262; www.squarebooks.com; Mon–Sat 9am–8pm, Sun 9am–5pm). Just off the square among the antiques shops are numerous bars popular with students.

WRITERS PAST AND PRESENT

Befitting a seat of learning, strong literary roots are planted here. William Faulkner, considered by many to be the American founder of the modern novel, made his home behind oak and rowan trees, in **Rowan Oak** (Old Taylor Road; tel: Error! Hyperlink reference not valid.662-234-3284; www.rowanoak.com; Tue–-Sat 10am–4pm, Sun 1pm–4pm). Faulkner extended the white wooden plantation-style house, mostly with his own hands. It is open for public viewing, although hours can be erratic and information hard to come by, but it is lovingly curated by Ole Miss, its present owners. The building and grounds, shaded by huge, cool trees, are enjoyable to stroll around and are open for touring.

Oxford has also been home to John Grisham, popular author of *The Firm*,

The Pelican Brief and *The Client*, successful books, mainly set in the South, that have become popular movies. His is the large yellow house just west of town south of MS 270. West on MS 278 for a little over 20 miles (32km), then north for about 30 miles (48km) on I-55 is **Arkabutla Lake**, popular for water sports, hiking, and camping, and a great spot to watch the local quail, wood ducks, and white-tail deer.

Just over 7 miles (11km) north and a left turn off I-55, is the country town of **Hernando ❽**. From the bluff at the west edge of town is a panoramic view of the Mississippi Delta, much as the explorer De Soto first saw in 1542 when he discovered for the Europeans this verdant plain, stretching out as far as the eye could see.

JERRY LEE LEWIS

Farther north about 5 miles (8km) on I-55, in **Nesbit ❾** is the **Jerry Lee Lewis Ranch** (1595 Malone Road; tel: 901-488-1823; www.thelewisranch.com; Thur–Sat 12am–5pm). Signed on the high, white security gates as, 'The

Lyceum Building at the University of Mississippi, Oxford.

The Devil's Crossroads sign in Clarksdale, where a trio of electric guitars mark the spot where musician Robert Johnson allegedly sold his soul to the devil in return for the ability to play the blues.

Double decker, paddle boat serves as a visitors' center for Greenville, Mississippi.

Killer,' over symbols of pianos, the Killer himself is unlikely to make an appearance, but many memorabilia of the singer's work is in evidence here. So, too, are some of his vintage Harley-Davidson motorcycles, his huge swimming pool in the shape of a grand piano, and his favorite dog, a chihuahua called Tapioca.

West of MS 31 and Goodman Road is a small home that claims to be 'Elvis's Honeymoon Cottage (5921 Goodman Road) in **Horn Lake.** This modest white house with black shutters is where the King brought his young bride, Priscilla, after their Las Vegas wedding in 1967. This location draws many Elvii wishing to check all notable locations off of their list.

MISSISSIPPI BLUES TOUR

The Delta spreads from the lobby of the Peabody Hotel in Memphis to Catfish Row in Vicksburg. In between, in these fertile cotton fields, the blues were born

US Highway 61 – the Blue Highway – runs north to south right through the Mississippi Delta, and was immortalized in the title of Bob Dylan's album Highway 61 Revisited. As well as connecting much of Mississippi, the road took players from the Delta to the riches of Memphis. State Highways 61 and 49 were the tracks of trade for Delta musicians in the first half of the 20th century, linking most of the major music venues, and where 61 crosses Highway 49 in Clarksdale is a large crossroads sign, with three blue guitars. Clarksdale is the hub of the Delta blues. When the blues was bursting out, it was said that: 'if you could make it in Clarksdale, you could make it in Memphis or Chicago.'

MUDDY WATERS TO GREENVILLE

North of Vicksburg on Highway 61 where it intersects with Highway 1, a sign may appear at the roadside saying, 'Rolling Fork, home of McKinley (Muddy Waters) Morganfield.' Or it may not, folks are apt to poach them. Muddy Waters was born in **Rolling Fork** ❿ on April 14, 1915, as a memorial on the south side of the **Courthouse Square** attests. Father of the Chicago electric blues style, Muddy learned to play around Stovall, Mississippi, where he was sent to live with his grandmother at an early age, and in nearby Clarksdale. Visitors can get a taste of local cuisine at the nearby Annual Leland Crawfish Festival (www.lelandchamber.com) each May.

Head north on Highway 61, and turn left on Highway 82 to **Greenville** ⓫, the largest city in the Delta. Greenville plays host to the biggest and oldest festival, the Mississippi Delta Blues Festival, each September. The first stop should be at the intersection of Highway 82 and Reed Road. The intersection is easy to spot, as it has a pristine replica of a stern-wheel riverboat. This is the **River Road Queen Welcome Center** (tel: 662-332-2378; hours vary, call ahead). The interior maintains the theme, and the upper floor houses

a Mississippi river road exhibit. Like much of the state, Greenville has deep literary traditions, to which the **Greenville Writers Exhibit** pays tribute in the library (341 Main Street). Main Street dead-ends at the **Mississippi Levee**. Completed in 1912, this was an engineering feat taller and longer than the Great Wall of China.

The Nelson Street area is probably as close an evocation as there is to the 1920s atmosphere of Memphis's Beale Street. There are bars with bands, singers, and records, and people hustling through the night. Plus, juke, or 'jook' joints, simple rooms with space for dancing and the place to hear the most authentic music (the word 'jook' is thought to be a contraction of 'juice,' with something of a sexual context). Ike and Tina Turner played at **Perry's Flowing Fountain**, also thought to be the original Anna Mae's Café from the 1985 Little Milton song. (Nelson) aficionados rate this among the top juke joints. Juke streets are often worked by drug dealers and pimps, catering to a mostly white clientele; politely declining offers of trade will usually suffice. Nelson Street's **Doe's Eat Place** (tel: 662-334-3315; www.doeseatplace. com; Mon–Sat 5–9pm) has porterhouse steak described by Men's Journal as 'the best thing to eat in America.' Another worthy option in Greenville is **Downtown Grille** (tel: 662-702-5161; www.downtowngrille525.com) on Washington Avenue. Dishes like charbroiled oysters, gumbo, crawfish cakes, and fried green tomatoes are sure to give the palate a true taste of the South. Don't forget to save room for dessert as the white chocolate chip bread pudding is always a hit.

On the way to Indianola, back on Highway 82, the town of **Leland** ⑫ has **three murals** depicting some of the local blues greats. Johnny Winter and his brother Edgar were both born here, and their father was once the mayor. They feature with Jimmie Reed and many others on the painting at Main Street and 4th. A block along at Main Street and 3rd is a brash, graphic mural honoring five decades of B.B. King's blues testimony. Leland

Rolling Fork, where famous bluesman Muddy Waters was born in 1915.

Row houses in Greenwood.

also honors local animator Jim Henson with much Muppet memorabilia in the **Birthplace of the Frog** (South Deer Creek Drive, tel: 662-686-2687; Mon–Sat 10am–4pm, Sun 2pm–5pm).

MISSISSIPPI MOJO

Head east on Highway 82 to **Indianola** ⑬. Albert King was born here on April 25, 1923, and B.B. King (no relation) was born just outside it on September 16, 1925. Riley (Blues Boy) King, as he was known in the early days, or 'the Beale Street Blues Boy,' transformed the electric blues with guitar, bass, drums and piano or mouth organ, into a massive traveling revue, later known as the B.B. King Orchestra. B.B. played a free outdoor concert in **B.B. King Park** on Roosevelt Street every year until his death in 2015. Indianola was also where Charley Patton died on April 28, 1934, and his grave can be seen in the New Jerusalem Church in **Holly Ridge**. Like so many bluesmen, Patton's grave went unmarked for some time, the marker provided by his record company having been purloined. The

present headstone was furnished with help from musician John Fogerty.

The area around **Greenwood** offers no fewer than three graves for Robert Johnson (see page 169), two at Morgan City, and in Quito south of Highway 82. Past Ita Bena, fittingly between Quito and Morgan City where his two gravestones are, is a **Robert Johnson Monument**.

The third grave is a few miles north of Greenwood at Little Zion Church. The neat white church has no sign, but an address marker reading 63530. Unlike the other two, the grave here is unmarked, in keeping with most of the Johnson lore. This is, however, the site credited by blues scholars including John Hammond, Steve LaVere, and Steve Cheseborough.

The first blues heard by W.C. Handy was the spot 'where the Southern Cross the Dog,' and **Moorhead** is where that is. The Southern and the Dog are, or were, the railroad tracks that made a perfectly perpendicular intersection. Tutwiler station was where he was snoozing when the Clarksdale train

was nine hours late. He was awoken by 'a lean, loose-jointed negro' singing *Where the Southern Crosses the Dog* and playing a guitar with a slide, a sound he described as 'the weirdest music I had ever heard.' Handy researched and developed the sound, becoming known as the Father of the Blues. The Tutwiler Arts Project has commissioned a number of **blues murals**, and the **commemorative plaque** at the station gives the date of Handy's meeting as 1895, but the event is well documented as having been in 1903. When you stop by a restaurant, order catfish if it's on the menu; this one-street town is enriched by catfish farming in the surrounding lakes. Just outside Tutwiler, by the foundation stones of the Whitfield M.B. church, is the marker that Lillian McMurray of Trumpet Records in Jackson (see page 162) erected for **Sonny Boy Williamson's grave**.

Rosedale evokes the Robert Johnson line 'Going Down to Rosedale/Take my rider by my side,' which the rock group Cream appropriated into the song Crossroads; nearby **Beulah** was the location for the crossroads in the 1986 movie of the same name. Rosedale is also a part of the famed Mississippi Blues Trail, so look for markers while in town.

Take MS 8 to **Dockery Plantation**, 25 miles (40km) away. Charley Patton lived and worked here, as did Pops Staples, patriarch of the Staples Singers. Sometimes known as the 'King of the Delta Blues' and certainly one of the early innovators, Patton was a source of inspiration to Howlin' Wolf, Son House, and John Lee Hooker. This is where he told Robert Johnson to: 'quit that noise before all the peoples leave.'

CLARKSDALE

In early August, the **Clarksdale Sunflower Festival** (www.sunflowerfest.org) is in distinguished company by featuring Mississippi musicians playing authentic Delta blues. Slide guitars, mouthharps and thumping rhythm sections drive the beats, and gravelly throats still wail the good-time songs in juke joints and bars all year round. As well

Mural of Mississippi jazz musician Robert Johnson.

⌀ CROSSROADS

Robert Johnson was taking a little time to build a reputation as a bluesman a good one, anyway: He was playing on Dockery Plantation one night when Charley Patton told him to 'Quit that noise before all the peoples leave.' Son House held a similarly meagre opinion of Johnson's efforts.

It all changed one night in Stovall, north of Clarksdale, when Johnson played in front of House and Willie Brown. Son House said later: 'When he finished, all our mouths were standing open. I said: 'Well, ain't that fast. Man, he's gone now'.'

House is believed to have started the rumour that Johnson acquired his astonishing prowess in a deal struck with the Devil. It was thought that the Devil could be met, and would be available for bargaining, if a player took his guitar to crossroads at midnight and began to pick the strings. The Devil would appear in the form of a Black man, take the instrument and tune it. Fluid licks of unheard splendor would then drip from the player's fingers, in exchange for the ownership of his soul.

The publishers of this book in no way advocate any form of dealing with Satan, as he is well known to be untrustworthy. Tuning, however, can be a help.

as being the home of the blues, **Clarks-dale** was the home of Tennessee Williams, and a literary festival is held annually in his honor. Clarksdale isn't a large town, and many of its best sites are grouped near each other, in an area known as Blues Alley. The **Delta Blues Museum** (1 Blues Alley; tel: 662-627-6820; www.deltabluesmuseum.org; Mon–Sat 10am–5pm), founded by Sid Graves, and aided by contributions from Texans ZZ Top, is at the epicenter. Most of the great Delta bluesmen are celebrated here, and the story of plantation life, so bound up with the evolution of the music, is well described, too. The gift shop offers scarce contemporary and older recordings, as well as a wealth of memorabilia.

The actor Morgan Freeman, a local resident, owns a popular club in Clarksdale: the relaxed, bare-wood furnished **Ground Zero** (387 Delta Avenue, tel: 662-621-9009; www.groundzerobluesclub.com; hours vary), which features local as well as traveling acts. Freeman himself can often be seen here.

Started in 2022, **Cathead Delta Blues Arts** (252 Delta Avenue, tel: 662-624-5992; www.cathead.biz; hours vary) promotes Mississippi, and particularly Delta artists of all kinds; paintings, photography, recordings and sculptures display much of the creativity of the area. Nearby, **Stackhouse Records** occupied the building resembling a riverboat. Those that want to hear live music should head to Red's Lounge (tel: 662-627-3166), where blues, juke, and nightlife combine in a classically Southern way. Folks can dance, sing, or clap to live music nightly.

Wade Walton's Barbershop on Issaquena Avenue was where W.C. Handy, Sonny Boy Williamson, and John Lee Hooker got their hair cut and swapped tales and licks. Farther along the same road, a plaque marks the location of **W.C. Handy's home**. Across the street is the **Greyhound** station that was the starting point for many bluesmen's journeys to Memphis and Chicago. The original location of the local radio station **WROX** (257 Delta Avenue) was where Early Wright

Ground Zero Blues Club.

became Mississippi's first Black DJ in 1947. Ike Turner started as a janitor and was later a DJ at WROX. The station still broadcasts on 1450AM.

Just across the railroad tracks is the New World District, where numerous jukes took up residence to entertain the ears of various patrons. This, being the 'wrong side of the tracks,' is where visitors are apt to be advised not to go, but good manners and discretion should be an adequate guide. Just across the tracks (under the bridge, in fact), a block along and a block to the left, is where old Highway 61 crossed with old Highway 49. If there was a Robert Johnson crossroads, and if it was in Clarksdale (both unlikely), this is where it would have been. The **Riverside Hotel** (615 Sunflower Avenue, tel: 601-624-9163; www.riversideclarksdale.com) is rich in blues history. The local Black hospital was in the right-hand side of the building, and when Bessie Smith met with a ghastly automobile accident in 1937, it was here that she was brought, and later died. Ike Turner claims to have resided in every room in the hotel. John F Kennedy, Jr also stayed here when hiding from the press. **Abe's Bar-B-Q** is a popular pork joint, just below the three blue guitars of the modern, much photographed but inaccurate **Crossroads sign**.

On the Hopson Plantation (tel: 662-624-5756; www.hopsonplantation. com) was America's first mechanized planting, picking and baling operation, and the Commissary is now a great place for a late drink or two, often with impromptu music supplied by guests from **Hopson's B&B (Bed & Beer) Shack Up Inn**. The inn offers unique accommodation in restored sharecropper cabins, complete with air-conditioning, and a couple of shacks that even have pianos. If you want to meet local musicians, this is one of the best place to stay in the area. To reach Hopson's from the Delta Blues Museum, take Sunflower Avenue and turn left onto US 61, then travel south onto US 49 a couple of miles until you see the sign.

TUNICA AND ROBINSONVILLE

US 61 leads to the town of **Tunica** ⑮. In 1992, there were 20 hotel rooms in Tunica County. Little over a decade later there were more than 6,000, such is the impact of legalized gambling. Tunica's **Blue and White Restaurant** has been serving authentic Mississippi cooking since 1924; Elvis was a regular, as are ZZ Top and other fans of turnip greens, grits, and red-eye gravy. The café is by the corner of US 61 and MS4 and open from 5am (tel: 662-363-1371; www.blueandwhiterestaurant.com). **Robinsonville** ⑯ is little more than a strip of casinos just north of Tunica. One of the most notable is the Horseshoe Hotel & Casino (tel: 800-303-7463), which is owned by Caesars, and has a spa and several restaurants on site. The on-site Bluesville often hosts headline acts that perform pop, rock, and country music.

A road in Clarksdale, home to blues music.

Shrimping boat at sunset
in Florida.

THE GULF COAST

A silver thread meandering along the Florida Panhandle, Alabama and Mississippi, the Gulf Coast is the sunshine playground of the South.

This magical silver strip of America's southern Gulf shore stretches from Florida through Alabama and Mississippi, all the way to Louisiana. Soft sea breezes caress the palms and grasses, long spits of sugar-white sands slip gently into the bright emerald waters of the Gulf of Mexico and the network of bays and lagoons that form the Intracoastal Waterway.

These sunshine playgrounds of the South hide from invading Yankees behind the discouraging nickname of 'the Redneck Riviera.' Although cowboy hats and beery country & western bars are not too hard to find in the popular resorts of Florida's Pensacola Beach and Destin, there are also beautiful quiet spots like Navarre Beach, as well as fabulous nature reserves in the Gulf Islands National Seashore. The 160 miles (257km) of barrier islands from Santa Rosa Island, Florida, to Cat Island in Mississippi fall under the administration of the National Parks Service. These represent only 20 percent of the reserve, the other 80 percent being underwater. They provide campgrounds, nature trails, picnic and hiking areas, and maintain several Civil War forts.

For the more cultivated and formal expressions of nature, there's the subtropical splendor of Bellingrath Gardens. More modern man-made recreation, especially of the

adult-oriented kind, is taken to its extremes in the mini-Las Vegas neon nirvanas of Biloxi and Gulfport in Mississippi. The gaming rooms and lavish shows glitter and sizzle in front of the seaside backdrop.

Southern hospitality is particularly fine in the B&Bs of Mississippi and Alabama, welcomes in Florida are warm, and the accents of Southern cooking are at their best with the wealth of fresh fish and seafood generously provided by the Gulf waters. As Bobby Mahoney, proprietor of Mary Mahoney's

Main attractions
National Museum of Naval Aviation
The John C. Stennis Space Center
Biloxi
Panama City Beach

Map on page 174

A beach on the Florida Panhandle.

Old French House in Biloxi, Mississippi, says: 'How can you explain the incredible amount of crawfish and lobster coming out of the muddy waters round here? There's a lot of loving going on in the dark of that mud.'

FLORIDA PANHANDLE

The 24-mile (37km) spits of soft sand along I-98 from Carillon Beach to Okaloosa Island are collectively known as the Emerald Coast, or **Fort Walton Beaches**, with beaches on both sides of the strip. Unfortunately, the Florida Panhandle took a direct hit from Hurricane Michael in 2018, but a determined outlook and feverish rebuilding means that many places are back in business – or soon will be. Nevertheless, it's a good idea to call ahead before you visit.

Beginning the continuous dash of white sands that sweeps all the way to Pensacola is **Panama City Beach** ❶. Lining the seafront Miracle Mile, Panama City Beach is a family resort, the Redneck Riviera in full cry. The bars twang with both kinds of music – country and western. Thrill rides

clatter by the miniature golf courses, and boats and jet-skis dart through the salt spray, the aroma of fried crawfish wafting on the air. Panama City Beach is also known for golf, voted third-best 'Little Golf Town in the US' by Golf Digest. Try **Bay Point Golf Club** (tel: 850-235-6950; www.baypointgolfclub.com), which hosts PGA qualifying schools.

SEASIDE

Some 44 miles (71km) west on the coastal highway is the town of **Seaside**, a remarkably, almost eerily pretty, planned community, a pioneer of what it calls 'the new urbanism.' J.S. Smolian bought 80 acres (32 hectares) of land in 1946, but it was his grandson, Robert Davis, who dreamed up this little fantasy land, where controls are strict and building regulations are meticulously studied. You can rent bikes from **Seaside Transit Authority Bike Rentals** in Central Square (tel: 850-231-0035; www.seasidetransitauthority.com), where there are numerous cute eateries, and **Cabana Man** in George's Gorge (tel: 850-231-5046; www.cabanaman.com) hires out beach chairs,

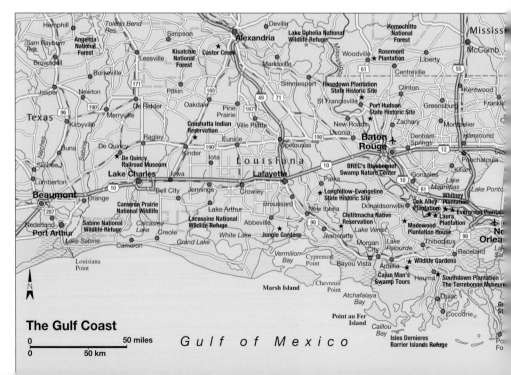

The Gulf Coast

0   50 miles

0   50 km

Gulf of Mexico

umbrellas, kayaks, and other beachy needs. A short way up the coast, **Grayton** is like a casual version of Seaside; a little less kept, a little more lived in. Trees overhang the small road and driveways are blown across with unbelievably white sand. On **Grayton Beach**, sushi fans particularly follow the neon to AJ's. Adjacent to the beach is a state park with cabins to rent (tel: 800-326-3521 for reservations). Back on 1-98, about 26 miles (42km) of soft, silvery white sand and deep green sea passes **Santa Rosa Beach**, a quiet, attractive little seafront town, to **Silver Sands Factory Stores**, which claims to be the US's largest concentration of designer outlets, with dozens of stellar names from Mallsville.

Another 8 miles (13km) farther on is the town of **Destin ②**. Offering an upscale version of the beach resort, Destin has large hotels, golf courses, and beach-town shops that proffer everything from beachwear and scuba kits to yachts. The nearby Eglin Air Force Base and test site is the world's largest, and Destin provides opportunities for the crew's recreation.

The busy but pretty marina gives harbor to well-maintained catamarans and fishing boats, and fishing is popular among tourists and off-duty Eglin jetjockeys alike. Visitors who are not Florida residents require a license for freshwater and seawater fishing, and they are available for three days, seven days or annually. Call 888-347-4356 to obtain a license. Deep-sea fishing trips are available from many companies, including Destin Princess (tel: 850-837-5088; www.destinpartyboatfishing.com). One of the local jet-jockeys said, 'If you want to know about the weather, just ask a pilot or a fisherman. What they get in Mobile today, we're gonna eat tomorrow.'

Turn inland, left, off 1-98 at Benning Drive for the huge **Gulfarium** (1010 Miracle Strip Parkway, tel: 850-243-9046; www.gulfarium.com; daily 9am–4.30pm), which has sea-life shows with dolphins, seals, sharks, moray eels, stingrays, and other water-dwellers. Rejoin the Miracle Strip Parkway (1-98) to the right and cross over the tall bridge. The hump in the middle allows

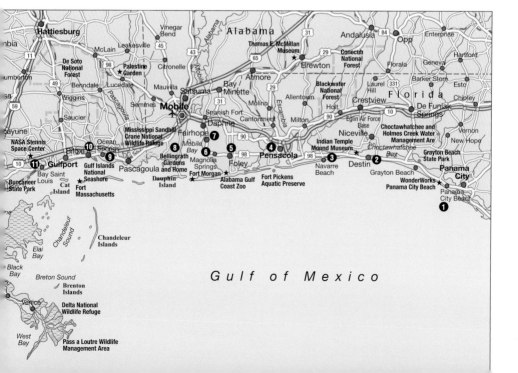

sailboats out to the Okaloosa Expanse and gives excellent views. A few miles farther along, 1-98 crosses the Intracoastal Waterway inland to **Fort Walton Beaches**.

In a shady garden off Highway 98 and built around a 223 by 178ft (68 by 54 meter) temple mound is the interesting **Indian Temple Mound Museum** (139 Miracle Strip Parkway, tel: 850-833-9595, Tue–Sat 10am–3pm). The mound itself was raised by Native Americans between AD 800 and 1400 and is the only surviving mound on the Gulf Coast. Native American technology, crafts, and artifacts are displayed with hands-on exhibits that kids love.

After Fort Walton Beach, I-98 continues on the north side of Santa Rosa Sound until Navarre, where a left turn will cross the sound again **to Navarre Beach** ❸. A few high-rise condos are beginning to huddle at each end of this otherwise unspoiled spot. Still popular with pelicans, and hardly more than a quarter of a mile long, Navarre Beach is quiet, slow, and laid-back. One diner said of the key lime pie at **Sailor's Grill**:

Fishing pier on Fort Walton Beach.

'I swear, this is the best. So good it's sinful.' Visitors to the grill (tel: 850-939-1092; www.juanaspagodas.com; daily 8am–9pm) are some connoisseurs of key lime pie. From here, the barrier island gets even slimmer, with the sugar-white sands of both coasts making for a pleasant drive, and buildings become more sparse. A few miles along is a picnic area with spots for swimming, and a park ranger's station. Sea oats and grasses fan the dunes, and sea birds skim the water.

FORT PICKENS

Pensacola Beach claims the longest pier on the Gulf of Mexico at 1471ft (448 meters). There's fishing off the pier for snapper and redfish. The more popular chain hotels like Ramada and Comfort Inn are well represented.

Reached through **Fort Pickens State Park**, a 6.5-mile (11km) spit of white sand with the Gulf close by on either side, is **Fort Pickens**. A museum describes the part that the fort played holding Mobile Bay for the Union during the Civil War. This area of land

has campgrounds and endless space for picnics or beach relaxation, hiking, and birdwatching. Returning from Fort Pickens, turn left and cross the toll bridge at Navarre Beach to **Gulf Breeze**. To the left are beach and fishing areas, and, to the right on I-98, the **Naval Live Oaks Nature Preserve** headquarters. The visitor center presents exhibits celebrating the distinctive live oak, so much a feature of the Southern states, and is the starting point for some of the hiking trails through the 1,378-acre (558-hectare) wooded park area. Among the woods are trails and remnants from the Native American cultures that resided here for at least 10,000 years.

PENSACOLA

Over the fine 3-mile (5km) bridge to **Pensacola ❹**, and a sharp and immediate turn-off to the right is the **Visitor Center** (1401 East Gregory Street; tel: 800-874-1234; www.visitpensacola.com; Mon–Fri 9am–5pm, Sat and Sun 9am–4pm), well-stocked with information on accommodations and local attractions, in addition to the rich history of this significant Southern coastal city. The grounds are good for picnics, with extensive views over Pensacola Bay. Pensacola's main historic districts – Palafox, Seville, and the North Hill Preservation district – offer numerous examples of Southern architectural and cultural influence, from modest colonial homes to mansions with wrought-iron filigree, as well as many museums.

From the visitor center, take the Bayfront Parkway and turn right on Adams Street to the large green square and the handsome **Old Christ Church**, a white wooden church with brown shutters, high, arched windows, and stained glass at the rear. This is the heart of the **Seville Historic District**, the oldest part of Pensacola. Historic house museums are dotted along **Government, Church, and Zaragosa streets**. The town's administration passed between states no fewer than 17 times in 300 years of history, as celebrated in the annual Fiesta of Five Flags around **Seville Square**.

The **Palafox Historic District** congregates around Palafox Street and Plaza Ferdinand. At one end of the tranquil plaza is a fountain, at the other, a bust of General Andrew Jackson to mark his receiving West Florida from Spain in 1817. The castellated honey-brick **Pensacola Museum of History** (330 South Jefferson Street; tel: 850-595-5990; www.historicpensacola.org; Tue–Sat 10am–4pm, Sun 12pm–4pm) fronts the square with neoclassical detail. Slightly north of here in the Palafox neigborhood, the **North Hill Preservation District** has more than 400 private historic homes, and an interesting mix of architecture. One of the world's finest collections of aircraft is kept at the **National Museum of Naval Aviation** (1750 Radford Boulevard; tel: 850-452-8450; www.navalaviationmuseum.org; daily 9am–4pm). This passes **Fort Barrancas**, first established by the British in 1763 and now operated as a museum as part of the National Seashore.

With 32 miles (51km) of white sand coastline between Mobile Bay and Perdido Bay, and the Gulf of Mexico on the south shore, the creation of the underrated **Intracoastal Waterway** in 1933 made **Gulf Shores** into an island. To reach **Perdido Key** on the island, follow SR 282 for about 9.5 miles (15km). 'Pleasure Islands' as the Key is now branded, offers the usual Redneck Riviera resort diversions, hurricane damage notwithstanding, alongside the beauty of Gulf Islands National Seashore, excellent for deep-sea fishers and golfers.

ALABAMA COAST

Continue on the coastal highway across the border into Alabama. Here the island communities of **Orange Beach** and **Gulf Shores** have fabulous broad stretches of sugar-white sand, backed by low-key resorts with pleasant hotels, beach houses, and seafood restaurants. Alternatively, take I-98 for about 20 miles (32km) to where the cute, old-style appearance of the town of **Foley** ❺ belies a little shopper's mecca. Antiques stores abound around the town itself, while not far away is the excellent complex housing the **Tanger Outlet Center** (2601 South McKenzie

Magnolia Springs.

Street, tel: 251-943-9303; www.tanger-outlet.com/foley). Tanger has scores of outlet stores that lure crowds from miles around, attracted by upscale bargains from stores like Kate Spade, Coach, Tommy Hilfiger, Le Creuset, Nike, Reebok, and J Crew.

Magnolia Springs 6 has the last water-borne mail delivery in the US, which gives a clue to the nature of this quiet community. The pace is unhurried, manners are gentle and old-fashioned, and it is a lovely base from which to explore the beautiful **Azalea Coast**. Home and birthplace to a number of authors including Winston Groom who wrote *Forrest Gump*, Fannie Flagg, author of *Fried Green Tomatoes at the Whistle Stop Cafe*, a community of writers and artists is thriving and growing in the shade of the live oaks.

One block left of where Highway 49 crosses I-98 is **Magnificent Magnolia** (tel: 251-965-6232), an art gallery that stimulates the muses of the locality, providing a nurturing retreat for writers and artists. In **Jesse's Restaurant** (14770 Oak Street, tel: 251-965-3827; www.jessesrestaurant.com) try a pecan-encrusted catfish Caesar salad or the excellent whiskey steak. David Worthington at **The Magnolia Springs Bed and Breakfast** (14469 Oak Street, tel: 251-965-7321; www.magnoliasprings.com) offers Southern B&B hospitality as gracefully as anyone could hope for, in a home that is on the National Register of Historic Places.

Continue on I-98 and turn left onto Alternate-98 along the lovely wooded coastline of Mobile Bay to **Punta Clara**, also known by the English translation, 'Point Clear.' On the left is the **Punta Clara Kitchen** (tel: 800-437-7868; www.puntaclara.com). A lovely candy-colored deck with a swinging sofa wraps around the rooms of cutesy antiques, from glasses to furniture, packed like The Old Curiosity Shop. The Candy Kitchen sells jams, local honey, fudge, peanut-butter crunch, lots of old-style American

favorite treats, and novelty candies like blue crabs that you can watch being made. Behind the Punta Clara Kitchen, the **Wash House Restaurant** serves crab cakes, swamp quail appetizers, tuna, snapper, and steak entrees with Southern accents, on white linen settings with silver cutlery.

A short way farther on Alternate-98 is the **Autograph Collection Grand Hotel Golf Resort and Spa**. Despite the ravages of fire and hurricanes, a Grand Hotel has stood here since the Civil War, when it was used as a hospital for wounded Confederates at Vicksburg.

North about 2.5 miles (4km), **Fairhope 7** is a little nest of prim, often-pretty streets, with pastel facades. Garbage cans have white wooden surrounds topped with flowers, and antiques parlors sell vintage linen. Art galleries and bookstores are everywhere. The sleepy residential community rolls down a steep bluff, with Creole-style cottages overlooking the bay. Nice walks by the sparkling bay meander through palms and live oak trees, while wooden piers jut in a line

Fairhope, Alabama.

into the water. The bay communities celebrate Mardi Gras with parades and floats, and Fairhope sprinkles a little visual class along the processions of floats with lights in the trees. This gives the town the look of a fairy-palace when glimpsed after dark.

Take the Scenic 98 road north, as the views of Mobile Bay are easily worth the detour. About 5 miles (9km) along, **Daphne** seems like a one-street town, more workaday than Fairhope, but the highway is shaded by trees, and there are also a good number of eateries, handy in Mardi Gras season when Fairhope is mobbed. Off the highway to the west are a beach and some little shops. Go back on I-98 for about 4 miles (7km) and make a right turn on I-90 to **Malbis** to see a stunning Greek Orthodox replica of a Byzantine Athenean church (28300 Highway 27, tel: 251-626-6739; hours limited, call ahead). Then return along I-90 and join I-10 across the bay, past Mobile (see page 148).

Bellingrath Gardens and Home ❽ (tel: 251-973-2217; www.bellingrath.org; daily 8am–5pm) is one of the Deep South's most beautiful gardens and more than worth the 20-mile (32km) excursion south to Theodore. Take I-10 west to exit 15-A, then follow the signs and turn south on Bellingrath Road. Bring comfortable walking shoes, take lots of photos, and plan to stay two to three hours. The flowers are best photographed in early morning or late afternoon.

When you leave the reception area, visit the Rose Garden and the Oriental area with teahouses and bright red bridges over a tranquil lake. Follow the path to Mirror Lake; the view across the water toward the home is one of the most photographed. Bellingrath Gardens is legendary for the 200 varieties of 250,000 azalea shrubs, 90,000 daffodils, countless tulips, and dogwood trees that bloom in the spring. Thousands of rosebushes fill the grounds with color in winter, while some 70,000 chrysanthemums provide a blaze of color in the fall. Yellow, white, bronze, red and pink mums cascade over the sides of bridges, walls, and planters and from the balconies of the house itself.

The tour of the 15-room home the Bellingraths built in 1937 is worth the additional time spent to see their collection of Persian rugs, silver, and furniture. The Chippendale dining table and chairs once belonged to Sir Thomas Lipton, the English shipping magnate.

MISSISSIPPI COAST

Off to the left on I-90, just before Ocean Springs, is the park entrance for the **Davis Bayou**. Follow Park Road about 4 miles (7km) to the attractive visitor center. In addition to information about camping, hiking and biking trails, birdwatching, and boating on the bayou, the center has a pretty exhibition of wildlife paintings from local artist Walter Anderson.

Take I-90 another few miles to **Ocean Springs** ❾. Just a short bridge

Bellingrath Gardens and Home.

away from the extravagant pleasure palaces of Biloxi, Ocean Springs is a quiet, relaxed and beautiful bayside home to an artistic and boating community. The atmosphere and desirable houses make it popular as a residence for upscale casino staff from its brash bayfront neighbor city.

Start from the far end of town at the **Ocean Springs Visitor Center**, prettily housed in the old train station and adorned outside with intriguing sculptures. The **Walter Anderson Museum of Art** (510 Washington Avenue, tel: 228-872-3164; www.walterandersonmuseum.org; Mon–Sat 11am–5pm, Sun 1pm–5pm) showcases Anderson's prolific artistic passions, by turns naive, psychedelic, and beautiful. Much of this reclusive artist's work was discovered only after his demise.

BILOXI

Along the **Biloxi** ❿ shoreline, a long stretch of mega-casinos, smaller versions of the Las Vegas hotel resorts, lean back on their pontoons and extend a willing and eager welcome. Among the bayfront casinos, **Margaritaville Resort Biloxi** is a class act. The barkeepers at the elegant lounge by the casino entrance shake up superb topshelf cocktails, and the Margueritas are particularly fine. Several mini-suites have large Jacuzzis in the rooms. The gaming rooms are pitched squarely at the value end of the market, offering friendly bar areas and competitive odds. **Beau Rivage** is a sister hotel to Steve Wynn's spectacular Las Vegas creation, Bellagio. There are glitters of similarity, and Beau Rivage doesn't want for luxurious appointments. The walls are hung with works of art, the spa and health center are beautifully designed and equipped, and the BetMGM Book Bar & Grill is a great place to grab a drink and watch a live game on the HDTVs.

In **Biloxi's Historic District**, called Vieux Marche (so near to Louisiana, a smattering of French is not uncommon) is a charming antiques market. Although known as 'The Mad Potter of Biloxi' in his lifetime, George E. Ohr's ceramics have been much admired by

Blues Comission sign in Ocean Springs.

One of the oldest buildings in Biloxi, Mississippi.

Biloxi Lighthouse.

Ohr-O'Keefe Museum of Art .

luminaries of the art world, including Andy Warhol. He is now known as 'America's most innovative potter.' The **Ohr-O'Keefe Museum of Art** (tel: 228-374-5547; www.georgeohr.org; Tue–Sat 10am–5pm, Sun 1pm-5pm) is dedicated to his work. The museum, which is well worth visiting, is named after Ohr and Annette O'Keefe, who was instrumental in raising funds for the museum. Designed by no other than Frank Gehry, the sculptural innovator of the Guggenheim Museum in Bilbao, Spain, the collection is well curated and the building is a sight to behold in its own right.

For those that wish to view Biloxi from the water, take a ride on the **Betsy Ann Riverboat** (tel: 228-229-4270; www.betsyannriverboat.com). Various cruise themes are available, such as Twisted Tiki Tours, the Historical and Ecological Tour, and a Hibachi Dinner Cruise. For the romantics at heart, the Sunset Cruise is always a hit because it combines the beauty of the water with the blazing colors of the nighttime sky.

Farther along Vieux Marche, the 1954 Taylor Building and its lovely neighbor, the Kreb Building, are an attractive pairing of Art Deco and Art Nouveau.

The pretty **Biloxi Lighthouse** is unusual for standing in the middle of a major road. There are restrooms at the foot of the lighthouse.

BEAUVOIR

A graceful and charming raised single-story antebellum home, with a presidential library in a more federal style, **Beauvoir** (2244 Beach Boulevard; tel: 228-388-4400; www.visitbeauvoir.org; daily 9am–5pm) is set back from the road and faces the sandy beach of the Gulf shore. This is the home of Jefferson Davis, referred to as the first president of the Confederacy, signalling that there may remain fond hopes for another.

Tours are about every 20 minutes, and waiting is on the gracious porch with half-a-dozen Southern-style rocking chairs. A small Museum of the Confederacy features memorabilia like

cannon, muskets, and uniforms. There are pictures from Davis's funeral featuring the horse-drawn hearse draped in black, with crossed rifles guarding the casket.

West along I-10, the unusual sight of cranes and silos on the gulf shows that **Gulfport** is a working town. Opportunities for recreation are available from a number of waterfront casinos, and relaxed dining at the attractive **Shaggy's Gulfport Beach** restaurant, sitting on stilts overlooking the marina, can provide consolation after a stint at the gaming tables.

The houses along the coast begin to stand taller and flex a little wider around **Pass Christian**; they settle back behind decorative gates and neat lawns. The comfy residences are set back from the road by a meridian of greenery and live oak trees. A large, elegant and modern Catholic church with exposed bells is hard to miss while in town. Follow I-90 and turn off after the long bridge to **Bay Saint Louis ⑪**, where the calm water turns silver. There are cute shops and a gorgeous **Amtrak station** in palm-shaded grounds. Houses are braced to the elements with frilly white latticework and large screened porches, and many of the newer houses are raised on stilts. The **Buccaneer State Park** has a campground near the water, in a wonderful, wooded setting.

Leave I-10 at Exit 2 for the **John C. Stennis Space Center** (1100 Balch Boulevard; tel: 228-688-3333; www.nasa.gov/centers/stennis; photo ID is required to tour the facility; see box). This massive site is NASA's primary rocket testing facility. A lunar module stands on stilts by the welcome center, and inside is a scale model of the space shuttle on a complete booster pack. Nearby are picnic grounds in a pretty wooded area. Shuttle buses leave every 15 minutes for the narrated tours of Stennis, which take in the huge acoustic buffer zone to America's largest rocket test complex. There are many fascinating exhibits, including a scale model of a complete Saturn 5-Apollo rocket stack, as well as some real rocket engines.

A beach home on stilts, along the Gulf of Mexico near Bay St. Louis.

⊘ ROCKET TESTING

The John C. Stennis Space Center, located on the Mississippi–Louisiana state border, is NASA's largest rocket engine testing facility. The site was originally chosen because of river access, a crucial component in transporting the enormous Apollo rocket motors; too grand in scale to be moved overland. The 13,500-acre (5,463-hectare) testing site is surrounded by a 125,000-acre (50,585-hectare) acoustic buffer zone, necessary to dissipate the roar of the rockets.

Since the site was officially opened in 1961, it has helped develop every major NASA rocket engine, including those for the Apollo missions to the moon and the Space Shuttle engines. Rolls Royce also operates aero-engine testing facilities here.

NASA'S BEST KEPT FACILITIES

Florida and Texas might be famed for NASA's launch and control centers, but the USA's earth-based space exploration experts can be found at facilities across the South.

You might not think of Mississippi as the backbone of NASA's rocket testing facilities, or indeed Alabama as America's best-kept collection of spacecraft, but you'd be wrong. For it is in these Southern states, with wilderness vast enough to drown out the sound of rocket testing, that NASA thrives.

THE JOHN C. STENNIS SPACE CENTER

All space rockets have to be tested somewhere. For NASA, this place is the John C. Stennis Space Center. It was here that the massive Apollo rocket thrusters were first tested before going on to send man to the moon.

The days of giant barges ferrying Apollo-sized rockets to this space center might be confined to history, but today this testing facility is a hub of activity; not just for NASA's next generation of space travel to Mars, but also for the likes of Rolls Royce, who share this facility for testing cutting-edge aircraft engines.

A billowing plume of steam signals a successful 450-second test of the RS-25 rocket engine at NASA's John C. Stennis Space Center.

Test complexes at the John C. Stennis Space Center.

An Apollo Saturn S-IC rocket stage is removed from the test stand at the John C. Stennis Space Center.

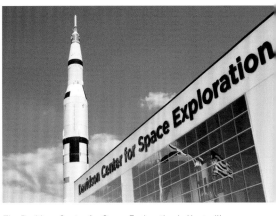

The Davidson Center for Space Exploration in Huntsville.

The US Space and Rocket Center Museum

Undeniably the largest museum of rockets on the planet, the US Space and Rocket Center Museum in Huntsville, Alabama, gives Cape Canaveral in Florida a run for its money. It's been a part of the South's space exploration-infused DNA since the early days of extra-terrestrial exploration, and its first exhibits date back to the second manned mission to the moon.

Today, there are almost 1,5000 pieces of space-exploring hardware on display at the museum, showcasing the collective efforts of NASA and the US military in pushing bravely ahead into the final frontier. Visitor favorites include the Space Shuttle Pathfinder and the military's sizeable Project Nike rockets, which constitute America's first attempt at ballistic missile defense.

However, it is the lunar achievements of the Apollo project that take center stage at the museum. The Apollo 16 lander capsule occupies pride of place, as the piece of human engineering that took us to the moon and back. Another popular exhibit is the grave of Miss Baker, a squirrel monkey NASA test subject, who successfully completed a suborbital test flight of the PGM-19 Jupiter rocket in 1959. After securing her place in history, Miss Baker became a much-loved and well cared for guest of the museum, until she passed away in 1984.

...unar landing rover at the Space and Rocket Center Museum.

...he Saturn V S-1C-15 rocket stage arrives at the John C. ...tennis Space Center on June 16, 2016.

Saturn V rocket and lunar landing module at the Space and Rocket Center Museum.

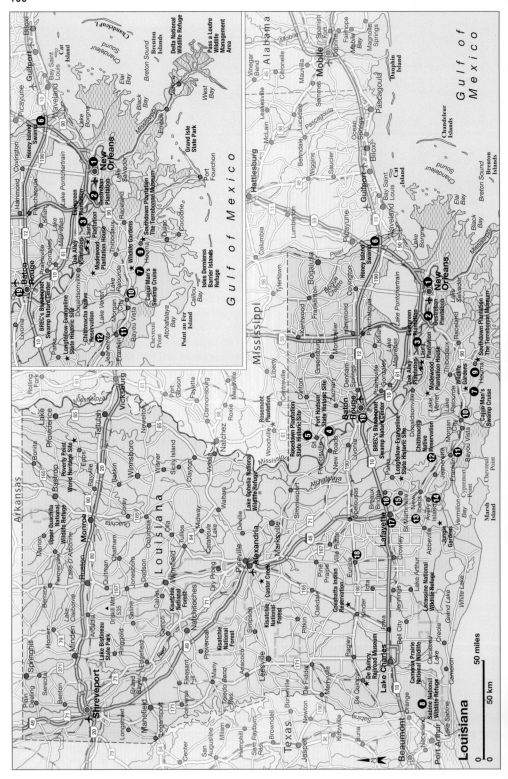

LOUISIANA

The fertile bowl of Louisiana teems between the Gulf of Mexico and the mighty Mississippi River, drizzled with swamps and bayous.

Alligators, egrets, and turtles bask in the steaming marsh grass, languishing in the mist. Bald cypress, palmetto, and black gum trees simmer in the swamplands under the tropical sun. Meanwhile, this vast natural hothouse has propagated equally lush human cultures. The diversity and spice of culinary creativity gives a taste of how rich a cultural feast Louisiana has to offer, with French sauces, Creole and Cajun slow cooking.

The three main cities are the Cajun capital Lafayette, the state capital Baton Rouge, and the Big Easy itself, New Orleans, all have their own distinct and unique ambience. The large Acadian Cultural Center in Lafayette, and the Acadian Memorial to le grand derangement in St Martinville tell of how French-Canadians transplanted to make the bayous their home, but in the towns around the River Teche, those stories have grown into a living modern reality. Cajun accordions and two-steps to lilting French lyrics are still at the heart of an exuberant social life. It's easy to find, with gumbo and *étoufée* on the side, especially in places like Breaux Bridge, Eunice, and New Iberia. As they say: *laissez les bontemps roulez.* ('let the good times roll').

Brash and beautiful Baton Rouge is an aggressive, modern city, but with a laid-back Louisiana drawl.

Louisiana swamp filled with cypress trees.

Baton Rouge also exemplifies a relaxed approach to political propriety, nowhere more so than in the Capitol building, itself a hot spot for debate and no holds barred confrontations.

New Orleans is the town that most of the world's musicians either wish they were from, or wish they could live in. You can stroll along just about any street and be seduced in about five paces by a beat, a riff, or the moan of a saxophone. Sample the simmering and sizzling delights of the French Quarter and, whatever the time of year,

Main attractions

New Orlean's French Quarter
Steamboat Natchez
The New Orleans Jazz Museum
Bourbon Street
Voodoo Museum
St Louis Cemetery No. 1
Cajun Country
Lafayette
Baton Rouge

Maps on pages 186, 190

somewhere there is bound to be a festival going on in what must surely be America's favorite party town. Most notably of course is Mardi Gras, which for some is just too much party, as well as, in April or May, perhaps the world's finest music festival, JazzFest.

For an immersion of history, take a trip through the splendor and grace of the antebellum and plantation homes along the Great River Road, up to the jewel-box town of St Francisville. These are places where vast acres of cotton fields with hundreds of enslaved people were ruled by either a kindly ole marse or a mean-eyed monster, long the popular stuff of novels and screenplays.

That hot, hot air, all that water, and the fecund black soil; the joy and sheer lust for life in Louisiana is irrepressible.

NEW ORLEANS

New Orleans  may be the birthplace of jazz, but it's Creole cooking, Spanish moss, steamboats and the French

St Louis Cathedral in New Orleans.

Quarter that spice the Big Easy's gumbo.

The 'City that Care Forgot' feels more like a Caribbean dominion than an American town. The almost constant festivals, the predominantly Black population, the exotic culture with an undercurrent of voodoo in the air; and the sound of music creeping and seeping out of every window and doorway, are all part of an atmosphere unique in the USA. Not for nothing is this America's favorite party town.

The Big Easy's most famous attraction is the **French Quarter**, the original colony of La Nouvelle Orleans, and its centerpiece is **Jackson Square**. Also called the Vieux Carre (Old Square), Jackson Square's buildings are small and colorful, with steep gables, sloping roofs, dormer windows, and graceful fanlight windows. Jackson Square was known to the French Creoles as Place d'Annes and to the Spanish Colonials as Plaza de Armas.

Stately **St Louis Cathedral** Ⓐ (tel: 504-525-9585, tours daily, except during services, www.saintlouiscathedral.org) is the square's most imposing building. The first church on this site was a small wooden structure, designed in 1724 by Adrien de Pauger, the French engineer who surveyed the original colony. It was named for Louis IX, the 13th-century saint-king of France who fought in two Crusades. The present cathedral dates from 1851.

SPANISH TREASURES

The two historic buildings flanking St Louis Cathedral are the **Cabildo** and the **Presbytere**. Both buildings date from the Spanish Colonial period and are now part of the **Louisiana State Museum** complex. The Presbytere (751 Chartres Street; tel: 504-568-6968; www.louisianastatemuseum.org/museum/presbytere; Tue–Sun 9am–4.00pm), on the right as you face the cathedral, was begun in 1795. The Casa Curial, as it was called by the Spanish, or

HURRICANE KATRINA

As the sun began to rise over the Gulf Coast on the morning of August 29, 2005, the world watched in horror as a massive hurricane hit New Orleans with a force that will never be forgotten, leaving scars that may never fully heal.

At first the strength and trajectory of the storm were uncertain, and it might even have bypassed New Orleans at one stage, but, after becoming a Category 5 hurricane over the Gulf of Mexico, Katrina hit the city to devastating effect. Nearly 2,000 people perished in the initial impact and subsequent flooding; many who survived lost absolutely everything. Property damage from Katrina, which spread from Florida to Texas, was estimated at as much as $180 billion. To give an idea of the force of the incoming water in New Orleans, entire houses were pushed off their foundations and propelled down the streets.

Low-lying New Orleans been under threat of flooding throughout its history and has always had levees along the waterline for protection. However, not only were inadequate, but they had been poorly maintained too, and Katrina's initial surge breached the defenses and consumed some 80 percent of the city.

Massive emergency measures came into play immediately, from local amateur radio buffs providing communications to a long list of NGOs, including the American Red Cross and the Salvation Army, rushing to the aid of the beleaguered population. However, they were unable to actually enter the city until it was deemed safe for them to do so, several days later. In the meantime, they collected the donations that began to pour in – more than $5 billion from individuals and corporate sources, along with pledges of money and other forms of help from many foreign countries.

Over the intervening years, some of those billions have been spent on the reconstruction of flood defenses to encircle the city, with over 350 miles (563km) of new levees, flood walls, and pumps, although some doubts have been expressed as to whether the planners took into account the threat of rising sea levels. Within the city, most buildings have been repaired or replaced, although there remain empty lots on some streets, and some evacuees never returned – the population today is still less than its pre-Katrina figure. But there are still historic and beautiful parts of New Orleans that weren't damaged at all, and the heart, soul, and character of the city has rebounded with all the charm and *joie de vivre* that has always made it a great place to visit.

Following the disaster, the agency that allots names to hurricanes removed Katrina from its list of options. It is to be hoped that there will also literally never be another Hurricane Katrina.

Devastation caused by Hurricane Katrina.

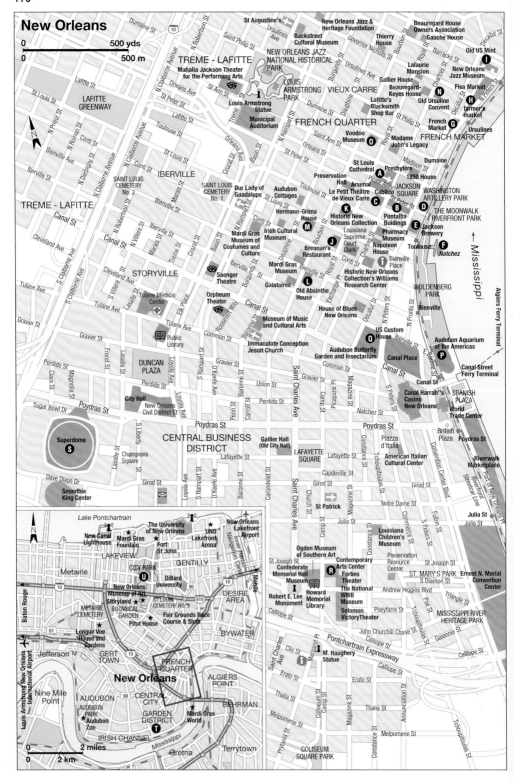

New Orleans

0 _____ 500 yds
0 _____ 500 m

LAFITTE GREENWAY

TREME - LAFITTE

Mahalia Jackson Theater for the Performing Arts

Louis Armstrong Statue

Municipal Auditorium

NEW ORLEANS JAZZ NATIONAL HISTORICAL PARK

LOUIS ARMSTRONG PARK

St Augustine's

New Orleans Jazz & Heritage Foundation

Backstreet Cultural Museum

Thierry House

Beauregard House Owners Association

Gauche House

Lalaurie Mansion

Gallier House

Beauregard-Keyes House

Old US Mint

New Orleans Jazz Museum

Flea Market

Old Ursuline Convent

farmer's market

VIEUX CARRE

Lafitte's Blacksmith Shop Bar

French Market

Ursulines

FRENCH QUARTER

FRENCH MARKET

Voodoo Museum

Madame John's Legacy

Dumaine

St Louis Cathedral

Presbytère

1850 House

Preservation Hall

Arsenal

Cabildo

JACKSON SQUARE

WASHINGTON ARTILLERY PARK

THE MOONWALK RIVERFRONT PARK

Le Petit Théâtre de Vieux Carré

Our Lady of Guadalupe

Audubon Cottages

Hermann-Grima House

Historic New Orleans Collection

Pontalba Buildings

Pharmacy Museum

Jackson Brewery

SAINT LOUIS CEMETERY No. 2

SAINT LOUIS CEMETERY No. 1

IBERVILLE

TREME - LAFITTE

Irish Cultural Museum

Louisiana Supreme Court Clerk

Napoleon House

Natchez

Mardi Gras Museum of Costumes and Culture

Brennan's Restaurant

Bienville Place

Historic New Orleans Collection's Williams Research Center

STORYVILLE

Saenger Theatre

Mardi Gras Museum

WOLDENBERG PARK

Galatoires

Old Absinthe House

Bienville

Tulane Medical Center

Orpheum Theater

House of Blues New Orleans

Museum of Music and Cultural Arts

US Custom House

Audubon Aquarium of the Americas

Public Library

Immaculate Conception Jesuit Church

Audubon Butterfly Garden and Insectarium

Canal Place

Canal Street Ferry Terminal

DUNCAN PLAZA

Canal St

SPANISH PLAZA

City Hall

New Orleans Civil District Ct

Canal Harrah's Casino New Orleans

World Trade Center

Superdome

CENTRAL BUSINESS DISTRICT

Gallier Hall (Old City Hall)

LAFAYETTE SQUARE

British Plaza

Piazza d'Italia

Poydras St

Riverwalk Marketplace

Champions Square

American Italian Cultural Center

Smoothie King Center

St Patrick

Julia St

Louisiana Children's Museum

Riverfront Streetcar Line

Ogden Museum of Southern Art

Contemporary Arts Center

Preservation Resource Center

ST. MARY'S PARK

Ernest N. Morial Convention Center

Lake Pontchartrain

New Canal Lighthouse

Mardi Gras Fountain

The University of New Orleans

UNO Lakefront Arena

New Orleans Lakefront Airport

Fort St John

LAKEVIEW

GENTILLY

Metairie

CITY PARK

Dillard University

DESIRE AREA

Mobile

New Orleans Museum of Art

Storyland

BOTANICAL GARDEN

ST. LOUIS CEMETERY NO. 3

Fair Grounds Race Course & Slots

Confederate Memorial Hall Museum

Forbes Theater

Robert E. Lee Monument

Howard Memorial Library

The National WWII Museum

METAIRIE CEMETERY

Longue Vue House and Gardens

Pitot House

BYWATER

Solomon VictoryTheater

MISSISSIPPI RIVER HERITAGE PARK

Jefferson

GERT TOWN

FRENCH QUARTER

M. Haughery Statue

Pontchartrain Expressway

Nine Mile Point

AUDUBON PARK

CENTRAL CITY

GARDEN DISTRICT

ALGIERS POINT

Audubon Zoo

Mardi Gras World

BEHRMAN

IRISH CHANNEL

0 _____ 2 miles
0 _____ 2 km

Gretna

Terrytown

COLISEUM SQUARE PARK

Baton Rouge

Louis Armstrong New Orleans International Airport

New Orleans

Mississippi

Presbytere to the French, was intended as a home for the priests who served the church but was never used for that purpose. A part of the museum complex since the early 20th century, the Presbytere houses an extensive **Mardi Gras exhibit**.

One of the most important structures in the city is the **Cabildo** (701 Chartres Street; tel: 504-568-6968; www.louisianastatemuseum.org/museum/cabildo; Tue–Sun 9am–4:00pm). Work began in 1795, but it wasn't fully completed until after the Americans took control of the city in 1803. Archaeologists discovered part of a wall from a 1750s police guardhouse that had been incorporated into the building, and it was in the room on the second floor called the Sala Capitular that transfer papers for the Louisiana Purchase were signed in 1803.

The buildings lining St Peter and St Ann streets are the **Pontalba Buildings** **B**, identical structures that were constructed in 1849 and 1850 and named for the colorful woman who financed and saw to their completion. Each building consists of 16 rowhouses: 12 units facing Jackson Square, two facing Decatur Street, and two facing Chartres Street. The 'lower' Pontalbas, on St Ann Street, are the property of the state of Louisiana, and the 'upper' Pontalbas on St Peter Street belong to the city of New Orleans. ('Lower' and 'upper' refer to the downriver and upriver sides of Jackson Square.) In the lower Pontalbas, the Louisiana State Museum maintains the **1850 House** (523 St Ann Street; tel: 504-524-9118; www.louisianastatemuseum.org/museum/1850-house; Tue–Sun (9:30am–4pm). The upper Pontalbas has several vintage clothing boutiques and various eateries. It also houses the New Orleans School of Cooking, where visitors need to stop by and try the fresh pralines, which are available to be shipped worldwide.

Across St Peter Street from the Cabildo is **Le Petit Theatre du Vieux**

Carre **C** (616 St Peter Street; tel: 504-522-2081; www.lepetittheatre.com), the oldest continually operating community theater in America, performing on this site since 1919. At 632 St Peter Street, a plaque declares that Tennessee Williams wrote *A Streetcar Named Desire* in an apartment in the building. Williams scholars claim that the playwright was inspired by the streetcar that used to rattle down Royal Street.

RIVERFRONT TO THE FRENCH MARKET

Just across Decatur Street is **Washington Artillery Park** **D**. This is a wonderful place to get a picture-postcard overview of Jackson Square and the Mississippi River. Street performers are often out in full force, and the mournful sound of a jazz trumpet is never far away. From here you can walk across the riverfront streetcar tracks to **Moonwalk**, a wooden walkway smack on the river. This is one of the finest places in town to watch the ever-changing parade of tugs, fanciful riverboats, and serious cargo ships

Pontalba Buildings.

Beignets at Cafe du Monde.

and tankers on the river, especially at sunset. Unfortunately, this is also a pretty good place to be harassed by panhandlers.

The large building nearby is the **Jackson (or Jax) Brewery** . The restored structure dates back to 1891, and for many years the popular Jax Beer was brewed on these premises; today it's a small mall in lush architectural surrounds. Two other sister properties house similar stores and eateries, many with views of the Mississippi River.

The ever-colorful **Steamboat Natchez** (tel: 504-569-1401; www.steamboatnatchez.com; offering harbor/jazz cruises and dinner/jazz cruises) docks behind the Jax Brewery at the Toulouse Street Wharf. An authentic paddlewheeler, this great floating white wedding cake offers delightful calliope concerts to passengers who take the sightseeing cruises. Nearby is **Cafe du Monde** (800 Decatur Street; tel: 504-587-0833; www.cafedumonde.com). Open early til late, the café is a New Orleans legend; it has been on this spot for more than 100 years and is the place for *café au lait* and *beignets* (little crispy doughnuts with messy powdered sugar on top). Café du Monde is the anchor of the **French Market** , a shopping complex with colonnades, arcades, and specialty stores.

Open-air cafés such as the Gazebo are great places to sample the sounds of Dixieland, and free concerts are regularly held in Dutch Alley. Concert schedules are available at the **Dutch Alley information kiosk** at the foot of St Philip Street. Park rangers at the Jean Lafitte National Historical Park offers free tours of the French Quarter and the Garden District, and supply information about the city and the region. Farmers have been bringing fresh produce to the **farmer's market** for more than 160 years. Sightseers and locals cram the aisles of the open-air shed, picking through bins of fresh fruits, vegetables, garlic, and pecans. There are also booths piled with wallets, jewelry, and other nonedible market goods. On weekends, a well-attended open-air flea market takes place at the rear of the farmer's market.

The **New Orleans Jazz Museum** can be found in the **Old US Mint** (400 Esplanade Avenue, tel: 504-568-6993; www.nolajazzmuseum.org; Tue–Sun 9am–4pm), which fronts onto Esplanade Avenue, has a fine jazz exhibit, including one of Loni Armstrong's first trumpets. The building houses an excellent jazz archive, which is available free to bona fide researchers. The mint, a massive three-story Greek-Revival structure, was constructed in 1835 on the site of an old Spanish fort. One of the first regional branches of the United States Mint, it produced about $5 million a month in coins. However, it was in operation for less than 30 years; the mint was closed in 1862 when Union forces occupied New Orleans during the War Between the States.

Steamboat Natchez.

ROYAL STREET

In the 19th century, the intersection of Conti and Royal streets was the banking center of the French Quarter. Money is the keynote here, and enjoyment of its pleasures is enhanced if you happen to have a lot of it, for this is the place to find upscale boutiques and fine restaurants.

The world-famous **Brennan's Restaurant** ❶ (tel: 504-525-9711; www.brennansneworleans.com) is located at 417 Royal Street. The building was constructed around the turn of the 19th century as a residence for the maternal grandfather of French Impressionist painter Edgar Degas. Shortly thereafter it was bought by the Banque de la Louisiane, as can be seen in the initials 'BL' that were worked into the fancy wrought-iron balcony. Across the street from Brennan's is a white marble building. This handsome structure, built between 1907 and 1909, now houses the **Louisiana Supreme Court**. It featured strongly in Oliver Stone's 1991 movie, *JFK*.

Across the street and down the block from the TV station WDSU, the excellent **Historic New Orleans Collection** ❸ (533 Royal Street; tel: 504-523-4662; www.hnoc.org; Tue–Sat 9.30am–4.30pm, Sun 10.30am–4.30pm) is pretty much what the name says it is: a collection of maps, documents, and memorabilia exhibiting the long and lively history of New Orleans. The Williams Gallery on the ground floor has changing exhibits of regional art, and there is an excellent research library here, while the building itself has connections with the Emperor Napoleon Bonaparte.

The corner of St Peter and Royal is said to be the most photographed place in New Orleans. The **Royal Cafe** is housed in one of the **LaBranche Buildings**, which were built around 1840 and are notable for their exquisite cast-iron galleries. There are actually 11 LaBranche Buildings lacing down the 600 block of St Peter Street to Cabildo

Alley. Cast iron was introduced in New Orleans in 1850; these buildings originally were undoubtedly festooned with simpler wrought (hand-worked) iron. At 915 Royal Street is another well-known and much photographed landmark, the Cornstalk Fence, behind which sits the fine **Cornstalk Hotel**. One of the quarter's many house-museums is the **Gallier House** (1118–1132 Royal Street; tel: 504-274-0748; www.hgghh.org; Fri–Mon 9:30am–3:30pm). It was built in 1857 by the well-known architect James Gallier, Jr, as a home for himself and his family. Gallier's father, James Gallier, Sr, was also a famous architect whose work can be seen all over town. Open for tours, the house is a fine example of how wellheeled Creoles of the 19th century lived.

The word 'Dixie' originated in New Orleans. It came from the French word for 'ten' (dix) on $10 bank notes. These notes were called 'dixies.'

BOURBON STREET BLUES

It's possible to hear **Bourbon Street** before you set foot in it. Within a

Old colonial houses in the French Quarter, decorated for Mardi Gras.

sixblock stretch you can hear hard rock, rhythm & blues, Dixieland, honky-tonk piano, Irish music, gut-bucket (lowdown mean blues), Cajun and zydeco, cancans, karaoke, and occasionally a bagpiper in full regalia.

It isn't even necessary to go inside to be entertained. Doors of clubs are flung wide open all year round, and the music pours out. Almost any place that serves mixed drinks has 'to go-cups,' so you can take your libation along as you stroll. Aside from the bars, a tour of Bourbon Street proper begins at the **Old Absinthe House** ❶ (240 Bourbon Street; tel: 504 523-3181; www.rue-bourbon.com/old-absinthe-house; daily 9am–3pm), a well-established institute of higher imbibing. The building was constructed in 1806 as a commercial-cum-residential structure and is typical of an entresol house. Entresol is a French word, meaning mezzanine, and in this context, it meant a half-story between the upper and lower floors. Sophisticated **Galatoire's 33 Bar and Steak** (215 Bourbon Street; tel: 504-335-3932; www.

galatoires33barandsteak.com; Wed–Sat 11:30am–9pm, Sun 12pm–9pm), one of the city's old-line French Creole restaurants, has been on Bourbon since its founding in the early 20th century and has been run by the same family ever since.

Just off Bourbon Street lies the **Hermann-Grima House** Ⓜ (820 St Louis Street, tel: 504-274-0750; www.hgghh.org; Wed–Mon 10am–4pm), another beautiful house-museum. The mansion itself is handsome, but of particular note are the restored outbuildings that surround pretty ornamental gardens. There is a 19th-century kitchen, where, during the winter months, Creole cooking demonstrations take place.

Antoine's (tel: 504-581-4422; www.antoines.com), one of the city's most famous restaurants, is located on St Louis Street, between Bourbon and Royal streets. In 1840, Antoine Alciatore founded this restaurant, and it's still operated by his descendants. Antoine's is housed in a lovely old building dating from 1868 that's lavishly decorated with pale-green ironwork. At Bourbon and St Philip streets, the musty old **Lafitte's Blacksmith Shop** (tel: 504-593-9761; www.lafittes-blacksmithshop.com; daily 10am–3am) is a little cottage that looks like it's about to collapse. Ownership records of this neighborhood bar date back to 1772, but it may be even older.

UPPER AND LOWER FRENCH QUARTER

Locals refer to the lower quarter and the upper quarter, because directions follow the flow of the river. The lower quarter is the area from Jackson Square to Esplanade Avenue, which is vaguely 'east' on a map; the upper quarter lies between Canal Street and Jackson Square. Local historians still argue over which is the oldest structure in the city's Vieux Carre, but it is true that the sole building to survive the devastating fire of 1788 intact is

Street musicians in New Orleans.

the fine **Old Ursuline Convent**  (1100 Chartres Street; tel: 504-529-3040; www.stlouiscathedral.org/convent-museum; Mon, Thurs–Sat 10am–2pm). The convent is the only remaining example in the city of pure French Creole architecture and one of the oldest buildings in the Mississippi Valley. The large structure was designed in 1745 by Ignance Francois Broutin for the Ursuline nuns who arrived here from France in 1727. The nuns prayed in the convent chapel during the 1815 Battle of New Orleans. Andrew Jackson, the hero of the battle, came to the convent afterward to thank them for their prayers. Across the street from the convent, the **BeauregardKeyes House** (tel: 504-523-7527; www.bkhouse. org; Mon–Sat 10am–3pm) is a house-museum with a lovely walled garden. The garden is included in the tour.

An only-in-New Orleans phenomenon is the spooky **Voodoo Museum** (724 Dumaine Street; tel: 504-680-0128; www.voodoomuseum.com; daily 10am–6pm). As well as palm-readings and voodoo tours, the museum offers night-time visits to 'voodoo rituals.' The museum itself features a creepy cornucopia of dolls, grisgris, and other mojo-stimulating specimens.

Some historians insist that the house known as **Madame John's Legacy** (632 Dumaine Street; tel: 504-568-6968; call for hours) predates the Old Ursuline Convent and should be crowned 'oldest in New Orleans.' The 700 block of St Peter Street has two establishments worth mentioning. Grungy, world-famous **Preservation Hall** at No. 726 is in a former stable and presents some of the best jazz in the world (tel: 504-522-2841; www.preservationhall.com). There's no bar, but you can get a 'to go-cup' next door from **Pat O'Brien's**, another well-known bar. Pat's is in an historic structure constructed around a stunning courtyard. It was built in 1791 and was used by the first Spanish Theatre to be founded in the United States.

BEYOND THE FRENCH QUARTER

For any visitors with time to spend, the leafy streets beyond the French

Pubs and bars line the French Quarter.

Quarter offer unparalleled delights, from overground cemeteries and fine garden homes to a city park and a lake. However, two fascinating attractions within sight of the French Quarter should be approached with some caution.

The stretch of **Rampart Street** between St Peter and Canal streets is fairly safe during daylight hours, but visitors should avoid walking alone on any section of Rampart after dark. Unfortunately, **Armstrong Park** should be avoided entirely except during big events held in the Mahalia Jackson Theatre for the Performing Arts or the nearby Municipal Auditorium. This is a shame, because from the French Quarter the lit-up entrance is very welcoming.

Old Congo Square, which many historians believe was the birthplace of jazz, is located in front of the Municipal Auditorium. Also called Beauregard Square, this is where 18th- and 19th-century enslaved people gathered each Sunday afternoon to chant and dance to the accompaniment of tam-tams. **Basin Street**, of song and legend, parallels Rampart Street. This, too, is an extremely unsavory, unsafe thoroughfare.

St Louis Cemetery No. 1, the city's oldest extant cemetery, is located on Basin Street behind Our Lady of Guadalupe Church. Cities of the Dead New Orleans' unique burial grounds are among the top sightseeing attractions in the city, but for personal safety, visitors should always visit the graveyards in the company of an organized group.

Informally known as Cities of the Dead, the cemeteries look like small towns with tiny windowless houses and buildings whose front doors are stark white marble slabs. In 1789, St Louis Cemetery No. 1 was established on the site of a previous one on St Peter Street, between Burgundy and Rampart streets. Its most famous inhabitant is Marie Laveau, the city's infamous voodoo queen, whose tomb is usually adorned with voodoo charms and brick-dust crosses.

St Louis Cemetery No. 2, which stretches between Iberville and St

St Louis Cemetery No. 1.

⊘ NICHOLAS CAGE

In 2009, despite being in good health, Hollywood actor Nicholas Cage decided to get his affairs in order – starting with a tomb in the city's most famous burial ground, St Louis Cemetery No.1. After purchasing the plot Cage commissioned a 9ft (2.7-metre) -tall stone pyramid, complete with the inscription: 'Omni Ab Uno'. This translates from Latin as 'Everything From One'. The actor has never spoken publicly about the reasons behind his pyramid purchase, but if you ask any local, they will tell you a theory or two. One of the most popular theories goes that Cage bought this plot to counter a curse that began when he bought the apparently haunted LaLaurie mansion. Legend has it that the pyramid's close proximity to grave of reputed Voodoo priestess Marie Laveau, negates the ill will of the ghosts from the LaLaurie mansion.

Louis streets along North Claiborne, was consecrated in 1823. It contains the tomb of pirate captain Dominique You, who fought with Andrew Jackson in the Battle of New Orleans. **St Louis Cemetery No. 3** is on Esplanade Avenue near the entrance to City Park. It opened in 1854. The entrance is through a broad, ornate iron gate, and the paved roads are wide enough for cars. There are several exquisite 'society' tombs here, including the ornate mausoleum of the Hellenic Orthodox Community.

CANAL STREET

Canal Street, one of the widest shopping streets in America, leads all the way from the Mississippi River to City Park Avenue, near City Park. A broad, treelined street with tall, graceful lampposts, it serves as a gateway to the river, a signpost toward the Central Business District, and the dividing line between Uptown and Downtown.

At the foot of Canal Street – that is, the riverside end of the street – the **Canal Street Wharf** and the **Poydras Street Wharf** along Spanish Plaza are the departure points for sightseeing riverboats. The structure anchored on Canal Street across from the wharf is the $40 million **Audubon Aquarium of the Americas** ❶ (tel: 504-565-3033; www.auduboninstitute.org; Thur–Mon 10am–5pm). The 1 million-gallon (3.75 million-liter) aquarium houses over 3,600 fish, reptiles, birds, and foliage indigenous to North, Central, and South America. Within the aquarium complex is an IMAX Theatre. Farther along, at 423 Canal Street is the gray, granite **US Custom House** ❷. Despite its austere exterior, the Custom House is worth a visit to see the Great Marble Hall, hailed as one of the finest examples of Greek Revival architecture in the US. The Custom House is also the home of the Audubon Institute's Insectarium.

THE WAREHOUSE AND CENTRAL BUSINESS DISTRICTS

At the upper end of Convention Center Boulevard and Riverwalk, in the area surrounding Julia Street, is the trendy **Warehouse District**, the leading center for visual arts in New Orleans. The revitalization of this district began in 1976, with the opening of the **Contemporary Arts Center** ❸ (900 Camp Street; tel: 504-528-3800; www.cacno.org; Mon and Wed–Sun 11am–5pm). As well as showcasing local artists, the center hosts drama, dance, and performance art shows. There's a flourishing style scene around the CAC, the nearby galleries and watering holes. When the nearby **National WWII Museum** (945 Magazine Street, tel: 504-528-1944; www.nationalww2museum.org; daily 9am–5pm) opened in 2000, it was marked by three days of hoopla, including re-enactments, flotillas, and celebrity appearances by, among others, Tom Hanks and Steven Spielberg. Housed in a vast former warehouse, the museum displays a wealth of exhibits, including memorabilia from the Normandy invasions of World War II.

Carnival colors of purple and green appear everywhere during Mardi Gras.

Catching a streetcar on Canal Street.

Across the street is the wonderful **Ogden Museum of Southern Art** (925 Camp Street, tel: 504-539-9650; www.ogdenmuseum.org; daily 10am–5pm). Affiliated with the Smithsonian Institute, this one-of-a-kind museum traces the story of the visual arts in the American South, and showcases the best of the past, present, and future of Southern culture.

Culture vultures can also visit two other museums. At 929 Camp Street, housed in a brooding Romanesque building, the **Confederate Memorial Hall Museum** (tel: 504-523-4522; www.confederatemuseum.com; Tue–Sat 10am–4pm) contains Civil War memorabilia, including personal effects of Jefferson Davis and Robert E. Lee.

The **Louisiana Children's Museum** (15 Henry Thomas Drive; tel: 504-523-1357; www.lcm.org; Wed–Sat 9.30am–4.30pm, Sun 11:30am–4.30pm) is a first-class facility offering hands-on exhibits that are both educational and fun.

In the earliest days, a vast plantation owned by the Jesuits extended upriver from what is now the French Quarter. This area comprises much of today's modern **Central Business District** (which locals call the CBD). Hunkering like a giant spaceship on Poydras Street among the skyscrapers is the **Superdome** (Sugar Bowl Drive; www.mbsuperdome.com). The dome is home to the New Orleans Saints football team and host of the famous annual Sugar Bowl college football game, as well as other events, such as Monster Jam and cultural festivals.

THE GARDEN DISTRICT

The **Garden District** ⑦ is bordered by Magazine Street, and Jackson, Louisiana, and St Charles avenues. It's possible to get a tempting taste of this sweet-smelling area by driving along the main thoroughfare, Prytania Street, which is lined with handsome 19th-century homes.

Much better is to take the **St Charles streetcar**, the oldest continuously operating street railway system in the world, get off at Jackson Avenue, and simply wander around. Although

Sculpture garden outside the New Orleans Museum of Art (NOMA).

⊙ MARIE LAVEAU

The life of world-famous Voodoo high priestess Marie Laveau can be traced back as far as 1801. Raised in the French Quarter of New Orleans, Laveau was the daughter of Marguerite Henry. It's difficult to determine where fact ends and fiction begins in the tale of Laveau's life and her alleged supernatural powers. However, to this day she is revered by many, and even feared by some, as Louisiana's most powerful witch. Some explain Marie's powers by painting her as a master of information, with dirt on everyone of influence in the city, gathered during her many years as a hair-dresser. Others maintain she was the real deal and worship her to this very day. Nowhere is this more apparent than in her mausoleum in Saint Louis Cemetery No. 1, which is forever adorned with lipstick kisses, candles, flowers, and charms.

there are too many fine structures to mention individually, not to be missed are the Pontchartrain Hotel, Colonel Short's Villa, and Commander's Palace restaurant. Architecture buffs should arrange to take one of the organized tours.

CITY PARK AND LAKE PONTCHARTRAIN

City Park ⓤ is one of the largest urban parks in the nation. Lying on the site of the old Louis Allard plantation, which accounts for its dreamy Old South appearance, the park contains the **New Orleans Museum of Art** (tel: 504-658-4100; www.noma.org; opens 10am daily, closing time varies), botanical gardens, an amusement park with an antique carousel, and lazy lagoons for fishing and boating. It also has more than 2,000 stately oak trees, dressed with frilly Spanish moss, which are among the loveliest in the South. The easiest way to reach City Park from the French Quarter is on Esplanade Avenue, which leads right to the entrance.

Cutting a wide swathe across the northern border of New Orleans is sparkling **Lake Pontchartrain**. Accessible from Downtown, via Elysian Fields Avenue or Canal Boulevard (an extension of Canal Street), Lakeshore Drive breezes along the lake for more than 5 miles (8km).

AROUND LOUISIANA

Antebellum plantations, Cajun music and alligators in the soup, Let the Good Times Roll down by the riverside and in the bayous of Acadia

The Southern manor home, with its vast acres of cotton fields and hundreds of enslaved people, ruled by a kindly ole marse or a mean-eyed monster, is the stuff of novelists and scriptwriters. The massive white-columned mansion shaded by moss-draped trees and sweetened with the scent of honeysuckle. Sweet (or sultry) young belles with milk-white skin, tiny waistlines and teasing eyes, gotten up in hoops and crinolines. Handsome, though sometimes sinister, cavaliers dashing off wherever they must, in order to fight for love, honor, or preferably both. **New Orleans** is surrounded by plantations, some with wistful names like Rosedown, some old and crumbling, some dolled up and fit for overnight guests. All, however, offer the requisite degree of romance, and a few even add in a mystery or two. Estates are generally open every day.

PLANTATION ROW

Louisiana's premier plantation country follows the Mississippi River from above Baton Rouge and ends around 23 miles (37 km) west of New Orleans. Pre-Civil War homes were built on the Great River Road to escape the dripping summer heat, and several offer bed & breakfast.

The closest plantation to New Orleans is **Destrehan** ❷ (13034 River Road, Destrehan; tel: 985-764-9315; www.destrehanplantation.org). Drive west on US 61 or I-10, take exit 310, and

Evergreen Plantation.

follow the signs. The oldest plantation in the Lower Mississippi Valley, this two-story house was built in 1787 by a free man of color. About 5 miles (8km) west of Destrehan, you can drive by gorgeous **San Francisco**, built in 1856 by Edmond Bozonier Marmillion. Frances Parkinson Keyes used San Francisco as the setting for her novel *Steamboat Gothic*.

The next three plantations – Evergreen, Laura, and Oak Alley – are on the west bank. On weekends you can take the Veterans Memorial Bridge across the river, but weekdays, enjoy a delightful ferry ride from Reserve over the waters to Edgard. Then head upriver on the **Great River Road** (LA 18) about 5 miles (8km) to **Evergreen Plantation** ❸ (4677 LA 18; www.evergreenplantation.org; not currently open for tours). The most intact Louisiana sugar plantation, Evergreen has 37 buildings on the National Register of Historic Places.

Upriver a little ways on LA 18 is **Laura Plantation** (2247 LA 18; tel: 225-265-7690; www.lauraplantation.com).

Laura was built in 1805 and was for many years managed by women. It was to this plantation that Senegalese enslaved people brought the Br'er Rabbit stories. **Oak Alley** (3645 LA 18; tel: 225-265-2151; www.oakalleyplantation.org), just 3 miles (5km) upriver of Laura, is perhaps the most photographed Louisiana plantation, and a frequent movie set. The white-columned house, built in 1837 behind a stately avenue of 28 oaks, has B&B rooms in small cabins, and a lovely restaurant. **Madewood** (4250 LA 308), too, is another lovely site to drive by. Painted pristine white, the house dates from 1846. On the west bank, 33 miles (53km) northwest of Madewood via LA 1 is Nottoway (31025 Hwy. 1, near White Castle; tel: 225-545-2730; www.nottoway.com). Nottoway is, quite simply, a knockout. Completed in 1859, and resembling a gigantic wedding cake, B&B accommodations are available, as is an excellent restaurant.

North of Baton Rouge on US 61, about 15 miles (24km) is the **Port Hudson State Historic Site** ❹ (236 Hwy. 61;

Rosedown Plantation.

tel: 225-654-3775; daily 9am–5pm). The 643-acre (260-hectare) site commemorates an 1863 battle, when 6,800 Confederates held off 30,000 Yankees for 48 days and nights – one of the longest sieges in US history. A boardwalk winds through an area that saw some of the fiercest fighting, and there are 6 miles (10km) of trails. About 35 miles (56km) north of Baton Rouge on US 61 is **St Francisville**. This charming little town with magnificent oak trees has been described as '2 miles long and 2 yards wide'. One of the most impressive mansions in the state is near the center of St Francisville. **Rosedown Plantation State Historic Site ❺** (12501 LA 10; tel: 225-635-3332) is a stunning house-museum, where the extensive grounds include centuries-old camellias and azaleas.

Several elegant homes line US 61 north of St Francisville, most among huge oaks, magnolias, and subtropical greenery, perfect for strolling in. **The Myrtles** (7747 US 61; tel: 225-635-6277; www.myrtlesplantation.com) is said to be 'America's Most Haunted House,' and on the site of a Native American burial ground. As well as daily tours, mystery tours of the house are conducted on weekends.

TOURING THE SWAMPS

New Orleans is an island in a wetlands Japing northward through salt, brackish, and freshwater marsh. For almost 300 years, the Crescent City has fought the Mississippi with levees, while exploiting the Delta's rich resources of food, fur, and oil, as well as its convenience for water transportation. Recently, environmental tourism has spawned numerous swamp tours. Most focus on wildlife and wetland ecology. All tourists want to see alligators, and most times they do, especially in the hot months that dominate the southern Louisiana calendar. Many operators can arrange transportation from New Orleans hotels.

The bayous meander and merge past alligators and walls of cypress, reaching through webs of twisted limbs and Spanish moss. Snakes, feral hogs, otters, deer and raccoons are spotted, as well as herons and egrets. Birds love the temperature, the canopy of cover, and the abundant food in Louisiana. The swamps are a feral wonderland, an adventure into the wilds of the earth's past.

Crawford Landing sits at the edge of **Honey Island Swamp ❻**, near Slidell on the north shore of Lake Pontchartrain, a 45-minute drive northeast of New Orleans. Dr Paul Wagner, a wetland ecologist and environmental consultant lived all his life at the edge of the swamp and founded his tour operation in 1982. He was the preserve manager in the White Kitchen Natural Area, a part of Honey Island Swamp, the premier cypress-tupelo gum swamp in Louisiana. **Honey Island Swamp Tours** (Crawford Landing at West Pearl River, Slidell; tel: 504-242-5877; www.honeyislandswamp.com) currently offers interesting, narrated boat tours.

⊘ Tip

Many plantations and their outbuildings have been converted into museums, bed-and-breakfasts or sweet-smelling restaurants. For a comprehensive list, go to the state website, www.louisianatravel.com.

Swamp tour.

A CAJUN MAN

Black Guidry plays Cajun tunes on his home-made accordion and guides the **Cajun Man's Swamp Cruise** (251 Marina Drive, Gibson; tel: 985-868-4625; www.cajunmanadventures.com) from deep-water **Bayou Black** marina, a 90-minute drive from New Orleans near Houma. These tour often take visitors to a little side bay where the long nose and intense eyes of a huge alligator pierce the green layer of duckweed. Some guides even summon the alligators with a guttural call. Also available are photo tours, eagle spotting tours, and tours specifically designed to maximize alligator viewing. Private tours and Cajun catering add-ons make the experience even more authentic.

The **Creole Nature Trail** (1205 N Lakeshore Drive; tel: 337-436-9588; www.creolenaturetrail.org) begins at **Sulphur**, 10 miles (16km) west of Lake Charles, over three hours' drive west from New Orleans, and provides a magnificent trip through vast wetlands. Its highlight is the **Sabine National Wildlife Refuge** , (www.

Sabine National Wildlife Refuge.

fws.gov/refuge/sabine), which is 125,000 acres (50,000 hectares) of salt and freshwater marsh. In the fall, the refuge is full of migratory birds. In hotter months, alligators appear. **Marsh Trail**, an elevated boardwalk, offers excellent views of waterfowl and wildlife. A pamphlet at the Sabine visitor's center lists 250 species of birds, from the common moorhen to the rare roseate spoonbill. The spoonbill is a large, pink bird, hunted relentlessly for its stunning plumage. In 1915 there were a mere 20 birds left in Carneron Parish. Numbers have increased since, although sightings are still rare. Conservation is at the heart of the wildlife refuge, which was started as a protective habitat and breeding ground for migratory birds and waterfowl.

FROM CANADA TO CAJUN COUNTRY

New Orleans was founded by French Creoles – the descendants of French people born 'in the colonies' – and the area west of the Crescent City was also settled by the French. However, the French of Cajun Country (which is also called Acadiana, or French Louisiana) have a different heritage from the Creoles.

In the early 17th century, the French had colonized the parts of Canada now the provinces of New Brunswick and Nova Scotia, then known as Acadia. In the mid-18th century, under British control, the Acadiens or 'Cajuns' were expelled for refusing to forsake their Catholic faith and swear allegiance to the British crown. The expulsion, known as *le grand derangement*, was romantically told by Henry Wadsworth Longfellow. His epic poem *Evangeline* tells of star-crossed lovers, parted by the *derangement*, who were reunited under a gigantic oak tree in St Martinville – but, tragically, too late.

The swiftest route from New Orleans into the heart of Cajun Country is via Interstate 10. The proud 'capital' of

French Louisiana is Lafayette (see page 206), 128 miles (205km) west of New Orleans, but it is fun to take a longer, more scenic route, to savor the Acadian flavor.

For the scenic route, drive south on US 90, which dips down to **Houma** ❾, 57 miles (92km) below New Orleans. Named for the Houmas Native Americans, Houma is a lazy little town among marshlands and bayous, an excellent departure point for swamp tours, and even a wetlands airplane tour. The **Houma/Terrebonne Tourist Commission** (114 Tourist Drive; tel: 985-868-2732; www.houmatravel.com; call ahead for hours) has a wealth of information about the area. Among the nearby attractions is the **Bayou Terrebonne Waterlife Museum** where the colorful interactive exhibits explore the wetlands, flora and fauna of this region.

Fourteen miles (22km) west of Houma, via US 90, the **Wildlife Gardens** offer walking and boat tours through the marshland, as well as simple cabins for overnight guests, right there

in the middle of the swamp. Strange dreams are guaranteed. Sprawled on the banks of the Atchafalaya River, 37 miles (60km) northwest of Houma via US 90, **Morgan City** ❿ served as the set for the first Tarzan movie, filmed in 1917. **Moonwalk**, atop the Great Wall – a flood wall that runs 22 miles (35km) alongside Front Street – is an observation deck for viewing the Atchafalaya, and gives historical displays of the environs.

Both US 90 and LA 182 lead to the pretty little town of **Franklin** ⓫, approached from the east beneath an arch of handsome live oak trees. Unique in this part of the Gallic bois, Franklin was settled not by Frenchmen, but by the English. The town has a wealth of beautiful white mansions, several open for tours and some offering B&B. Among Franklin's 'must sees' is **Grevemberg House Museum** (tel: 337-828-2092), an 1851 Greek Revival townhouse furnished with period antiques. The house displays Civil War artifacts, and charming antique toys. Take a few minutes to stroll around

Alligators sightings are almost guaranteed on a swamp tour.

White-faced ibis, Louisiana Marsh.

the **Franklin Historic District.** Franklin is a Main Street USA-type of town and designated by the National Trust for Historic Preservation. Three miles (5km) north of Franklin, in the town of Charenton, via LA 326 is the **Chitimacha Native Reservation** ⓬ (tel: 337-923-4973). The first indigenous people in Louisiana to be federally recognized, the reservation was established in 1925 after the group, which had numbered thousands, dwindled to just 50 people. The Chitimacha were famed for woven baskets, still made on the reservation, but the biggest attraction is the ever-expanding **Cypress Bayou Casino** (832 Martin Luther King Road; tel: 800-284-4386 www.cypressbayou.com). Open 24 hours, seven days a week, and invariably packed, gaming tables vie with video poker and slot machines, ever eager to relieve you of your dollars.

SHADOWS ON THE TECHE

The Spaniards who founded **New Iberia** ⓭, 25 miles (40km) northwest of Franklin, named it for the Iberian Peninsula of their homeland, but you'll see much more Acadian influence than Spanish. New Iberia is an attractive little town on the banks of the Teche. Information and advice is available at the Iberia Parish Tourist Commission (tel: 337-365-1540; Mon–Fri 8:30am–4:30pm).

New Iberia's outstanding attraction is **Shadows-on-the-Teche** (317 East Main Street; tel: 337-369-6446; www.shadowsontheteche.org; Thur–Sat 10am–4pm), Louisiana's only National Trust Historic House Museum & Gardens. With Bayou Teche in its backyard, and giant live oaks to shade it, Shadows was built in 1834 for sugar planter David Weeks. The furnishings are 19th-century Louisiana and European antiques. New Iberia is also home to America's oldest rice mill. Tours are conducted of the **Conrad Rice Mill** (307 Ann Street; tel: 337-364-7242; www.conradrice.com; Mon–Sat 9am–5pm), while the on-site **Konriko Country Store** sells Cajun food baskets, crafts, and other collectible gifts. New Iberia is just a short detour from one of South Louisiana's stellar attractions, Avery

Shadows-on-the-Teche.

ⓘ HOME OF HOT SAUCE

Famous all over the world, Tabasco sauce can be traced back to the early 19th century and its Louisiana creators, the McIlhenny family. The exact recipe is a closely guarded secret; essential ingredients include vinegar, salt, and Tabasco peppers. The tale of the small bottle now synonymous with the sauce is a charming one. Operating on something of a constrained budget, Edmund McIlhenny originally bottled his creation in old cologne bottles, discarded by a New Orleans glass supplier. The company has since outgrown such humble beginnings and today produces 750,000 bottles a day. In 2009 Queen Elizabeth II awarded the McIlhenny Company the Royal Warrant as Supplier of Tabasco Sauce to HM The Queen. Allegedly Her Majesty enjoys a Bloody Mary made with Louisiana's famous hot sauce.

Island, about 7 miles (11km) southwest of town. Go north on US 90 from New Iberia, take the LA 14 exit and turn left, then turn right on LA 329. There are no bridges or pontoons on the approach, and were it not for the signs, you would not even know that you'd reached an island.

A HOT LITTLE ISLAND

Avery Island ⑭ is synonymous with Tabasco sauce, the hot-hot condiment in kitchens and cafés the world over. Edmund McIlhenny concocted the sauce in the 1880s, and a fourth generation of McIlhennys now runs free tours of the **Tabasco Factory** (32 Wisteria Road; 337-373-6129; www.tabasco.com; daily 9am–4pm). Another relation, Edward Avery McIlhenny developed the 200-acre (81-hectare) **Jungle Gardens**, Avery Island's most spectacular attraction.

The gardens blaze with camellias, azaleas, and tropical plants – there is something in bloom year-round. In spring and summer, the bird sanctuary is aflutter with white egrets and herons, while in wintertime hordes of ducks come quacking from the chilly North.

Lovely **St Martinville** ⑮, the heart and soul of the Evangeline legend, lies 10 miles (16km) north of New Iberia. The St Martinville Tourist Information Center (tel: 337-394-2233; www.stmartinville.org) sits on the banks of the Teche, in the shadow of the fabled Evangeline Oak. A few steps from the oak, the **Acadian Memorial** commemorates le grand derangement of the Acadians with a huge mural. Massive bronze plaques are engraved with 3,000 refugees names, while an eternal flame burns in a peaceful garden on the riverbank. Adjacent is the vibrant AfricanAmerican Museum.

A block away, on the square, is **St Martin de Tours**, mother church of the Acadians; a statue of Evangeline stands in the churchyard. The neighboring **Petit Paris Museum** is small, but packed with artifacts and memorabilia from the area. Just outside the city limits, on LA 31, the star-crossed Acadian exile is remembered in the **Longfellow/Evangeline State Park**. Within the park is an interpretative center in a raised cottage, picnic grounds and barbecue grills, a craft shop, and a boat launch.

Continuing on LA 31 toward Breaux Bridge, after 2 miles (3km) is Cypress Island Road. Follow the signs to one of the state's best-kept secrets: **Lake Martin**, home to roseate spoonbills, blue herons, 'gators, nutria, and all kinds of exotic critters. **Breaux Bridge** ⑯, 5 miles (8km) farther along US 31, is famed for its Crawfish Festival held on the first weekend in May, when the population of around 8,000 swells with over 100,000 hungry visitors. Breaux Bridge is also home to **Café Sydnie Mae** (tel: 337-909-2377), which was named after a former Louisiana State Representative. It can get overrun with tours from New Orleans or Baton Rouge, but if that's the case,

⊙ Tip
If you're in Eunice on a Saturday night, stop by the Liberty Center, where Renzez-Vouz des Cajuns, a rowdy two-hour radio show, is often broadcast, mostly in French. Trust us, you don't have to know the language.

Attendees at the Crawfish Festival in Breaux Bridge.

go to legendary Cajun dance hall is **La Poussiere** (1215 Grand Point Avenue; tel: 337-332-1721).

COURIR DE MARDI GRAS

Lafayette ⓱, 10 miles (16km) west of Breaux Bridge on LA 94, is the big cheese in Cajun Country, with the region's greatest concentration of sites, sights, museums, restaurants, nightclubs, and lodging. It is also party central for the exuberant Cajun Mardi Gras. In the surrounding countryside, the Courir de Mardi Gras, or Mardi Gras Run, is a wild affair with masked riders thundering on horseback to farmhouses, gathering food for a big fete in the town square. The logical first stop is the Lafayette Convention & Visitors Bureau (1400 Northwest Evangeline Thruway; tel: 800-346-1958; www.lafayettetravel. com; call for hours). Next, the **Acadian Cultural Center** presents fun and informative exhibits on Cajun culture (501 Fisher Road; tel: 337-232-0789). Across the street from the Acadian Cultural Center is **Vermilionville** (300

Fisher Road; tel: 337-233-4077; Tues–Sun 10am–4pm), a huge Creole and Cajun living history experience with arts, crafts, cooking, and live Cajun music. The **Acadian Village** (200 Green Leaf Drive; tel: 337-981-2364; Mon–Sat 10am–4pm) is a smaller and more userfriendly folklife museum on the banks of a lazy bayou.

Just 35 miles (56km) northwest of Lafayette is **Eunice** ⓲, a typical Cajun town and home to Savoy Music Center (https://www.savoymusiccenter.com/: tel: 337-457-9563, see for opening hours) where a jam session takes place each Saturday morning. Rendez-Vous des Cajuns is a radio show broadcast from the **Liberty Center** on Saturday nights and is a great way to meet the local people. Much music and dancing, storytelling and bonhomie makes for great entertainment, especially over Mardi Gras.

BATON ROUGE

Only a few minutes' drive from glamorous plantations and ecoswamps, the cosmopolitan state capital makes it own modern mark on the banks of the Mississippi

Baton Rouge ⓳, the busy, modern capital of Louisiana, opens out like the flavors of a rich gumbo, flavors of the cultures spicing this Southern state.

The muddy Mississippi flows along the banks of the city's Downtown area and through a history of nations vying for control of the port's river trade route. Today, as America's fifth-largest tonnage port, Baton Rouge is still a queen of transportation and a diverse hub of commerce touting everything from Old South plantations and tasty Cajun food to the lush green landscape that makes it a 'city of trees.' Named by an early French explorer for a red stick marking Native American territorial boundaries, colonial Baton Rouge drew settlers from many European countries. It is now best known for the festivals, customs, and hospitality that

Violinist at Vermilionville.

so pleasingly coexist in this cultural melting pot.

A BIRD'S-EYE VIEW

The heart of Baton Rouge is around the historic Downtown area and the towering **State Capitol** (tel: 225-383-1825; tours available by reservation). The 1932 Art Deco building was designed for (he might even have said 'designed by') Huey P. Long, Louisiana's most flamboyant politician (see page 54). Entrance is by wonderfully grand, almost bombastic sweeping stone steps. The view from the 350ft (170-meter) -high 27th-floor observation deck lays out the port, the petrochemical industries along the river, and the homes and businesses of a sprawling nine-parish metropolitan area with 650,000 people. Winged allegorical figures on a 22nd-floor cutaway refer to Baton Rouge's hallmarks of Law, Science, Philosophy, and Art.

Inside the capitol's echoing marble lobby are visitors' desks dedicated to the city and Louisiana. Racks of brochures and informative guides direct visitors to the nearby oak-shaded plantation homes, and the rustic, rollicking Cajun country of the French Acadians. Browse the racks, and then slip into a guided tour of the ornate, intricately decorated capitol, and the myths and legends of Louisiana's raucous political history.

TAKE A WALKING TOUR

The Capitol's green, rolling grounds, rose garden, and glassy lakes preside over the city's center and its two historic neighborhoods. Adjacent to the front lawn is the 1805 **Spanish Town**, which features antebellum homes, charming cottages, and bungalows. Eight blocks south begin the gracious mansions and brightly painted houses of **Beauregard Town**. Enjoy a walking tour, or stop by the **Visit Baton Rouge Tourist Information Center** (359 3rd Street; tel: 225-383-1825; www.

visitbatonrouge.com) for maps of Downtown points of interest, and directions for catching the weekday trolley.

Between the two neighborhoods are the bustling businesses, state buildings, cafés and restaurants in the **Central Business District**, where friendly multicultural eateries welcome visitors with hearty plates of food. The CBD is bordered on the west by the river and two waterfront casinos, **Hollywood Casino Rouge** (tel: 225-709-7777) and the **Belle of Baton Rouge** (tel: 225-242-2600; www.belleofbatonrouge.com). Both offer splashy, high-end entertainment and delicious, low-cost Sunday jazz buffets.

One of the best views of the river's traffic of passing ships and barges, and the illuminated bridge at night, is from **Red Stick Plaza**. This is a promenade with sidewalks, lamplit benches, commemorative sculptures, and a dock projecting out over the water. Just below the plaza is the fine **Louisiana Arts and Science Museum** (tel: 225-344-5272; www.lasm.org; Wed–Fri 10am–3pm, Sat 10am–5pm, Sun

> **◎ Tip**
>
> Baton Rouge is near to both plantations and swampland. Nature lovers should consider the Baton Rouge Swamp Tours (tel: 225-383-1825; www.visitbatonrouge.com/things-to-do/tours/swamp-tours), just off Highland Road exit of Interstate 10.

Baton Rouge's Art Deco-style State Capitol building.

1–5pm). Located in an historic railroad depot, the museum hosts traveling exhibits, hands-on arts and space centers to entertain younger people, and a 60ft (18-meter) domed planetarium featuring a Space Theater with IMAX-type movies and laser shows.

Next door to the museum is the war hero, the **USS** *Kidd* (tel: 225-342-1942; www.usskidd.com; daily 9.30am–3.30pm), a floating destroyer restored to its glory days of 1942. The complex includes a Veterans Memorial Museum with two fighter planes, a large collection of model ships, and a black granite courtyard dedicated to the honor of Louisiana veterans.

Across River Road and up oak-lined North Boulevard is the graceful white neo-Gothic castle of the **Old State Capitol** (tel: 225-342-0500; www.louisianaoldstatecapitol.org; Tue–Fri 10am–4pm, Sat 9am–3pm; free). The 1882 spiral staircase climbs to a beautiful stained-glass dome. The **Center for Political and Governmental History** is the state's official repository of film and video archives and has a number of interactive exhibits. The vintage footage of Louisiana politicians, sometimes singing, sometimes ranting, is both instructive and entertaining. Two blocks down North Boulevard is the **Old Governor's Mansion** (502 North Boulevard; tel: 225-387-2464; www.preserve-louisiana.org; Tue–Fri 9am–4pm), with tours of the period bedrooms of four Louisiana governors, plus many amusing stories of the notorious Huey and Earl Long.

PLANTATIONS AND SWAMPS

Beyond the city's center and 3 miles (5km) down the Mississippi is **Magnolia Mound Plantation** (2161 Nicholson Drive; tel: 225-343-4955). This 1791 French Creole plantation has costumed tour guides and factual exhibits on slavery and old-time plantation medicines.

The **Rural Life Museum** (4650 Essen Lane; tel: 225-765-2437; www.lsu.edu/rurallife; daily 8am–5pm) is located along Interstate 10, 8 miles (13km) from Downtown. The museum is a replica of a working plantation, with a commissary, a blacksmith's shop, sugarhouse, gristmill, schoolhouse, overseer's house, and 25 acres (10 hectares) of formal gardens with statuary, winding paths, lakes, and plants indigenous to 19th-century Louisiana.

While the 'patriots' owned the city's plantations and mansions, the Cajun 'pioneers' of the low-lying swamps have long been Louisiana's backbone. See some of the beauty in this way of life at the **Bluebonnet Swamp Nature Center** (tel: 225-757-8905; Tue–Sat 9am–5pm, Sun noon–5pm). In this natural history park, a couple of miles of walkways meander through rich, green cypress-tupelo swamplands. There are turtles, alligators, and exotic birds to share the enjoyment with. And if you're lucky you might also be able to spot wild snakes, raccoons, rabbits, opossums, armadillos, squirrels, foxes, coyotes, deer and otter.

Wrought iron stairs in the Old State Capitol building.

LITERARY SOUTH

Taking his nom-de-plume from the state of Tennessee, born in Columbus, Mississippi, and writing in New Orleans in 1938, Tennessee Williams is the complete Southern writer. Born Thomas Lanier Williams in 1911, although he set A Streetcar Named Desire in New Orleans, the character of Blanche Dubois closely resembles Precious, the daughter of the Clark family in Clarksdale, Mississippi, where Williams spent much of his boyhood. The Glass Menagerie may have been inspired by the ornaments collected by another Clarksdale resident.

His tales turned on the fragilities and contradictions of his tortured eccentrics, and those puzzles may give a clue to the perplexing question of why the South gushes such a flood of literary prodigy. Truman Capote, Harper Lee, Eudora Welty, Richard Wright, and Donna Tartt are just a few from the long line of Southern literary luminaries.

The Southern voice has always found eager readers the world over, from Margaret Mitchell's Civil War plantation epic Gone with the Wind, to Anne Rice's tales of the vampire Lestadt, John Grisham's legal twists and torts, and the North Carolina landscape of Charles Frazier's Cold Mountain.

The story of the modern Southern novel, and even the modern American novel, traces up a wooded gravel drive in Oxford, Mississippi, to the white timber house where William Faulkner declared himself 'sole owner and proprietor' of his fictitious Yoknapatawpha county. In As I Lay Dying he detailed the inhabitants' thoughts and daily minutiae, in a manner often compared with James Joyce.

Tom Wolfe, a native of Richmond, Virginia, pioneered a form called The New Journalism, honed during his writing for Rolling Stone magazine. His essays on the wives of test pilots in the space program, later collected into The Right Stuff, used a stream-of-consciousness narrative with a documentary descriptive style. Owing more to Faulkner than to news reporting, he later developed his voice in his landmark entanglements of Wall Street traders, The Bonfire of the Vanities.

New Orleanian John Kennedy Toole committed suicide in 1969 in Biloxi, Mississippi, in desperate frustration at not being able to publish The Confederacy of Ounces. Convinced of the merit in his work, his mother pursued publishers until the Louisiana University Press took it up in 1980, gaining Toole posthumous critical acclaim and the 1981 Pulitzer Prize for literature. His second novel, The Neon Bible, considered the finer by some, followed. 'Southern Gothic' literature, examining the sublime and the grotesque in reality, is exemplified by Savannah-born writer Flannery O'Connor. One of the few writers to cross the chasm between 'literary fiction' and horror, her 1952 story Wise Blood, later filmed by John Huston, is of a preacher offering a doctrine, 'where the blind don't see and the lame don't walk and what's dead stays that way.'

Southern novels are often run through with a black vein. Even The Confederacy of Dunces is a comedy with dark, sometimes hollow laughs. But the stories and words of the South continue to chime with a poetry that still resonates far abroad.

Tennessee Williams in 1945.

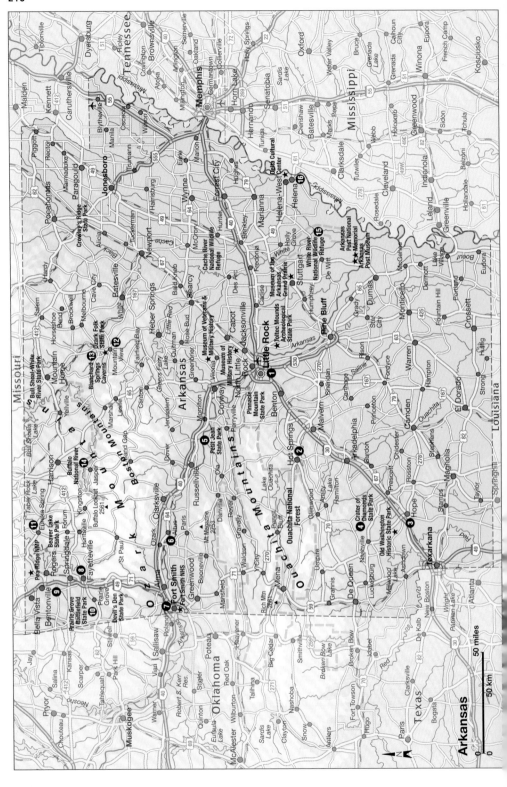

Arkansas

ARKANSAS

A detailed guide to the entire state, with principal sites cross-referenced by number to the maps

Arkansas, the home of former president Bill Clinton, is known as The Natural State, but was once nicknamed The Land of Opportunity – a name that still fits the state well. From the capital city of Little Rock, visitors can explore history and art museums, golf at award-winning courses, or fish for trophy bass in the Arkansas River. In the evenings there are live musical or theatrical performances and fine dining to enjoy. With a vehicle, it's easy to reach a state park with hiking trails, stunning river valley views, sailboats to rent, or fishing at a nearby lake. A 30-minute drive would put those with a love of the outdoors on a hiking trail in a national forest.

Even near Little Rock, outdoor opportunities abound. Within a two-hour drive are seven major lakes to choose between, including the crystal-clear Lake Ouachita, and Greers Ferry Lake. Flowing from Greers Ferry, the Little Red River boasts big rainbow trout and the world-record German brown trout. And several rivers that offer canoeing and kayaking are within a relatively short drive.

Day trips from Little Rock, though, can easily turn into overnight trips. Cities like Hot Springs, which is home to a national park, spas, thoroughbred racing, a botanical garden, and a theme park, have lodging options ranging from luxury downtown hotels to quaint bed-and-breakfast inns. A drive to western Arkansas leads past the state's wine country and to Fort Smith, a city with a history closely following that of the Wild West. In the eastern part of the state, visitors can learn how bottomland forests were transformed into some of the most productive farmlands in the nation, or how the area cultivated a rich tradition of blues music.

Arkansas is also home to 21 state parks, offering a variety of recreational and educational opportunities. Three state parks have lodges, and several

Main attractions

William J. Clinton Library and Museum
Central High School
Pinnacle Mountain
Lake Ouachita
Hot Springs National Park
Crater of Diamonds State Park
Wiederkehr Wine Cellars
Fort Smith
Prairie Grove Battlefield State Park

**Maps on pages
210, 213**

Canoeing on the Buffalo River.

⊘ Fact

Surrounded by 30 acres (12-hectares) of parkland, the William J. Clinton Library and Museum was purposely built jutting out into the Arkansas River, reflecting President Clinton's campaign promise to 'build a bridge to the 21st century.'

have hiking trails, campsites, cabins, or marinas with rental boats. Some preserve Civil War battlefields or folk music and crafts, while others are dedicated to interpreting the lives of the Native Americans who first inhabited the land. And, because Arkansas has more than 600,000 surface acres (240,000 hectares) of lakes and 9,700 miles (15,600km) of streams, several of the parks are on the water and offer accommodations with awe-inspiring views. What may be most appealing about Arkansas, though, is that just when travelers think they've seen it all, there's always something else just waiting to be discovered. It could be a pristine waterfall, or a quirky store in a mountain hamlet. It might even be a gem at the only diamond mine in the world open to the public. But that's to be expected in The Land of Opportunity.

LITTLE ROCK

Named for a small outcropping in the Arkansas River, **Little Rock ❶** has grown into a forward-looking city of the 21st century.

Travelling up the Arkansas River, French explorer Rene-Robert Cavalier de LaSalle spied towering bluffs near the first rock outcrop he had seen since departing the Mississippi River. He called the bluffs the 'Big Rock' and the outcropping the 'Little Rock.' What LaSalle encountered in 1682 is the place where the Arkansas River Valley rises from the Delta and meets the Ouachita Mountains to the south and the Ozark Mountains to the north – and the geographic center of what was to become, in 1836, the state of Arkansas.

Little Rock (pop. 183,133) reached the world's attention when then-Arkansas governor Bill Clinton became president in 1992, and again in 1996. Much of the world focused again on Little Rock when the **William J. Clinton Library and Museum ❹** (tel: 501-374-4242; www.clintonlibrary.gov; Mon–Sat 9am–5pm, Sun 1–5pm) opened on the banks of the Arkansas River. The library center, which is located in a 30-acre (12-hectare) park and houses a 20,000sq ft (1,860sq meter) museum, epitomizes Little Rock's Downtown revitalization efforts. Once dominated by dilapidated warehouses, the **River Market District** has been transformed into a vibrant area with stores, art galleries, restaurants, and bars featuring live music – all within walking distance of the presidential library.

HISTORICAL CENTER

It's no surprise that much of the state's history is centered around Little Rock. Downtown, and peculiarly located near skyscrapers, the **Historic Arkansas Museum ❸** (200 East Third Street; www.historicarkansas.org; Tue–Sat 9am–5pm, Sun 1–5pm) comprises five pre-Civil War buildings, including the city's oldest – the Hinderliter Grog Shop (c.1827). Guides in period attire provide tours of the grounds. The museum here features exhibits including native art and furniture. A few blocks away, the **Old State House Museum ❻** (300

The State Capitol of Little Rock with Buffalo River behind.

West Markham; tel: 501-324-9685; www. oldstatehouse.com; Tues–Sat 9am–5pm, Sun 1–5pm; free) served as Arkansas's capitol from 1836 to 1911. The building, which is the oldest capitol west of the Mississippi River, is where Clinton made his presidential acceptance speeches. Housed in the museum are exhibits on the state's role in the Civil War and Clinton's rise to the presidency, as well as dresses worn by Arkansas' first ladies.

Not far from the Old State House, guided tours are available at the **Arkansas State Capitol**, which is modeled after the nation's Capitol building. Also Downtown, the **Arkansas Museum of Fine Arts D** (tel: 501-372-4000; www. arkansasartscenter.org; Mon–Fri 10am–5pm; free), which has internationally recognized collections, and the **Repertory Theatre E** (tel: 501-378-0405; www. therep.org), which has produced more than 60 world theatrical premieres, are but two reasons Little Rock is often considered the center of the arts in Arkansas. **Robinson Auditorium** hosts performances by the Arkansas Symphony Orchestra as well as concerts

by top performers. The **River Market's Museum of Discovery F** (501-396-7050; www.museumofdiscovery.org; Tue–Sat 9am–5pm, Sun 1–5pm) is a fun place for children and adults to learn about the sciences and see anthropological artifacts and exhibit, many of which deal with the state. Across the river is the **Simmons Bank Arena G** (tel: 501-975-9000 www.simmonsbankarena.com), where Elton John, Reba McEntire, and other big-name performers have entertained, and which hosts major sporting events.

In west Little Rock, **Wildwood Park for the Performing Arts H** (20919 Denny Road; tel: 501-821-7275; www. wildwoodpark.org) includes six gardens and is the largest park in the Southeast dedicated to the performing arts. Lanterns! (www.wildwoodpark.org/ lanterns) every April is a three-day festival with entertainment, food, and drinks from around the world.

CENTRAL HIGH SCHOOL

In 1957, the national media descended on Little Rock as nine young men and women became the first Black

Little Rock's Old State House.

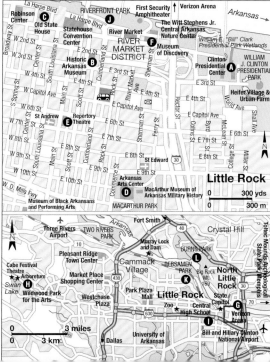

students to attend **Central High School** at 14th and Park streets. At the time, Arkansas, which had integrated Little Rock's public transportation system years before, was considered moderate on civil rights issues in comparison to its Southern counterparts. But when 'The Little Rock Nine' attempted to enter the school, Arkansas's governor, responding to protests among whites, enlisted the Arkansas National Guard to block the students' efforts, before President Eisenhower sent in federal troops to enforce the desegregation, prompting international headlines.

Across the street from the school, which is now a National Historic Site, is a helpful Visitors' Center (2120 W Daisy L Gatson Bates Drive; tel: 501-374-1957; www.nps.gov/chsc; Tue–Sat 9am–4.30pm), located in a renovated Mobil Service Station that features exhibits, including original newsreels, about the landmark crisis.

Interesting local history, though, began long, long before. About 10 miles (16km) southeast on US 165, then 400 yds/meters south on Highway 386,

Native Americans left their mark at what is now the **Toltec Mounds Archeological State Park** (tel: 501-961-9442; Wed–Sat 8am–5pm, Sun 1–5pm), where, from AD 600 to 1500, they built mounds rising from the flat, fertile land they had found and farmed. Toltec is near the **Plantation Agriculture Museum** (www.arkansasstateparks.com/parks/plantation-agriculture-museum), which interprets the state's long history of cotton farming.

PARKS AND THE OUTDOORS

At Juliuus Breckling **Riverfront Park** (400 President Clinton Ave.) walkers enjoying views of the Arkansas River can also learn about and see the 'Little Rock.' The park's Riverfest Amphitheatre regularly hosts concerts, and the entire park bustles with festivity and music during Riverfest, held each Memorial Day weekend. Farther upstream, cyclists and runners enjoy the paved trails at **Rebsamen Park** , where golfers can take a swing at its 18-hole public golf course just across the river from the 'Big Rock.' North Little Rock's **Burns Park** ,

Memorial to the Little Rock Nine in the grounds of the Arkansas State Capitol building

⊘ LITTLE ROCK NINE

The original plan to racially integrate high schools in Little Rock can be traced back to the attorney Richard B. McCulloch. It was to be a very cautious and gradual approach, beginning with one high school in 1957, before slowly being extended to a small selection of other junior high schools three years later.

The third and final phase was tabled to begin in 1963, with a limited desegregation of the grade schools in Little Rock. There was a great deal of opposition to the plan from all sides and in early 1956, the National Association for the Advancement of Colored People filed a lawsuit against it. This alliance of opposition to McCulloch's plan contributed in no small part to the 1957 crisis at Central High School.

one of the largest municipal parks in the US, has among its outdoor offerings a paved trail along the river, hiking trails, campgrounds, picnicking areas, and two 18-hole golf courses. Just west of Little Rock, **Pinnacle Mountain** dominates the landscape and is home to a state park that has a visitor center (tel: 501-868-5806) with exhibits on the area's geology and flora and fauna. The park also has hiking trails, including one that climbs the park's namesake peak and one that affords panoramic views of the Arkansas River.

AROUND ARKANSAS

With gems like Hot Springs and Eureka Springs, and real diamonds for the taking, there's a lot to enjoy between the Ozark Mountains and the Mississippi Delta.

As the Ozark and Ouachita mountains rise from the vast Mississippi Delta, so stories, songs, tales, and towns have risen with them as tall, proud, and diverse as the landscape. Arkansas is, in parts, both Old South and Wild West. Some of the early innovators of the blues drew their influences here, while immigrants, isolated among the hills of the Ozarks, nurtured and developed a tradition of folk music that is still alive. The land itself earned Arkansas the nickname of 'The Natural State,' as it has lush and varied landscapes of hills, lakes, and trails for outdoor adventure. **Little Rock's** central location makes a perfect base for exploring the crags and corners of the state.

HOT SPRINGS AND BEYOND

Visitors to **Hot Springs ❷** (pop. 35,750), 55 miles (86km) southwest of Little Rock via Interstate 30 and US 270, are amply and agreeably rewarded. Since 1904, Oaklawn Racing Casino Resort has held thoroughbred races from March through May, and simulcast racing through the rest of the year. The city also has award-winning golf courses, some of the state's best festivals, the Mid-America Science

Museum, Magic Springs Theme Park, and Garvan Woodland Gardens on the shores of a sparkling lake. Fishing and water sports are available, as Hot Springs borders Lake Hamilton and is near one of the largest reservoirs in Arkansas, Lake Ouachita. Both lakes have resorts and marinas with rental boats and fishing-guide services.

The main draw for this attractive resort town, though, is the hot springs themselves, which have attracted the good, the glitterati, and the notorious over the decades, including gangster Al Capone, who took to the waters and conducted business from the still lovely **Arlington Hotel** (239 Central Avenue; tel: 501-623-7771; www.arlingtonhotel. com). In 1832, Congress declared the land around the 47 natural springs a national preserve. Today, the visitor center at **Hot Springs National Park** (tel: 501-620-6715; www.nps.gov/hosp/index.htm; daily 5am–10pm) is housed in the **Fordyce**, one of eight opulent bathhouses along what is known as **Bathhouse Row**. The Fordyce looks much as it did when it was completed in 1915

Bathhouse Row, Hot Springs.

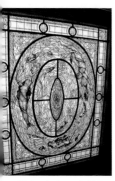

Stained-glass skylight at Fordyce Bath House, Hot Springs.

and has exhibits on the history of Hot Springs and the bathing experience. The staff can offer information on the park's campgrounds, picnic areas, and hiking trails. Also on the row, the elegant **Buckstaff** still offers traditional baths and massages.

The town's distinctive atmosphere and Art Deco architecture has attracted an artsy crowd. Boutiques, art galleries, and restaurants are located on and near magnolia-lined Bathhouse Row, while a 1950s movie theater is the headquarters for a nationally-attended documentary film festival. South of Hot Springs, 20 miles (32km) on Highway 7, **DeGray Lake** is a fishing and watersports resort, with cabins and campgrounds, plus a state park with a 90-room lodge, 18-hole golf course, campsites, horseback riding, and a marina with rental boats.

Farther south, along I-30 at **Hope ❸**, the 'Bill Clinton Trail' from Little Rock and Hot Springs (Clinton's boyhood home) offers tours of his birthplace as well as, in August, the Hope Watermelon Festival. Nearby, **Old**

Diamond hunting at Crater of Diamonds State Park.

Washington Historic State Park (tel: 870-983-2684) has 25 pre-Civil War buildings and was the state's Confederate capital from 1863 – after Union troops captured Little Rock – until 1865. Interpreters in period dress greet guests at the 1836 courthouse and homes with 19th-century furniture. The park's restaurant serves traditional Southern fare in the tavern, dating from 1832.

The only diamond mine in the world where visitors may keep gems they find is the **Crater of Diamonds State Park ❹** (tel: 870-285-3113; daily 8am–4pm).

Since the first diamond was discovered in 1906, more than 75,000 have been unearthed, including the 40.23-carat 'Uncle Sam' diamond. Exhibits and films at the park describe the area's geology and showcase diamonds, and interpreters give tips for prospecting. Diamond seekers be warned, though – summertime temperatures on the park's open field can be extreme. The park is just off of Highway 26 near Murfreesboro, 43 miles (69km) from I-30.

FROM LITTLE ROCK WEST AND NORTH

Arkansas' varied landscape gives wonderful views traveling west all the way from the edge of the Delta along the Arkansas River Valley, where Arkansas's first state park (opened in 1932) tops Petit Jean Mountain. Off I-40 on Highway 154 about 69 miles (111km) from Little Rock, many of the stone structures at **Petit Jean State Park ❺** – a 24-room lodge, cabins, and bridges – were built by the Depression-era Civilian Conservation Corps (see page 54). At Petit Jean are campgrounds, hiking trails, and scenic overlooks.

Swiss-German immigrants found the rich soil around the small town of **Altus ❻** ideal for winegrowing. The oldest of the wineries here, **Wiederkehr Wine Cellars** (www.wiederkehrwines.com), has been family owned since 1880, and offers free tastings, guided tours and bottles for sale in the gift shop. German fare is served at a restaurant in the original 1880 cellar. Three other wineries offer similar services in Altus, 116 miles (187km) from Little Rock, and a few miles south of I-40.

In 1817, the US military built **Fort Smith 7** on the western frontier to keep peace between the Cherokee and Osage Native American people, after their relocation to Native Territory just west over the Arkansas River. In 1851, a federal court with jurisdiction over half of Arkansas and the entire Native Territory, a vast area, was established at the fort. Today, the museum at the **Fort Smith National Historic Site** (tel: 479-783-3961; daily 9am–5pm) interprets the fort's history and tells stories of outlaws drawn to the frontier and the US marshals who upheld the law. The most notorious lawman, 'Hangin' Judge' Isaac Parker, sentenced 160 criminals to death. The site has a re-creation of Parker's courtroom and the original 'Hell on the Border' jail. There's a real Wild West feel.

As a busy river port, the city of **Fort Smith** attracted a varied clientele. **Miss Laura's** in the Belle Grove Historic District is reportedly the only former house of prostitution on the National Register of Historic Places, and now serves as the city's visitor center (2 North B Street; tel: 800 637-1477; www.fortsmith. org/miss-lauras-visitor-center; Mon–Sat 10am–4pm, Sun 1:30–4.30pm). Inside, travelers can pick up maps and information, as well as learn about its rowdy past. Across the river are the antiques shops in historic Van Buren and, on the **Arkansas and Missouri Railroad** (tel: 479-784-8600), restored vintage passenger cars take half- or full-day round-trips through the Ozark Mountains.

FAYETTEVILLE

With bridges towering above deep valleys, I-540 makes a swift and pleasant 58-mile (93-km) drive from Fort Smith to **Fayetteville 8**, home to the University of Arkansas. Fayetteville, along with three neighboring cities, is one of the fastest-growing metropolitan areas in the nation. Behind much of this growth is the world's largest retailer, Wal-Mart, headquartered 27 miles (43km) north

The Fort Smith National Historic site.

Sam Walton's pick-up truck and the Walmart Museum in Bentonville.

in **Bentonville** ❾. The cute museum, located in one of the company's original 'five and dime' stores on the square in downtown Bentonville, provides insights into the phenomenal rise of Sam Walton's family-owned business. The square also offers a couple of good places for a down-home lunch.

Arts, culture, and nightlife are anchored in Fayetteville by Dickson Street. On and around Dickson are art galleries, boutiques, restaurants, bars with live music and the Walton Arts Center, where symphony orchestra and other performances take place. **Devil's Den State Park**, which has campsites, cabins, trails and vistas revered by outdoor enthusiasts, is just 25 miles (40km) from Fayetteville, while huge and deep **Beaver Lake** is only a few miles away. Just west of Fayetteville on US 62, **Prairie Grove Battlefield State Park** ❿ encompasses 500 acres (200 hectares) and is known as one of the nation's best-preserved Civil War battlefields. The largest Civil War battle west of the Mississippi River took place at **Pea Ridge**, now a national

Eureka Springs.

military park (see page 93). A drive-through tour with recorded messages gives both the Yankee and Confederate perspective. The battlefield is located on US 62, 34 miles (55km) east of Fayetteville.

Thirty-two miles (51km) east of Pea Ridge via US 62, lovely **Eureka Springs** ⓫ began to flourish in the late 1800s as people were drawn by the purported healing powers of the resort town's natural springs. The town, with winding streets lined with unusual shops, eateries and art galleries, has embraced its Victorian heritage so successfully that the National Trust for Historic Preservation named Eureka one of its 'Dozen Distinct Destinations.'

Carrying on a heritage of different sorts, the **Ozark Folk Center** (1032 Park Avenue; tel: 870-269-3851; www.ozarkfolkcenter.com; call ahead for opening times) at **Mountain View** ⓬ is the only park in the US dedicated to preserving Southern folk ways of life. Folk music concerts (in season) are held in its auditorium, and the park has a gift shop, a restaurant, lodge rooms, and a crafts village where country skills are demonstrated. During warmer months, folk musicians converge on the courthouse lawn on Mountain View's town square for impromptu sessions. Mountain View is located on Ark. 9, 122 miles (196km) from Eureka Springs or 105 miles (169km) from Little Rock.

Just 15 miles (24km) north, **Blanchard Springs Caverns** ⓭ (tel: 870-757-2211; call for current hours) is ranked among the top 10 caves in the country. Famed for its trout-filled waters, the White River also flows near the town. Water released from the massive dam at **Bull Shoals Lake** – some 64 miles (103km) north near the Missouri border – is cold and teems with German brown, rainbow and cutthroat trout. As is true with Arkansas's other popular trout streams, resorts and outfitters are located along the White River. North of Little Rock near

Heber Springs, the Little Red River boasts the world-record German brown trout. It flows from Greers Ferry Lake, is popular for watersports, and is home to the hybridstriped bass and walleye.

The main natural asset of the Ozark Mountains is the **Buffalo National River** ⑭, America's first federally protected stream. The Buffalo, the most popular of more than a dozen float streams in Arkansas, is known for its campgrounds and hiking trails skirting the river. Numerous outfitters along the Buffalo provide canoe and cabin rentals.

THE ARKANSAS DELTA

In stark contrast to Arkansas's mountain ranges is its Delta region, which covers roughly the eastern third of the state. Here, two national scenic byways run north and south and provide insight into the history and slower-paced life of the region. **Crowley's Ridge Parkway** is named for the only 'highlands' in the Arkansas Delta it follows. The 200-mile (320km) route begins in northeast Arkansas and ends at the Mississippi River at the town of Helena, passing by or near five state parks, the St Francis National Forest, and several museums. On Arkansas' eastern border, the **Great River Road** skirts the Mississippi and some of the most productive farmland in the nation. The route also passes near **Arkansas Post National Memorial** (tel: 870-548-2207), which commemorates the first permanent European settlement in the lower Mississippi River Valley, and passes through the **White River National Wildlife Refuge** ⑮, where a visitor center at St Charles houses exhibits on the river, Native Americans, and wildlife. Near the Great River Road, **Stuttgart's Museum of the Arkansas Grand Prairie** tells how the area became the nation's most productive ricegrowing region, and how duck-hunting earned national recognition.

KING BISCUIT TIME

While cotton is king in the Delta, more than just soybeans and rice have been cultivated in this rich land. Blues music is deep-rooted in the southern Mississippi River Valley. The best place to learn about the Arkansans who've contributed to the genre is in **Helena** ⑯, 119 miles (192km) from Little Rock and less than an hour's drive from Memphis; Mississippi's legendary Highway 61 (see page 166) is just over the river. Helena's **Delta Cultural Center** (141 Cherry Street; tel: 870-338-4350; www.deltaculturalcenter.com; Tue–Sat 9am–5pm) contains exhibits on the Civil War, agriculture, slavery, and the Mississippi River, as well as features on local bluesmen like Louis Jordan, Howlin' Wolf, and Sonny Boy Williamson, original DJ for the influential radio show, 'King Biscuit Time.'

The show made the names of many blues pioneers, and broadcasts to this day. The *King Biscuit Time* show is the longest-running blues radio broadcast in the world, and visitors can watch as it's aired live each weekday at 12.15pm. The station, KFFA, also hosts the King Biscuit Blues Festival. Held every October since 1986, it is the largest free outdoors blues festival in the nation.

Ellis Cedell Davis's 1954 guitar and the knife he used as a slide on display at the Delta Cultural Center in Helena.

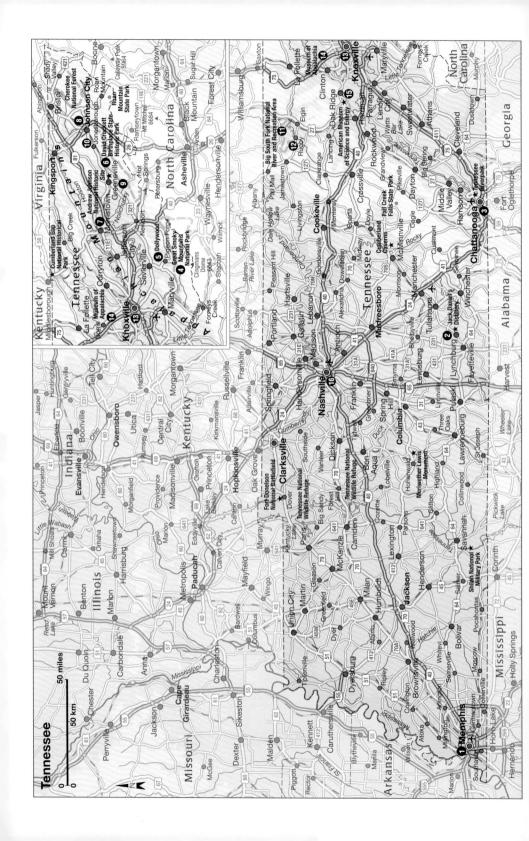

TENNESSEE

Admitted into the Union in 1796, Tennessee was an early destination for frontiersmen: Davy Crockett began life and exploration near Jonesborough.

Andrew Johnson, a Greeneville native, kept his Senate seat even though Tennessee seceded from the Union, and became president after Lincoln's assassination. Seventh President Andrew Jackson's 'rough and ready' reputation is confounded by the elegance of his Nashville home, The Hermitage. Among the mountains of Tennessee, the Great Smokies rise majestically. The half-million acre (200,000-hectare) national park is a terrain practically unchanged in hundreds of years. The hills are steep and rugged, the forests dense, sheer cliffs offer magnificent scenery, and lush vegetation is everywhere, with an extraordinary variety of birds, reptiles, and mammals.

A joy to explore, Tennessee is only 520 miles (840km) wide and 120 miles (190km) deep. Distances are short, and major cities are only a few hours' drive apart. Fast highways cross the state, and the Tennessee Scenic Parkway System gives 2,300 miles (3,700km) of wellmarked, mostly two-lane roads, with historic sites and excellent recreational areas, plus the wonderful Natchez Trace Parkway.

Tennessee is not only for the 'great outdoors' though. This Southern state offers modern man-made diversions: Memphis, worldfamous as the home of rock'n'roll and the King himself, has

a glass pyramid for its namesake, and the splendid, sobering National Civil Rights Museum. Nashville, sparkling capital of country music, was known as the Athens of the South, and boasts a Parthenon from the 1896 state centennial, an exact replica of the Greek original.

From the mountainous east to the Mississippi River, Tennessee, 'the Volunteer State,' presents visitors with an alphabet of attractions and activities: The American Museum of Science and Energy, Beale Street in

Main attractions

Beale Street
National Civil Rights
 Museum
Graceland
Jack Daniel's Distillery
Rock City Gardens
Chattanooga Choo Choo
 Rail Station
The Great Smoky
 Mountains
Dollywood
Big South Fork

Map on pages 220, 223

Sun Studio in Memphis.

Memphis, Chickamauga Civil War battlefield, Dollywood, Elvis, Fort Donelson, Graceland, The Hermitage, Iron Mountain Stoneware, Jack Daniel's Bourbon Distillery, kayaking on wild rivers, Lookout Mountain, the Museum of Appalachia, the National Civil Rights Museum, Opryland, a Parthenon and a Pyramid, quiet mountain trails, Rocky Mount, the Sunsphere, Knoxville, Tennessee Walking Horses, the Union Soldiers' monument at Greeneville, Victorian houses, James White's Fort, xylophones in Nashville's Symphony Orchestra, the Sgt Alvin York monument, Zoo Choo at the Knoxville Zoo.

Music, mountains, heritage, history, National Scenic Byways, and Elvis Presley, too. With all this in just one state, who could fail to be charmed by the magic of Tennessee?

MEMPHIS

With the birthplace of rock'n'roll, the mansion of The King, and a pyramid by the river, the home of the World Barbecue Championship is still 'Soulsville, USA.'

The Peabody Memphis hotel.

Memphis ❶ is a town deep in the American cultural flow. Since the completion of the railroad in 1857, when the port became the South's link to the Atlantic Ocean, Memphis has been a place where people, ideas and cultures met and mixed. In the last two centuries, emancipation from slavery, some of the great American musical movements, both Black and white, and a meeting point in the unstoppable currents of the civil rights movement, all burst through Memphis. Still a major trading region, Memphis is home to FedEx and the global freight company, and the Memphis Cotton Exchange remains the largest spot cotton market in the US. Also America's largest trading and processing center for hardwoods, agribusiness and distribution through the ports are vital components in Memphis's thriving economy.

A proud echo from Egypt, where Memphis's name was inspired, is a spectacular indoor stadium in the shape of a Pyramid. Downtown there are trolleys to ride, ducks to watch waddling in one of the great landmark hotels, and good Southern cooking to be nourished and comforted by, in the town that hosts the world barbecue championships, what *USA Today* calls, 'one of America's friendliest cities.'

REVITALIZATION

The **Main Street Trolley** (tel: 901-274-6282; www.memphistravel.com/main-street-trolley) has revitalized Memphis' public transportation. The Memphis Area Transit Authority expanded this efficient service through Main Street and Downtown using vintage and historic carriages, giving atmosphere to this agreeable way to shake across town. Trolleys run between Central Station in the south of town, along Riverside Drive past the Pyramid in the north of the city, and along Front, Main, Second, and Third streets.

For the major musical sites, Sun Studio (see page 224) operates a free shuttle, calling at the Rock 'n'

Soul Museum, Beale Street, the Stax museum, Heartbreak Hotel, and Graceland Plaza. The bus departs hourly from 11am until 6pm.

The infamous **Memphis Pyramid** **A** (1 Bass Pro Drive) can be found in the Pinch Historic District. **Mud Island River Park** **B** (125 North Front Street; daily) is across a short bridge. The five-block River Walk is a model of the Mississippi's 1,000-mile (1,600km) journey from Cairo, Illinois, to its mouth at New Orleans. Outdoor events and concerts are also staged in the park. Within the park is the **Mississippi River Museum** (tel: 901-576-7230; call for current

hours), which further describes the natural and cultural history of the Lower Mississippi River Valley. From Mud Island, riverboat tours are available on the *Memphis Queen*.

Drive to Auction Avenue, and then turn left at North Second Street to **Slave Haven Underground Railroad Museum** **C** (826 North Second Street; tel: 901-527-3427; www.slavehavenmemphis.com; Mon–Sat 10am–4pm). On display are the trap doors and secret tunnels used by enslaved people who took refuge at this plantation, one of the important stations of the Underground Railroad. Reserve ahead for tours.

Memphis Glass Pyramid.

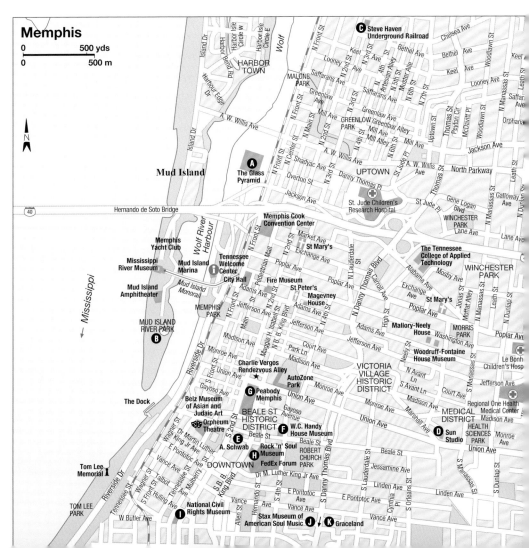

Fact

Sun Studio is the widely acclaimed and acknowledged birthplace of rock'n'roll, but it wasn't just Elvis who danced the boards and recorded hit tunes here. It was in this studio that Ike Turner recorded *Rocket 88* and Johnny Cash laid down the global smash hit *I Walk the Line*.

South along Second Street and left onto Union Avenue leads to the yellow logo and green blind of **Sun Studio** (706 Union Avenue; 901-521-0664; www.sunstudio.com; Sun–Thur 10am–5:15pm, Fri & Sat 10am–6:15pm), legendary producer Sam Phillips's cradle of rock'n'roll (see page 88). Tours pass displays of vintage recording equipment and memorabilia from the tiny studio, which has been open for business for over 50 years. The studio is small and functional, but the echoes of Ike Turner, Jerry Lee Lewis, Roy Orbison, Johnny Cash, Carl Perkins, and The King are almost audible. Tour guides are enthusiasts and/or musicians themselves, making this one of the more enjoyable tours in Memphis, maybe in the entire South. If you're in a car, go a short distance on Myrtle Street, turn right on Beale Street, then drive for five minutes to reach the entertainment district of **Beale Street**, which has been welcoming music lovers and party people since the 1800s. The street is a tourist attraction, but it only got that way because it drew players like Muddy Waters, John Lee Hooker, and Memphis Minnie up from the Mississippi Delta.

These few blocks of Beale Street are lined with clubs, bars, and restaurants. Most of the clubs offer a $20 wristband, which gives admission to the street's other clubs. **B.B. King's Blues Club** features both local and headline acts, and B.B. would make regular appearances here right up until his passing in 2015. The **Blues City Cafe and Band Box** is acclaimed for its hot tamales, Southern fried catfish, and over-broiled steaks, favored by President Clinton when he was in town. The **Rum Boogie Cafe** features a red-hot houseband, and the stage has seen action from Stevie Ray Vaughan and Aerosmith, to name but two. The main criterion for bar selection is 'who's playing tonight?'

A visit to Beale Street would be incomplete without seeing the **A. Schwab** store, definitely one of the world's more unusual souvenir opportunities. Here since 1876, Schwab offers clothing and hats, as well as a useful selection of voodoo requisites. On the corner of Beale and 4th streets, the **W.C. Handy House Museum** (www.wchandymemphis.org/wchandy.html) is a shotgun shack where this acknowledged father of the blues raised six children. Nearby, Handy is also honored in the **W.C. Handy Performing Arts Park**. The park is a popular venue for outdoor events, festivals, and spontaneous jam sessions. Like any place where tourists throng, take a measure of street-savvy along to Beale Street, day or night.

DUCKS DELUXE

A block north of Beale Street is Memphis's most famous landmark, the **Peabody Memphis** (149 Union Avenue; tel: 901-529-4000; www.peabodymemphis.com). The two-story colonnaded open lobby is tiled with marble, surrounded by polished statues of elephants, and has an Italian marble fountain as its centerpiece, by the cocktail bar. The fountain pool is the daytime playground

Main Street Trolley in Memphis.

for five of the hotel's most pampered guests – the Peabody ducks. Arriving in procession across a red carpet from the elevator at 11am every morning, at 5pm they waddle back again for the ride up to their penthouse on the roof. Among the stores in the lobby is **Lansky's**, the men's outfitter to The King (Elvis, that is), formerly located on Beale Street.

Grown out of the side of the hotel, **Peabody Place** is a gleaming 300,000sq ft (28,000sq meter) super mall developed by the Belz Corporation, who reputedly own more real estate in Memphis than the state of Tennessee. A short walk south along Second Street leads to the Smithsonian's **Rock 'n' Soul Museum** ⊕, (191 Beale Street; tel: 901-205-2533; www.memphisrocknsoul.org; Wed–Sun 10am–5pm). Highly interactive displays draw out the story of the blues emerging from the cotton gins, via the radio, into the emerging teenage consciousness of the 1940s and 1950s. The Killer, Jerry Lee Lewis, is quoted as saying, 'without the co-operation of total resentment on the part of parents, rock'n'roll would never have survived.' Music plays from jukebox selections around the museum cases all the way from Memphis Minnie through James Brown to Gil Scott Heron, so allow several hours to wander around and enjoy the extravaganza.

At the same address, the **Gibson Showcase Factory** is a showroom for many of the popular guitar manufacturer's more exotic offerings. Since their founding over 100 years ago by mandolin maker Orville Gibson, the brand has played an important role in popular music. Informative guided tours of the Memphis factory are available, and showcase instruments are on display in the store. The adjacent Gibson Lounge (tel: 901-944-7998) is good venue for visiting top-line performers of blues, jazz, country, rock, and rock'n'roll. Tickets are normally only available at the door, on the night. Shows are on most nights of the week.

SOMBER SITE

About half a mile south along Second Street, turn right at Huling Avenue to the **National Civil Rights Museum** ❶ (450 Mulberry Street; tel: 901-521-9699; www.civilrightsmuseum.org; Wed–Mon 9am–5pm). It is built around the courtyard of the Lorraine Motel, and specifically the balcony where Martin Luther King, Jr was assassinated by a rifle-shot from the building opposite on Monday, April 4, 1968. The shot was, as with most of the 1960s political assassinations, alleged to have come from a lone gunman, James Earl Ray in this case.

The clear and moving exhibits eloquently chronicle the civil rights struggle in the US, beginning in 1619. The 1955 Montgomery bus boycott is described aboard an actual bus, where the seat occupied by Rosa Parks, and its significance, is illustrated. Some of the terrifying violence from the early 1960s in Birmingham, Alabama, is displayed in newsreel footage.

Room 306 of the Lorraine Motel, the room Dr King occupied on that April

Beale Street.

morning, is preserved intact, the bed unmade, a desk set with breakfast things, just as it was on that day, seen through a glass wall from the adjacent room. Heard in the background is a recording of Mahalia Jackson singing Precious Lord, *Take my Hand*. King had heard a choir rehearsing the song for that evening's meeting, and called down to them to 'Sing the song real good tonight,' shortly before the fatal shooting. Mahalia Jackson sang the song at King's funeral.

The **Stax Museum of American Soul Music ❶** (926 East McLemore Avenue; tel: 901-261-6338; www.staxmuseum.com; Tue–Sun 10am–5pm) is southeast of Downtown, on the site of the original Capitol movie theater. One of the most influential recording stables of the soul era is celebrated here. The history of 'Soulsville, USA' shows more than 2,000 exhibits, including copies of all of the Stax recordings, and much memorabilia from this explosive talent pool. Albert King's famous purple 'Flying V' guitar is on show, along with one of his more extravagantly frilly shirts, as is

Isaac Hayes's peacock-blue Cadillac Eldorado, trimmed in gold and named *Superfly*, naturally.

The Sun Studio shuttle, or a 10-minute drive south of Downtown, leads to **Graceland ❸** (Elvis Presley Boulevard; tel: 901-332-3322; www.graceland.com; daily 9am–4pm). With over one million visitors each year, Graceland is second only to the White House as the most visited private residence in the US; prepare to wait in long lines to enter, often next to impersonators in leather jackets and quiffs. For such a megastar, and in comparison to the opulence of today's celebrities, the 23-room Graceland seems surprisingly modest. As soon as Elvis had made enough money in 1957, he bought the mansionette for $102,500 as a home for himself and his parents. He kept the name, which came from the niece of the original owner, but added the musically-themed gates the same year. The interior style is unrestrained, over-the-top, distinctly 1970s, and generally eye-popping. More somberly, Elvis, and his parents Gladys and Vernon, are buried in the small, quiet Meditation Garden at the rear of the house, alongside a marker for Jessie Garron Presley, Elvis's stillborn twin brother.

HOUND DOG

Across the road is The King's impressive auto museum, showcasing a Stutz Bearcat and a Blackhawk, and more Cadillac fins than you could shake a hip at. A little farther along, Elvis's two aircraft, the Lisa Marie and Hound Dog II, are also open for inspection.

AROUND TENNESSEE

Sample the cellars of the Jack Daniel's Distillery, choo-choo into Chattanooga, or wander the pine-scented hills to Pigeon Forge and Dollywood.

After the bright lights of Memphis, the rolling mountains of Tennessee are waiting to be explored. Civil War history is presented with Southern panache

Tourists visit Elvis Presley's Graceland Mansion.

along this route, which begins with a long straight drive down I-64 from Memphis to East Tennessee, loops through mountain roads, and ends at Knoxville – just a short drive from Nashville.

LYNCHBURG

The 100-mile (60km) drive from **Memphis** to Lynchburg is quicker than it seems, as the road is well maintained. Still, the **Natchez Trace Parkway**, once one of the most heavily traveled – and dangerous – roads on the Southwest frontier, offers a pleasing change of pace (see pages 161 and 227). These Native American trails wound their way from the middle of the state toward Natchez, Mississippi, a distance of around 400 miles (640km). The trail fell into disuse after riverways replaced overland travel as the primary means of transportation. At milepost 385.9, the **Meriwether Lewis Monument** marks the gravesite of the famous explorer who did so much to chart these frontiers.

The first stop is **Lynchburg ❷**, but considering the town's primary export, it may be as well to park the car, stay the night, and prepare to sleep it off. The **Jack Daniel's Distillery** (tel: 931-759-6357; daily 9am–4.30pm) makes sour-mash whiskey in this tiny town (pop. 361, according to the label on the bottle, around 6,000 in reality). Jack Daniel's calls itself America's oldest registered distillery; charcoal mellowing with hard sugar maple is why Tennessee whiskey differs from most Kentucky bourbons. Tours include a stop at Mister Jack's original office, which contains 'the safe that killed him.' Your tour guide will be happy to explain how this event came about.

Chattanooga ❸ is a short way south on SR 50. The city's Downtown revival was thanks to an abundant but formerly neglected resource: looping through the city, the Tennessee River had few recreational opportunities, but now the **Tennessee Riverpark** is

a 22-mile (35km) greenbelt highlighting the city's stunning natural beauty. Beginning at the Chickamauga Dam, it extends through Downtown to the scenic Tennessee River Gorge, and includes mini-parks, hiking trails, historical sites, playgrounds, and fishing piers. Walkways provide access to the Tennessee Aquarium, the Hunter Museum of Art, and many other attractions.

The **Tennessee Aquarium** (tel: 800-262-0695; www.tnaqua.org; Sun–Fri 10am–5pm, Sat 10am–6pm) is built around a spectacular 60ft (18-meter) canyon and contains two living forests and 22 tanks. Visitors follow the Tennessee River's course from its source in the Appalachian Mountains to the Gulf of Mexico. At the aquarium, river otters and alligators inhabit the river areas; stingrays, sharks, and colouful ocean fish patrol the Gulf of Mexico. Next door, the **Creative Discovery Museum** (tel: 423-756-2738; daily 10am–5pm) offers hands-on educational fun for kids and adults. This interactive museum includes an Artist's

☉ THE NATCHEZ TRACE

This 8,000-year-old trail wanders south from Nashville, through Tennessee, and clips the corner of Alabama. From here it snakes by Tulepo, Mississippi, and continues all the way to Natchez. The Trace began life as a series trails trampled by buffalo between feeding grounds. By the late 18th and early 19th centuries, as many as 10,000 'Kaintucks' (boatmen from anywhere north of Natchez) regularly braved the Trace. Delivering cargo in New Orleans and often selling their boats in Natchez, they took a rifle, a bottle of whisky, and a pack of cards, and either rode or hiked the trail back north. In the other direction, pioneers bound for Mississippi came south, and by 1800 a mail service followed the paths.

The remoteness of the trail, located in deep forest and dense undergrowth, together with many ferocious wild animals in the woodland made the Trace harsh and unforgiving territory, where a slight injury could easily become life threatening. There were also the hazards of murderous bandits, and the hostile Native Americans. As a result the Trace earned itself the nickname: 'the Devil's Backbone'. During the 1820s, trade developed on the Mississippi River and use of the Trace declined. The woods and brush began to reclaim it, until its restoration by the National Park Service, along with a scenic drive called the Natchez Trace Parkway.

Studio, a Musician's Workshop, and a Field Scientist's Laboratory, where visitors can excavate for dinosaur hones.

The **Hunter Museum of Art** (tel: 423-267-0968; www.huntermuseum.org; Mon, Wed–Sat 10am–5pm, Sun noon–5pm) is as renowned for its setting on a 90ft (30-meter) limestone bluff above the river as for its outstanding collection of American art. The museum is split between a 1904 Classical-Revival mansion, and a contemporary building with large windows overlooking the river. The buildings connect by an interior elliptical staircase and a rooftop sculpture garden. Artists include Mary Cassatt, Childe Hassam, Thomas Hart Benton, Ansel Adams, and Albert Bierstadt, plus many international touring exhibitions. Across from the Hunter, the **Houston Museum of Decorative Arts** (tel: 423-267-7176, www.thehoustonmuseum.org; Tue–Sat noon–4pm) displays Anna Safely Houston's 10,000 pieces of antique glass, china, and furniture.

Train enthusiasts shouldn't miss the **Tennessee Valley Railroad Museum** (tel: 423-894-8028; www.tvrail.com;

Point Park Civil War Cannon Monument on Lookout Mountain, Chattanooga.

Wed–Sun 9am–3:30pm). The 40-acre (16-hectare) outdoor museum, just outside the city, is a railroader's dream, with a marvelous collection of classic locomotives, Pullman sleeping cars, dining cars, and cabooses. Chattanooga's key role in the outcome of the Civil War is commemorated in the moving **Chickamauga and Chattanooga National Military Park** (see page 96).

At Rock City Gardens (tel: 706-820-2531; www.seerockcity.com; daily 8.30am–6pm) on Lookout Mountain, Lover's Leap claims a view over seven states. A trail pinches through Fat Man's Squeeze and over the Swing-Along Bridge, across a yawning canyon. At nearby Ruby Falls, an underground passageway leads to a soaring, illuminated waterfall. A ride on the **Lookout Mountain Incline Railway** (tel: 423-821-4224; www.ridetheincline.com; Mon–Fri 9am–6pm, Sat and Sun 9am–7pm) is the scary but scenic way to reach the mountaintop. The world's oldest and steepest incline railway – opened in 1895 – scales a steep 72.7 percent grade and affords panoramic views of the city through glass-roofed rail cars.

There are also uncrowded places for fishing, boating, swimming, and watersports on southeast Tennessee's Hiawassee Scenic River, Tellico River, and Tellico Lake, created by the Tennessee Valley Authority.

THE GREAT SMOKY MOUNTAINS

To the northeast is the main attraction of east Tennessee. Not Dollywood, although that's here too – it's the Great Smoky Mountains. Everyone who comes here has a favorite trail: waterfall, flower, or view. These comforting old mountains, beginning in Tennessee and ending in North Carolina, straddle the state boundaries as they go, and inspire very strong attachments. The fantastic **Great Smoky Mountains National Park** ❹ was carved out of 500,000 acres (200,000 hectares) of private land only about 90 years ago: People return to their old homes to reunite with families, fill a jug with clear spring water, or lay flowers on the grave of a loved one. When the first white settlers entered the region in the late 1700s, the Smokies were inhabited by the Cherokee Native Americans, who named the mountains Shaconage, 'place of the blue smoke.' The Cherokee built homes from logs and settled in villages along the Oconaluftee River and Deep Creek. Their famous chief, Sequoyah, devised a written alphabet, and the Cherokee published their own newspaper.

EARLY SETTLERS

The arrival of Europeans, mostly of Scots-Irish heritage, in the 18th century spelled the demise of Cherokee society. Between 1783 and 1819, frontiersmen flooded through the gaps in the mountains, Revolutionary War veterans received land grants in the Smokies, and treaties were signed that left the Cherokee with only a scant remnant of their ancient homeland.

Visitors are attracted to the wild streams and waterfalls, excellent trails, including a 70-mile (112km) stretch of the **Appalachian Trail**; and the black bears, bobcats, red wolves, white-tailed deer, and other wildlife that use the Smokies both as refuge and as nursery ground. From the Smokies' windswept crest, Newfound Gap Road winds down the north face of the mountains, following the tumbling water of the West Prong of the Little Pigeon River as it flows into Sugarlands Valley.

After gathering information from **Sugarlands Visitor Center** (tel: 865-436-7318; daily 9am–5pm), follow Little River Road for an excursion to **Cades Cove**, which has one of the country's best collections of pioneer homes and farmsteads in an 'open-air museum.' Farmers in Cades Cove took most of their wheat and corn to be ground at the **John Cable Mill**, powered by a large wooden water wheel near the **Cades Cove Visitor Center**. John Cable's daughter, known as 'Aunt' Becky, lived most of her life in the nearby two-story frame house built in 1879.

Farmhouse at Cades Cove dating back to the early 1820s.

⊘ CHOO CHOO

Glenn Miller made the song *Chattanooga Choo Choo* an international hit in the 1941 movie *Sun Valley Serenade* directed by H. Bruce Humberstone. It celebrated Chattanooga's railroad heritage, which was centered around the grand, Beaux Arts-style Terminal Station, built in the early 1900s.

Nowadays, the station is the busy hub of the 30-acre (12-hectare) Chattanooga Choo Choo complex, which features vintage sleeping cars turned into unique hotel accommodations, restaurants, stores, tennis courts, gardens, a model railroad, and a 1915 steam locomotive that served the Chattanooga & Southern Railroad. It's particularly good place to spend the holidays with a festive Winter Wonderland featuring ice skating, twinkling lights and even Santa himself.

Other houses on or near the 11-mile (18km) Cades Cove loop are open to the public, including the **John Oliver Place, Elijah Oliver Place**, **Tipton Place**, and **Carter Shields Cabin**. These houses make it easy to imagine just what life was like a century ago. The walls still carry a strong smell of kerosene and the faint odor of apples.

Cades Cove is so popular that bumper-to-bumper traffic is a perpetual problem on the loop road. The best solution is to detour onto gravel country roads, like Sparks Lane, park the car and take a picnic basket into the green pastures. Early morning is a magical time to see the cove; the sun burns swirling mist off the surrounding mountains, and spider webs sparkle with dew among the grass. Bluebirds perch on fence posts, and the horses, cattle, and deer graze, oblivious to human presence.

The highest peak in the Smokies is **Clingmans Dome**, towering high at 6,643ft (2,025 meters) and straddling the Tennessee/North Carolina border. At Newfound Gap, a mile above sea level, take the 7-mile (11km) spur road west to the Clingmans Dome parking lot, where a half-mile trail leads to a concrete observation tower. Be prepared: at these heights, fog is common, and long vistas may be obscured. On a clear day, however, the great ramparts of the Smokies spread out with blue ridge after blue ridge, separated by deep ravines. Their softness is deceptive; this is rough country.

After a hike in the Great Smoky Mountains you may need **Gatlinburg's** creature comforts. The town has dozens of hotels and motels; stores on The Parkway, its crowded main drag, sell everything from finely made mountain handicrafts and musical instruments to tacky souvenirs, T-shirts, fudge, and taffy. Popular restaurants specialize in hearty meals of freshly caught trout, or bountiful breakfasts to get you off on a solid footing. An aerial tramway transports visitors 2.5 miles (4km) to **Ober Gatlinburg** (tel: 865-436-5423; daily 9.40am–5:40pm), a mountaintop amusement complex with a skating rink, craft shops, cafés, live entertainment, and winter skiing. Some of the best quality mountain crafts are created by members of the **Great Smoky Mountains Arts and Crafts Community** (tel: 865-436-6921; www.gatlinburgcrafts. com; daily 10am–5pm). Their studios and shops are on an 8-mile (13km) loop of Glades and Buckhorn roads, 4 miles (6km) from downtown Gatlinburg.

DOLLYWOOD

Dolly Parton's **Dollywood** ❺ also features handicrafts (tel: 800-365-5996; www.dollywood.com; hours vary, check website) at the theme park, nearby in **Pigeon Forge**. Dollywood's several stages set the countryside a-hummin' with live country & western, bluegrass, gospel, and pop music, with special appearances by big-name stars. The park is also brimming with rides and restaurants.

Rollercoaster at Dollywood.

Another early American legend – David 'Davy' Crockett – was born in 1786 in a log cabin on Limestone Creek, between Greeneville and Johnson City. Humorist, explorer, and martyr at the Texas Alamo, Crockett once described himself as 'common as bear spoor in a barley patch.' His one-room, dirt-floor cabin has been reconstructed in the **Davy Crockett Birthplace State Park** ⑥ (tel: 423-257-2167), where there are bounteous picnic spots by the creek and lots of places to camp.

Crockett fans can follow his trail to **Morristown** ⑦, where coonskin caps, buckskins and a likeness of 'Ole Betsy,' his favorite 'shootin' iron,' are on the walls of his father's reconstructed tavern, now open as the **Crockett Tavern Museum** (tel: 423-587-9900; Tue–Sat 11am–5pm).

At the **Rocky Mount State Historic Park** ⑧, Crockett and the frontier are very much alive (423-538-7396; www.rockymountmuseum.com; Wed–Sat 11am–5pm) at Piney Flats, north of Johnson City. The two-story main house was constructed in the 1770s as the first capitol of the Territory of the US south of the Ohio River. Guides in colonial dress weave flax into yarn, cook on an open hearth, and lead you back in time.

In **Greeneville** ⑨, instead of the Confederate Johnny Reb usually stationed at Southern courthouses, a Union army man stands guard on the pedestal. He symbolizes east Tennessee's strong Union sentiments during the Civil War. The region's Union loyalties are also personified by Greeneville's most famous son, Andrew Johnson. When the war began, Johnson was the only Southerner to remain in the US Senate. He became Abraham Lincoln's vice president in 1864, and after Lincoln's assassination in 1865, the 17th president. The **Andrew Johnson National Historic Site** (tel: 423-638-3551; www.nps.gov/anjo; Tue–Sat 9am–4pm; free) includes his log-cabin tailor shop, two homes, and his tomb. Founded in 1779

and cradled in the Blue Ridge Mountain foothills, **Jonesborough** ⑩ is Tennessee's oldest town. After the Revolution, it was briefly capital of the would-be-state of Franklin. For the first weekend of October, its beautifully preserved homes, churches, and public buildings are the backdrop for the National Storytelling Festival.

BIG SOUTH FORK

In east Tennessee, 10 million people come every year to Great Smoky Mountains National Park, but less than a tenth of them discover the peace and seclusion on offer in the wilds of the **Big South Fork National River and Recreation Area** ⑪.

Big South Fork sprawls over 10,000 acres (4,000 hectares) of rugged grandeur that belongs to the Cumberland Mountains of northern Tennessee and southern Kentucky. Most of its wooded ravines, rocky gorges, and white-water rivers are well away from paved roads, on trails accessible only by foot, horseback, and four-wheel-drive. Operated by the US Park Service, the useful **Bandy**

The Cumberland River at Big South Fork National River and Recreation Area.

Creek Recreation Area has campsites, picnic pavilions, showers, and rest rooms. Train buffs shouldn't miss the **Big South Fork Scenic Railway**, a two-hour journey through a deep tunnel and beautiful gorge, and along the picturesque banks of Roaring Paunch Creek.

It is possible to go even further back in time to the Victorian English village of **Rugby** ⓬. In 1880, Thomas Hughes, a social reformer, established Rugby as a haven for younger sons of English gentry. Under Victorian primogeniture tradition, firstborn sons usually inherited their fathers' estates, compelling siblings to enter 'respectable' professions such as medicine or law. Rugby allowed the disinherited to take up farming and other trades without social stigma. Victorian homes, stores, an Anglican church, a 7,000-book library, and a schoolhouse were built for the 450 villagers. The experiment failed, but the village endured. More than 20 original structures re-create the age of Dickens and Queen Victoria. The colony's rise and fall is chronicled at the Rugby schoolhouse visitor center.

HIGHLAND WINES

The lacy cascades of **Fall Creek Falls** are among the joys of roving the Cumberlands, the eastern USA's second-highest waterfall. **Jamestown** has a surprising taste of Tennessee at the **Highland Manor Winery** (tel: 931-879-9463; www.highlandmanorwinery.com; Mon–Sat 10am–6pm, Sun 12pm–6pm), with entertainment at the Cumberland County Playhouse.

East of the Cumberlands, the Appalachian Mountains jut up to southwestern Virginia and southeastern Kentucky. In the late 1700s and early 1800s, Upper East Tennessee, as the area is known, was the new nation's western frontier. In 1775, Daniel Boone expanded the frontier by opening the Wilderness Road through **Cumberland Gap**. Wagon trains followed, then late last century Boone's trail was asphalted for the heavy traffic on what had become part of US25. In a happy turnabout, in 1996, the Cumberland Gap Tunnel was opened to divert the highway away from the historic trail. The National Park Service is now slowly removing the asphalt and replanting the trail to how it was in Boone's era. Threaded with hiking trails, it is set to become part of the 21,000-acre (8,500-hectare) **Cumberland Gap National Historical Park** (tel: 606-248-2817; www.nps.gov/cuga). Gift shops, restaurants, and an on-the-spot wedding chapel can be found in the little town of Cumberland Gap, which borders the park.

KNOXVILLE

Knoxville ⓭, with a metro population of around 185,000, is the urban gateway to the Smokies. Students on the University of Tennessee's (UT) main campus give the city a youthful flavor. The city especially comes alive on Saturdays in the fall, when 96,000 fans, dressed in bright "UT orange," cheer on the Volunteers football team. Those in search of intellectual stimulation can enjoy the university's films, lecture

Fall Creek Falls.

series, or concerts. UT's **McClung Museum of Natural History & Culture** (tel: 865-974-2144; mcclungmuseum.utk.edu; Tue–Thur 9am–5pm) is a field day for curious minds of all ages. Its well-displayed collections illuminate Tennessee's past through anthropology, archaeology, and natural history.

The town of Knoxville also has many cultural and recreational amenities. **Blount Mansion** (tel: 865-525-2375; www.blountmansion.org; Wed–Sat 10am–4pm), almost hidden among downtown Knoxville's modern buildings, is one of Tennessee's most revered historic shrines. Here in 1796, Territorial Governor William Blount, assisted by Andrew Jackson and other prominent minds, drafted the constitution that made Tennessee America's 16th state.

James White's Fort (tel: 865-525-6514; www.jameswhitesfort.org; Mon–Fri 9.30am–4pm), within musket range of Blount Mansion, was the area's first settlement. General James White built the sturdy log stockade in 1786. The fort's seven buildings bring the history to life with exhibits of pioneer weapons and furnishings.

The city has also revived some of its more recent past. After the Civil War, merchants, wholesalers, and industrialists made their fortunes behind the ornate brick facades around Jackson Avenue and Central Street. Forgotten for decades, the **Old City** has come back to life with restaurants, cafés, music clubs, artists' lofts, antiques shops, art galleries, trendy apparel boutiques, and what-not stores that attract fun-seekers day and night.

World's Fair Park (tel: 865-215-1158; www.worldsfairpark.org; daily 6am–midnight) is a legacy of the 1982 event that brought visitors from near and far. It's pretty easy to find: just look for the 26-story **Sunsphere**, crowned by a golden glass ball.

Stop at the Knoxville Convention and Visitors Bureau at the entrance, then ride the elevator to the observation deck for a panoramic view of the city and the lazy, hazy Smoky Mountains.

The **Knoxville Museum of Art** (tel: 865-525-6101; www.knoxart.org; Tue–Sat 10am–5pm, Sun 1–5pm; free), has permanent collections of art by regional and international artists. The museum has a sculpture garden, gift shop, and café.

The natural habitats of the **Knoxville Zoo** (tel: 865-637-5331; www.zooknoxville.org; daily 9am–5pm) contain more than 1,000 exotic birds and animals. Exhibits include Gorilla Valley, Cheetah Savannah, and a river habitat for playful otters. Youngsters will particularly enjoy the Zoo Choo Train and Bird Show, or the rare chance to ride a camel.

A BETTER MOUSETRAP

The **Museum of Appalachia**  (tel: 865-494-7680; www.museumofappalachia.org; Mon-Fri 9am–5pm, Sat and Sun 9am-6pm) keeps the cultural heritage of the Southern Appalachians alive in the town of **Norris**, north of Knoxville. Among the 250,000 artifacts featured are some unusual inventions like the

A Tennessee Volunteers fan.

Market day in Knoxville.

OAK RIDGE

The birthplace of the atomic bomb was an unlikely one: the small town of Oak Ridge was built in secret by the US Army corps as a base for the Manhattan Project.

The town of Oak Bridge owes its very existence to the World War II Manhattan Project, the purpose of which was to develop the atomic bomb. Oak Ridge was established as a production site of the now-infamous Manhattan Project by the Americans, Canadians, and the British in 1942. The location was chosen for a number of reasons: it was remote but close enough to road and rail links; the nearby Norris Dam could be relied upon to provide ample

AEC administration building, 1945.

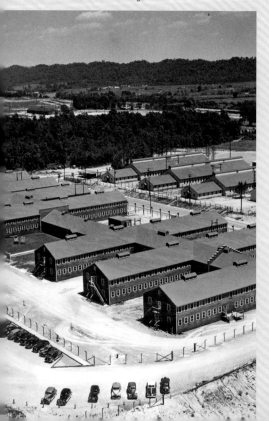

water and electricity; and crucially, the 17-mile (27km) -long site was contained within a valley, providing a natural barrier should the experiment go horribly wrong.

Subject to gagging orders but not Tennessee state law, the town grew quietly and quickly, from a population of just 3,000 in 1942, to more than 75,000 in 1945. The land was owned outright by the military, which administered everything from healthcare to grocery supplies, much to the chagrin of Tennessee Governor Prentice Cooper. The Governor was not a fan of being told what to do, or of the annual loss of half a million dollars in property taxes.

Architect John Merrill was contracted by the army to design the town in secret, and soon, with the backing of the army engineering corps, 300 miles (480km) of roads, 13 supermarkets, 10 schools, a library, and dozens of restaurants were created. Movie theaters, train stations, and thousands of prefabricated homes also appeared at a great pace, however because of the town's rapid expansion, there was a chronic shortage of housing and basic supplies throughout World War II.

Despite such a large population, information about work assignments was deliberately fragmented, and the majority of Oak Ridge residents didn't realize what they were working on until the first atomic bomb was used against Japan, in August 1945.

Two years after the war ended, the United States military turned the town over to civilian control, however the US Atomic Energy Commission retained ultimate authority. Of the four plants built here to separate plutonium, two are still standing and are now used for research and materials storage. The Oak Ridge National Laboratory is housed here and is home to the supercomputer Titan – one of the fastest supercomputers on the planet.

You have to be an American citizen to tour the original facilities, and it's a popular tour with limited seasonal availability to boot. There's even a waiting list, so if you'd like to visit and learn more, you need to put your name down well in advance. There are strict ID requirements also. Those wishing to arrange a tour need to contact the facility to make all arrangements at 865-294-4531.

self-resetting mousetrap. Fiddlers, guitarists, and maestros of the dulcimer, harmonica, and washtub bass are usually in fine form on the porch of the 1840s **Great House.**

Oak Ridge , west of Knoxville, was the birthplace of the Atomic Age. During World War II, this 'secret city' was created as part of the Manhattan Project to develop the atomic bomb. Now the modern city of almost 30,000 people welcomes visitors to the energy-related museums and other attractions. There is also a 38-mile (60km) Oak Ridge Self-Guided Motor Tour. Pick up maps and information from the Oak Ridge Convention and Visitors' Bureau, and begin the tour next door at the **American Museum of Science and Energy** (865-294-4531; www.amse.org; Mon–Sat 9am–5pm, Sun 1pm–5pm).

The museum's 200 exhibits include quizzes, computer games, and do-it-yourself experiments relating to everything from fossil fuels to nuclear fission. Other attractions include the **Children's Museum** (tel: 865-482-1074; www.childrensmuseumofoakridge.org; Tue–Fri 10am–4pm, Sun 1–4pm); a hands-on Southern Appalachians heritage center; the **Oak Ridge Art Center** (tel: 865-482-1441; www.oakridgeartcenter.org; Tue–Fri 9am–5pm, Sat–Mon 1–4pm; free), with permanent and touring collections; and the University of Tennessee's bright, sweet-smelling **Arboretum**.

NASHVILLE

Called the Athens of the South for its academia, and Music City USA for its recording studios, **Nashville ^** has a twang that tickles the head and the feet.

Nashville is a blend of New South progress with Old South charm, 21st-century attractions, and a history rich in the music that has brought worldwide fame to the capital of Tennessee. The city has art galleries, museums, and entertainment venues of all kinds, from large outdoor amphitheaters and high-capacity indoor concert venues, to small, out-of-the-way places where famous entertainers are often gigging or just sitting in. Aspiring singers and songwriters come to master their craft and strive for recognition too.

The settlement that was to become the city of Nashville was founded on Christmas Day, 1779, when James Robertson crossed the Cumberland River with a small group of men and made camp on the overlooking bluffs. Here they built Fort Nashborough. Less than a year later, a larger group of settlers arrived by the Cumberland River. On May 1, 1780, Tennessee's first government was established with a document known as the Cumberland Compact, a set of rules created and agreed by the 200 settlers who called the area home.

What had formerly been a part of North Carolina became Tennessee, the 16th state in the new Union on June 1, 1796. Nashville became the state capital of Tennessee around 47 years later, in 1843.

Nashville skyline view from the Shelby Street pedestrian bridge.

Nashville was a frontier town from the beginning, a small outpost of rugged pioneers in a decidedly hostile environment, under frequent assault from Native American people who had banded together, determined to destroy the small settlement. Winters were harsh, with constant food shortages, sickness, and little help from outside. Despite these hardships, the town grew quickly, with Davidson Academy established in 1785, Blount College in 1794, and Nashville's first newspaper, the Tennessee Gazette, started in 1797.

Nashville's early growth came from the westward expansion of the original colonies, and its key position on the Cumberland River. The river served as a highway, bringing goods and new residents, and transforming small Fort Nash borough into a full-scale city with rail service, schools, a hospital, and merchants. Nashville has been nicknamed alternately 'the Athens of the South,' for its institutions of higher learning, and 'Music City, USA,' for the many recording studios, the

headquarters of Gibson and Epiphone guitars, and the Grand Ole Opry.

ON BROADWAY

Nashville was designed, like many river cities, with a main street running east to west, ending at the riverbank. In Nashville, this street is **Broadway**. Streets beginning at the river and leading off either side of Broadway start as 1st Avenue, 2nd Avenue, and so on. They are designated either 1st Avenue North, or 1st Avenue South, depending on whether they are north or south of Broadway. As a result, it's easy to orient yourself in the area, and much of downtown Nashville is within a comfortable seven-block walking distance. Broadway between 1st and 7th Avenue will serve as a good point of reference, as the street is always an easy place to orient from. The Cumberland River bank is a good place to start. **Riverfront Park** is at the riverbank where Broadway intersects 1st Avenue. It has parking for those who prefer to leave their cars and walk around Downtown, but there are also parking lots

Nightlife on Broadway.

throughout the area. There's an excellent view across the river of the football stadium, home of Nashville's NFL team, the Tennessee Titans. Facing the river to the right is the **Shelby Street Bridge,** now a pedestrian walkway to the east bank (accessible at 4th Avenue South and McGavock Street).

WILD HORSE SALOON

Fort Nashborough (daily 9am–4pm; free) is less than a block from Riverfront Park up 1st Avenue North. The 1930s wood re-creation of the original fort provides a depiction of rugged pioneer life on the Cumberland. Back at Riverfront Park, it's a brief walk up Broadway to 2nd Avenue North, literally the next block. Nashville's **Hard Rock Cafe** is on the right. Turning right off Broadway onto 2nd Avenue North is the epicenter of Nashville's **Historic District**, the main tourist center for the city. Here are many familiar restaurants, as well as souvenir shops and thriving entertainment venues. Also on 2nd Avenue North is the famous **Wild Horse Saloon** (tel: 615-902-8200; www.wildhorsesaloon.com). Nashville's premier country music club is also a great spot for lunch or dinner. A walk through the area showcases many places for great Southern food, drinks, and entertainment.

At the summit of 2nd Avenue North is **Public Square**, the former site of the original Nashville courthouse and once the heart of the city. Returning to Broadway there are restaurants, nightclubs, and souvenir shops lining both sides of the street.

At 316 Broadway, between 3rd and 4th Avenue North, is **Hatch Show Print** (tel: 615-577-7710; www.hatchshowprint.com; daily 9.30am–5:30pm), America's oldest continuously operating letterpress shop, and a perfect place to shop for reproductions of music and show posters. At the corner of 4th Avenue North and Broadway is Gruhn Guitars, one of the world's most esteemed vintage guitar stores. There's guaranteed good pickin' here.

Just beyond Gruhn Guitars, at 422 Broadway, is **Tootsie's Orchid Lounge** (tel: 615-726-0463; www.tootsies.net; daily 9:30am–3pm). Tootsie's is Music City's premier honky-tonk, a traditional watering hole for Opry performers between shows. Ahead on the right is 5th Avenue North. Turn right, and the 1892 **Ryman Auditorium** immediately appears. It was the second but most famous home of the Grand Ole Opry (from 1943 to 1974). Two blocks up 5th Avenue North on the right, at the corner with Church Street, is the **Downtown Presbyterian Church**. Designed by William Strickland, also the architect of the State Capitol, this church is one of the best examples of Egyptian Revival architecture in America. This is also where Andrew Jackson was honored after his victory at the Battle of New Orleans in 1815. Farther up 5th Avenue at Deaderick Street is the **Tennessee State Museum** (tel: 615-741-2692; www.tnmuseum.org; Tue–Sat 10am–5pm, Sun 1–5pm; free).

Ryman Auditorium, Nashville.

TENNESSEE MARBLE

Up the hill to the left is **Legislative Plaza**, a vast open area. Up the steps is the Greek Revival **War Memorial Building** with an auditorium, and the **Military Museum** (Wed–Sat 10am–5pm). To the right at the top of the hill is the Tennessee **State Capitol** (www.nashvilledowntown.com/go/tennessee-state-capitol; Mon–Fri 9am–4pm), completed in 1859. The building is a highly notable American example of Greek Revival architecture and is constructed of Tennessee marble with iron roof braces. The lush grounds of the Capitol building are populated with statues, and the tombs of President James K. Polk and his First Lady wife are also here.

Across Broadway at 5th Avenue is the **Bridgestone Arena**, Nashville's largest concert arena. Inside on the ground level are the **Visitors Information Center** (tel: 615-770-2000; www.bridgestonearena.com), and the **Tennessee Sports Hall of Fame and Museum** (tel: 615-242-4750; www.tshf.net; Tue–Sat 10am–4pm). The museum comprehensively illustrates the history of local sports and sports figures from the 1800s to the present, and features lots of memorabilia. The Visitors Information Center has books, T-shirts, and other souvenirs for sale.

Most importantly, the lobby has a kiosk stuffed with informative pamphlets and brochures covering many of the historic, cultural, and educational attractions that the city has to offer. These brochures provide directions, hours of operation and admission costs. Continuing along 5th Avenue South, you will immediately see the architecturally bold **Country Music Hall of Fame** (tel: 615-416-2001; www.countrymusichalloffame.org; daily 9am–5pm). Highly recommended for music fans, even those who might not be aficionados of country or country & western, there are displays of costumes, instruments and automobiles, as well as films, photographs, and ephemera documenting the lives and lifestyles of famous country, blues, blue-grass, folk, rockabilly, and gospel artists. There is also a restaurant and a souvenir shop on the premises, with an extensive selection of related books and recorded music. Parking is available adjacent to the museum.

On Broadway beyond 7th Avenue, some kind of transportation is recommended. First up on the left side of Broadway at 901 is the 24,000-sq-ft (2,230-sq-meter) **Frist Center for the Visual Arts** (https://fristartmuseum.org) , Nashville's prime gallery for touring exhibitions. Continuing along Broadway away from the river, the next building on the left is the massive stone **Union Station**. Now a landmark hotel, the lobby and mezzanine level are certainly worth a peek. In another mile, Broadway forks and there are sites to see to the right and the left.

MUSIC ROW

For Music Row, take a left off Broadway onto 17th Avenue South. At the top of the hill a mile farther, is Wedgewood Avenue. Directly across Wedgewood is Belmont

Exhibition at the Country Music Hall of Fame and Museum.

University campus. One of the South's most significant antebellum mansions, the 150-year-old **Belmont Mansion** (tel: 615-460-5459; www.belmontmansion.com; Mon, Thur–Sat 10am–3:30pm, Sun 11am–3:30pm) is on the campus. Its owner, Adelicia Acklen, was one of America's richest women before, during, and after the Civil War. She managed to keep both Union and Confederate forces from appropriating her wealth, bore 10 children, outlived her three husbands (she is buried with all three of them), and died shopping in New York. She must surely have been one of the more colorful figures from American history.

Turn left at Wedgewood Avenue, then back down 16th Avenue South to the other half of Music Row. You will dead-end into a traffic circle graced in the center with *Musica*, a 40ft (12-meter) statue of dancing nudes. Around the traffic circle and down the hill on Demonbreun Street are a number of sidewalk cafés and coffee shops. Otherwise, follow the traffic circle for 180 degrees and return to Broadway.

If you take the right fork, Broadway becomes West End Avenue, then Harding Road, and eventually Highway 100, but it's all the same road. **Vanderbilt University** is on the left, at 21st Avenue. Then comes pretty, tranquil **Centennial Park** with its life-size replica of **The Parthenon**, now an art gallery (www.nashvilleparthenon.com; closed Mon and Tue) on the right. The area is known as a mecca for vintage and modern guitar fans. West End Avenue becomes Harding Road in about 3 miles (5km). On the left at 5025 Harding Road is the **Belle Meade Plantation** (tel: 615-356-0501; www.bellemeadeplantation.com; daily 9am–5pm), a Greek Revival mansion with a fine old barn where championship horses were bred in the 19th century. Along Highway 100, turn left on Cheek for the sweet-smelling, peaceful and lovingly manicured **Cheekwood Botanical Gardens and Museum of Art** (https://cheekwood.org; daily 9am–5pm).

MUSIC CITY

Printer's Alley, located off Church Street between 3rd and 4th avenues north, was once the center of Nashville's nightlife. Today, it still houses nightclubs and restaurants descended from the venues of the 1940s and 1950s. **The Exit/In** (tel: 615-321-3340; www.exitin.com) at 2208 Elliston Place, is known as Nashville's 'Music Forum.' Nearly every famous act in pop, rock, country, and blues has played it at one time or another. The **Bluebird Cafe** (tel: 615-383-1461; www.bluebirdcafe.com) is a small but respected room, mainly for acoustic music. It is located at 4104 Hillsboro Road in the Green Hills Area (reservations suggested).

Back Downtown, the **Tennessee Performing Arts Center** (tel: 615-782-4040; www.tpac.org) at 505 Deaderick Street is likely to stage anything from plays to headline vocalists. With popular musicals playing sell-out shows being the real draw.

Andrew Jackson's tomb. It's just 15 minutes from Downtown. Take 1-40 east to Exit 221.

Visitors head towards the entrance of The Parthenon.

240

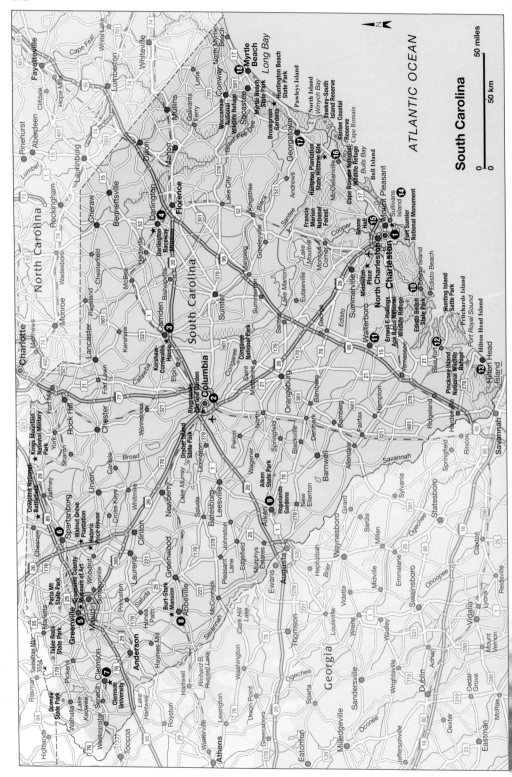

South Carolina

SOUTH CAROLINA

South Carolina is making an appropriately leisurely
and graceful transition from old to new South.

In Charleston, the South Carolina Aquarium is already the biggest tourist draw in the 'palmetto state,' and the revitalized waterfront has sprouted an IMAX theater among its attractions. Also, big attractions are a number of green championship golf courses, including Jack Nicklaus's Turtle Point, Tom Fazzio's Osprey Point, and the world-famous Ocean Ryder Cup Course.

South Carolina is home to the USA's first master-planned resort and residential community, bordered by loblolly pine, palmetto trees, and oak; Sea Pines cut the path that towns like Seaside and Disney's Celebration in Florida have followed. The Spoleto Festival, a 17-day event as modern as they come, has been described by the Washington Post as 'America's most comprehensive arts festival.'

Charleston – which played a key role in both the American Revolution and the Civil War – has spearheaded this revitalization, but the city still tends to the historical roots that run so deep in South Carolinan soil. South Carolina was the first state to secede from the Union in 1860, and the first to fire a shot in the conflict called, in these parts, 'The War of Northern Aggression.' Wealthy South Carolina planters had much to lose by continued association with the North and its fierce

opposition to the large plantation way of life. Several members of Jefferson Davis's cabinet and staff came from South Carolina.

Founded by the British in 1670, the original settlement of Charles Towne governed territory including what is now North Carolina, South Carolina, Georgia, and upper Florida. Ten years later it moved to its present location, now the city of Charleston. South Carolina saw much military action during the Revolutionary War, and relics are scattered throughout the state. But it

Main attractions

The Spoleto Festival
Charleston's Open Air
  Market
Battery and White Point
  Gardens
Fort Sumter
South Carolina Aquarium
Magnolia Plantation
Darlington Raceway
Sea Pines
Myrtle Beach

Maps on pages
240, 243

Trees draped in Spanish moss, Edisto Island.

suffered more during that 'other war,' and was a particular target for revenge.

The Southern signatures of leafy, climbing kudzu and romantic, ethereal canopies of Spanish moss still shade the white-columned mansions. Moist breezes even now are best relieved by tall glasses of lemonade, and the accent still wraps soft, soothing, and charming around the ears like cotton. Even the old African-English Gullah dialect persists among some Black communities in Charleston, as it does on the island of St Helena.

So, the more it changes, the more it stays the same, and what Johann David Schoepf wrote of South Carolina in 1783 still holds true: 'There prevails here a finer manner of life, and on the whole, there are more evidences of courtesy than in the northern cities.'

CHARLESTON

Hidden within an intricate system of deep-water creeks and salt marshes is **Charleston ❶**, a town as constant as the tides that have driven its fortune for 300 years.

Historic homes in downtown Charleston.

Pirate attacks, wars, fires, earthquakes, tornadoes, and hurricanes have ravaged this lovely city for centuries, but Charlestonians have always picked up the pieces, and in great style. Often recognized as one of the most desirable places in which to live in America, the clop of horses crossing cobblestone streets or the rustling of a summer breeze through palmetto trees instantly conjures a hint of the reasons why.

In 1670, a ship full of English colonists arrived and founded Charles Towne (now open to the public – see page 250) on the Ashley River, 5 miles (8km) upstream from Charleston's present location. Named after Charles II, Charles Towne endured 10 hard years of battling malaria, heat, flooding, and the Kiawah Native Americans. The colonists packed their bags and headed for the hills, moving to the peninsula we now know as Charleston.

The **Charleston Visitor Center ❹** (375 Meeting Street; tel: 800-868-8118; daily 8.30am–5pm) is a useful first stop on any tour of the town. Built in 1856 as a South Carolina Railroad freight depot, the center is one of the oldest railroad structures in the US. Here are opportunities to find the answers to questions, take advantage of the public restrooms (rare in the Historic District), and enjoy a 20-minute orientation film about the city. Then, leave the car here and hop aboard one of the many transportation options.

Across Meeting Street from the Visitor Center is the first and the oldest museum in the US, the **Charleston Museum ❸** (tel: 843-722-2996; Mon–Sat 9am–5pm, Sun noon–5pm). It features permanent and occasional exhibits focusing on Charleston, the Low Country, and the state. The museum-owned **Joseph Manigault House** next door offers tours of its restored interior and exterior. Built in 1803, the house is considered one of the finest examples of Federal-style architecture in the world and is a National Historic Landmark.

THE SWAMP FOX

Parallel to Meeting and on the other side of the Visitor Center is King Street, the city's central business artery. Traveling south on Upper King toward Calhoun Street, **Marion Square Park** is on the left. The park takes its name from American Revolutionary hero Francis Marion, the 'Swamp Fox,' known for eluding British officers in the Low Country swamps where he had hunted since childhood.

Facing the park stands the **Old Citadel** ⊙ – original site of one of the oldest military colleges in the nation, constructed in 1842. Now at a newer location farther north on the peninsula, the Citadel lost its battle to preserve single-gender education in the name of tradition, and in 1996 reluctantly admitted women cadets. Located at 171 Moultrie Street by the 65-acre (26-hectare), Victorian-style **Hampton Park**, the Citadel has a free on-campus museum of its own. It also presents a Dress Parade by the South Carolina Corps of Cadets most Friday afternoons throughout the academic year.

FESTIVALS

A city of festivals, Charleston's biggest is the **Spoleto Festival USA**. During the Spoleto and Piccolo Spoleto arts festivals each year, usually held at the end of May and early June, all the city's a

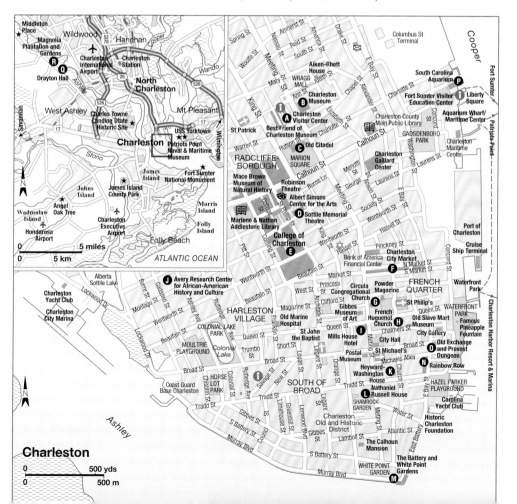

Charleston

stage, and there's absolutely no telling what delights there will be to see and hear: dance, experimental theater, opera, chamber music, performance art, crafts, and visual-arts shows. This is certainly the best time to experience Charleston, but keep in mind that there will be huge crowds, and hotels and airplane reservations need to be made well in advance. Calhoun Street was named for John C. Calhoun, an important statesman before the Civil War and vice-president of the United States under Andrew Jackson, and whose statue keeps watch from a pedestal in the park. Calhoun is the entrance to **Middle King Street**. An area heavily populated by College of Charleston (CofC) students, the student-oriented businesses – record shops, coffee houses, bars, and inexpensive restaurants – make it a perfect spot for browsing, grazing, and other forms of generally creative loafing.

From its earliest days, Charleston has been a city known for tolerance and the appreciation of life's little pleasures, and some of its larger pleasures too. By the early-to-mid-18th century, Charleston was one of the wealthiest ports in the Southeast. Exporting cotton, rice, and indigo from its 'golden coast,' Charleston imported in return the riches of Europe and the West Indies. Lured by a lavish lifestyle, grand homes, exquisite taste, and religious freedom not found in other colonies – hence its nickname the Holy City – artists and immigrants, seamen and merchants, rich and poor flocked here for profit and a good time. That was how it earned its other nickname – the Unholy City.

THE COLLEGE OF CHARLESTON

Taking a right off King Street into George Street leads past the classical-style **Sottile Theatre** ⓓ. Owned by CofC and opened as the Sottile Theater, one of the many local movie houses operating in Charleston in the 1920s, it's where *Gone with the Wind* had its local premiere.

On the next block, the herring-bone brick pattern of the walkway reveals that this is the midst of the **College of**

Horse-drawn carriage taking tourists through Charleston.

ⓞ JOHN C. CALHOUN

The seventh Vice President of the United States began his career in politics back in 1810, when the voters of Charleston elected him to the House of Representatives. John C. Calhoun vehemently opposed the influence of the British and advocated against America's neutrality in the Napoleonic Wars.

He would go on to become known as the cast-iron-man, for his controversial and unwavering defence of the right to own enslaved people and the view that slavery was a wholly positive thing, for both enslaved people and slave owners. Such was the controversy surrounding Calhoun that when he eventually died, his friends hid his body overnight in a church, and buried him secretly in an unmarked grave, fearing desecration by Federal troops during the Civil War.

Charleston campus. Founded in 1770, CofC was the first municipal college in the country. Crossing St Philip Street to the entrance and core of the college, the **Old Main Campus**, a National Historic Landmark, appears on the right. It includes the **Porter's Lodge**, which for many years was the residence of the college janitor whose goats roamed the College Green behind, until a student riot over the animals put an end to the affair in the 1850s. It now houses faculty offices. Through the triple arches and Doric columns is the two-story stuccoed brick **Towell Library; Randolph Hall**, where the first classes took place; and **The Cistern**, where CofC graduates, clad in white evening dress, receive their diplomas each May.

Back on King Street, interesting and unusual specialty stores lead down to Market Street. Straight ahead is **Lower King Street**. King Street is also the location of the well-known **Charleston Grill** (224 King Street; tel: 843-577-4522; www.charlestongrill.com), originally made famous by former chef, Louis Osteen, who has now moved on and is regarded as a hugely important figure in the Charleston culinary scene. Every restaurant that he works with immediately becomes the place to eat. After a block, Market Street encounters Meeting Street where the 1841 Roman Revival-style **Market Hall** stands, across the way from the entrance to the **City Market** ❸. The market has been in operation since just shortly after the Revolutionary War.

OPEN-AIR MARKET

The market trails for a few blocks behind Market Hall and contains open-air sheds in which craftsmen, collectors, artisans, and others peddle everything from jewelry and clothes, to sweetgrass baskets, artwork, T-shirts, and 13 Bean Soup mix. (This is a traditional Low Country favorite, along with Hoppin' John, black beans and rice, and shrimp and grits). They say there's a two-year waiting list for a spot to sell goods at the market.

The **Gibbes Museum of Art** (tel: 843-722-2706; www.gibbesmuseum.org; Mon–Sat 10am–5pm, Sun 1pm–5pm) houses one of the finest collections of American art in the Southeast, and includes an outdoor sculpture garden. Across the street is the **Circular Congregational Church** ❺, which dates from 1681. The original church, made of white brick, was called White Meeting House, and gave its name to Meeting Street. This church features some of the most interesting tombstones in the city. The local fascination with cemeteries may seem odd, but Charleston has some of the best, and considering how locals love a bit of ancestor worship, it isn't so very strange. Embossed with lounging skeletons atop gray slate, the stones in this cemetery rival those of the adjoining **St Philip Church** on Church Street. The **Dock Street Theatre**, at 135 Church Street, was the first formal theater in the country. It has its own gallery inside and a courtyard out back, which often features the

> **Ⓘ Fact**
>
> Charlestonians declared their independence from the British at the Old Exchange and Provost Dungeon. In the process, they made the building one of the most historic sites in the whole state. A series of bitter battles began almost immediately after independence was declared.

Charleston City Market.

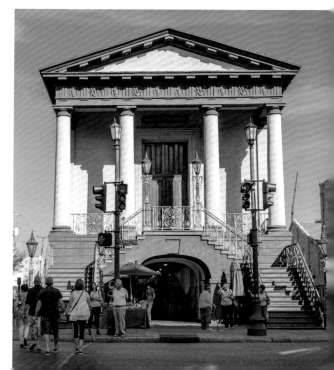

⊙ Tip

Charleston was built for carriages, not cars, so leave yours behind at the Visitor Center where there's free parking. Not only are the streets teeming with bicyclists, students, tourists, and traders, they are also prone to flooding.

Sundown Poetry Series during the Piccolo Spoleto Festival.

Across from the theater is the dominating Gothic Revival **French Huguenot Church** , set up in 1681 by French Protestant refugees. At one time, the church services were scheduled according to the tides, so that plantation owners, who traveled to the church mainly by boat, were able to arrive safely at the service in time for the opening hymn.

Up along Queen Street from the Dock Street Theater is the **Queen Street Playhouse**, home to South Carolina's longest running theater company the Footlight Players. Commanding the corner of Queen and Meeting streets is the magnificent **Mills House Hotel** Ⓗ (tel: 843-577-2400; www.millshouse.com). The original structure dates back to 1853, and it is one of the most elegant hotels Downtown. Robert E. Lee stayed here during his visit to Charleston in 1861. From the balcony, Lee watched as the most devastating fire in the town's history burst out of the Ansonborough neighborhood and raged through the

The busy intersection at Charleston's Market and Meeting streets.

city, devouring more than 500 buildings in its path. Beside the Mills House on Meeting Street is the Greek Revival **Hibernian Hall**. Built in 1840 and one of the oldest Irish fraternal societies in America, this is the venue for the famous St Cecilia Society Ball.

Chalmers Street on the left along Meeting, near Broad Street, is the longest of the numerous cobblestone streets in the city. Along it stands the **Fireproof Building**, home to the South Carolina Historic Society, and **Washington Square Park**, which was once lined with houses of ill repute. Also on Chalmers Street, in what is now the **Old Slave Mart Museum**, horses, steamships, and, regrettably, enslaved people were auctioned until 1863.

GULLAH

Many of the Black people in today's Charleston are direct descendants of the first enslaved Africans, brought to the city for their expertise in rice cultivation; rice became essential to the Charleston plantation system. Hired out as blacksmiths, masons, and artisans when they were not needed on the plantations, these enslaved people helped build the Charleston we know today, and their influence still permeates the city.

This is easily seen in the growing number of African-American galleries; at the **Avery Research Center for African-American History and Culture** ❶ at 125 Bull Street; in piazza ceilings painted 'haint blue' to ward off evil spirits; in the tight coils of the sweetgrass baskets that have been woven by the female descendants of enslaved people at the market, and at Broad Street for the past 300 years; in the wrought-iron gates of the **Philip Simmons Garden** from craftsman Philip Simmons, honored by the Smithsonian; and during the MOJA arts festival held each October. The Avery Center has established an excellent website linking the city's African-American sites and culture, where more information is available at www.africanamericancharleston.com.

Traces of the heritage are also evident in the conversations of the local people. Called Gullah, this distinctive Creole language has developed from a blend of dialects and was spoken on many plantations. West African intonations pepper the English-derived language, and its idiomatic expressions make it sometimes difficult to understand. Pure Gullah is dying out now, but its presence is still heard in the streets of 'Chaa 'stun,' as they say. Tours of many of the town's Gullah-inspired sites can be arranged; for information in advance, go to www.gullahtours.com.

At the intersection of Meeting and Broad streets rests the **Charleston County Courthouse**, **City Hall**, the **US Post Office** and **St Michael's Episcopal Church**, the oldest church building in the city. George Washington and Robert E. Lee worshipped here, and two signatories of the US Constitution are buried in the churchyard.

NAMED BY RIPLEY'S

The intersection continues to be called **The Four Corners of Law** after the Ripley's Believe It or Not strip coined the term because each corner represented a different legal branch – city, state, federal, and God's law. It's the only place where you can get married, divorced, pay your taxes, and pick up the mail, all in the same place, or at least reputedly so. Broad Street is known as the 'Wall Street of Charleston' because of the city being originally walled and surrounded by a moat, with Broad Street as its northernmost boundary.

Broad Street, lined with palmettos, flagstone sidewalks, and Charleston's real estate, law, and banking offices, comprises the city's financial center. Taking a left off Meeting Street, then a right off Broad onto Church Street, earthquake bolts are apparent on the sides of many of the buildings. Installed after the disastrous earthquake of August 31, 1886, each bolt stabilizes a metal rod running the length of the house between floors. Many Charlestonians employed this method to reinforce their homes after the 7.5 Richter Scale quake destroyed more than 100 buildings and damaged 90 percent of the city.

Along this portion of Church Street is **Cabbage Row**, on which DuBose Heyward based a fictional Catfish Row in his novel *Porgy*, which George Gershwin later turned into the wildly successful opera *Porgy and Bess*. The pre-Revolutionary string of double tenements were home to nearly 100 African-Americans, who frequently offered cabbages for sale from their window sills. Heyward based his character Porgy on Sammy Smalls, a crippled tenant. Today, the buildings are mainly occupied by gift shops.

Next door is the **Heyward-Washington House ❶**, owned by the Charleston local prominent rice planter Daniel Heyward. His son Thomas, who also lived here, was one of the 56 esteemed gentlemen who left their signatures to

Pavilion at White Point Garden.

PORGY

The origins of this novel, play, and, opera can be traced back to Charleston. The music heard on the city's street would come to shape it on the stage.

Author DuBose Heyward based much of his novel *Porgy* on Charleston's Cabbage Row, which in print and on stage, would become immortalized as Catfish Row. The novel began its transition into a play and then an opera after the composer George Gershwin read the novel in 1926. He immediately reached out to Heywood to champion an on-stage adaptation.

After eight years and many conversations with Gershwin, Heywood warmed to the idea but insisted that before a single note was played, Gershwin had to visit Charleston. It is a good job that he did too, because the music Gershwin heard on his journey through Charleston – a mix of folk songs passed down from generation to generation – is what inspired the entire libretto for the stage adaptation, *Porgy and Bess*.

Sammy Davis Jr in the 1959 film version of Porgy.

The songs sung in the stage adaption closely follow the tale that unfolds in the novel. Porgy is a homeless and disabled beggar, trying to survive in the mean slums of Charleston. Despite his lot in life, he never strays from his devotion and continuous attempts to rescue Bess from the evil clutches of her abusive and jealous lover Crown, and her drug dealer, a character called Sportin' Life.

Controversy surrounded the opera from the very first performance in 1935. The almost all-back cast did not receive a warm welcome at the time and many African Americans feared that a rare opportunity for a moment in the spotlight had been squandered.

Despite the initial controversy however, *Porgy and Bess* would go on to gain international notoriety and acclaim, with tours that spanned Europe and even Russia. The production has been championed by powerful literary figures, including Truman Capote and Harper Lee.

Today *Porgy and Bess* is a popular Oscar-winning film and there have been several 21st-century stage adaptations. It is clear that the world's love affair with the pair, and the mean streets of 1920s Charleston, endures to this day.

the American Declaration of Independence. Back on Meeting Street is the Federalstyle **Nathaniel Russell House** Ⓚ at No. 51. Owned and operated by the Historic Charleston Foundation, this is one of America's most important neoclassical houses. Built in 1808, it features handsome oval rooms, an impressive free-flying staircase spiraling unsupported for three floors, elaborate plasterwork ornamentation, and the kind of genteel period furnishings favored at the time by the merchant elite.

This is just one of the many museum-houses in the city which have been bought, restored, and maintained by local preservation groups. Lists of places that are open to visit are available from the visitor center (see page 242).

THE BATTERY

Continuing along Meeting or King streets towards the water leads to **The Battery & White Point Garden** Ⓛ. Shaded by massive live oak trees, with a large white gazebo at the center, the gardens are often used for weddings.

White Point Gardens got its name from the mounds of oyster shells that once covered this southernmost tip of the peninsula. Stede Bonnet was hung for piracy not far from this park, and Anne Bonny, the first pistol-wielding woman pirate – a Charleston debutante and subject of great local scandal still discussed at dinner parties today – often enjoyed a good Cooper River skinny dip in the chilly water just over the Battery wall.

The cannons and statues in the park commemorate city and state heroes and the many wars in which Charleston has fought. The **South Battery** grand homes that face the park catch the harbor breezes from their two-story piazzas. Walk along the promenade lining the Battery wall and stop at the brass marker laid in the curve of the sidewalk. One of the most significant sites from the Civil War can be seen from this vantage point. The target of the opening shots of the war, now maintained in the **Fort Sumter National Monument**, is way out over the water at the mouth of the harbor (see page 91, and below

People walking on the Battery.

⊘ FIRST FEMALE PIRATE

Anne Bonny is first female pirate recorded in history, with a fierce reputation to boot. Originally from Ireland, Bonny, in partnership with the infamous Calico Jack Rackman, plundered the Caribbean for the early part of the 18th century. At their first meeting, Rackman was so enamoured that he offered Bonny's husband a handsome sum in exchange for his wife. When her husband refused, the pair escaped the island together and Bonny became a part of Rackman's crew.

Bonny was a more than capable fighter, proving herself in combat during countless raids alongside their male crew. When the ship was eventually captured by the British Navy, the crew were hauled to Jamaica where everyone, apart from a heavily pregnant Bonny, was executed. Her sentence was paused until after she gave birth.

⊙ Tip

Charleston street names have eccentric pronunciations: Legare Street is pronounced 'Legree'; Huger Street is 'Yougee'; Hasell Street is pronounced 'Hazel'; and Vanderhorst Street is 'Vandrost'.

for boat information). **East Battery**, also called High Battery, is a picturesque street lined with grand mansions and the Regency-style **Edmondston-Alston House**, which is open to the public. Farther along the street is **Rainbow Row** , the longest stretch of pre-Revolutionary houses sharing the same wall in the US. It contains 14 residences and is the most photographed scene in Charleston.

At the foot of Broad, the street turns into East Bay Street at **the Old Exchange and Provost Dungeon** . The building was constructed by the British during the Golden Age of Charles Towne and was used to hold imprisoned pirates and Native Americans in the lower level. In March 1776, South Carolina declared its independence from colonial rule on the Exchange steps.

East Bay Street past the Old Exchange is definitely a place to go prepared with an appetite; it's one of the central dining spots in the city and thronged with popular and well-known eateries.

Down East Bay from **Waterfront Park**, with its pineapple-shaped fountain, is the **US Custom House**, where the Provincial Congress met in 1775 to set up the first independent government established in America.

A few blocks north on East Bay and heading toward the water leads to the corner of Calhoun and Concord, where the state's most visited attraction, the **South Carolina Aquarium** (tel: 843-577-3474; www.scaquarium.org; daily 9am–5pm) is located. When the aquarium opened in 2000, it spearheaded a revitalization of this part of the waterfront, now known as **Aquarium Wharf**.

As well as an **IMAX Theatre**, there's the National Park Service's **Fort Sumter Visitor Center**, a mainland reference point for information about the fort's historic role in the 'late unpleasantness' as Charlestonians refer to the conflict, and from where boats depart for trips to the site.

PLANTATION PARADISE

A Low Country tradition was for planters to pack up their bags and retreat to their townhouses in the city in order to escape the heat of sweltering Southern summers. Today, these plantations, located anywhere from 10 to 30 miles (16 to 48km) from Charleston, are open to the public everyday and offer a glimpse into a different world.

Three plantations or gardens are located off Highway 61, northwest of the city by the Ashley River. An interesting first stop, however, is the original settlement of Charleston, the **Charles Towne Landing State Historic Site** (1500 Old Town Road, Highway 171; tel: 843-852-4200; daily 9am–5pm). Benefitting from extensive and on-going renovation, this site and nature preserve has a reproduction 17th-century sailing vessel, an animal forest, and lovely Low Country vistas. Two of South Carolina's most beautiful plantations were built by a single family, the Draytons. Over four years, between 1738

The famous Pineapple Fountain, in Waterfront Park.

and 1742, John Drayton built **Drayton Hall** ❷ (tel: 843-769-2600; www.draytonhall.org; Wed-Mon 9:30am-3:30pm), one of the finest examples of colonial architecture in America, and the only one of the plantation houses on the Ashley River to survive the Civil War intact.

The house remained in the family until 1974, when it was purchased by the National Trust. The house's style is characterized by the classical hallmarks of symmetry and bold detail, and the two-story portico is believed to be the first of its kind built in America. The National Trust has made a point of leaving the house unfurnished, which provides the perfect opportunity to study the fine architectural details.

MAGNOLIA PLANTATION

Nearby **Magnolia Plantation and Gardens** ❸ (tel: 843-571-1266; www.magnoliaplantation.com; daily 9am–5pm) has been owned for over 10 generations by the Drayton family, and has one of the country's oldest and loveliest gardens (c.1680). The year-round blooms include America's largest display of azaleas and camellias. More than a century ago, tourists were clambering aboard steamboats and chugging up the river just for a visit to the magnificent grounds.

Middleton Place (tel: 843-556-6020; daily 9am–5pm) is America's oldest landscaped garden (c.1740). Although the house was burned during the 'late unpleasantness,' certain parts have been rebuilt. The stableyard often features craftsmen practicing old plantation trades.

AROUND SOUTH CAROLINA

Home of thoroughbred champions and little towns in a time-warp of American history, South Carolina is a Revolutionary rural idyll

Well away from the narrow cobblestone streets and fine plantation homes of Charleston, South Carolina is a pleasant patchwork of orchards and farms, hills, and rugged mountain foothills. The Chattooga River, where Burt Reynolds and Jon Voight battled whitewater rapids in John Boorman's 1972 movie, Deliverance, rips along the state's northwestern border with Georgia. Around the state, hospitable rivers and streams, and mammoth lakes welcome fishermen, swimmers, and sailors. Football is king at Clemson University and the University of South Carolina; stock-car racing rules at Darlington. Thoroughbred steeplechases and fox hunts are the favored sports in Aiken and Camden. Some of the towns are older than the state itself and were battlegrounds of the Revolution and the Civil War.

COLUMBIA

South Carolina's state capital is the town of **Columbia** ❹, lying on the Congaree River in the heart of the state, and with a metropolitan population of over 150,000. The University of South Carolina's main campus lends vitality to this old and new city. Founded

Drayton Hall.

Rear entrance to the Robert Mills House in Columbia.

The South Carolina State House, Columbia.

in 1786, Columbia has many historical land marks, museums, and a 50,000-acre (20,000-hectare) lake right on its doorstep.

The **Columbia SC Visitors Center** (tel: 803-545-0002; www.experiencecolumbiasc.com, Mon–Fri 9am–5pm), at 1120 Lincoln Street, is a good place to start. Watch the orientation film and pick up information on attractions, hotels, restaurants, and tours, then walk across the street to the Capitol.

The **Italian Renaissance South Carolina State House** (tel: 803-734-5049; Mon–Fri 9am–5pm, Sat 10am–4pm) was still under construction when it was shelled by Sherman's Union troops in May 1865. Bronze stars cover the cannonball scars. The **African-American Historical Monument** was the first of its kind on any state house grounds in the US. Dedicated in 2001, it traces the history of African Americans from the Middle Passage to the fight for freedom in the Civil War and the more recent struggles for civil rights.

Civil War enthusiasts are bound to enjoy the flags, uniforms, weapons, and soldiers' personal effects in the **Confederate Relic Room and Museum** (tel: 803-737-8095; www.crr.sc.gov; Tue–Sat 10am–5pm) in the War Memorial Building on the neighboring University of South Carolina campus. The museum also exhibits 18th- and 19thcentury women's fashions, old money, stamps, and everyday domestic items. The **McKissick Museum** (tel: 803-777-7251; Mon–Fri 8.30am–5pm, Sat 11am–3pm), in the university's early 1800s Horseshoe complex, highlights Southern folk arts, culture, and natural history. The museum's historical artifacts include the Howard Gemstone Collection and the Bernard Bamch Silver Collection. In the same area, the **Robert Mills Historic House and Park** (tel: 803-252-1770; Tue, Fri and Sat 10am–1pm, Sun 1–3pm), built in 1823, commemorates the Columbia-bred architect of the Washington Monument in Washington, DC.

At the **Columbia Museum of Art** (tel: 803-799-2810; www.columbiamuseum.org; Fri-Wed 10am–5pm, Thur 10am–8pm) you can see contemporary, medieval, Baroque, and Renaissance paintings, sculpture, and decorative arts, and a children's gallery. Also Downtown, the **South Carolina State Museum** (tel: 803-898-4921; www.scmuseum.org; Tue–Sat 10am–5pm, Sun noon–5pm) makes an interesting use of an 1890s textile plant. Four floors of the old Columbia Mills – one of the world's first totally electrified textile mills – are filled with historical displays and hands-on exhibits. You can touch the 30-million-year-old tooth of a great white shark, see a laser show, or study a replica of the world's first submarine: a Confederate vessel that sank on its maiden voyage from Charleston.

Riverbanks Zoo and Garden (tel: 803-779-8717; www.riverbanks.org; daily 9am–5pm) takes a safari through rainforests and deserts, goes under the seas and then through a Southern farm. Ranked among the nation's best

zoos, Riverbanks' natural habitats are home to more than 2,000 birds, reptiles, and animals – many of them high on endangered species lists. Across the Saluda River from the zoo, the gardens have 70 acres (28 hectares) of woodlands, historic ruins, and plant collections to explore.

After a busy day of sightseeing, the restaurants, nightclubs, and unusual stores in the Five Points neighborhood, near Downtown, and the university, offer a good evening out. When Columbians want to unwind on water, they take a short drive west to Lake Murray. Around the lake's 540-mile (870km) shoreline are marinas, fishing docks, full-service campgrounds, playgrounds, swimming, and water-skiing. Many recreational amenities and lodgings are in **Dreher Island State Park** (tel: 803-364-4152; daily 9am–5pm), which is connected to the mainland by a causeway and bridges. Nature lovers may also enjoy an outing at **Congaree National Park** (tel: 803-776-4396; daily 9am-5pm; free), east of Columbia. The 22,000-acre (9,000-hectare) sanctuary teems with wildlife and has two boardwalks for viewing. Fishing, hiking, canoeing, and camping are available, too.

CAMDEN

In 1732, **Camden** ❸, a half-hour east of Columbia, was chartered by King George II as the first official permanent settlement in South Carolina's interior. When the American Revolution broke out, Camdenites renounced their allegiance to the Crown, and in August, 1780, His Majesty's Commander in Chief in the Colonies, Lord General Charles Cornwallis, was sent to subdue the rebellious patriots. For nearly a year after winning the Battle of Camden, Cornwallis enjoyed the amenities of Camden's finest residence, the three-story Georgian Colonial mansion built by wealthy merchant Joseph Kershaw. Scarred and burned

during the Civil War, the **Kershaw-Cornwallis House** has been recreated with furnishings donated by Kershaw's descendants. The house is part of the 92-acre (37-hectare) **Historic Camden Revolutionary War Site** (tel: 803-432-9841; www.historiccamden.org; Tue–Sat 10am–4:30pm, Sun 1–4pm), which includes a powder magazine, log cabins, picnic areas, and a crafts shop. The **Camden Historic District** includes more than 60 homes, churches, and buildings dotted around the picturesque town of 6,900 people. There are selfguided walking and driving tours, or guided tours can be arranged through the Kershaw County Chamber of Commerce (tel: 803-432-2525; www.kershawcountychamber.org; Mon–Fri 9am–5pm). The fascinating **Bonds Conway House** (811 Fair Street; tel: 803-425-1123; call for an appointment) was the home of Bonds Conway, the first African American in Camden to purchase his freedom and that of his family. He was an accomplished architect, and his house is now home of the Kershaw County Historical Society.

Congaree National Park.

After the Civil War, Camden's mild climate attracted Northern horse breeders who built beautiful in-town estates and fostered the passion for equestrian sports. The year's two big steeplechases are the Carolina Cup in late March, and the Colonial Cup in late November. Both attract legions of horsefolk and floods of partying tailgaters, who arrange their finest tea-service, silver, and china around the **Springdale Race Course** (tel: 800-780-8117; Mon–Fri, Sept–May, hours vary, phone ahead) to enjoy extravagant picnics.

Don't miss the National Steeplechase Museum at the racecourse, which exhibits items from the cup championships. For races of a different stripe, come to **Darlington ❹**, east of Camden and north of Florence, when stock cars roar around the **Darlington Raceway** (tel: 843-395-8900; www.darlingtonraceway.com). If a race isn't running, there are champion cars in the **Darlington Raceway Stock Car Museum** at the same venue (tel: tel: 866-459-7223; daily 10am–4pm).

UPCOUNTRY

Greenville and Spartanburg are two dynamic cities in the state's north-western Upcountry. **Greenville ❺** (pop. about 70,000) is proud of its city parks (more than 60) and excellent zoo. Several blocks of Main Street are traffic-free and lined with antique, apparel and gift shops. A short drive from the city, Paris Mountain, Caesars Head, and Table Rock state parks have recreational lakes, picnic areas, and campgrounds in the wooded Blue Ridge Mountain foothills. **Table Rock State Park** (tel: 864-878-9813; Sun–Thur 7am–7pm, Fri and Sat 7am–9pm) gets its name from the distinctive round dome of Table Rock Mountain, one of the Upcountry's best-known landmarks. The two-lane, 130-mile (210km) **Cherokee Foothills Scenic Highway** (SC 11), is a picture-postcard route to those and other state parks, historic sites, and woodland hiking trails. The Scenic Highway loops north across the state, from I-85 at the Georgia border to I-85 at Gaffney.

Greenville proposes several options for art lovers. The **Greenville County Museum of Art** (tel: 864-271-7570; www.gcma.org; Wed–Sat 10am–5pm) displays fine collections of Southern and American paintings, sculpture, photography, and fabric art. The Bob Jones Museum and Gallery (tel: 864-770-1331; www.bjumg.org; call for hours) exhibits more than 400 religious paintings by Rembrandt, Titian, Rubens, Van Dyck, and other European artists from the 13th to the 19th centuries.

Walnut Grove Plantation (tel: 864-576-6546; Sat 11am–5pm, Sun 2pm–5pm) has graced the countryside near **Spartanburg ❻** since 1765. The elegant main house is restored and furnished with period antiques. Also on the grounds are a doctor's office, smokehouse, gristmill, and a family burial ground. Spartanburg's other historic shrines open to the public include the 1795 Historic **Price House**

Main Street in downtown Greenville.

(tel: 864-576-6546; Sat 11am–5pm, Sun 2pm–-5pm) and the 1790 **Jammie Seay House** (tel: 864-596-3501), which is open by appointment only.

At **Clemson University** ❼, 3 miles (5km) from **Pendleton**, stop at Tilman Hall Visitor Center for maps to help explore the museums, gardens, and historic buildings on the wooded, 1,500-acre (600-hectare) campus. Or stroll among the 2,200 varieties of ornamental plants in the sweet-smelling **State Botanical Garden** (tel: 864-656-3405; www.clemson.edu/public/scbg/visit/visitors-center.html; daily 10am–5pm). Walkways lead by a Chinese pagoda, an arboretum, gristmill, and lakeside teahouse, and a number of the trails are adapted for the blind.

Fort Hill (tel: 864-656-2475, hours vary, call ahead), on the campus, was the manor home of John C. Calhoun, US vice-president under Andrew Jackson and John Quincy Adams, and one of the South's most notable 19th-century statesmen. The mansion was part of plantation land donated by Calhoun's heirs to the state for its agricultural university.

ABBEVILLE

Abbeville ❽, southeast of Pendleton and Clemson, is a charming town in a time warp, where sitting on a bench in the public square evokes 240 years of American history. Designed in oblong, 18th-century style by a homesick Frenchman who named the town after his hometown, the square is attractively planted with seasonal flowers. Its most imposing monument is a Confederate memorial obelisk. 'Old Bob' is a cast-iron bell that has, over the years, summoned Abbevillians to all manner of happy and sad observances. Old Bob probably pealed joyously in 1860, when South Carolina's first organized pro-secession rally was held here, but must have tolled mournfully in May, 1865 – three weeks after the surrender at Appomattox – when Con federate

president Jefferson Davis convened his war cabinet for the last time at the **Burt-Stark Mansion** (tel: 864-366-0166; hours vary), now a museum. A stroll around the square takes you through a raft of antiques shops, the 1842 Trinity Episcopal Church, the handsomely restored 1880s Belmont Inn, and the turn-of-the-19th-century **Opera House** (tel: 864-366-9673; www.abbevillecitysc.com; open seasonally). Once a forum for traveling vaudeville troupes – Fanny Brice, Al Jolson, and Jimmy Durante graced its stage – the Opera House now hosts theatrical productions most weekends. One of the best collections of Native American art outside the Southwest is held at the **Dr Samuel R. Poliakoff Collection of Western Art** (tel: 864-459-4009; hours vary).

AIKEN

Aiken ❾, like Camden, is enamored of horses. Thoroughbreds have been training in Aiken's mild, pine-scented climate since the mid-19th century. Out standing 'graduates' include Kelso,

◷ **Fact**

Founded in 1790 by affluent coastal planters, Pendleton seems like a postcard from an early American photo album: around the grassy village green, weathered brick buildings house antiques shops and an eclectic mix of restaurants.

Table Rock State Park.

Horse of the Year five years running in the 1960s; the 1981 Kentucky Derby winner, Pleasant Colony; and 1993 Derby champion Sea Hero. The **Aiken Thoroughbred Racing Hall of Fame and Museum** (tel: 803-642-7631; www.aikenracinghalloffame.com; call for hours) honors these and other Aiken-trained blue bloods. Located in a former carriage house at **Hopelands Gardens**, the hall salutes the champions with racing silks, photos, paintings, trophies, and other memorabilia. After visiting, you can enjoy Hopelands' native trees and flowers, wetlands, and outdoor sculptures. On certain summer evenings from May through August, the air trills with jazz, bluegrass, classical, and other musical charms.

The city's horse mania reaches a fever pitch during three weekends in March when the Aiken Triple Crown fills historic Aiken Mile Track with harness, steeplechase, and flat races. Needless to say, the 'Triple' also puts Aiken's high society into high gear. Champagne brunches, teas, lunches, suppers, and balls go on practically

non-stop throughout the month. Even if you don't get an invitation to one of the gala events, be sure to take a driving tour through the **Aiken Winter Colony Historic Districts**, where 'cottages' routinely have 50 to 90 rooms, and, of course, stables. As you drive Whiskey Road, Easy Street, and other paved roads and bridle paths, you'll pass many training farms and polo fields. These are especially active from November through April.

DuPont Planetarium (tel: 803-641-3654; call for opening times), in the Ruth Patrick Science Education Center on the campus of USC Aiken, produces programs in its tilted dome. The **Aiken County Historical Museum** (tel: 803-642-2015; Tue–Sat 10am–5pm, Sun 2–5pm), housed in a 1930s Winter Colony mansion called Banksia, exhibits its Native American artifacts, an old-timey drugstore, and rooms furnished in period style. At **Aiken State Natural Area** (tel: 803-649-2857; daily 9am–7:45pm), 16 miles (26km) east of the city, it's easy to relax on any of the four lakes and enjoy camping, swimming,

Horse at Aiken.

⊙ THE AIKEN TRIPLE

Dating back to the 1940s, The Aiken Triple Crown is the equestrian event of the year in these parts. Made up of the Aiken Trials, the Aiken Steeplechase, and the Pacers and Polo match events, the event draws in thousands of spectators, from hundreds of miles in every direction. The spectacle also includes a carriage parade, a spectacular set of exclusive opening parties, and much more.

After two years of disruption due to the Covid-19 pandemic the event is back on and had a successful trial event in March of 2022. The event gets very busy, and it's expected to be even more so in the coming years as people look forward to being able to attend again, Try and bag yourself a ticket early. Usually the event falls in May.

boating, and nature trails. There's also plentiful recreation to be had at the big lakes created by impoundments of the Savannah River on the border between South Carolina and Georgia.

SOUTH CAROLINA COAST

Shell-covered shores by sleepy coastal towns in no hurry to catch up, industry here means casting a net or catering to world-class golfers

If you listen to the accounts of those who grew up along South Carolina's coast, you'll discover a place rich in simplicity and close to the earth. Weather-worn cottages face a shell-covered shore, and shrimp boats head out to sea. Riverside plantations anchor avenues of oak, and sea-island African Americans keep alive the spirituals and Gullah language of their enslaved ancestors. The coast is a golden ribbon of tidal creeks and marshes separated by waves of green-and-gold spartina grass. It is a geography formed by earthquakes, hurricanes, tidal pools, wars, and a people too proud to give up. Secluded beaches and islands remain, but the modern world is catching up. Development may raise the standard of living for some lucky few, but for the rest a plot of soil, a cast net, and the peace to roam an island without walls is more than enough to make life full and enriching.

SOUTH OF CHARLESTON

Taking US 17 south from Charleston and down SC 20 through **Johns Island**, you pass the St. Johns Yacht Harbor (once home of the Stono Native Americans); Fenwick Hall (whose proprietor once entertained pirates); Wadmalaw Island, famous for the **Charleston Tea Gardem** (tel: 843-559-0383; charlestonteagarden.com; Mon–Sat 10am–4pm, Sun noon–4pm) – the only one in the United States; and **Rockville** (known as Wadmalaw Island's 'Little Nantucket'). Once on **Kiawah Island**, head for Beachwalker Park. Its wide

boardwalk winds through a tangle of oaks, pines, palmettos, and yucca plants before reaching a 10-mile (16km) beach bordered by private condos.

As for golf, test your skills at Jack Nicklaus's Turtle Point; Tom Fazzio's Osprey Point; or the famed **Ocean Course** (tel: 800-654-2924) – site for Ryder Cup matches. If that isn't enough, move to **Seabrook Island** (tel: 843-768-2500; www.discoverseabrook. com) next door with 3 miles (5km) of beaches, two championship courses, and 200 villas.

Follow US 17 south about 15 miles (24km) to SC 174, which leads through a moss-covered archway of oak trees to **Edisto Island ⑩**, one of the oldest settlements in South Carolina. Once home to the Edisto Native Americans and prosperous sea-island cotton planters, Edisto Island still preserves remnants of the past. Visitors can find broken arrowheads, pottery, and sharks' teeth at a Native American shell mound on the beach (please leave what you find). The privately owned, **Windsor Hill**

Championship golf at the Ocean Course on Kiawah Island.

Plantation (circa 1857), stands as a typical representation of a sea-island home built up on piers to catch the cooling breeze and to avoid tempestuous tides. Where US 17 meets with the Atlantic, **Edisto Beach State Park** offers a mile of prime, seashellcovered beach and 1,255 acres (505 hectares) of oak Low Country folk art.

Back on US 17, head inland on SC 64 to the town of **Walterboro** ⓫. Its main street is typical of many small, Southern towns, complete with a jail, courthouse, post office, pharmacy, barbershop, and a few specialty stores. Settled in 1784, its prosperity as the largest railroad depot on the Savannah-to-Charleston line in the mid-1890s can still be seen in its luxurious, antebellum and Victorian homes shaded by plentiful hickory trees. Thee are several churches dating back before the 18th century. The **Colleton Museum** (tel: 843-549-2303; www.colletonmuseum.org; Tue noon–6pm, Wed–Fri 10am–5pm, Sat 10am–2pm) and the **South Carolina Artisans Center** (tel: 843-549-0011; www.scartisanscenter.com; Mon–Sat 9am–5pm; free) are both great places to view Low Country folk art. The 133ft (41-meter) landmark tower slit with narrow windows at the edge of town is not, as some may suggest, a former prison, but rather a 100,000-gallon (380,000-liter) water tower.

BEAUFORT

Take SC 303 back to US 17 and head south toward Beaufort through the ACE Basin, where the Ashepoo, Combahee, and Edisto rivers form one of the largest estuarine systems on the east coast. Travel down US 21 past the horse farms, marshlands, and vegetable farms of Port Royal Island. When you reach Beaufort itself, head down Boundary Street until you reach Henry C. Chambers Waterfront Park and nearby historic Bay Street lined with specialty stores and boasting the town's favorite eateries and night-time hang-outs.

Established in 1711, **Beaufort** ⓬ (pronounced Bew-fort) is the second-oldest town in South Carolina. Its pre-Revolutionary homes are constructed of tabby and oyster shells, limestone, wooden pegs, and homemade nails. Its grand, antebellum homes point to a time of prosperity during the American Revolution. Most of Beaufort's historic homes are privately owned, with the exception of the Federal-style **Verdier House**, built by a wealthy merchant in 1790. Along with Beaufort's historic churches (including the Old Sheldon Church ruins north of town), The **Beaufort History Museum** (tel: 843-525-8500; Mon--Fri 10am–4pm, Sat 10am–3pm) is worth a visit for its history as home of the Beaufort Voluntary Artillery – one of the oldest military units in the nation. The sea islands surrounding Beaufort feature semi-tropical wildland and carry overtones of a Gullah heritage still alive today (see page 246). The 19th-century lighthouse on Hunting Island offers

Shrimp boat near Beaufort.

a sweeping view of the coastline and state park below.

HILTON HEAD

Take SC 170 out of Beaufort heading south until you reach SC 278. Travel down this highway past the historic town of Bluffton, the scenic Pinckney Island National Wildlife Refuge until you reach **Hilton Head Island ⑬**, 30 miles (48km) south of Beaufort.

Until the 1956 construction of a bridge linking the island to the mainland, Hilton Head resembled many of the other sea islands – isolated, rural, and poor, with a population descended from.enslaved peole In a region where change comes slowly, Hilton Head startled Low Country residents – and Hilton natives – with its sudden economic boom, and the many changes that prosperity brought.

Hilton Head has the nation's first master-planned resort and residential community, Sea Pines. Just one of the island's many resort 'plantations' featuring golf, tennis, and water sports, **Sea Pines** also encompasses a forest preserve. The resort's **Harbour Town Yacht Basin and Marina** is a luxurious affair with its numerous specialty stores.

Bordered by loblolly pine, palmetto trees, and oak, Hilton Head's beaches shelter endangered, 200lb (90kg) loggerhead turtles, who bury their eggs in the soft sand on summer nights. Bottle-nosed dolphins are easy to spot, away from the public-access beaches. **The Coastal Discovery Museum** (tel: 843-689-6767; www.coastaldiscovery.org; Mon–Fri 9am–4.30pm) has hands-on nature exhibits, tours, and cruises exploring the local wildlife.

NORTH OF CHARLESTON

North on US 17 from Charleston, take North SC 703 to **Sullivan's Island ⑭**. The drive winds by waves of whistling spartina grass and over the Intracoastal Waterway right onto the island's Middle Street. All establishments are as rough-and-tumble as the island itself, so don't worry about tracking in the sand.

At the tip of the island facing Fort Sumter (where the first shots of the Civil War were fired, see pages 91 and 249) in Charleston Harbor, **Fort Moultrie** (tel: 843-883-3123; Wed–Sun 9am–5pm) is on the site of the 1776 fort that withstood the British in the American Revolution, thanks to bullet-absorbing palmetto-logs – hence the palmetto emblem on the state flag.

Head back in the opposite direction on Middle Street for the **Isle of Palms**, with activities including biking, water sports, shrimping, and crabbing. On the northeast end of the island, the **Wild Dunes Resort** offers extensive golf and tennis opportunities.

Back on US 17 just north of Charleston, **Mount Pleasant,** with a string of dockside seafood restaurants on Shem Creek, is the next town. Along the way, wooden roadside stands sell the area's famous hand-woven sweetgrass baskets, a Gullah tradition. Unlike the

Lighthouse at Hilton Head.

austere plantations farther north, **Boone Hall** (tel: 843-884-4371; www.boonehallplantation.com; Mon–Sat 9am–5pm, Sun noon–5pm) is most people's idea of a genuine antebellum residence. The hall's breathtaking avenue of live oaks draped with Spanish moss is said to have inspired the plantation entrance for the movie Gone with the Wind. The present house was rebuilt in 1935, but the surrounding buildings are much older, dating to around the mid-1700s, and include a smokehouse and a gin house. Of particular note are the nine original slave cabins considered to be one of the best-preserved 'slave streets' remaining.

Driving on US 17 toward McClellanville, pass through **Francis Marion National Forest**, which covers over 250,000 acres (100,000 hectares). Logging companies fight with environmentalists over the area, but don't get the wrong idea – thousands of acres have been preserved for endangered plants and animals, and hiking, camping, and canoeing facilities are reserved for lovers of the outdoors.

To experience more wilderness, venture out on SC 584 to **Moore's Landing**, where you can take an easy boat ride to **Cape Romain National Wildlife Refuge** (tel: 843-928-3264). A 22-mile (35km) stretch of barrier islands, Cape Romain encompasses 90 million acres (36 million hectares) of land and water populated only by dolphins, egrets, pelicans, herons, and other wildlife, viewed by boat, nature trail, and walking along the beach.

Bordered by the Francis Marion National Forest and the Cape Romain National Wildlife Refuge, is the small fishing village of **McClellanville**. Its history dates back to a hurricane-torn 1822 settlement. The shrimp boats, clam dredges, and oyster boats moving in and out of the local shrimp docks hark back to 1900 when McClellanville was the United States' largest exporter of oysters.

GHOST CAPITAL OF THE SOUTH

Georgetown is the third-oldest city in the state. This historic seaport's revitalized Downtown area features a Harborwalk on the Sampit River, and the town's Historic District keeps alive a vibrant past. Many residents think of it as a 'little Charleston', complete with historic homes, sea-going vessels, and numerous B&B inns located Downtown and on Winyah Bay. It's also the ghost capital of the South – nearly every historic home has stories to tell of a resident spirit or two.

With the exception of the **Kaminski House Museum** (tel: 843-546-7706; www.kaminskimuseum.org; Mon–Sat 10am–5pm), which has a fine collection of 18th-century antiques, many homes are not open to the public but could be noted on any walking or driving tour. The **Rice Museum**, Prince George-Winyah Episcopal Church, and the Georgetown County Courthouse do allow visitors inside.

Famous for its handcrafted hammocks, **Pawley's Island** was used by

Historic home in Georgetown.

1800s plantation owners to escape the threat of malaria during the summer months. Although the hurricane of 1822 destroyed many of the earlier buildings, Pawley's remains the epitome of South Carolina beach towns, with its paint-peeled cottages standing watch over Myrtle Avenue. **Murrells Inlet** is the oldest fishing village in the state as well as the owner of the title 'the seafood capital of South Carolina.' Don't even think about leaving without sampling some of the seafood from one of the restaurants along this stretch of US 17. The catch is so fresh it practically swims into your plate.

GOLF COAST

Myrtle Beach ⓲ visitors, young and old, whirl on the dance floors of the popular **Myrtle Beach Pavilion Park** (tel: 843-839-0303; www.pavilionparks.com ; daily 11am–9pm), while thrill seekers plunge to the earth on the Drop Tower. The most important ride, though, is a vintage Herschel-Spillman Merry-Go-Round. Built in 1912, it is one of fewer than 100 hand-carved carousels in the US.

On Ocean Boulevard, **Ripley's Believe It or Not Museum** (tel: 843-916-0888; www.ripleys.com/myrtlebeach; daily 10am–9pm) also includes an **Aquarium** and the **Moving Theater**. **Dolly Parton's Pirates Voyage Dinner and Show** (formerly the **Dixie Stampede**) (tel: 843-497-9700; www.piratesvoyage.com) gives an Old South spark to dinner theater.

Myrtle Beach is just one stop along the 60-mile (100km) stretch of beach called the **Grand Strand** that runs from the northern tip of South Carolina down to Georgetown. This strip has been called the 'golf coast,' with more than 75 championship golf courses and resorts.

Only 3 miles (5km) to the south, the 312-acre (126-hectare) **Myrtle Beach State Park** is South Carolina's most popular state park. No surprise, really, with around 350 campsites, a 730ft (220-meter) fishing pier, and the popular Sculptured Oak Nature Trail to divert and entertain all who stop by. There's also bike trails, dedicated swimming spots and much more.

Myrtle Beach Pavilion Amusement Park.

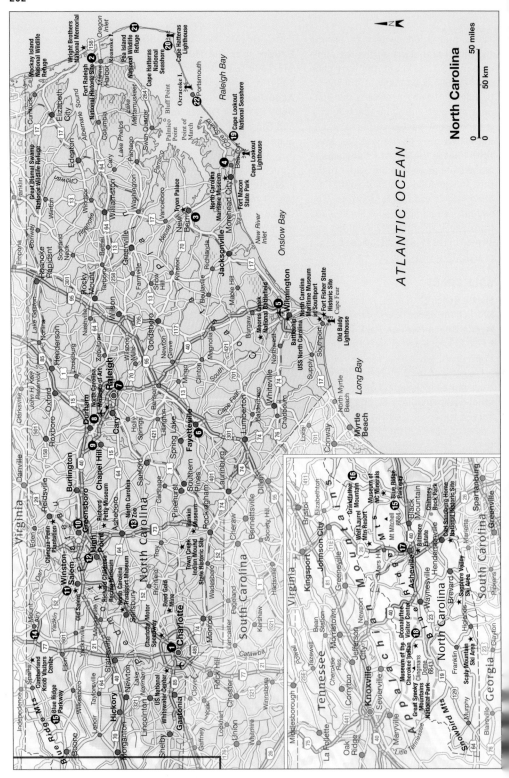

North Carolina

ATLANTIC OCEAN

NORTH CAROLINA

Standing at the four corners of Trade and Tryon in Charlotte are huge sculptures entitled Transportation, Commerce, Industry, and the Future.

Transportation is personified by a railroad worker, and Commerce by a gold miner spilling money on the head of a banker. A woman of the mills represents Industry, a child peeking from her skirts hinting at past child labor. A mother holding a child represents the Future of the city. The new South is proclaiming itself in North Carolina – fresh, rejuvenated, and mindful of the homage that is due to its past. The International Civil Rights Center and Museum in Greensboro, and the Stagville Center in Durham are among the many living tributes to the Black history of the South, and the evidence of the colonial South survives in forts and mansions throughout the state.

But North Carolina's eyes fix firmly on the prizes of the future. Textiles, tobacco, and tourism have been North Carolina's main industries until late, but banking and the clean-room high-tech industries have become a larger presence in recent years. Pure quartz crystals mined near Spruce Pine become key components in many of the world's computer chips, and Raleigh-Durham's Research Triangle Park leads the world with biotech innovation. Charlotte has grown to become one of the nerve centers of the world's banking. For visitors, North Carolina is blessed with wild and wonderful coastal regions, romantically rolling

hills, and the Blue Ridge Mountains that provided inspiration for Charles Frazier's *Cold Mountain*. The moderate four-season climate makes visits beautiful. Five interstate highways (26, 40, 77, 85, and 95) offer easy access to the state, and five airports (Charlotte, Raleigh-Durham, Greensboro, Asheville, and Wilmington) connect North Carolina to the rest of the world. Stretching westward over 500 miles (800km) from Manteo to Murphy, the state has an abundance of scenic byways, designated by easy-to-follow

⦿ Main attractions
Bechtler Museum of
  Modern Art
Levine Museum of the
  New South
Nascar Racing
Elizabeth City
Birthplace of Pepsi Cola
USS North Carolina
The Great Smoky
  Mountains Railroad
Wright Brothers National
  Memorial

⦿ Maps on pages
262, 265

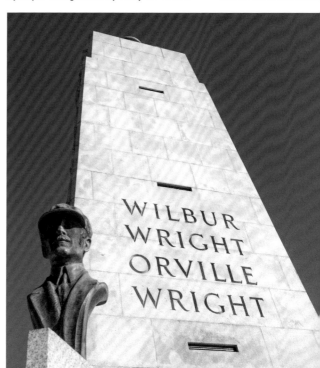

Wright Brothers National Memorial.

highway markers, and out-of-the-way places perfect for exploring. The rugged Atlantic coastline is marked by the barrier islands that have wrecked thousands of ships and offers spectacular views and walks near a wistful line of lighthouses, erected to guide and guard the shipping lanes.

Asheville has adopted the forward-looking nickname of 'The Land of the Sky,' of late, and the state is still known to many as 'the TarHeel State.' The origins of the Tar-Heel moniker are unclear but may be derived from how the defending forces resolutely stuck their heels down in front of the British during the Revolutionary War. Still, whatever it chooses to call itself, North Carolina is a beautiful and very friendly place to visit.

CHARLOTTE

North Carolina's Queen City and the newest star in the South's firmament, **Charlotte ❶** has grown from a sleepy little backwater into an international banking monarch, home to the headquarters of the internationally

Downtown Charlotte.

prominent Bank of America. It has sprouted a crown of skyscrapers befitting its nickname, but between its soaring skyline and its shady canopy of willow oaks, the city also deserves a reputation as one of the South's most beautiful modern cities. Named the 'Best City to Live In' by the National Council of Mayors, Charlotte is one of the fastest-growing urban areas in the US. Over 800,000 people live within the city limits, with 1.9 million in the metro areas.

INDUSTRY AND THE FUTURE

The Square, where Trade and Tryon streets cross, marks the heart of the city. Here the county's first courthouse reared on long pilings from the mud in 1768. Even before that, the crossroads figured significantly in the area's history. An ancient buffalo trail used by Native Americans crossed the Great Wagon Road from Pennsylvania here. Four statues ring The Square, representing Charlotte's history and heritage on a grand scale. Crafted by Raymond Kaskey, the monumental bronzes are representations of Transportation, Commerce, Industry, and The Future, the city's bywords, both of yesterday and of today. The majority of Charlotte's cultural and entertainment offerings occupy the 12 blocks surrounding The Square. Restaurants, hotels, nightclubs, museums, and galleries line the streets in every direction. Although the **Center City** is easy and pleasant to walk around, with wide, well-lit sidewalks, free Gold Rush trolley buses can also take you within a block of most attractions.

On the southeast corner of the Square stands the 60-story **Bank of America Corporate Center ❶** (100 North Tryon Street), world headquarters of the nation's largest consumer bank, and Charlotte's tallest skyscraper. Walk through the marble lobby, dominated by three fresco panels by local artist Ben Long, to **Founders**

Hall, a lofty atrium lined with stores and restaurants. On the second-floor balcony is the box-office of the **Blumenthal Performing Arts Center** (tel: 704-372-1000; www.blumenthalarts.org) the city's premier performance venue and home stage of the acclaimed North Carolina Dance Theatre. The Bank of America lobby is just one of several public buildings and churches around the city with frescos by North Carolina artist Ben Long. Charlotte has more frescos – a form of art nearly forgotten since the Renaissance – than any other city outside of Italy. At the entrance of the former **Transamerica Square** in the 400 block of North Tryon Street, Long created a frescoed dome, depicting North Carolina places and people,

including former Bank of America CEO Hugh McColl. More frescoes are in the **First Presbyterian Church** (200 West Trade Street; tel: 704-332-5123; www.firstpres-charlotte.org) and the lobby of the **Charlotte-Mecklenburg Law Enforcement Center** (601 East Trade Street; tel: 704-336-7600).

A STROLL DOWN TRYON

Heading south on Tryon Street from The Square passes some of the newest and oldest buildings in the city. **Thomas Polk Park**, named for Charlotte's founder, is a good place to start on The Square's southwest corner. The tiny park's waterfall makes a refreshing stop on Charlotte's steamy summer days.

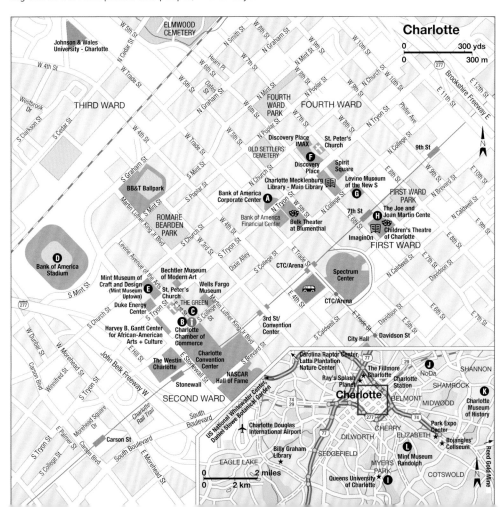

Bronze statue of the
Carolina Panther,
outside the Panthers'
home ground, the Bank
of America Stadium.

NASCAR Hall of Fame.

Three blocks south, look for the modest entrance to the **Latta Arcade** (316 South Tryon Street), one of Center City's few remaining commercial buildings from the early 20th century. The elegant glass-roofed arcade leads to narrow, pedestrian-only Brevard Court, lined with stores and restaurants, a scene straight out of Charles Dickens. Next door, the **Charlotte Chamber of Commerce** (tel: 704-980-8272; www.charlottechamber.com; Mon–Thur 9am–4pm), the city's official visitor center, offers stacks of information on the city. Maps of historic Fourth Ward and the city's many works of public art, and guided tours are available from here. The tall buildings dominating the area here make up the headquarters of the third-largest consumer bank in the US, the **Wells Fargo Center.** Locals joke that the south end of Tryon belongs to Wells Fargo, while Bank of America holds sway north of The Square.

THE GREEN

The Green , Wachovia's most ambitious effort to date, is a park that stretches across the block from South Tryon to the entrance of the **Charlotte Convention Center** (501 South College Street; tel: 704-339-6000; www.charlotteconventionctr.com). On the park's south side, a fun fountain of spouting fish leads to an unusual and entertaining audio path, with motion-activated sounds.

The magnificent Radcliffe condominiums, million-dollar pieds-a-terre for Charlotte's glitterati, line the north side of the Green. This is the lair of sport celebs such as Bob Johnson, founder of the BET network and owner of the NBA Charlotte Bobcats, and NASCAR star Jeff Gordon. The historic 1920s store, **Radtcliffe's Flowers** (435 South Tryon Street), that gave the project its name, today is a charming restaurant. The **Bank of America Stadium** (800 South Mint Street; tel: 704-358-7000; www.panthers.com/stadium), dominating the landscape a couple of blocks to the west, is home of the NFL Carolina Panthers. Pairs of snarling black panthers with bronze fangs flank the stylish sport facility's entrances. Stop by the Panther's Team Store (Mon–Fri 11am–6pm, Sat 12–4pm, seasonally) for Panther gear, or for tours of the stadium.

THE NORTH END

In the blocks north of The Square, NationsBank, now Bank of America, changed the face of Charlotte's Downtown area. Most of its museums, and a cluster of galleries, dining, and nightlife are near the **Spectrum Center** (East Trade and North 5th streets; tel: 704-688-9000; www.spectrumcentercharlotte.com), the go to concert venue for all big acts on tour.

At the **Mint Museum of Craft+ Design** (Tryon Street, tel: 704-337-2000; www.mintmuseum.org; call for hours), a Dale Chihuly-designed chandelier graces the lobby of one of the country's premier showcases of wood, ceramic, glass, and fiber

art objects. The museum anchors an ever-expanding string of galleries and museums at Tryon's north end. Next door, in the Art Deco-inspired Truist Building, the **Sonia and Isaac Luski Gallery** (tel: 704-973-4500) features several art mediums, including paintings and glasswork.

The **McColl Center for Visual Art** (721 North Tryon Street; tel: 704-332-5535; www.mccollcenter.org; Fri 11am–6pm, Sat and Sun 12pm–5pm); the **Light Factory Photo Arts Center** (700 N Tryon Street; tel: 704-333-9755; www.lightfactory.org; Wed–Sat 11am–3pm), and the fine **Harvey B. Gantt Center for African-American Arts + Culture** (551 S Tryon St; tel: 704-547-3700; hours vary, call ahead), with a notable collection by Black artists, are all within a few blocks. The jewel in the crown however has to be a recent addition to Charlotte's art scene, the **Bechtler Museum of Modern Art** (420 South Tryon Street; tel: 704-353-9200; www.bechtler.org; hours vary) Mixing music, artwork thought to be lost forever, and the best traveling exhibits in the world, the admission fee is worth every cent. The blocks to the west of North Tryon are Charlotte's oldest residential neighborhood, the **Fourth Ward**. Ornate Victorian homes restored to their original splendor line the shady sidewalks, making for a wonderful stroll, as long as it's not too hot. An IMAX theater and exhibits from dinosaurs to space exploration make learning fun at **Discovery Place** ❻ (301 North Tryon Street; tel: 704-372-6261; www.science.discoveryplace.org; Mon, Fri, and Sat 10:30am–4:30pm), one of the top hands-on science museums in the country.

The **Levine Museum of the New South** ❺ (200 East 7th Street; tel: 704-333-1887; www.museumofthenewsouth.org; hours vary) presents a multimedia journey through the South and the city's heritage, from its days as a textiles capital to its current status

as a banking superpower. Special exhibits follow the career of native son, the preacher Billy Graham, and the rise of the motorsports industry. Behind the museum stands one of Charlotte's unique mixed-use buildings, **7th Street Station** (225 East 7th Street). A gourmet grocery and restaurants occupy the street level; above, a parking garage offers complimentary parking. Colorful panels decorate the outside of the building. Touch them and they respond with a chime... or a giggle.

The Station is one of the major stops on the Charlotte Trolley line. Across the tracks lies Charlotte's best attraction for children, **ImaginOn: The Joe and Joan Martin Center**❽ (East Seventh and Brevard streets; tel: 704-416-4600; www.imaginon.org; Mon–Thur 9am–8pm, Sat 9am–5pm). A joint project of the local Children's Theatre and the Charlotte/Mecklenburg Public Library, the center brings stories to life in a rich and entertaining setting.

Other attractions in the area especially attractive to younger visitors

The Bechtler Museum of Modern Art.

The Levine Museum of the New South, at 200 East 7th Street, presents a multimedia journey through both Charlotte and the South's distinctive history. If you only have time for one museum visit during your trip to Charlotte, make it this one.

include an indoor waterpark, Ray's **Splash Planet** (215 North Sycamore Street; tel: 704-432-4729; hours vary).

A TROLLEY RUNS THROUGH IT

Riding Charlotte's painstakingly restored electric trolley is a highlight of any city visit. The trolley parallels Church Street through the Center City beginning at North 9th Street, then plunges through the Charlotte Convention Center, before passing over I-277 into **Historic South End**. Running daily into the evening hours, the trolley is a favorite way for visitors and locals to see the sights.

Once the heart of Charlotte's textiles industry, the renovated mills and warehouses of South End now house numerous dining and entertainment options. Hop aboard an antique trolley car for a do-it-yourself pub crawl or ride to the end of the line. The South End also has a quaint vibe filled with local flair in the form of ice cream shops, cafes, and restaurants, all of which are the perfect way to end your trolley journey.

The spring blooming season (March and April) finds Charlotte residents and visitors alike cruising the streets of historic neighborhoods close to the Center City. **Myers Park** ❶, where most streets seem to be named Queens Road, has some of the city's most spectacular mansions. Beyond lies **South Park**, the area's top destination for upscale shopping.

East Boulevard, stretching from South Boulevard to Queens Road West, runs through the heart of historic **Dilworth** past restored Queen Anne mansions and a row of restaurants. At Freedom Park (1900 East Boulevard; tel: 980-314-1002), a favorite spot for strolling, paved paths circle a lake, passing groves of cherry trees and a children's nature museum. To experience more of Carolina's fabulous flora, visit **Daniel Stowe Botanical Garden** (Belmont Street; tel: 704-825-4490; www.dsbg.org; Wed–Sun 10am–4pm), one of the South's must-see horticultural showcases.

NODA ARTS DISTRICT

Artists in search of inexpensive studio space redeemed a run-down mill village just north of Downtown, turning it into a bohemian community of studios and galleries they dubbed **NoDa** ❶. Upscale condominiums followed, and today a dynamic art scene centers around North Davidson and 36th streets. Coffee shops, theaters, and some of the city's best art galleries teem with an eclectic mixture of locals during the Gallery Crawls, which are held on the first and third Friday of every month.

Long before this current renaissance, there was another Charlotte, with a historical story dating back to colonial times. Citizens adopted the Mecklenburg Declaration of Independence on May 20, 1775, a year before the Continental Congress signed their more famous Declaration. Charlotte witnessed the country's first gold rush

The Billy Graham Library in Charlotte.

after Conrad Reed found a huge gold nugget on his family's farm. So much gold came out of the area's mines that the first branch of the US Mint was established here.

Explore the region's early history at the **Charlotte Museum of History**  (3500 Shamrock Road; tel: 704-568-1774; www.charlottemuseum.org; Thur–Sat 11am–5pm). On the museum grounds is the **Hezekiah Alexander House**, the oldest stone building in the county and home of one of the signers of the 'Meck Dec.' The interior, open for guided tours, contains many period furnishings. At **Reed Gold Mine** (Midland; tel: 704-721-4653; www.historicsites.nc.gov/all-sites/reed-gold-mine; Tue–Sat 9am–5pm) in Cabarras County, now a state historic site, you can learn how gold was prospected and processed, tour the tunnels, and pan for gold yourself.

The **Mint Museum Randolph** (2730 Randolph Road; tel: 704-337-2000; hours vary) is housed in the original Mint building. This branch of the Mint hosts important traveling exhibitions in addition to its own massive collections of European porcelain, South American Pre-Columbian, and Spanish Baroque art.

BILLY GRAHAM TERRITORY

One of Charlotte's most famous sons returned to his roots with the opening of the **Billy Graham Library** (tel: 704-401-2432; www.billygraham.org) off the Billy Graham Parkway in southwest Charlotte. The campus features the evangelist's childhood home, as well as a museum documenting his many crusades and the official archive of his writings.

For a sampler of the region's charms, **Latta Plantation Nature Preserve** (Huntersville; tel: 980-314-7878; daily 7am–5:30pm), 12 miles (19km) north of town, makes an excellent destination. This star of the Mecklenburg County Park and Recreation system includes a historic **plantation house** and the **Carolina Raptor Center** (tel: 704-875-6521; hours vary, call ahead), home to injured birds of prey. Nature trails stretch down to the shores of

NASCAR race at the Charlotte Motor Speedway.

⊘ THE LAND OF NASCAR

For stock-car racing fans, Charlotte is a pilgrimage. With 90 percent of all active NASCAR race teams based in the area, and Lowe's Motor Speedway, home of two important Nextel Cup races, on Charlotte's northeast border, the region offers race fan more sights per mile than any other. At the Speedway, take a narrated tour of Lowe's famous tri-oval, offered daily. Learn to drive a real race car at the Richard Petty Driving Experience. For a lesser investment, pilot a miniature car at the NASCAR SpeedPark in nearby Concord Mills Mall (I-85, exit 49).

Near the Speedway, the Hedrick Motorsports Museum and Team Shop and Roush Racing recall the stars and cars that made racing history. Of course, this is the perfect accompaniment to the NASCAR Hall of Fame in downtown Charlotte.

Just 23 miles (37km) north on I-77, the town of Mooresville (pop 19,000) bills itself as 'Race City USA'. Make your first stop the North Carolina Auto Racing Hall of Fame to pick up a map of the many race shops that welcome visitors. One site not to be missed is Dale Earnhardt Inc., the Taj Mahal of garages.

About an hour north on I-85 lie two other landmarks: the Richard Petty Museum in Randleman and the Richard Childress Racing Museum in Welcome, dedicated to the memory of driver Dale Earnhardt.

Mountain Island Lake, where you can rent a canoe or kayak. It's the perfect place to spend another North Carolina day.

AROUND NORTH CAROLINA

The flourishing fortunes of Pepsi-Cola and the biotech Research Triangle Park bring a touch of modernity to a region known in the past mainly for tobacco cultivation and the towering Smoky Mountains.

From the wild dunes of the Outer Banks to the highest mountains in the east, North Carolina offers some of the most varied, and most scenic, vistas in the South. Its history is equally varied, stretching from the site of the first British colony on the continent to research laboratories where today's biotech breakthroughs are made.

This chapter follows the development of the state, beginning by the sea and then moving westwards. From centrally located **Charlotte**, Interstate 85 runs toward Greensboro (see page 274), then tours east toward the sea and west to the mountains.

Scene from The Lost Colony, a historical drama telling the story of the Roanoke settlement at the Waterfront Theater.

THE ROANOKE MYSTERY

Twenty years before Jamestown and 43 years before the Pilgrims landed on Plymouth Rock, British settlers chose Roanoke Island, between the mainland and the Outer Banks, as the site of the first English colony in the New World. They named their settlement after their patron, the adventurer Sir Walter Raleigh, and began to build. But the colony came to a mysterious end. When Governor John White returned after a three-year absence, he found the fort abandoned, and the colonists gone. The word 'Croatoan' carved on a post provided the only clue to their disappearance.

Controversy has raged ever since about the fate of the colonists, but the mystery remains. During the summer months, the state's original outdoor drama, **The Lost Colony** (tel: 252-473-6000; www.thelostcolony.org; June-Aug), recounts the history of the Roanoke settlement and speculates on its fate. The play has fared better than the colony itself. Written by Pulitzer Prize-winner Paul Green, it has run every summer since 1937 at the Waterside Theater, on the grounds of **Fort Raleigh National Historic Site ❷** (tel: 252-473-2111; www.nps.gov/fora; Sun–Fri 9am–5pm, Sat 6am– 5pm), itself a reconstruction of the 1585 palisade.

From Roanoke Island, continue to the Outer Banks (see page 279), just minutes away, or turn inland and wander through the state's eastern counties, an intricate maze of inlets and tidal rivers. The abundance of marshes makes this one of the best bird-watching areas on the East Coast. Huge flocks of snow geese and swans winter in these wetlands, also inhabited by alligator, deer, red wolves, and black bear.

Early settlers established towns along the rivers of eastern Carolina, and some of the most interesting lie along US 17, the highway through eastern Carolina, running 285 miles

(459km) from Virginia to South Carolina. Throughout the region are scenic harbors and waterfronts that captivate photographers.

Towns worth a visit include **Elizabeth City**, a seaport at the edge of the Great Dismal Swamp, 20 miles (32km) from the Virginia border, and Edenton, said to be one of the prettiest towns in the South, **Bath**, the colony's first incorporated town (1705), retains many of its original buildings, In **New Bern ❸** (pop, 29,000), costumed guides re-create the gracious life of North Carolina's royal governors at Tryon Palace (tel: 800-767-1560; www.tryonpalace.org; Mon–Sat 9am–5pm, Sun noon–5pm). The magnificent Georgian mansion, rebuilt from the original plans, was one of the finest buildings in the colonies. New Bern also gave Pepsi-Cola to the world; you can sip a bit of history at the re-created soda fountain, Birthplace of Pepsi Cola (256 Middle Street; tel: 252-636-5898; Mon–Sat 10am–6pm, Sun noon–4pm; free) where the formula was invented in 1898.

From New Bern, it is 37 miles (60km) down US 70 to Morehead City and **Beaufort ❹** (pronounced in North Carolina 'BO-furt'), once the colony's largest seaport. The area rings with tales of the pirate Blackbeard, who ran his ship, the Queen Anne's Revenge, ashore near Beaufort. The **North Carolina Maritime Museum** (315 Front Street; tel: 252-504-7740; www. ncmaritimemuseumbeaufort.com; Mon–Sat 10am–5pm, Sun 12–5pm) displays items from the wreck.

THE CAPE FEAR COAST

Along the coast south about 90 miles (145km) is **Wilmington ❺** (pop. 119,000), North Carolina's largest port, founded in 1739. Wilmington celebrates its history in one of the nation's largest historic commercial districts, extending 200 blocks along the Cape Fear River. Lovingly restored stores, restaurants, galleries, inns, and museums, make for one of the most vibrant scenes in the state. The *Battleship USS North Carolina* (tel: 910-399-9100; www.battleshipnc.com; daily 8am–5pm), veteran of many World War II Pacific engagements, dominates the shore on

The USS North Carolina, moored at Wilmington.

⊘ THE USS NORTH

She was the fourth US Navy vessel to bear the name, and to this day, is among the most successful and tested warships in the world. She was the first newly constructed battleship to enter service during World War II and took part in – and survived – every naval battle in the Pacific conflict. This record earned the *USS North Carolina* 15 battle stars, making her the most decorated warship of World War II. Her primary duty of care throughout her years of service was the protection of aircraft carriers: her defense of the *USS Enterprise* during the 1942 Battle of the Solomon Islands is widely acknowledged as the only reason the *Enterprise* got out in one piece herself. Before she was retired and permanently moored in Wilmington, she sailed more than 300,000 nautical miles (555,600km).

the far side, and a vintage navy launch taxis visitors across. The Battleship is the site of a spectacular 4th of July party with a huge fireworks display.

During the Civil War, Wilmington was the last port remaining open to the Confederacy. Blockade-runners supplied Richmond and the Confederate armies until the 1865 fall of **Fort Fisher** (Kure Beach; tel: 910-251-7340; www.historicsites.nc.gov/all-sites/fort-fisher; Tue–Thur and Sat 9am–4:45pm). Wilmington today is North Carolina's movie capital, with over 1,000 film-related projects produced. Weekend tours of the **EUE/Screen Gems Studios** (tel: 910-343-3500; www.euescreengems.com) are available during the summer months.

A handful of North Carolina's most popular beaches, including Carolina, Wrightsville, and Kure, are just minutes from Wilmington. At **Carolina Beach State Park** (tel: 910-458-8206; daily dawn–dusk), the Flytrap Trail leads past beds of carnivorous plants, native only to the Cape Fear watershed. One further stop along US 17 is a particular delight for foodies. **Calabash** (pop. 1,500), just before the South Carolina border, lends its name to a famous lightly breaded and fried seafood. Steamed oysters are another local specialty. Interstate 40 runs 420 miles (676km) across North Carolina, from Wilmington to the Tennessee border. Passing through four of the state's major cities, it is a handy corridor for exploration, but for all that North Carolina offers, consider some side trips, too.

The 'Old North' state is noted for its natural beauty, so branch off the beaten path by land or sea. Paddling a canoe or kayak or rafting are inviting options. Even novices enjoy the easy paddling in eastern North Carolina's blackwater rivers, where paddle trails lead through stands of cypress trees hundreds of years old, hung with Spanish moss. Farther west, paddles become more challenging, culminating with some of the best whitewater runs in the country on the Nantahala, New, French Broad and other mountain rivers. The **Nantahala Outdoor Center** (tel: 828-785-5082; www.noc.com; hours vary) organizes trips for every ability. Hiking is also a lovely way to see the sights, especially in western North Carolina, where thousands of miles of footpaths, including the Appalachian Trail, wind over the mountains.

THE SANDHILLS TO THE CENTER OF THE STATE

Ancient sand dunes form a unique ecosystem in southeast North Carolina. Home of the longleaf pine and the endangered red-cockaded woodpecker, the area is also a famous golfing destination. For dedicated golfers, a pilgrimage to the **Pinehurst Resort** (tel: 844-330-1669; www.pinehurst.com) to play the legendary Number 2 is a must. Designed by Donald Ross in 1907, this course consistently ranks among the top 10 in the country.

A military history detour beckons through nearby **Fayetteville 6** (pop.

State Capitol Building, Raleigh.

210,000) and **Fort Bragg**, where museums detail the history of America's fighting forces, including the state-of-the-art **Airborne and Special Operations Museum Foundation** (tel: 910-643-2778; www.asomf.org; Tue–Sat 10am–4pm, Sun noon–4pm).

Raleigh, Durham, and Chapel Hill form a rough triangle bounded by 1-85, 1-40, and 1-95 about 90 miles (145km) west of Wilmington. This is the heartland and favorite jumping ground of the legendary Atlantic Athletic Conference of basketball fame. The North Carolina State Wolfpack of Raleigh, the Carolina Tarheels of Chapel Hill, and the Duke Blue Devils of Durham are some of the most successful teams in college hoops.

RALEIGH-DURHAM

This area has an abundance of excellent state- and university-sponsored museums, gardens, and other attractions, all of which charge no admission, making this a terrific destination for travelers on a budget. **Raleigh ⑦** (pop. 460,000), is North Carolina's capital city, with an active arts and entertainment scene.

The **North Carolina Museum of Art** (tel: 919-839-6262; Wed–Sun 10am–5pm; free) the **North Carolina Museum of Natural Sciences** (tel: 919-707-9800; www.naturalsciences.org; Tue–Sun 10am–5pm; free) and its neighbor, the **North Carolina Museum of History** (tel: 919-807-7000; www.ncmuseumofhistory.org; Mon–Sat 9am–5pm; free), are some of the highlights of over a dozen free museums, tours and gardens in Raleigh.

Durham ⑧ (pop. 270,000), once a thriving tobacco capital, today grabs headlines as the home of **Duke University** and its famous medical center, endowed by the immense Duke tobacco fortune. A stroll through the magnolia trees that line the neo-Gothic West Campus reveals many treasures, including **Duke Chapel** (tel:

919-681-9488; call for hours) where patriarch Washington Duke lies in marble state; the extensive **Sarah P. Duke Gardens** (tel: 919-684-3698; www.gardens.duke.edu); and the **Nasher Museum of Art** (www.nasher.duke.edu; Tue–Sat 10am–5pm, Sun noon–5pm; free).

Chapel Hill ⑨ (pop. 60,000) remains the quintessential college town. The University of North Carolina, founded here in 1789, is the nation's oldest state supported college. Stroll down Franklin Street to soak up the student vibe. Notable sights on campus include the **North Carolina Botanical Garden** (tel: 919-962-0522; Tue–Thur and Sat 9am–5pm, Sun 1–5pm; free), the office of Chapel Hill alum Charles Kuralt and the Memorabilia Room at the Dean E. Smith Center (tel: 800-722-4335), where athlete supremo Michael Jordan's jersey holds center court. There's another important triangle within the Triangle, the world-famous **Research Triangle Park** (RTP). This special business park, set aside for high-tech companies, hothouses some of the top biotech research facilities in the nation.

The Duke Chapel.

Pick up a driving-tour brochure at the Durham Visitor Center (tel: 919-687-0288; Tue–Thur and Sat 10am–5pm).

THE TRIAD HEARTLAND

About an hour's drive to the west of the Triangle, the combined interstates 1-40 and 1-85 bring you to Greensboro, Winston-Salem, and High Point, the major towns of the Triad. Early settlers of these rolling Piedmont hills came from sects seeking religious freedom, an influence that continues today.

Quakers founded **Greensboro** ❿ (pop. 225,000), named after the 'Quaker General' Nathanael Greene, who inflicted a costly victory on British general Cornwallis during the American Revolution. **Guilford Courthouse National Military Park** (tel: 336-288-1776; Wed–Sun 9am–5pm) presents a compelling re-creation of the hotly contested battle. In 1960, the city made a landmark contribution to the civil rights movement when the 'Greensboro Four' staged the first sit-in at the local Woolworth's, now maintained as the **International Civil Rights Center and Museum** (tel: 336-274-9199; www.sitinmovement.org; Mon–Sat 10am–6pm).

Moravians settled the Wachovia tract, now the city of **Winston-Salem** ⓫ (pop. 245,000), in the mid-l 700s, and presentations in the historic part of the city, at **Old Salem Museums and Gardens** (tel: 336-721-7300; www.oldsalem.org; Wed–Sat 9am–2pm) re-create their culture, led by docents in period attire. From the present-day Czech Republic, the Moravians first put down roots in Bethlehem, Pennsylvania, and later moved to North Carolina at the invitation of a lord proprietor who wanted industrious people who could make a contribution to the area. On the grounds are a Toy Museum, and a museum of early Southern decor. Sample the famous Moravian cookies at Winkler Bakery or sip coffee at E. A. Vogler.

High Point ⓬ (pop. 110,000) has over 120 furniture factories, including the 15 largest in the world, and proudly calls itself the 'Home Furnishings Capital of the World.' Unbelievable discounts on furnishings attract shoppers from near and far. Many also enjoy a souvenir photograph at a local landmark, the **World's Largest Chest of Drawers**, at 508 Hamilton Street. A half-hour drive down I-73/74 from the Triad leads to one of the state's most popular destinations – the **North Carolina Zoo** ⓭ (tel: 800-488-0444; www.nczoo.org; daily 9am–5pm) in **Asheboro**. The nation's largest natural-habitat zoo exhibits animals from Africa and North America. The polar bears, seen entertainingly through an underwater window, are a local favorite.

Fans of fine pots will want to continue a further 12 miles (19km) down I-73 to **Seagrove**, the pottery capital of the South. More than 100 potteries in the area fire pieces from North Carolina's distinctive red clay. Seagrove's busy **North Carolina Pottery Center** (tel: 336-873-8430; www.ncpotterycenter.org; Tue–Sat 10am–4pm) provides

Woman in traditional Moravian dress at Old Salem.

maps to area potteries, and exhibits some of the finest examples of North Carolina clay art, including the popular 'face jugs.'

US 64 west from Asheboro leads to **Lexington** (pop. 19,000), a major capital of barbecue. Come hungry. Nearly two dozen specialty restaurants here serve 'chopped pig' cooked over a hickory fire and topped with a secret sauce. The little town of **Mount Airy** ⓮ (pop. 10,000), 35 miles (56km) north of Winston-Salem on I-74, came to fame when native son Andy Griffith used it as the model for Mayberry, the fictional town of his romantically rural TV series. Fans today find the town largely unspoiled. You can savor a pork-chop sandwich at **Snappy Lunch** or have a haircut at **Floyd's City Barber Shop**. The **Andy Griffith Museum** in the Mount Airy Visitor Center (tel: 336-786-1604; Mon–Sat 9am–5pm, Sun 1–5pm) displays a wealth of Andy's personal memorabilia. Mount Airy is also a noted center for bluegrass and old-time music. Shows and jam sessions feature the region's top fiddlers and banjo pickers, and take place every week, yearround. Admission is usually free.

BLUE RIDGE PARKWAY

The **Blue Ridge Parkway** ⓯ runs through 469 miles (755km) of dramatic mountain scenery, joining Shenandoah National Park in Virginia with Great Smoky Mountains National Park on the North Carolina/Tennessee border. Although the parkway is open year-round, some sections may be closed in winter due to snow. Check with the National Park Service (tel: 828-298-0398) for up-to-the-minute weather conditions.

Traffic backups often tie up the 252 miles (405km) of the parkway in North Carolina, especially during the fall foliage season. The two-lane road is winding and often narrow, with low speed limits and steep grades. If possible, allow several days to tour. Also, bring a sweater, even in summer; temperatures are often 10 degrees or more cooler than in the Carolina lowlands. If you plan on hiking in the mountains,

The Blue Ridge Parkway during fall.

⊘ THE BLACK SOUTH

The historic monuments marking the real sacrifice of the past, are now at long last, being created. For generations, the South ignored, and even belittled, its Black heritage. Now, memorials to Black history have become important stops for visitors of all colors. The Black South is the foundation of the region's very existence. In the early years, it was mainly the Black population who paved the streets, built the buildings, and toiled in the fields that brought wealth to the region.

There are over 500 historic sites of significance throughout the South. Some represent the shameful legacy of slavery and the struggle for civil rights; others pay tribute to the Black South's uplifting music and art. They evoke mythic figures such as Casey Jones, Mr Bojangles, Kunta Kinte, and Porgy and Bess. As a collection, they represent the substantial contribution Southern Black people have made to the United States. Many regional tourist boards now provide brochures of important sites of black heritage, and walking trails.

Important sites are detailed throughout this book, but of particular significance are the Martin Luther King National Historic Site, Atlanta (see page 120), the National Civil Rights Museum, Memphis (see page 225), and the artful Gullah Tours around Charleston (see page 247). See also the feature on civil rights in Alabama, page 140.

HOLLYWOOD AND NORTH CAROLINE

Hollywood has had long-standing love affair with North Carolina, which has been the backdrop of countless blockbusters.

The rich landscapes of the South, from the Appalachian Mountains through the South Carolina swamps across the Mississippi Delta all the way to darkly exotic New Orleans, have for years offered movie-makers backdrops for romance and adventure. Played by Gregory Peck, small-town lawyer, Atticus Finch brought Southern issues vividly to a head in the 1962 movie of Harper Lee's Alabama story, *To Kill A Mockingbird*. The tender tale is believed to be drawn from that most reclusive of author's childhood in Monroeville. A childhood she shared, incidentally, with the rather less reclusive Truman Capote, screenwriter of *Breakfast at Tiffany's* and a collaborator on a deeply sinister adaptation of Henry James's 1898 story *The Turn of the Screw*, filmed in 1961 as *The Innocents*.

The contradictions, rivalries, and bitter ironies of the Civil War in Georgia combined for the 1939

Jessica Tandy and Morgan Freeman star in Driving Miss Daisy.

classic that's still thought of as the quintessential Southern romance; the film of Margaret Mitchell's *Gone with the Wind* tallied up eight Oscars in Hollywood. 'The War' continues to provide a thoughtprovoking context, and as the majority of the battles were fought on Confederate land, the South is always the cinema setting. Robert F. Maxwell's four-hour behemoth *Gods and Generals* made a serious attempt to get inside Rebel hero Stonewall Jackson's camp. With its terrific length, and a point-of-view that may have unsettled some audiences, even Robert Duvall's meticulous portrayal of the general couldn't win large audiences.

The adaptation of *Cold Mountain* may have suffered a similar fate; movie-goers seem a little reluctant to stand in line for reappraisals of the war. Using only a few shots of the Blue Ridge Mountains, the film crew decamped to the chilly, less-expensive hills of Romania to use as a substitute for evocative North Carolina. The film was better received in Europe than in America.

Successful modern films with Southern themes continue to emphasize the romantic, tragic, comedic, and Gothic elements that are so much a part of the image of Dixie. The South Carolina swamplands lent a terrifying 'parallel universe' reality to John Boorman's 1972 fear-fest, *Deliverance*. In 1989, Bruce Beresford scooped up three Oscars for *Driving Miss Daisy*, the amiable comedy of a Jewish woman (Jessica Tandy) and her relationship with her Black chauffeur.

The Southern gift of storytelling was highlighted in 1991 with Fannie Flagg's tale of reminiscence, *Fried Green Tomatoes at the Whistle Stop Cafe*, fetching another Southern Oscar statuette nomination for Miss Tandy. John Grisham's legal pot-boilers have also met with considerable success, with *The Firm*, *The Pelican Brief*, *The Client*, and *The Runaway Jury* all set against Southern backdrops like Memphis and New Orleans.

Plots turning on Southern manners and mores have seduced cinemagoers since the silver screen first flickered alight, and Southern sentiments, accents, and manners will no doubt go on providing screenwriters with inexhaustible creative inspiration.

pack foul-weather gear, water, and high-energy snacks. Concrete mileposts – marked 'MP' – announce distances along the parkway. NC 89, running 20 miles (32km) west from Mount Airy, enters at MP 217, close to the Virginia border, near **Cumberland Knob Visitor Center**. Fabulous overlooks, trails, and campgrounds encourage frequent stops to explore and learn more about the cultural and natural history of the Southern Appalachians, and also to savor the stupendous views. Although wildflowers bloom along the parkway throughout the summer, the mountain laurel, rhododendron, and flame azaleas are most magnificent in June and July. Some of the best places to see them are **Doughton Park** at MP 238 and **Craggy Gardens** at MP 364, where acres of purple and pink blossoms delight the eye.

The Southern Highlands Craft Guild displays traditional mountain handicrafts at a number of attractive stops along the parkway, including **Flat Top Manor** (tel: 828-8-5330; call for hours; closed winter) in Moses Cone Park, MP 294 near Blowing Rock; and the **Folk Art Center** (tel: 828-298-7928; daily 10am–5pm) just outside Asheville at MP 382.

THE HIGH COUNTRY

The Boone/Blowing Rock area (MP 291) makes a good overnight stop near the parkway's north end. An outdoor drama, *Horn in the West* (tel: 828-264-2120, June–Aug), recounts the life of pioneer and local hero Daniel Boone.

Charles Kuralt, a state native and host of over 600 On the Road TV travel shows, loved this area. Follow his footsteps to **Grandfather Mountain** ⓰ (tel: 800-468-7325; www.grandfather. com; hours vary), a United Nations Biosphere Preserve noted for families of black bears and a mile-high hanging bridge. Kuralt liked to hang out by the pot-bellied stove at **Mast General**

Store in Valle Crucis. Virgin stands of white pine and hemlock and groves of flowering rhododendron line the short trail to spectacular **Linville Falls** (tel: 828-765-1045; daily dawn–dusk).

The **Museum of North Carolina Minerals** (tel: 828-765-2761; daily 9am–5pm; free) at MP 331 displays minerals and gemstones, including emeralds, diamonds, and rubies, mined in the Carolina mountains. NC 128 branches off at MP 355 to **Mount Mitchell State Park** (tel: 828-675-4611) where a paved road leads to the top of the highest peak in the eastern United States at 6,684ft (2,037 meters). An exhibit hall (May–Oct) near the summit explores the mountain's geology, history, and weather.

MOUNTAIN CROSSROADS

Asheville ⓱ (pop. 90,000), located at the intersection of I-40, I-26, and the Blue Ridge Parkway (MP 380), provides an excellent staging area for journeys into the surrounding mountains. It is also the home of one of North Carolina's most famous attractions, the

The grand Biltmore Estate.

magnificent **Biltmore Estate** (tel: 800-411-3812; www.biltmore.com; daily 9am–5pm). The 250-room French Renaissance chateau built by George Vanderbilt in 1895 is considered by many to be the United States' grandest castle. Plan to spend a full day exploring the house and extensive gardens, and sampling wines at the popular Biltmore Winery.

Cosmopolitan Asheville's renovated Art Deco Downtown area is awash with boutiques, coffee houses, craft shops, galleries, and a variety of dining options. There is definitely a scene here, with more artists and young professionals moving in each month. Asheville's city centerpiece, **Asheville Museum of Science** (tel: 828-254-7162; hours vary), houses a complex of museums including the Asheville Museum of Art and the Colburn Gem and Mineral Museum. Out front, on Pack Square, look for a replica of the winged statue immortalized in Thomas Wolfe's classic *Look Homeward, Angel*. Wolfe, a native, evoked many of the city's locations in his autobiographical novel. His mother's boarding house, where much of the story takes place, is preserved as a part of the **Thomas Wolfe Memorial** (tel: 828-253-8304; www.wolfememorial.com; Tue–Sat 9am–5pm).

Less than an hour's drive outside Asheville, **Chimney Rock Park** (tel: 828-625-9611; www.chimneyrockpark.com) has a stunning view of the Carolina Piedmont and **Lake Lure**, selected by National Geographic as one of the 10 most beautiful artificial lakes. Walk up or take the 26-story elevator to the top of the natural granite tower.

THE SOUTHERN HIGHLANDS

Beyond Asheville, the Blue Ridge Parkway continues for 90 more winding miles (145km) through the Pisgah and Nantahala National Forests, a journey that can take most of a day, before reaching the final milepost, 469, just outside Cherokee and Great Smoky Mountains National Park. Travelers on a schedule may prefer the more direct route via I-40, US 23/74 and US 19 (50 miles, 80km), which reaches Cherokee in less than two hours.

The home of the eastern branch of the Cherokee Nation has a story to tell. The Native Americans here descend from the remnant of the indigenous people who avoided forced removal to Oklahoma in 1838. An outdoor drama presentation, Unto These Hills (tel: 828-497-1532; www.cherokeehistorical.org; June–Aug), recounts the history of the Cherokee, from the arrival of the Spanish in 1540 to the tragic 'Trail of Tears' that took thousands of lives on the long, forced march west.

There are more heartbreaking tales about the Trail of Tears at the **Museum of the Cherokee Indian** (tel: 828-497-3481; www.mci.org; daily 9am–5pm). **Oconaluftee Indian Village** (tel: 828-497-2315; daily 9am–5pm) re-creates the daily life of the indigenous people in the 1750s. The deluxe-but money-draining **Harrah's Cherokee Casino**

American flag on top of Chimney Rock.

(tel: 828-497-7777), on the reservation, offers blackjack, slots, and stage shows. Fortunately, profits benefit the indigenous people.

Behind Cherokee rise the Great Smokies, the largest untamed wilderness remaining in the eastern United States, also the most visited of all the national parks, with 9 million visitors annually. The 33-mile (53km) road over Newfound Gap to Gatlinburg, Tennessee, the main route through the park, often backs up with traffic, especially when one of the resident black bears puts in an appearance. Stop at **Oconaluftee Visitor Center** (tel: 828-497-1904; daily 9am–5pm), 2 miles (3km) north of Cherokee, for maps and information.

THE ROOF OF THE SOUTH

West of Cherokee, the North Carolina Mountains stretch for many more miles through a country of waterfalls, ruby mines, and villages full of summer visitors and antiques shops. Scenic byways invite you to roam, or you can take the **Great Smoky Mountains Railroad** (800-872-4681; www.gsmr.com; year-round) from Dillsboro for a spine-tingling trip through steep gorges.

Here on the roof of the South, the borders of Georgia, Tennessee, North and South Carolina lie close together. The scenery is wild, and cultural roots run deep. Festivals of music and dance, and schools that teach traditional crafts, along with luxurious resorts and historic inns, all preserve the unique heritage of North Carolina's Southern Highlands.

THE OUTER BANKS

With wide, water-thrashed beaches and sea oats along low sand dunes, the islands of the Outer Banks retain a certain wildness despite encroaching development

A string of narrow islands and peninsulas along the far eastern shore, the Outer Banks emerge like the head

of a whale breaching into the Atlantic. Two coastlines, **Cape Hatteras National Seashore** ⑱ and **Cape Lookout National Seashore** ⑲, preserve 120 miles (190km) of these beaches on Bodie, Hatteras and Ocracoke islands, and Core and Shackleford banks. While most coastal islands lie within 10 miles (16km) of shore, the Outer Banks belong to the realm of the sea. In places, 30 miles (48km) of water separate Hatteras Island from the mainland. The Outer Banks are perfect for peace, isolation, national parks, water sports, fishing, hang-gliding, and getting away from it all. Lodging and other visitor amenities are available in the areas not designated as National Seashores; for details of these, contact the **Outer Banks Visitors Bureau** (tel: 877-629-4386; www.outerbanks.org; daily 9am–5pm).

NATIONAL SEASHORES

The National Seashores of the Outer Banks have their own personalities, distinct from the rest of the state. The islands have wide, water-thrashed

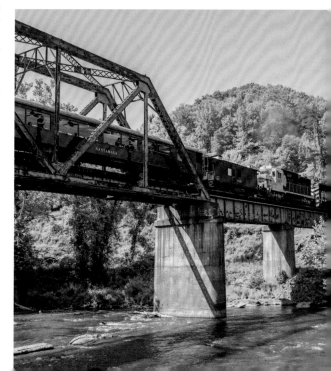

The Great Smoky Mountains Railroad train passes over the Tuckasegee River as it leaves Bryson City.

⊘ Fact

December 2023 marks the 120th anniversary of the Wright Brothers powered flight. These anniversaries are celebrated locally with vintage aircraft shows and military fly-overs.

beaches. Scattered patches of sea oats and beach grasses bind low dunes behind them. Clumps of shrubby marsh elder and bayberry dot the swales. Most trees lean away from the sea, a feature formed by the relentless salt spray that stunts the branches on windward sides.

Two strong navigational currents pass off the Outer Banks. The Gulf Stream flows north from Florida at a speed of about 4 knots. It swings east near **Cape Hatteras**, providing a perfect send-off for ships bound for Europe. The cooler Virginia Coastal Drift flows closer to shore. Near the crook in **Hatteras Island**, navigational hazards in the form of submerged and shifting sandbars reach 8–10 miles (13–16km) out to sea. Early ship captains dreaded this passage; the islands are so low that, to read natural landmarks, they had to remain close to shore. But they dared not venture near Diamond Shoals, the 'graveyard of the Atlantic.' Over the centuries, more than 600 ships ended their journeys disastrously here.

To warn ships of hazardous waters, the construction of lighthouses was a high priority during colonial times. Cape Hatteras got its first lighthouse, a 90ft (27-meter) sandstone tower, in 1803. The present one was completed in 1870. With 1.25 million bricks, it towers 208ft (63 meters) above the beach and the seagulls, the tallest lighthouse in the United States.

When it was built, the **Cape Hatteras Lighthouse** stood 1,500ft (450 meters) from shore. Decades of erosion have brought waves within 200ft (60 meters) of its base. The keeper's quarters house a museum and a visitor center (tel: 252-473-2111; daily 9am–5pm). Lighthouses mark other portions of the Outer Banks. All have distinctive exterior patterns and flash for different time periods at night so that navigators can identify them. The squat, whitewashed **Ocracoke Lighthouse** was built in 1823, the oldest still operating in North Carolina. Diamond-patterned **Cape Lookout Lighthouse** ⓴, completed in 1859, warns sailors of the low-lying Core

Bodie Island Lighthouse, seen from across the Marsh boardwalk.

Banks. The horizontally striped **Bodie Island Lighthouse**, in service since 1872, guards Oregon Inlet. During the late 19th century, the US Life-Saving Service established guard stations at 8-mile (13km) intervals along the banks. Patrolmen paced the beaches, scouting for ships in distress. When a vessel grounded, they rushed to its aid with a lifeboat and rescue equipment. Two of the original life-saving stations, **Chicamacomico** (at Rodanthe) and **Little Kinnakeet** (near Avon) remain. At Chicamacomico, park interpreters re-enact lifesaving drills on some afternoons in summer.

Cape Hatteras's islands are linked by Route 12. The **Bodie Island** and Hatteras Island sections of the seashore surround **Pea Island National Wildlife Refuge ㉑**. Observation platforms and several short trails lead from the highway to excellent viewpoints for watching the Canada and snow geese, whistling swans, and migratory ducks that spend the winter at the refuge. Pull-offs along Route 12 offer access to the beach, while long piers at **Rodanthe**, **Avon**, and **Frisco** give anglers a rare opportunity to cast for deep-water fish, which are not normally caught in the surf.

FIRST IN FLIGHT

Near **Kitty Hawk** is **Kill Devil Hills** – named, some say, after a drink that would kill even the Devil – and the granite **Wright Brothers National Memorial** (tel: 252-473-2111; daily 9am–5pm), which commemorates the first powered airplane flight by brothers Orville and Wilbur Wright on December 17, 1903.

At **Nags Head**, many visitors stop for a walk on **Jockeys Ridge**, a towering and unstabilized sand dune that migrates from time-to-time with the prevailing winds. Access to **Ocracoke Island**, at the southern end of Cape Hatteras, can only be reached by ferry from Hatteras; for more information on ferry schedules, telephone: 800-293-3779.

Ocracoke is also the departure point for the historic village of **Portsmouth ㉒**, at the north end of Cape Lookout. Early residents of Portsmouth made their living 'lightering' (transferring) cargo from oceangoing vessels to boats that served Core and Pamlico sounds. The town is quiet now. A self-guiding trail winds among remaining structures, providing a glimpse into its former life.

Except for the visitor center on **Harkers Island**, **Cape Lookout** is waterbound. Visitors can take excursion boats from Barkers Island to the lighthouse on **Core Banks**, or from Beaufort to the west end of Shackleford Banks. As off-road vehicles are allowed only on certain beaches, Cape Lookout's islands beckon backcountry hikers and campers.

Take all the necessary supplies you will need and plenty of water along with you and be sure to arrange a return pick-up time with the ferry operator beforehand.

Sunrise over the sand dunes at Corolla Beach.

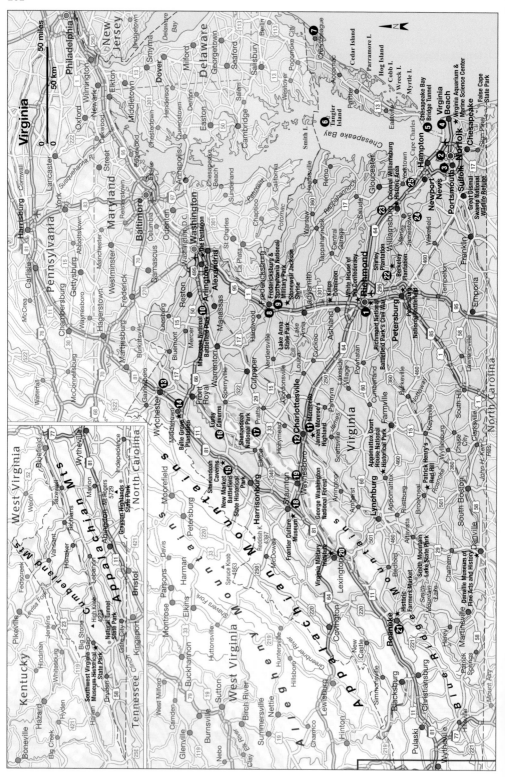

VIRGINIA

Thomas Jefferson wrote in a letter in 1791: 'On the whole, I find nothing anywhere else... which Virginia need envy to any part of the world.'

Jefferson was referring, in this instance, to the weather, but since he was an acknowledged master-builder, ardent gardener, and architect of several of his state's most elegant buildings, we hold his truths on Virginia to be self-evident.

An emerald jewel in the crown of the new South, the northern hills of Virginia are rapidly becoming a garden suburb for the nation's Capitol, Washington, DC. Escapees from the 'company town' travel to weekend homes near Richmond, Fredericksburg, and even sleepy little Luray. The 17.5mile (28km) Chesapeake Bay Bridge-Tunnel is one of the engineering wonders of the modern world, and the rising sweep of the bridge makes for a truly memorable drive.

Although one of the last Southern states to secede from the Union, in many ways Virginia was the worst affected. As many historians point out, over half the battles fought in the war took place in its green rolling hills. George Washington, the young country's first president, was born here. Jefferson, elected in 1801, ushered in an era commonly known as the Virginia Dynasty, and for the next 25 years the leader of the nation would be elected from the ranks of Virginia gentlemen. Another leader of a different nation felt so strongly about the land that he gave

up a career to follow a cause: Robert E. Lee was offered the command of the Union forces in the War Between the States. He could not bear to take up arms against his Virginia kinsmen, however. History books the world over record the heavy consequences that followed his decision.

So what is it about Virginia that so stirred these men of distinction and now motivates the movers and shakers who toil in DC? The very things that any visitor cannot fail to appreciate: blue hazy mountains with trickling

⊙ Main attractions

Richmond's Court End
Shockoe Slip
Richmond National
    Battlefield Park
The Edgar Allan Poe
    Museum
Virginia Museum of Fine
    Arts
Virginia Beach
Monticello
Shenandoah Caverns
Natural Bridge

◉ Maps on pages 282, 284

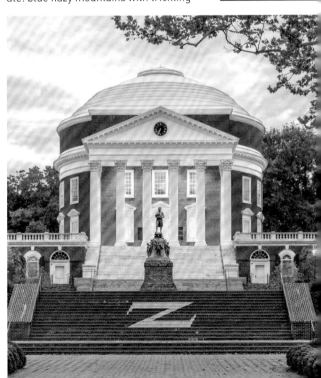

Rotunda at the University of Virginia.

waterfalls, and deer so unafraid that they wander right up to strangers; small towns where, even today, children use rubber inner tubes to float on the clear mountain creeks, and a sea with fine shell-laden golden sands, stretching for miles along the coast.

In this state of great beauty and great men, the last word could best be left to another of them. The poet Walt Whitman was moved to write in 1865: 'Dilapidated, fenceless, and trodden with war as Virginia is, wherever I move across her surface, I find myself roused to surprise and admiration.'

RICHMOND

It was once the capital of the Confederacy, and later the home of Mr Bojangles. Now the movers and shakers of the nation's capital are equally at home in **Richmond ①**.

Richmond is at the heart of the New South, and still embodies all the best of the Old South. More than a billion dollars of shiny new buildings grace the Downtown skyline, while on the backstreets the leafy neighborhoods

are graceful, resplendent with restored mansions, new museums, rejuvenated warehouses reborn as art galleries, and Downtown apartments. Bestriding the James River, the city has spread south, but most of the interesting sites are located on the north side, following the city's colonial layout of 1737.

Less than an hour's drive from Williamsburg (see page 298) to the east and Jefferson's Monticello to the west (see page 292), Richmond makes a perfect base for exploring central Virginia. The city's importance cannot be overestimated, as it is both the former capital of the old Confederacy and a hub of the northern New South.

DOWNTOWN DELIGHTS

In many ways, **Franklin Street** could be called the 'Gateway to Downtown Richmond.' Landmarks such as the Commonwealth Club provide the perfect prelude to how the old blends so well with the new. All along Franklin Street, historic houses saved from the wrecking ball now serve as private residences or as offices for organizations

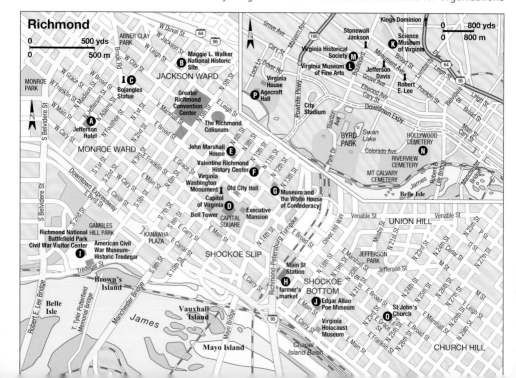

like the Garden Club of Virginia, the Junior League of Richmond, and the Woman's Club. Notable among them is the **Jefferson Hotel** Ⓐ (101 West Franklin Street; tel: 804-788-8000; www.jeffersonhotel.com), a Downtown landmark since 1895 and still dispensing old-world hospitality. **Main Street** is where Richmond means business: all along this road you'll find industrial, business, financial, government, and legal offices.

The historical district around **Broad Street** features 19th- and 20th-century commercial buildings that have become fine stores and apartments. This section has also been dubbed 'President's Row' because of the presidential streets running across it, names that ring throughout the colonial history of America: Adams, Jefferson, Madison, and Monroe.

Broad Street itself presents a mini-history of architecture, from Romanesque to Art Deco, and leads Downtown to **Capitol Square**. This area has seen the arrival of ventures like the **Richmond Coliseum** and a busy convention center.

Just a few blocks from the Coliseum is the historical district known as **Jackson Ward**, a quintessential urban neighborhood with wonderful cast-iron architecture that shouldn't be missed, but should be approached with caution late at night. Jackson Ward had its heyday in the 1900s, and the area was home to many prominent African Americans. The fine **Maggie L. Walker National Historic Site** Ⓑ (600 North 2nd Street; tel: 804-771-2017; Tue–Sat 9am–4:30pm; free) is a memorial to one of the most successful Black businesswomen in the post-Civil War South, with four previously derelict buildings undergoing restoration by the National Park Service.

Not far away is the **Bill 'Bojangles' Robinson Statue** Ⓒ. This commemorates 'Bojangles,' the fast-as-lightening tap dancer who grew up in Jackson Ward before finding fame with his feet.

He is caught in a typical pose, dancing down a flight of steps. The **Black History Museum and Cultural Center** on W Leigh Street (tel: 804-780-9093; www.blackhistorymuseum.org; Tue–Sat 10am–5pm) details African-American experiences in the Old Dominion.

COURT END

Within an eight-block section of the Downtown area is **Court End**, containing National Historic Landmarks, excellent museums, and many buildings on the National Register of Historic Places.

The focal point of Court End's past is the **Capitol of Virginia** Ⓓ at 9th and Grace streets, the second-oldest working capitol in the United States (Maryland is the first). Designed by Thomas Jefferson and modeled after a Roman temple in Nimes, France, it was later used as the model for the nation's Capitol building in Washington, DC. Free guided tours are available.

Other buildings of interest surround the Capitol. The **Executive Mansion** is the home of Virginia's governor.

Bill 'Bojangles' Robinson statue in Jackson Ward.

Statue of George Washington in the Virginia Capitol Building.

Richmond's **Old City Hall** on Capitol Square is in the Gothic Revival style and houses the courtroom from which the area derives its name. **Morton's Row** along Governor Street provides a look at the Italianate residences that used to surround Capitol Square (these are now state offices). Farther along on the Court End tour is the **John Marshall House** ⑤ at 9th and Marshall streets. This was Marshall's residence for the 45 years during which he served as Secretary of State, Ambassador to France, and Chief Justice of the Supreme Court of the United States.

The **Wickham House** on Clay Street provides a glimpse into the life of John Wickham, Richmond's wealthiest citizen when he built the house in 1812. It is maintained by the **Valentine Richmond History Center** ⑥, which relates Richmond's varied history through excellent exhibits and slides. At 1201 East Clay Street is the **White House of the Confederacy** ⑦ (tel: 804-649-1861; www.acwm.org; Fri–Mon 10:15am–4pm; free), providing further insight into Richmond's unparalled role during the Civil War. The home served as the residence of Jefferson Davis, president of the Confederacy from 1861 to 1865, and the museum houses the largest Confederate collection in the nation. Most of the exhibits from the war were contributed by local veterans, and in the early days of the museum, they, or their descendants, often worked as guides.

SHOCKOE

South of Capitol Square and down by the riverside is **Shockoe Slip**. No other area in town better displays Richmond's integration of the past and present to produce an enjoyable future. In the 19th century, Shockoe Slip was a lively area full of stores and tobacco warehouses but fell into decay as commerce along the James River slowed. Today, the Slip is active again, but now it's full of diners, shoppers, and strollers taking full advantage of the revitalization. This is also the scene in **Shockoe Bottom**, a warehouse district southeast along the river that saw a renewed growth after the completion of new a flood wall to protect the area from the danger of high waters.

Trendy restaurants, offices, and residences are housed in renovated red-brick buildings from the earlier commercial boom. For example, the old **Belle Bossieux Building** (now a popular restaurant) on 18th Street, was built as a row of stores with residences above. It was designed by Edmund Bossieux, a New Orleans native who obviously liked the city's architectural style. The **farmers' market** ⑧, one of the oldest continuously operating in the country, is held by the intersection of 17th and Main streets. Virginian farmers have been bringing fresh farm produce to market here for more than 200 years. Be sure to stock up before leaving town.

The **Virginia Holocaust Museum** ⑨ (E Cary Street; 804-257-5400: Mon–Fri 9am–5pm, Sat and Sun 11am–5pm) tells the story of the Holocaust through real

The James River, with Richmond in the background.

accounts of victims. Visitors can register online to reserve a spot, and both parking and admission to the museum is free. (see pages 93 and 98).

An eerie contrast to the lively Shockoe Bottom commercial scene is provided by the **Edgar Allan Poe Museum** ❶ (1914–16 East Main Street; tel: 804-648-5523; www.poemuseum. org; Tue–Sat 10am–5pm, Sun 11am–5pm). Richmond's oldest structure is now a fascinating memorial to one of America's finest writers. It presents the life and career of this strange, but talented, local author.

METROPOLITAN RICHMOND

If time allows, there are many attractions that are also worth seeing farther away from the city center. Head northwest up Broad Street for two striking museums: housed in the former Broad Street Train Station is the **Science Museum of Virginia** ❸ (2500 West Broad Street; tel: 804-864-1400; www.smv.org; Tue–Sun 9.30am–5pm). With an engaging and informative presentation of science, this is a venue that the whole family can appreciate. There are very few 'Do Not Touch' signs here; instead, visitors are encouraged to observe, interact, and experience the impact of science on life. The museum is best known for its IMAX dome. Adjacent to the Science Museum is the **Children's Museum of Richmond** (tel: 804-474-7000; www.c-mor.org; Tue–Sun 9.30am–5pm), perfect for visitors from six months to 12 years old.

On the statue-laced **Monument Avenue** are many tributes to the South, including General Robert E. Lee astride his horse, *Traveller*, erected in 1890. Also along the avenue are some of Richmond's most beautiful metropolitan homes, a testament to the city's former gentle and gracious beauty. Nearby, the **Fan District**, so-called because of the shape of its streets, also has some lovely renovated Victorian homes, plus lots of local restaurants.

The **Virginia Museum of Fine Arts** ❶ (200 N Arthur Ashe Blvd; tel: 804-340-1400; www.vmfa.museum; daily 10am–5pm; free) is by the broad and spacious avenue appropriately called **The Boulevard**. In addition to its modern art, the collection of Fabergé jeweled Easter eggs and 'objects of fantasy' is one of the largest in the country. One block away on North Boulevard is the **Virginia Historical Society** ❿, which has an excellent museum.

South of the Fan District is the **Hollywood Cemetery** ❶. Rolling hills, and bluffs overlooking the James River afford the serene and forested cemetery with the perfect setting for a sobering walk-through history. The site provides the resting places for more than 18,000 Confederate soldiers, including Confederate president Jefferson Davis, and US presidents James Monroe and John Tyler.

GIVE ME LIBERTY OR GIVE ME DEATH!

On the other side of Downtown, **St John's Church** ❶ (2401 East Broad

O Tip
The Virginia Museum of Fine Arts has a positive impact on the Richmond community, which has included working to preserve historic buildings. Such improvements included the historic Robinson House, which was completed in 2020 and serves as a tourism center and history exhibit.

At the Virginia Historical Society.

HOLLYWOOD CEMETERY

Richmond's most well-known cemetery is a final resting place and memorial for those who died in the Civil War.

The Hollywood Cemetery was aesthetically inspired by Boston's Mount Auburn. The design was commission to architect John Notman, which he delivered in 1849, along with the site's name, Hollywood, inspired by the holly trees on the surrounding hillsides.

Without doubt, the most striking sight in the cemetery is the Monument for the Confederate War Dead. Standing at 90ft (27 meters) high, this giant granite pyramid was built to honor the 18,000 Confederate troops who enlisted and never made it home.

Ask any local about the legend surrounding the pyramid's top stone and they'll be sure to stop what they're doing and regale you with the tale. Legend has it that no-one could determine just how to place the capstone atop such a high monument, aside from the notorious criminal Thomas Stanley. Convict Stanley had been working on the pyramid's construction when he made the offer that if he were to be freed, he would share his solution. There's no firm historical record to substantiate the legend. However, the fact that the pyramid was completed confirms to believers among Richmond's residents that Stanley did his part.

In recent years, the future of the Confederate War Dead Monument has been called into question, with a renewed focus on whether it, and others like it, should be preserved or removed completely. In 2017, the topic of Confederate monuments became associated with the Charlottesville white supremacy rally, and the violence that ensued.

The Hollywood Cemetery is also the resting ground for a number of presidents. The fifth US president, James Monroe, was reinterred from New York City by Virginia Governor Henry Wise in 1858. John Tyler, the 10th US president is also buried here, as is Jefferson Davis – the only President of the Confederate States.

Monuments and former presidents are not the only draw to the cemetery. Many of the tombs in the Hollywood Cemetery have their own ghoulish legends attached, including tales of hauntings, paranormal activity, and sightings of ethereal individuals. Among the most reported sightings, is that of a dog standing guard over the grave of its owner, a little girl.

Richmond's Hollywood Cemetery.

Street; tel: 804-648-5015; www.historicstjohnschurch.org) stands on historic **Church Hill**, overlooking the city skyline. Here Patrick Henry made his famous 'Give me liberty or give me death!' speech. Guided tours allow visitors to stand where Patrick Henry spoke to an audience including George Washington, Thomas Jefferson, and Benjamin Harrison on that day in 1775. The speech is often re-created on Sundays.

There's more to Richmond a little farther afield. The **West End** takes in both the west side of the city and part of Henrico County. The highlight is **Agecroft Hall ❷** (4305 Sulgrave Road; tel: 804-353-4241; www.agecrofthall.org; Thur–Sun 11:30am–4pm), a restored 15thcentury English manor house and gardens. It's perfect for a day excursion out of town, as is a cruise aboard a 20th-century paddlewheeler. The scenic trip along the James River offers dining and entertainment opportunities. Alternatively, the whole family might enjoy **Paramount's Kings Dominion**, 20 miles (32km) north of Richmond on I-95, an amusement park with 12 rollercoasters and the tallest Drop Ride in North America.

AROUND VIRGINIA

A modern naval center, swimming ponies, beautiful homes and natural beauty – there's history and culture unsurpassed in the shade of the Blue Ridge Mountains

Virginia begins at the ocean, and ends in the Blue Ridge Mountains, and its development has mirrored its topography. In the 1600s, colonial settlers founded Jamestown, and later Williamsburg, on the far eastern shore. Slowly, as the state prospered, they spread themselves with their families westward. Our route around the state follows this pioneering trail, and commences, as the colonists did, by the ocean. Fortunately for travelers, the state capital, Richmond, is convenient to both the mountains and the sea.

SEA BREEZES

For more than 300 years, the ocean has sustained and romanced the **Tidewater** area, the region in southeastern Virginia along the inlets and river coves to the sea. The busy town of **Norfolk ❷** is right at the heart of the region and serves as a good base for exploration. **Waterside** is a marketplace with stores that stretch along the waterfront; from the promenade a selection of harbor tours are available on a number of vessels. **Nauticus** (tel: 757-664-1000; www.nauticus.org; Tue–Sat 10am–5pm, Sun noon–5pm) is a three-level maritime museum featuring one-of-a-kind interactive exhibits, which take visitors on an adventure of marine discovery.

The **Norfolk Naval Base** opened in 1917 on a tiny site and has extended to 5,200 sprawling acres (2,100 hectares), playing a major role in the history of the military, and growing to become the capital base for the United States Navy.

The salty tang of the sea is never far away in these parts. Across the river in **Portsmouth ❸**, more military history awaits. The **Portsmouth Naval**

Nauticus and the USS Wisconsin, Norfolk.

Shipyard Museum was established in 1949 in the shipyard itself, and later moved to its current waterfront site. Just around the corner from the shipyards is the bright red **Lightship Museum**.

On a peninsula, the towns of Newport News and Hampton have been military bases, huge shipbuilding facilities, and a port of embarkation and debarkation for troops through American history. In keeping with its strategic importance, there are a number of museums devoted to the military, and some dedicated to transportation. The **Hampton History Museum** (tel: 757-727-1102; www.hampton.gov/119/Hampton-History-Museum; Mon–Sat 10am–5pm, Sun 1–5pm) has displays telling of the arrival of Captain John Smith and the demise of Blackbeard the Pirate.

Jutting out into the ocean, **Virginia Beach ❹** is the Atlantic coast's longest resort beach, stretching along a golden 28 miles (45km). The sand and surf are, of course Virginia Beach's major attractions, and the ever-popular hot dog stands, huge amphitheater,

razzle-dazzle nightlife, and general bonhomie are never far away. But there's more to this resort; the **Virginia Beach Maritime Historical Museum**, for instance. The building was originally a US Life-Saving/Coast Guard Station, and now houses nautical artifacts, scrimshaw, ship models, photographs, marine memorabilia, and a great little gift shop for coastal souvenirs.

THE EASTERN SHORE

The Eastern Shore is a distinctive part of Virginia; the people, places, and food make this land between Chesapeake Bay and the Atlantic Ocean a very separate place. Coming from Virginia's Tidewater area, a typical drive starts with the **Chesapeake Bay Bridge-Tunnel ❺** and heads north. The Bridge-Tunnel is one of the engineering wonders of the world, running 17.5 miles (28km) across the wide-sweeping bay. On reaching the area, use US 13 to explore until something appeals, then turn off the main road into another way of life.

The pretty upscale town of **Cape Charles** provides a quick introduction to the Eastern Shore, while little fishing towns like **Oyster** and **Cherrystone** give a perfect glimpse of life as it has been lived for decades. Historic **Eastville** features beautiful homes, government buildings, and churches, all within an easy stroll or drive off attractive Courthouse Green. Quiet **Pungoteague**, which means 'Place of Fine Sand,' is the location of several stately old homes and the oldest church on the Eastern Shore, **St George's Episcopal Church**, which dates from 1738.

The busier **Wachapreague** ('Little City by the Sea') waterfront is popular with both fishermen and tourists. **Onancock**, 'Foggy Place,' is great for an hour or so of exploration. Market Street has attractive shops and leads to the wharf where the **Hopkins & Brothers** store has been a Virginia landmark since it first opened in 1842.

⊙ THE CHINCOTEAGUE PONY SWIM

Tangier Island's most famous event takes place during summer in the town of Chincoteague. The wild ponies of neighbouring Assateague Island are thought to be the descendants of Spanish ponies, whose owners were shipwrecked on the Way to Peru.

Some may have bred with runaway horses from the camps of the early colonialists. Roaming freely all year round, the animals achieved national fame with the publication of Marguerite Henry's book Misty of Chincoteague, and tourists have been flocking to see the ponies ever since, most of which are owned by members of the Chincoteague fire department.

In the last week of July, firemen herd the excess foals across the narrow channel to Chincoteague in an event that causes much mirth and even a post of betting among the spectators as they speculate on which pony will swim the fastest. The following day ponies are driven along Chincoteague's Main Street for the annual animal auction, which is held as a fundraiser for the (volunteer) fire department. To witness this unusual spectacle, a hotel room needs to be booked months – or even years – in advance, as the event has become extremely popular. Everything starts bright and early at 8am at the Woodland Trail parking lot on Assateague.

The wharf is also an embarkation point for boat trips to **Tangier Island** ❻, one of the state's most unusual tourist destinations. The island was first sighted by Captain John Smith in 1608 and has remained relatively unchanged for decades (some say centuries). Local fishermen and their families speak with an accent that has persisted in the community since their Elizabethan ancestors arrived from Cornwall, in southwestern England.

Up by the Maryland border, the town of **Chincoteague** ❼ is an island community that has made its living on the water and, now, from tourism. Main Street has an old-fashioned feel to it, and side streets provide good dining, shopping, rooms to rent, and hugely popular annual events, such as the Chincoteague Pony Swim.

RICHMOND TOWARD WASHINGTON, DC

Thanks to the proximity of Washington, DC, Northern Virginia is distinct from the rest of the state. The political machinery, businesses, and people make this region a great deal busier than the outlying areas.

Heading toward Washington, DC, from Richmond on busy I-95, is the pretty, historic city of **Fredericksburg** ❽. Once considered part of Central Virginia, the suburbs and commuter zeal of the nation's capital have spread so far from the city limits that Fredericksburg, 50 miles (80km) away, has been annexed by Northern Virginia. Still, it's easy to understand why upscale Washingtonians would want to live here.

The town was founded on the banks of the Rappahannock River in 1728. Historic sites are on every street corner: the **Rising Sun Tavern**; the **Mercer Apothecary Shop** with its shelves filled with Dr Mercer's medicine bottles; and the **Mary Washington House**, purchased by George for his mother. Many of Mrs Washington's belongings remain, as well as a beautiful English

garden in the back. George's only sister, Betty, lived in nearby Kenmore, an elegant 18thcentury plantation home. The **Fredericksburg & Spotsylvania National Military Park** ❾ is made up of no fewer than four battlefields, 17 miles (27km) from town. The Civil War hit Northern Virginia perhaps harder than any other part of the South – or the North, for that matter. Up to 60 percent of all the military encounters took place in the border state of Virginia, and poignant reminders of the conflict are everywhere. Causalities here, combined with those at Manassas, southwest of Washington, were heart wrenching: more than 37,000 young men were killed or wounded in the fighting (see page 91).

Both **Manassas and Middleburg** ❿, 45 miles (70km) west of Washington, DC, lie in the region referred to by some as Hunt Country. Anyone interested in horses will feel right at home in the pleasant pasture land and well-heeled, equestrian atmosphere surrounding this pretty town. The old-fashioned streets are best explored on

Fredericksburg.

The Chincoteague Pony Swim.

Tip

On the outskirts of Washington is Potomac Mills (2700 Potomac Hills Circle; tel: 703-496-9330), a mega mall with more than 200 retail and outlet stores and daily discounts of 20–70 percent. There are 25 places to eat, plus an 18-screen movie theater complex.

foot (if not on horseback) and many of its restaurants serve Virginia wine from local vineyards.

RICHMOND TO MONTICELLO

Thomas Jefferson's home, **Monticello** ⓫ (tel: 434-984-9800; www.monticello. org; Thur–Mon 8:30am–6:30pm, Tue and Wed 8:30am–5:30pm) lies about an hour's drive west of Richmond off busy Interstate 64. Designed and built by the architect and statesman between 1768 and 1809, Jefferson saw to it that Monticello (Italian for 'little mountain') was unlike any other American house of its day. It is indisputably one of the nation's architectural masterpieces, and one of the few American homes on UNESCO's World Heritage List (along with such treasures as the Taj Mahal, the Pyramids, Versailles, and the Great Wall of China).

The neoclassical style is highlighted by the dramatic dome, which appears on the back of the US nickel. Jefferson hated the architecture of Williamsburg and said that if the British-inspired houses had not had roofs they would be mistaken for brick kilns. Hence his penchant for domes, which he mounted on several important buildings.

The entrance hall was the president's private museum, displaying, among other artifacts, items collected by Lewis and Clark during their expedition to the West. A tour of the house and grounds reveals much about the man, his home, his role as architect of several houses, and also about Virginia and US history. Jefferson is buried under the obelisk that he designed for himself.

Monticello can be seen from James Monroe's lovely home, **Ash Lawn-Highland** (tel: 434-293-8000; www.highland.org; daily 9:30am–4:30pm), only 2 miles (3km) away. Thomas Jefferson designed Ash Lawn for his great friend James Monroe, who was the fifth president.

Monticello is located along what has come to be called the **Constitution Route**, established in 1975 to recognize its historic significance for Virginia. Four US presidents (Jefferson, Madison, Monroe, and Zachary Taylor) and 11 Virginia governors were either born or built their

Monticello.

estates along this road. The Constitution Route runs right through the university town of **Charlottesville ⑫**. The town revolves around the **University of Virginia**, including Jefferson's renowned **Rotunda** (that dome again). Jefferson planned the university as the first secular college in America, and, at the same time laid out the university's 'academical village' around graceful, languid lawns. Charlottesville itself has been discovered by Washington, DC's intelligentsia and media folk, many of whom have country retreats in the area. As a result, the town's stores and restaurants are sophisticated and expensive compared to the rest of rural Virginia. The town gained global notoriety in 2017, when it was the scene of a white supremacist rally. Participants marched under Nazi and Confederate flags to oppose the removal of a statue of Confederate General Robert E. Lee. One person was killed in the ensuing violence.

The countryside north of Charlottesville features some of Virginia's finest vineyards set into rolling hills. From Charlottesville, it's only a short drive to the town of Waynesboro (see page 295), where there is a choice to travel along the beautiful Shenandoah Valley, either to the North or the South.

THE SHENANDOAH VALLEY

The country charm of the Shenandoah Valley attracts thousands of visitors annually, especially during the fall, when the leaves of the trees turn to burnt oranges and reds. The valley reaches from north to south, from West Virginia down through the state, and ends at the lovely town of Roanoke. Long famous in song and history, Shenandoah is flanked by green wooded hills and the misty Blue Ridge Mountains, which rise 3,000–5,000ft (900–1,500 meters). The valley runs about 200 miles (320km) long and is 10–20 miles (16–32km) wide.

I-81 runs the entire length, but Route 11 is more pleasurable, ambling through small towns, past wineries and subterranean caverns, historic sites, and pretty inns that recall a more leisurely time. **Winchester ⑬** makes a good introduction to the valley. Vitally important during the Civil War, Winchester changed hands 72 times during the skirmishes, and was the scene of six major battles. The Winchester-Frederick County Visitor Center is located in the **Hollingsworth Mill House**, just off I-81. It adjoins one of Winchester's three important museums, **Abrams Delight**, built in 1754 by one of the earliest settlers.

George Washington's Office Museum in the Downtown area is a small log cabin that Washington used as an office in 1755 and 1756 while he supervised the construction of Fort Loudoun as protection against Native Americans and the French. Just north on Braddock Street, **Stonewall Jackson's Headquarters Museum** serves as a third draw for museum and history buffs. Early spring is a glorious time to visit Winchester, when the area turns into a pale blossom heaven, as

Fall in Shenandoah National Park.

petals from the clusters of fruit trees drift languidly on the breeze and float lazily to the ground. This celestial event is celebrated in an annual **Apple Blossom Festival**.

PLANTATIONS AND ANTIQUES

Most visitors to **Middletown**  head straight for the **Wayside Inn** for a great meal (try the peanut soup) and to spend the night, or to while away the time before heading to your next destination. Due east of Washington, DC, Middletown in recent years has begun to mirror the preoccupations of its increasingly upscale clientele.

Just south of Middletown, the **Belle Grove Plantation** (tel: 540-869-2028; www.bellegrove.org; Sat 10am–4pm, Sun 1–5pm) is worthy of an excursion. The house, built in 1794, is significant because of Thomas Jefferson's involvement in its design. About 10 minutes' drive down the road from Belle Grove is **Strasburg,** rightfully known as 'The Antique Capital of the Blue Ridge.' The **Strasburg Emporium** and other small stores give ample opportunity to shop

Skyline Drive, Shenandoah National Park.

'til you drop. Beyond Strasburg, the Shenandoah Valley opens out, the Blue Mountain ridges sloping up to the skies on both sides. Farther south, **Shenandoah Caverns** surprise many people with their netherworld beauty and stunning lighting. Descend by elevator to Bacon Hall, where the formations here look remarkably like strips of bacon.

TEENAGE REBELS

The New Market area played a key role in the Civil War. The **New Market Battlefield Historical Park**  honors the brave charge made by teenage cadets recruited from the Virginia Military Institute to join their older brothers-in-arms on the battlefield. The cadets helped to rally the troops, and on May 15, 1864, contributed to a major Confederate victory. There are extensive background exhibits and a poignant walking tour.

Many people are lured to the small town of Luray by the **Luray Caverns**  (tel: 540-743-6551; www.luraycaverns.com; daily 9am–6pm). These large, somewhat spooky caves were discovered by

⊘ SHENANDOAH NATIONAL PARK

Shenandoah National Park is a long, narrow corridor of ridges and valleys clothed in dense forest and laced with streams and waterfalls. Running along the backbone of the Blue Ridge Mountains is the Skyline Drive, a 105-mile (160km) scenic highway that serves as the park's main thoroughfare. The effort to create a national park in the Blue Ridge was launched in the 1920s, and construction of the Skyline Drive began in 1931. Several of the campgrounds, picnic areas, and lodging amenities were built by the Civilian Conservation Corps (see page 54). The park was dedicated in 1936.

A second major project, the Blue Ridge Parkway, was also started in the 1930s. Often described as 'the most graceful road in America', the Parkway stretches 469 miles (755km) along the backbone of the Appalachian Mountains between Shenandoah and Great Smoky Mountain national parks, crossing Virginia into North Carolina. Along the way are countless overlooks, historic sites, wayside exhibits, hiking trails, and museums. Both roads are marked by mileposts, with a speed limit that means a leisurely pace is strictly enforced which gives you plenty of time to soak up the scenery and enjoy the drive. Together, these two roads form the longest and one of the most stunning views in the United States.

a local entrepreneur in 1878 and have since been the site of several subterranean weddings. Couples are serenaded by a huge 'stalacpipe' organ, mentioned in the *Guinness Book of Records*, which plays notes when air is pushed through the stalactites by electronically controlled, rubber-tipped plungers. When visiting the caverns, be sure to take a sweater as it is chilly underground, even when it's blazing hot outside. An impressive car collection and a gigantic maze are also on the premises.

Luray, a gateway to the **Shenandoah National Park** ⑰, is dominated by a beautiful hotel on a hill, The **Mimslyn Inn** (tel: 540-743-5105; www.mimslyninn. com). Despite its imposing position, this hostelry with an elegant dining room and indoor roof terrace is cozy and welcoming. A very pleasant and fairly inexpensive country inn, there is a relaxed, local Virginia atmosphere at the lobby bar, and around the rocking chairs on the veranda.

After passing through the busy university city of Harrisonburg, the quieter college town of **Staunton** ⑱ awaits. This hilly town has a restored railroad depot, and the **Woodrow Wilson Presidential Library**, which details the life and times of the 28th president. The most popular exhibit is his Pierce-Arrow limousine. Staunton is also the home of the **Frontier Culture Museum**. This hugely successful undertaking features 18th- and 19th-century working farms transplanted from England, Germany, Northern Ireland, and America, offering insights into country life.

SOUTHERN ARTIST

A half-hour to the east of Staunton, the town of **Waynesboro** ⑲ is known as the home of Southern artist P. Buckley Moss. Her stick-figure paintings are collected throughout the world, and the **P. Buckley Moss Museum** in Waynesboro displays and sells much of her work. Around Waynesboro, it's easy to pick up I-64, the big interstate that heads east toward Charlottesville and Monticello, then continues on towards Richmond (see page 284).

History lures travelers to **Lexington** ⑳, the prettiest town in the valley, if not in Virginia itself. A 19th-century college town, Lexington is home to both the **Virginia Military Institute (VMI)** and **Washington and Lee University**. Despite its military heritage, the town is not at all rigid or stuffy. Locals are unfailingly pleasant and helpful, and the antiques shops (including delightful second-hand bookstores) make it a lovely place to stroll. VMI was founded in 1839 and is the oldest state-supported military college in the US, earning it the sobriquet 'The West Point of the South.' Stonewall Jackson taught here. Treeshaded Washington and Lee University was founded in 1749. Tiptoe quietly into **Lee Chapel** to see the final resting place of Robert E. Lee. The visitor center, the **Stonewall Jackson House**, Jackson's pre-Civil War home, and the **Stonewall Jackson Memorial Cemetery** are all within walking distance.

see page 284

Impressive stalactites at Luray Caverns.

Just 14 miles (22km) south of Lexington, Natural Bridge is known as one of the seven natural wonders of the world. This 215-ft (65-meter) high stone arch, carved by water over the centuries, stands as one of the valley's most famous sites. Its popularity owes as much to marketing as to nature, though; there are plenty of sites as beautiful – and less commercialized – up in the mountains of Shenandoah National Park (see page 295).

STAR CITY OF THE SOUTH

Roanoke ㉑ is the valley's largest city, the southern end of the rolling, pine-scented ravine. Known as the 'Star City of the South,' its emblem, a huge 88ft (27-meter) neon star on **Mill Mountain**, overlooks the city and the valley. Roanoke is known for its historic **Farmers' Market**, where growers have brought fresh fruits, vegetables, and flowers by country road for nearly 125 years. The little Downtown area around the marketplace has been spruced up a treat, and the **Center in the Square**, a multilevel arts center, throbs with life

and live performances. Other attractions include the **Virginia Museum of Transportation** (big trains and other vehicles) and the **Harrison Museum of African American Culture**. A fitting end to any Shenandoah Valley visit.

COLONIAL VIRGINIA

Just a pretty drive away from Richmond are sturdy brick plantation homes; Williamsburg, capital of the former colony; Yorktown, and Jamestown, which celebrated its 400th anniversary in 2007

When many Virginia visitors think of the Old Dominion, they think of colonial Williamsburg, which, along with its two stately companions, Jamestown and Yorktown, form Virginia's Historic Triangle, the oldest part of the state and among the oldest places in the US. The three sites, which make up the **Colonial National Historical Park**, are linked by the lovely 23-mile (35km) **Colonial Parkway**, a road that meanders through forests and fields. Although I-64 makes the Williamsburg area only an hour away from Richmond, the most

Lee University Hall, Lexington.

interesting route from the capital follows the Plantation Road (Route 5). In a drive of less than 60 miles (95km), the road between Richmond and Williamsburg winds through more than 300 years of Virginian and American history.

PLANTATION ROAD

Only 18 miles (29km) from Richmond's soaring skyline is the finest plantation in the area. As with many stately mansions, the road up to Historic Shirley ❷ (tel: 804-829-5121; www.historicshirley.com; Tue-Sat 10am–4pm) is, fittingly, along a tree-lined drive. Shirley was founded in 1613, just six years after the settlers arrived in Jamestown, making it the oldest plantation in Virginia. The brick structure is one of the nation's prime examples of Queen Anne architecture.

It has been the home of the Carter family since 1723; Anne Hill Carter was the mother of Robert E. Lee and was born at Shirley. Many prominent Virginians enjoyed hospitality here, including George Washington and Thomas Jefferson. Look for the plethora of pineapples, an international symbol of hospitality, in the hand-carved woodwork of the house and the pineapple pinial on the peak of the rooftop. The tour is good value, and the stroll along the river is invigorating.

Leading up to **Berkeley Plantation** (tel: 804-829-6018; www.berkeleyplantation.com; daily 9.30am–4:30pm) is a short dirt road that was designed for carriages. A sign requests that motorists drive 'leisurely.' Berkeley dates from 1726 and has played host to George Washington, the succeeding nine US presidents, and thousands of tourists. Colonial-clad tour guides point out that the military song *Taps* was composed here in 1862, while Union forces were encamped at the plantation during the Civil War. William Henry Harrison, Governor Benjamin Harrison's third son, was born at Berkeley and grew up to become the famous Native American fighter

'Tippecanoe,' the ninth president of the United States, and grandfather of Benjamin Harrison, the 23rd president.

By taking a fork in the road from Berkeley, you'll arrive at **Westover Gardens**. The plantation, built about 1730, is not open to the public, but its grounds, on the banks of the James River, are perfect for strolling. The best view is seen by walking across the lawn instead of following the path. The small structure by the ice house has passageways leading to the river, dug in case of attack by Native Americans.

Next on the route is **Evelynton** (tel: 800-473-5075). Even if plantation interiors don't appeal, take the road up to the house to enjoy the outside, the greenhouse, and the gift shop. The escorted tours inform about the family's patriarch, Edmund Ruffin, who fired the first shot of the Civil War at Fort Sumter. He also earned the title, the 'Father of American Agronomy,' by virtually saving 19th-century Virginia from a bleak agricultural economy.

The last plantation before Williamsburg is **Sherwood Forest Plantation**

⊙ Tip

There's more to Williamsburg than just history. The Williamsburg Winery is the state's largest, and tours and tastings take place every day. Busch Gardens Williamsburg regularly wins the 'Most Beautiful Theme Park' award, while Premium Outlets has more than 130 stores with discounted goods.

The Natural Bridge.

(tel: 804-829-5377; www.sherwoodforest. org; daily 9am–5pm), former home of President John Tyler, and said to be the longest frame house in America. It has been a working plantation for almost 250 years and is still occupied by members of the Tyler family. The family's pet graveyard can be seen nearby.

WILLIAMSBURG

Williamsburg ㉓ (tel: 757-229-6511; www.visitwilliamsburg.com) was once the capital of a colony that extended, it is said, all the way to the present-day state of Minnesota. The Colonial Williamsburg Foundation now looks after around 85 percent of the 220-acre (90-hectare) town laid out by Royal Governor Francis Nicholson. Bisected by mile-long **Duke of Gloucester Street**, the **Colonial Williamsburg Historical Area** (tel: 855-771-3290; colonialwilliamsburg.com; daily 8:45am–5pm) contains 88 original structures, 50 major reconstructions, and 40 exhibition buildings. There are also 90 acres (35 hectares) of gardens and greens, several museums, not to mention nearby **Carter's Grove**, which features a 1754 mansion, **Wolstenholme Towne**, with a museum, a slave quarter, and a reception center. In colonial Virginia, there's much to see, as you would imagine from a destination that has employed 3,500 archaeologists, researchers, historians, and historical interpreters.

Any visit should begin at the **visitor center** (101 Visitor Center Drive; tel: 855-771-5217; www.colonialwilliamsburg.com; daily 8.45am–5pm) and *Williamsburg – The Story of a Patriot*, a 35-minute film. The best way to see often-crowded Williamsburg – the town gets 4 million visitors in a busy tourist year – is to arrive just before the center closes at night and buy admission tickets for the next day.

One of America's first planned cities, Williamsburg was constructed between 1698 and 1707, after the abandonment of Jamestown. It was conceived as a gentle country town, so each house on the main street was surrounded by half an acre of land to allow for the smokehouse, stable, dairy, orchard, and slave quarters. It was a prosperous market town, with the

Horse-drawn carriage tour in Williamsburg.

College of William and Mary at one end, and the Capitol at the other end. The residence of the crown's representative in the colony of Virginia was the grand, centrally located Governor's Palace.

The town may look and feel something like a stylish, upscale theme park minus the cotton candy, but it's a great place to depart from the strains and stresses of 21st-century life and become immersed into a slower, and more langorous style and pace.

JAMESTOWN

Jamestown ❷ (tel: 757-856-1250; www. historicjamestowne.org) was the original site of the first permanent English settlement in the New World. In 1997, archaeologists discovered the remains of the original 1607 British fort, unearthing tens of thousands of relics, including a human skeleton. The excavation was seen as one of the most important finds in recent times. The ruins of a 1640s church tower, and the excavated site of the old capital, are also worth seeing. The settlers' story is told through film and full-size re-creations of ships and outdoor settings at the Jamestown Settlement Museum (tel: 757-253-4838; daily 9am–5pm), where costumed interpreters portray life at the beginning of the 17th century.

YORKTOWN

Yorktown ❷ lying 14 miles (20km) along the Colonial Parkway from Williamsburg, is the historic site of the last major battle of the Revolutionary War and, in 1781, the surrender of Lord Cornwallis to General George Washington. The visitor center (1000 Colonial Parkway; tel: 757-898-2410; daily 9am–5pm) presents a film about the history of the town and is the place to begin a Battlefield Tour. From the top of the visitor center, look out over the earthworks that mark the lines of the battlefield. The Historic Area's Main Street has gracious homes dating from when York town prospered as a tobacco port. The Nelson Home, where a signatory of the Declaration of Independence lived, was built in 1711. Nearby, the Yorktown Victory Center tells the story of the American Revolution through a film and outdoor living history exhibitions.

Replica ship at the Jamestown Settlement Museum.

The Shack Up Inn, Clarksdale, Mississippi.

USA THE SOUTH

TRAVEL TIPS

TRANSPORTATION

A – Z

FURTHER READING

TRANSPORTATION

By air

If it is too impractical because to drive to the destinations listed in this book, an easy alternative is to fly. The major hubs in these Southern states are:

Georgia: Hartsfield-Jackson, Atlanta.

Alabama: Birmingham-Shuttlesworth International Airport, Birmingham.

Mississippi: Jackson Evers International Airport, Jackson.

Louisiana: Louis Armstrong New Orleans International Airport.

Arkansas: Arkansas International Airport-Byh, Blytheville.

Tennessee: Memphis International Airport and Nashville International Airport.

North Carolina: Charlotte Douglas International Airport, Charlotte.

South Carolina: Charleston International Airport.

Virginia: Richmond International Airport.

Traffic in Jackson Square, New Orleans.

Among the international and domestic airlines that serve these airports are:

Air Canada: tel: 888.247-2262; www.aircanada.com

American Airlines: tel: 800-433-7300; www.aa.com

British Airways: tel: 800-247-9297; www.britishairways.com

Delta: tel: 800-221-1212: www.delta.com

Frontier Airlines: tel: 800-401-9000; www.flyfrontier.com

JetBlue: tel: 800-538-2583; www.jetblue.com

United: tel: 1-800-864-8331 www.united.com

The following commuter airlines offer services within the region:

Allegiant Airlines: tel: 702-505-8888; www.allegiantair.com

Southwest: tel: 800-435-9792; www.southwest.com

Airport taxes

Domestic flights include up to 20 percent in additional taxes to cover US Excise Tax (7.5 percent), security costs, and airport and facility fees.

Airlines include this in the final total for the plane fare.

By rail

Although passenger services were greatly curtailed in the South during the latter part of the 20th century, it is still possible to travel by rail. Amtrak is the major rail passenger carrier in the US, and its network links many cities, but sadly bypasses many more. However, there are still some excellent routes that glide through breathtaking scenery. Whilst not the fastest or cheapest way of getting around America, riding the rails can still be a leisurely and highly enjoyable experience, provided you have the time and money. Many of the South's Gulf Coast cities are linked by Amtrak. Details about Amtrak's train service can be obtained by calling 800-872-7245 or at www.amtrak.com.

By bus

The national long-distance bus service, Greyhound, provides an impressive network of ground travel, offering daily services to major towns and cities. Routes and schedules are subject to change, so it is a good idea to check all arrangements with local stations in advance. Most cities also have municipal bus systems. Reservations and local bus station details are available by calling 214-849-8100 or visiting www.greyhound.com.

As both Greyhound and municipal stations are often located in somewhat run down areas, try to stay alert and do not wander too far, particularly after dark. Plan your journey for daylight arrival if possible. The buses themselves are safe and reasonably comfortable; choosing a seat near to the driver will discourage unwanted attention from any fellow passengers.

By taxi

Taxi service is available at major airports, and bus and train stations, connecting the cities of the southern states to hotels and other major tourist destinations. The most affordable and convenient options, however, are Uber and Lyft, accessible by smartphone app.

GETTING AROUND

On foot

With so many national parks, hiking trails, and outdoor activities on offer, the Southern states are the perfect place to park your car, strap on your hiking boots and set off on foot to enjoy the great outdoors. Most big city and regional tourism offices produce and distribute free walking tour guides, so be sure to look out for these on your visit. In the national parks of the South, you will also see hiking routes mapped out and labeled, according to difficulty, altitude, and accessibility for those with disabilities.

Cycling

Mountain biking and road cycling are prevalent pastimes in the South. Many of the major cities in these states have put a great deal of time and money into developing dedicated cycle routes, throughout their metropolitan streets. A great example of this is the city of Chattanooga, Tennessee, where the riverside cycle paths draw bicycle enthusiasts from miles around. You'll also find cycle rental facilities in most of the national parks listed in this guide; these mountain bikes are well maintained and by renting them, you're supporting conservation efforts throughout the parks.

By car

The infrastructure in the US is often best suited to cars and the Southern states are no exception. The major roads and interstate routes are well maintained, but the backcountry roads are sometimes forgotten about, so if you plan on going off road or exploring farther afield, a 4WD SUV with a high clearance will be helpful.

Car rental

The majority of car rental companies require drivers to be at least 21 years old, with a valid driver's license and a major credit card. A deposit will be withheld on your credit card for the duration of the car rental and refunded when you return the vehicle in good condition. Be aware that returning the car without a full tank of gas will result in an exorbitant amount charged directly to your credit card, often up to ten times what you would pay at the gas station.

You will find car rental agencies in most cities and airports, offering everything from basic economy models to luxury sports cars. It's almost always cheaper to arrange a rental in advance, so look out for fly-drive deals when you're booking plane tickets to a destination.

Be vigilant when the agents at the car rental offices run through your insurance options. If your credit card or personal car insurance does not include a car rental option, you must take out coverage. Major car rental companies include:

Alamo: Tel: 888-233-8749; www.alamo.com

Avis: Tel: 800-352-7900; www.avis.com

Budget: 800-214-6094; www.budget.com

Dollar: Tel: 800-800-5252; www.dollar.com

Enterprise: Tel: 800-266-9565; www.enterprise.com

Hertz: Tel: 800-654-4173; www.hertz.com

National: Tel: 844-393-9989; www.nationalcar.com

Thrifty: Tel: 800-334-1705; www.thrifty.com

Distances and driving times

The routes in this book cover a great distance across some of the largest states in the south. They stick to the primary roads and, with the exception of a few notable remote attractions, are designed to take in the main sights along the way.

Try to limit your driving to 3 or 4 hours a day (200 miles/321km). Aim to get the bulk of it out of the way in the morning, in order to allow the maximum amount of time to enjoy your daily destinations.

Take regular breaks and stock up on coffee and supplies if you're not accustomed to driving long

Cyclist in Charleston.

distances on a regular basis. Avoid driving late at night in areas that you don't know well, as they may not be well-lit, or lit at all in some cases.

Driving in remote areas

If you're going off road or are planning a trip that takes you onto backroads, it pays to be prepared for all eventualities. If your itinerary takes you away from towns and opportunities to restock on supplies, make sure you have plenty of water and provisions for the duration of your journey. Car essentials, such as a spare tire, an extra can of gas, a toolkit, and roadside hazard markers are also a good idea. If you do break down in a remote area and you can't signal for help, don't leave your car. A vehicle not only provides shelter: it's also easier to spot than a person. Most importantly, before you set off, make sure someone knows your route and make arrangements to check in with them on a regular basis. In doing so, they'll know if and when to send in the cavalry to help out.

Safety tips for motorists

Make sure you have a good map or a navigation system that allows you to save directions for use offline, should you lose your data connection or network coverage. Dialling 511 in any state will connect you with the Traveler Information Service, which provides up-to-date information regarding road closures, construction, delays, diversions, public transportation, and weather hazards.

A-Z

A

Accommodations

Chain hotels and motels are reliable and convenient but tend to lack unique character. You can, however, usually depend on a clean, comfortable room for a reasonable price. In general, prices range from $75 to $150 per room depending on the location, the season, and additional amenities.

When making a reservation, ask about special weekend or corporate rates and 'package deals'. Hotel staff in the US are notorious for quoting only the most expensive rates, but many hotels offer a variety of discounts and promotions. If you have the time to do a little research, you may find that B&Bs offer better service and more hospitality (not to mention a good breakfast, including grits, to get you going in the morning) for roughly the same price as a chain hotel. Often run by families with thorough local knowledge, they're likely to enhance your stay. For the DIY option, your go-to should be Airbnb. However, if you're looking for something with a little more curated Southern charm, try www.bbonline.com or www.bnb-finder.com.

Admission charges

Entrance fees at most museums and tourist attractions range from as little as $3 all the way to upward to $40. Discounts are often available for children under 12, seniors over 65, veterans, and families. Official state tourism boards have extensive and regularly updated details online about food, tourism, travel, and activity deals. The Southern state most renowned for free museums is Virginia.

B

Budgeting for your trip

The Deep South is much more affordable than other parts of the US, even more so if you stick to activities like exploring the national parks and the free self-guided walking tours on offer in most of the major cities. A cheap motel or hotel, across the South, will fit nicely into an accommodation budget of $40 to $70 per room, per night. For a good quality hotel, expect to pay between $100 and $175 a night. For a more high-end experience, expect a room to set you back anywhere between $250 and $500 a night. During the peak of summer, when the prospect of visiting outdoor attractions in near 90 percent humidity looms, a lot of the major hotel chains will slash their rates to keep the tourists coming through their doors. Be on the lookout for seasonal deals like this, especially in states like Mississippi and Louisiana.

For your daily food budget, you can get by on a minimum of around $40 a day per person, if you avoid drinking alcohol, frequent Southern supermarket chains like Publix and Aldi, and only eat out at diners, or fast-food drive-thrus. Meals in nicer restaurants do, of course, vary in price and value, but individual main courses are normally set at $25–$45, per dish.

Gas prices can be volatile across all of the US, but especially in the Deep South, with the price-per-gallon being affected by impending hurricanes and other factors. The 'normal' price-per-gallon however, is around the $3.75 mark. Most economy rental cars will do up to 350 miles (563km) on a full tank but if you're stopping and starting on small country roads and not sticking

to 65mph (105kmh) on the interstate, plan for increased fuel consumption. It's worth comparing prices at different gas stations too. Sheetz, 7/11, and Wawa will often better the price-per-gallon of their competitors, like Shell or BP.

C

Climate

The Deep South spans two time zones and various climates, but all states enjoy wonderfully sunny summers. Louisiana and the Florida Panhandle enjoy the mildest cold season, while Akansas, Tennessee, North Carolina, and Virginia all see snow and ice. Sandwiched in the middle, Mississippi, Alabama, Georgia, and South Carolina enjoy a little from both camps, making the weather in these central states the hardest to predict. Hurricanes are a fact of life the farther south you travel between June 1 and November 30, while tornadoes form as far north as Tennessee.

Louisiana and the Florida Panhandle

Annual rainfall across both states averages around 60ins (152cm), the majority of which falls during the near-tropical summer months. Average temperatures across the two states reach well above 90°F (32°C) in the summer and fall to 61°F (16°C) in winter. The winter might sound mild but when you combine humidity and light winds with that average temperature, you'll need a sweater and pants.

Mississippi, Alabama, Georgia and South Carolina

The annual rainfall across these four great states ranges from 54 to 60 inches annually (37–152cm).

Average temperatures reach 85°F (29°C) in the summer and fall to 50°F (10°C) in winter. Exposed to the ocean, the winter in South Carolina will feel cooler than the land-locked Mississippi, Alabama, and Georgia. Snow is a rare occurrence in Georgia, but when it does arrive, travel disruption is widespread.

Arkansas, Tennessee, North Carolina and Virginia

Across these four states, the average annual rainfall varies from 43 to 50 inches (110–127cm) annually. Average temperatures across the states reach 75°F (24°C) in the summer but drop sharply to freezing and below in the winter months: 10°F (-12°C) is not uncommon and snow has to be dealt with on the roads, train tracks, and runways each year.

What to Wear

The dress standard across the Deep South is informal and practical: the more comfortable you are the better. Shorts and capris will suffice in most summer situations. During the winter, especially in Arkansas, Tennessee, North Carolina, and Virginia, there's no shame whatsoever in wearing as many winter layers as humanly possible, to keep out the bitter cold. In the warmer and more humid states, microfiber base layers are a good investment to help guard against the evening winter chills.

Crime and safety

Many places in the South have their fair share of crime. Common sense will be your most effective weapon: try to avoid walking alone at night – at the very least stick to livelier, more brightly lit thorough-fares and walk confidently. Keep an eye on your belongings at all times when in public. Never leave your car unlocked or small children by themselves. Avoid leaving luggage and other valuables in plain sight in a parked car: instead lock them safely in the trunk or take them with you. If you have any valuables, you may want to lock them in the hotel safe.

Take particular care when using bank ATMs at night. Make sure you carry your cell phone with you at all times, just in case you need to call for help. Don't carry large sums of cash or wear expensive jewelry.

In the event of a traffic accident, remain with your vehicle, call the emergency services, and wait for them to arrive. It is illegal to leave the scene of an accident before the police arrive. Law requires wearing a seatbelt at all times in all states; laws vary from state to state for children, but use a safety seat or booster for kids under 4'9" (145 cm). If you are caught driving under the influence of alcohol or drugs, there are stiff penalties including jail time and large fines.

Customs regulations

Everyone entering the United States must pass through US Customs and Border Protection. You may bring with you the following duty-free items: one liter of alcohol if you are 21 or over; 200 cigarettes, 50 cigars or 2kg of tobacco for personal use if you're over 18; and gifts worth up to $100 ($800 for US citizens). Travelers with more than $10,000 in US, foreign currency, or travelers' cheques, must declare these upon entry. Meat or meat products, illegal drugs, firearms, seeds, plants, and fruits are not permitted and must be disposed of before entering the country. For more information, contact US Customs and Border Protection: tel: 877-277-5511; www.cbp.gov.

E

Eating out

It's impossible to categorise the cuisines of the Deep South. It's best to go into each state with an open mind, and a healthy appetite. Catfish is king in Tennessee, crawfish takes pride and place in Mississippi, New Orleans pairs its world-famous gumbo with po'boy sandwiches, and in the Panhandle, blackened Red Snapper is a regular, and delicious staple. The easiest and most efficient way to see what's good locally is to consult the tried, tasted, and tested restaurants in the Walking Eye App, or open Uber Eats as you drive from state to state, to peruse highly-rated eateries.

Electricity

Standard electricity in North America is 110–115 volts, 60 cycles AC. An adapter is necessary for most appliances from overseas, aside from Canada and Japan.

Embassies and consulates

Foreign embassies are all located in Washington, DC. They include:
Australia (Tel: 202-797-3000; www.usa.embassy.gov.au)
Canada (Tel: 202-682-1740; travel.gc.ca/assistance/embassies-consulates)

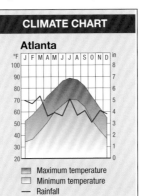

CLIMATE CHART

New Orleans

- Maximum temperature
- Minimum temperature
- Rainfall

CLIMATE CHART

Atlanta

- Maximum temperature
- Minimum temperature
- Rainfall

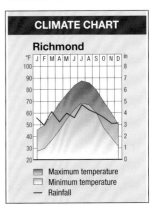

CLIMATE CHART

Richmond

- Maximum temperature
- Minimum temperature
- Rainfall

France (Tel: 202-944-6000; www.fran-ceintheus.org)
Germany (Tel: 202-298-4000; www.germany.info/embassy)
UK (Tel: 202-588-6500; www.gov.uk/world/organisations/british-embassy-washington)
Ireland (Tel: 202-462-3939; www.embassyofireland.org)
New Zealand (Tel: 202-328-4800; www.mfat.govt.nz)
South Africa (Tel: 202-232-4400; www.saembassy.org)
Contact the US State Department for street addresses and the embassy and consulate information of other countries (Tel: 202-647-4000; www.state.gov/s/cpr/rls)

Emergencies

In case of extreme emergencies, dial 911.

Etiquette

Southern hospitality can be seen in almost every interaction across the Deep South, but don't take this as a cue to be complacent in the hospitality that you dole out on your journeys and explorations. If you're seen to be cold or dismissive here, you'll soon encounter the sharp tongues of the South. Racism, division, and chauvinism are all apparent but not tolerated in social gatherings. In the same vein, any topic of conversation that has the potential to cause conflict – especially politics and religion – are by default, left at the door. In this great nation made up of immigrants from all over the world, cultural heritage and family trees are popular (and safe) topics of conversation.

H

Health and medical care

Travel restrictions relating to the Covid-19 pandemic are ongoing and subject to change at any given moment. Make sure to check the most up-to-date guidance at https://travel.state.gov/content/travel/en/traveladvisories/covid-19-travel-information.html before you fly. At the time of writing all travelers above the age of two are required to show evidence of a negative Covid-19 test taken 24hrs before you fly.

Medical services are extremely expensive all over the US. Always arrange fully comprehensive travel insurance to cover any emergencies. Check the small print first: coverage may exclude treatment for water-, winter-, or mountain sports accidents, unless these have been specifically included. If you need medical assistance, consult WebMD (www.doctor.webmd.com) for the physician or pharmacist nearest to you. In large cities, there is usually a physician referral service number listed. If you need immediate attention, go directly to a hospital emergency room (most are open 24 hours a day). You may be asked to produce proof of insurance cover before being treated.

Care should be taken to avoid dehydration and overexposure to the sun. This can happen rapidly even on cloudy days. A high-factor sun lotion, hat, and water bottle are essential accessories.

Heat exposure

The heat and humidity throughout the South can be not only uncomfortable, but also dangerous. If spending the day outdoors, carry water and take rest in the shade. Otherwise, mint juleps, iced tea, and light clothing are the only remedies for the South's sultry summers.

L

LGBTQ+ travelers

In many respects the Deep South is a very conservative area. Public displays of affection, whether straight or gay, may attract unwanted and unpleasant attention. Gay-friendly establishments may be in short supply, but discreet couples should be able to fully enjoy the South. There will be no problem in New Orleans. The LGBTQ+ community have made good progress in the Deep South in recent years, but it's best to test the waters discreetly. A good way to measure this is the degree to which you see the annual pride celebrations promoted on social media and on state tourism websites. The bigger the budget and the larger the photo albums, the more comfortable you can afford to feel in each location.

M

Media

Newspapers

The Deep South is a place where traditions are respected, supported and maintained, which is great news for the newspapers across these states. In fact, many of these publications in the South enjoy healthy circulation figures and buck the national trend of decline. In today's digital age, most of the papers offer free online editions. Whether digital or in print, a good local newspaper is still one of the best ways to get to know the city and state you're visiting. Below is a list of the best local newspapers in each state:
Georgia
The Atlanta Journal Constitution; www.ajc.com
Alabama
The Birmingham News; www.al.com/birmingham
Mississippi
The Clarion Ledger; www.clarionledger.com
Louisiana
Baton Rouge Advocate; www.theadvocate.com
Arkansas
Northwest Arkansas Democrat-Gazette; www.arkansasonline.com
Tennessee
Knoxville News Sentinel; www.knoxnews.com
North Carolina
The Charlotte Observer; www.charlotteobserver.com
South Carolina
Asheville Citizen-Time; www.citizen-times.com
Virginia
The Virginian-Pilot; www.pilotonline.com

Money

Although rarely obligatory, many workers in the service industries in the US rely on tips for a large part of their income. General rates are:
Waiters: 15–20 percent
Bartenders: $1 a drink
Taxi Drivers: 15 percent
Airport/hotel Baggage Handlers: around $2 per bag
Chambermaids: for overnight stays it is not necessary to tip, for longer stays a minimum of $3–4 per day will ensure you are all well looked after
Doormen: $3–4 for helping unload a car or other services

Hairdressers, manicurists, and masseurs 15 percent

Credit cards are accepted almost everywhere: most hotels, restaurants, and stores take the major ones, such as American Express, MasterCard and Visa. Along with outof-state or overseas bank cards, they can also be used to withdraw money at ATMs. Travelers' checks are still widely accepted, although you may have to provide proof of identification when cashing them at banks.

Before you leave home, check which ATM system will accept your card and the conversion charges you will incur per transaction. It's always best to have some cash with you. Most hotels offer in-room safes, so you can store this here in case of emergency.

Opening hours

Banks: 9am–5pm, weekdays. Some stay open until 6pm and on Saturdays.
Post Offices: 8am–4 or 5.30pm, weekdays, Saturday closed or closing earlier and opening later.
Stores: Shopping centers and malls are generally open 10am–9pm. Downtown area stores often close at 5–6pm. Most cities have 24-hour restaurants, convenience stores, and supermarkets.

Postal services

Even the most remote towns are served by the United States Postal Service. Smaller post offices are limited to business hours (Monday–Friday 9am–5pm), although central, inner-city branches may have extended opening times and open on Saturdays. Stamps are sold at all post offices, plus at some convenience stores, filling stations, hotels, and transportation terminals, usually from vending machines. Be sure to have some change handy.

Express Mail

For reasonably quick delivery at a modest price, ask for priority mail. For overnight deliveries, try US Express Mail. Many people prefer to use one

of several domestic and international courier services, including:
Fedex: tel: 800-463-3339; www.fedex.com
DHL: tel: 800-225-5345; www.dhl.com
United Parcel Service: tel: 800-742-5877; www.ups.com

Poste Restante

Visitors can receive mail at Southern post offices if it is addressed to them, care of 'General Delivery,' followed by the city name and (very important) the zip code. You must pick up this mail in person within a week or two of its arrival, with a form of photo identification.

Public holidays

As with many other countries, the US has gradually shifted most of its public holidays to the Monday closest to the actual dates, creating a number of three-day weekends throughout the year. Major holidays such as Christmas and the New Year are celebrated on the actual day. Keep in mind that during public holidays, post offices, banks, government offices, and many private businesses are closed. Major holidays include:
New Year's Day: January 1
Martin Luther King Jr Day: Third Monday in January
Presidents' Day: Third Monday in February
Good Friday: March/April – date varies
Easter Sunday: March/April – date varies
Cinco de Mayo: May 5
Memorial Day: Last Monday in May
Independence Day: July 4
Labor Day: First Monday in September
Columbus Day/Indigenous Peoples'

Pensacola Boardwalk.

Day: Second Monday in October
Veterans Day: November 11
Thanksgiving: Fourth Thursday in November
Christmas Day: December 25

Religious services

There's no official state religion in the US, but in the Deep South, Christianity is still a prevalent part of daily life. You can join practically any Sunday service in any Southern state, and receive a warm welcome, but be respectful of the legacy of yesterday's racial divisions in today's church services: they are no longer segregated by law, but many are still separated by choice.

Shopping

'Buy local' is a phrase you'll hear often and with enthusiasm across the Deep South, and in the era of the giant retailers like Amazon and Walmart, it's heartening to see so much support for locally owned businesses. If you can afford to support the local stores, it's a nice way to make sure your dollars are going directly to local employees and supply chains.

Telephones

Public payphones have largely disappeared from malls, gas stations, and

Episcopal church in Charleston.

transportation hubs, but if you do find one, and you don't have the correct change, dial 1-800-COLLECT. You'll be prompted to enter your credit card number and after doing so, you can place your call.

American cell phones use GSM 1900 – a different frequency from other countries, so even if you buy an American sim card, it is unlikely this will work in phones from overseas. The most affordable options for data, calls, and text messaging abroad, are bolt-on travel packages, arranged for and bought in advance from the phone operator in your home country.

Dialing Abroad

To dial abroad (Canada follows the US system), first dial the international access code 011, followed by the individual country code.

Country codes
Australia: 61
Ireland: 353
New Zealand: 64
South Africa: 27
United Kingdom: 44

Time zones

The Deep South spans two time zones: Eastern (which is Greenwich Mean Time minus five hours) and Central (Greenwich Mean Time minus six hours).

Tourist information

State tourism offices

Georgia
Explore Georgia

www.exploregeorgia.org
Atlanta
Atlanta Convention & Visitors Bureau
Tel: 404-521-6600
www.atlanta.net
Athens
Athens Convention & Visitors Bureau
300 N Thomas St, Athens
Tel: 706-357-4430
www.visitathensga.com
Macon
Visit Macon
450 Martin Luther King Jr Blvd, Macon
Tel: 478-743-1074
www.maconga.org
Savannah
Visit Savannah
101 E Bay St, Savannah
Tel: 912-644-6400
www.visitsavannah.com

Alabama
Alabama Tourism Department
tourism.alabama.gov
Birmingham
Greater Birmingham Convention & Visitors Bureau
950 22nd St. North, Suite 550, Birmingham
Tel: 205-458-8000
www.birminghamal.org
Huntsville
Huntsville/Madison County Visitor Center
500 Church St NW, Huntsville
Tel: 256-551-2230
www.huntsville.org
Selma
Selma Welcome Center
14 Broad St, Selma
Tel: 334-874-4864
Mobile
Visit Mobile Welcome Center
1 South Water Street, Mobile
Tel: 251-208-2000
www.mobile.org

Mississippi
Visit Mississippi
www.visitmississippi.org
Vicksburg
Visit Vicksburg
52 Old Hwy 27, Vicksburg
Tel: 800-221-3536
www.visitvicksburg.com
Natchez
Natchez Tourism Department
500 Main Street, Suite 1, Natchez
Tel: 601-492-3000
www.visitnatchez.org
Jackson
Visit Jackson

308 East Pearl Street, Suite 301, Jackson
Tel: 800-354-7695
www.visitjackson.com
Biloxi
Biloxi Visitors Center
1050 Beach Blvd, Biloxi
Tel: 228-374-3105
www.biloxi.ms.us

Florida
Pensacola
Visit Pensacola
1401 E Gregory St, Pensacola
Tel: 800-874-1234
www.visitpensacola.com

Louisiana
Louisiana Travel
www.louisianatravel.com
New Orleans
New Orleans & Company
2020 St Charles Ave, New Orleans
Tel: 800-672-6124
www.neworleans.com
Lafayette
Tourist Information Center
1400 NW Evangeline Throughway, Lafayette
Tel: 800-346-1958
www.lafayettetravel.com
Baton Rouge
Visit Baton Rouge
359 3rd St, Baton Rouge
Tel: 225-383-1825
www.visitbatonrouge.com

Arkansas
Discover Arkansas
www.arkansas.com
Little Rock
Little Rock Convention & Visitors Bureau
101 S Spring St, Little Rock
Tel: 501-376-4781
www.littlerock.com

Tennessee
Tennessee Department of Tourist Development
www.tnvacation.com
Memphis
Memphis Tourism
47 Union Ave, Memphis
Tel: 901-543-5300
www.memphistravel.com
Chattanooga
Chattanooga Visitors Center
215 Broad St, Chattanooga
Tel: 800-322-3344
www.chattanoogafun.com
Knoxville
Visit Knoxville
301 S Gay St, Knoxville
Tel: 865-523-7263

www.visitknoxville.com

Nashville
Nashville Visitors Center
500 11th Avenue N Suite 650, Nashville
Tel: 615-259-4730
www.visitmusiccity.com

South Carolina
Discover South Carolina
www.discoversouthcarolina.com
Charleston
Charleston Area Convention and Visitors Bureau
423 King St, Charleston
Tel: 800-774-0006
www.charlestoncvb.com
Columbia
Columbia Regional Visitors Center
1010 Lincoln St, Columbia
Tel: 800-545-0002
www.experiencecolumbiasc.com
Beaufort
Beaufort Area Visitor Center
713 Craven St, Beaufort
Tel: 843-525-8500
www.beaufortsc.org
Greenville
Visit Greenville SC Visitor Center
206 S Main St, Greenville
Tel: 800-717-0023
www.visitgreenvillesc.com

North Carolina
Visit North Carolina
www.visitnc.com
Charlotte
Charlotte Visitor Info Center
501 S College St, Charlotte
Tel: 704-339-6040
www.charlottesgotalot.com
Wilmington
Wilmington and Beaches Convention and Visitors Bureau
1 Estell Lee Place, Wilmington
Tel: 910-341-4030
www.wilmingtonandbeaches.com
Raleigh-Durham

Greater Raleigh Convention and Visitors Bureau
One Bank of America Plaza, 421 Fayetteville St Ste. 1505, Raleigh
Tel: 800-849-8499
www.visitraleigh.com

Virginia
Virginia Is for Lovers
www.virginia.org
Richmond
Richmond Visitors Center
405 N 3rd St, Richmond
Tel: 804-782-2777
www.visitrichmondva.com
Williamsburg
Colonial Williamsburg Regional Visitors Center
101-A Visitor Center Drive
Williamsburg, VA 23185
Tel: 855-771-3290
www.colonialwilliamsburg.com/visitor-center

Tour operators and travel agents

There's a vast array of nationwide tour operators and travel agents in the US, offering general and bespoke travel itineraries. You can select the one best suited to your trip from the **US Tour Operators Association** (www.ustoa.com) and the **National Tour Association** (www.ntaonline.com). It's also a good idea to connect with the visitor center at your destination, to inquire about their network of locally tried, tested, and trusted listings.

Travelers with disabilities

Under the Americans with Disabilities Act (ADA), hotels built after 1995 and containing more than five rooms must by law be usable by persons with disabilities. Accommodations built before this time and smaller lodgings are exempt, so it's worth calling ahead before you confirm any reservations. Many hotels provide voice-over television services, special alarm clocks, and adapted security measures. Attractions and restaurants are required by law to build ramps for those with limited mobility. Many major attractions also provide wheelchairs specially adapted to their terrain and visitor routes. The most in-depth and up-to-date resource on this topic is The Society for Accessible Travel and Hospitality (tel: 212-447-7284; www.sath.org).

V

Visas and passports

Foreign travelers to the US must carry a valid passport, and a round-trip ticket is normally required. A visa is necessary for visits of more than 90 days; those who require a visa should apply at the American Embassy or Consulate in the city or country where they permanently reside.

Tourists or business travelers from countries participating in the Visa Waiver Program, can stay up to 90-days in the US without a visa. Travelers who are eligible for the program must register online at the website of the Electronic System for Travel Authorization, or ESTA (tel: 202-325-8000; https://esta.cbp.dhs.gov/esta) at least one week before they travel. An approved application remains valid for two years, or until the traveler's passport expires. It also entitles the holder to multiple entries into the US during this period.

W

Weights and measures

The US operates on the imperial system of weights and measures. Metric is rarely used. Below is a conversion chart:
1 inch = 2.54 centimeters
1 foot= 30.48 centimeters
1 mile= 1.609 kilometers
1 quart = 1.136 liters
1 ounce = 28.40 grams
1 pound = 0.453 kilograms
1 yard= 0.9144 meters

Mountaineer Inn in Asheville, North Carolina.

FURTHER READING

FICTION

Billy by Albert French. Moving novel about a 10-year-old Black boy convicted of murdering a white girl in Mississippi in 1937.

The Complete Stories by Flannery O'Connor. One of the South's leading writers, Georgia-born O'Connor is known for her novel *Wise Blood*, powerfully filmed by John Huston, but this collection of short stories shows the true range of her talent.

Fried Green Tomatoes at the Whistle Stop Cafe by Fannie Flagg. Flagg's acclaimed account of the life of the 80-year-old Cleo Threadgoode, from Whistle Stop, Alabama.

Intruders in the Dust by William Faulkner. It is hard to choose from the Nobel Laureate's work, but this thriller-like story of an elderly Black farmer arrested for the murder of a white man is especially accessible.

Life on the Mississippi by Mark Twain. The seminal and beautifully written story of Samuel Clemen's journey as a riverboat pilot.

The Secret Life of Bees by Sue Monk Kidd. Set on a peach farm in South Carolina in the 1960s, this is a beautiful tale of a girl's maturing, and her awareness of racism.

A Time to Kill by John Grisham. A gripping tale of a series of rcial killings in a small town in Mississippi.

To Kill a Mockingbird by Harper Lee. Classic novel set in the Deep South of the 1930s, about a Black man accused of raping a white girl and defended by an honorable white lawyer, played in the movie by Gregory Peck. Set in a fictionalized version of Lee's home town, Monroeville, Alabama.

GENERAL NON-FICTION

Midnight in the Garden of Good and Evil by John Berendt. This 'factual' account of a murder in steamy Savannah in 1981 became a cult best-seller, and there are even now 'Midnight' tours of the town.

Praying for Sheetrock by Melissa Fay Greene. True story of the 1970s political awakening of the tiny Black community of Sheetrock, in McIntosh County, Georgia.

Redbirds: Memories from the South by Rick Bragg. Bragg's account of how he grew up in poverty in rural Alabama, and went on to become a Pulitzer Prize-winning novelist.

Sitting Up with the Dead by Pamela Petro. The author travels across the South from the Carolinas to Louisiana, in search of the traditional oral storytellers and listening to their tales.

⊘ Send us your thoughts

We do our best to ensure the information in our books is as accurate and up-to-date as possible. The books are updated on a regular basis using destination experts, who painstakingly add, amend and correct as required. However, some details (such as opening times or travel pass costs) are particularly liable to change, and we are ultimately reliant on our readers to put us in the picture.

We welcome your feed back, especially your experience of using the book "on the road", and if you came across a great new attraction we missed.

We will acknowledge all contributions and offer an Insight Guide to the best messages received.

Please write to us at:
Insight Guides
PO Box 7910
London SE1 1WE

Or email us at:
hello@insightguides.com

HISTORY & CIVIL RIGHTS

Heritage of the South by Tim Jacobson. The history of Dixie from the Native Americans until now.

Mine Eyes Have Seen the Glory by Douglas Brinkley. Biography of Rosa Parks, the dignified woman who began the Montgomery Bus Boycott when she refused to give up her seat on the bus to a white man.

Stride Toward Freedom by Martin Luther King Jr. Dr King's account of the early days of the Civil Rights struggle, in particular the pivotal 1955–6 Montgomery Bus Boycott.

MUSIC

The Blues Highway by Richard Knight. A travel and music guide of a route stretching from New Orleans to Chicago, though much inevitably focuses on the South's rock, jazz, country, and blues roots.

Blues Traveling: The Holy Sites of Delta Blues by Steve Cheseborough. A detailed guide to the blues landmarks of Mississippi and the surrounding area, from the backroads to the big city.

Good Rockin' Tonight by Colin Escott with Martin Hawkins. Marvelous account of the birth of rock'n'roll at Sun Records in Memphis, Tennessee, where Elvis, Johnny Cash, Roy Orbison, Jerry Lee Lewis, and Carl Perkins all made their earliest recordings.

It Came from Memphis by Robert Gordon. The roots of rock'n'roll, and much else besides, in an offbeat trawl through Memphis's recent history.

TRAVEL

Backroad Buffets & Country Cafes by Don O'Briant. A guide to the best in backroads cooking.

In God's Country by Douglas Kennedy. London-based journalist and novelist travels through the Bible Belt.

No Place Like Home by Gary Younge. A journalist who grew up in Britain journeys through the South and explores the notion of racial identity.

Recommended Country Inns – the South by Carol and Dan Thalimer. Dreamy places to lay your head.

A Turn in the South by V.S. Naipaul. Nobel Prize-winning novelist's memorable journey through the South, from Graceland to the struggles of the Civil Rights Movement.

CREDITS

PHOTO CREDITS

AWL Images 0/1, 8BL, 10/11, 12/13, 14/15, 16, 102/103, 104/105, 106/107, 108, 300
Carol M. Highsmith 4, 64/65, 68, 87, 88, 109, 114, 117, 120, 133, 135T, 136, 137, 137T, 138B, 143, 144, 145T, 145B, 146, 147, 148, 149B, 150T, 150B, 153, 157B, 157T, 160, 166T, 168, 169, 170, 171, 183, 197T, 204, 252T, 256, 260, 261, 263, 268, 270, 302T, 308, 309
Everett Collection/Shutterstock 42, 155
Georgia Department of Economic Development 124B, 126
Gerald Herbert/AP/REX/Shutterstock 164
Getty Images 6BL, 8M, 20B, 22B, 23T, 23B, 26, 27, 28, 29, 34, 38, 44, 45, 46, 47, 48, 51, 56, 57, 58, 61, 62, 63, 67, 69,

70, 71, 72, 73, 77, 78, 79, 80, 81, 82, 83, 84, 85, 86, 89, 90, 95, 98, 99, 116, 127, 139, 140, 141, 167, 178, 189, 206, 209, 219, 234, 238, 253, 257, 269, 287, 288, 291B
iStock 7TL, 9, 17, 30, 36, 75, 92, 113T, 113B, 115, 129B, 130, 131T, 131B, 158, 161, 162, 165, 173, 176/177, 187, 188, 192B, 194, 203T, 211, 212, 213, 223, 224, 232, 233T, 233B, 235, 241, 242, 244, 245, 246, 249, 251, 259, 264, 277, 281, 283, 285B, 286, 289, 296, 302B, 303, 304
NASA 184/185T, 184BR, 184BL, 185BL
Public domain 18/19, 20T, 21T, 21B, 22T, 24, 25, 31, 32, 35, 52, 54
Shutterstock 6MR, 6MR, 7TR, 7ML, 7BL, 7BR, 8BR, 33, 37, 39, 40/41T, 40BL, 40BR, 41TR, 41ML, 41BL, 41BR,

43, 49, 50, 53, 55, 59, 60, 66, 74, 76, 91, 93, 94, 96, 97, 111, 118, 119, 121, 122, 123, 125, 128, 129T, 135B, 142, 149T, 151, 156, 159, 163, 166B, 172, 179, 180, 181T, 181B, 182T, 182B, 185ML, 185BR, 185TR, 191, 192T, 193, 195, 196, 197B, 198, 199, 200, 201, 202, 203B, 205, 207, 208, 214, 215, 216B, 216T, 217, 218T, 218B, 221, 222, 225, 226, 228, 229, 231, 236, 237, 239, 247, 248, 250, 252B, 254, 255, 258, 266T, 272, 273, 274, 275, 278, 280, 285T, 291T, 292, 293, 294, 295, 297, 298, 299, 307
Six Flags 124T
The Coca-Cola Company 6ML
The Dollywood Company 230
VisitNC.com 7MR, 266B, 267, 271, 279
Warner Bros/The Zanuck Company/Kobal/REX/Shutterstock 276

COVER CREDITS

Front cover: Charleston, South Carolina, *shutterstock*
Back cover: monument in oldtown Savannah *Shutterstock*
Front flap: (from top) Rainbow Row in Charleston *Shutterstock*; Gus's World

Famous Fried Chicken in Memphis *Shutterstock*; Heron in North Carolina *Shutterstock*; Atlanta *Shutterstock*
Back flap: Lower Broadway, Nashville *Shutterstock*

INSIGHT GUIDE CREDITS

Distribution
UK, Ireland and Europe
Apa Publications (UK) Ltd;
sales@insightguides.com
United States and Canada
Ingram Publisher Services;
ips@ingramcontent.com
Australia and New Zealand
Booktopia;
retailer@booktopia.com.au
Worldwide
Apa Publications (UK) Ltd;
sales@insightguides.com
Special Sales, Content Licensing and CoPublishing
Insight Guides can be purchased in bulk quantities at discounted prices. We can create special editions, personalised jackets and corporate imprints tailored to your needs. sales@insightguides.com www.insightguides.biz

Printed in China

All Rights Reserved
© 2022 Apa Digital AG
License edition © Apa Publications Ltd UK

First Edition 2004
Third Edition 2022

www.insightguides.com

Editor: Beth Williams
Author: Jennifer Prince
Picture Editor: Tom Smyth
Cartography: updated by Carte
Layout: Greg Madejak
Head of DTP and Pre-Press: Katie Bennett
Head of Publishing: Kate Drynan

CONTRIBUTORS

This title was updated by **Jennifer Prince**, a freelance travel writer based in Virginia. Jennifer Prince's work is featured on several national travel sites, such as Travel + Leisure, National Geographic, AFAR, Lonely Planet, and Conde Nast Traveler. She thrives on off-the-beaten-path itineraries and is passionate about finding microstories to bring destinations to life. Jennifer currently lives in Virginia with her husband, and other than travel and writing, she enjoys 80s music, vintage things,

fostering kittens, and time with her family.

Beth Williams commissioned and edited this title.

This edition builds on the work of previous authors including **Robert Savage, Martha Ellen Zenfell, David Whelan, Lee Sentell, Renee Wright, Jay G. Harrod, Judy Pennington, Honey Naylor and Scott Faragher**.

Penny Phenix indexed this edition.

ABOUT INSIGHT GUIDES

Insight Guides have more than 45 years' experience of publishing high-quality, visual travel guides. We produce 400 full-colour titles, in both print and digital form, covering more than 200 destinations across the globe, in a variety of formats to meet your different needs.

    Insight Guides are written by local authors, whose expertise is evident in the extensive historical and cultural

background features. Each destination is carefully researched by regional experts to ensure our guides provide the very latest information. All the reviews in **Insight Guides** are independent; we strive to maintain an impartial view. Our reviews are carefully selected to guide you to the best places to eat, go out and shop, so you can be confident that when we say a place is special, we really mean it.

Legend

City maps

	Freeway/Highway/Motorway
	Divided Highway
	Main Roads
	Minor Roads
	Pedestrian Roads
	Steps
	Footpath
	Railway
	Funicular Railway
	Cable Car
	Tunnel
	City Wall
	Important Building
	Built Up Area
	Other Land
	Transport Hub
	Park
	Pedestrian Area
	Bus Station
	Tourist Information
	Main Post Office
	Cathedral/Church
	Mosque
	Synagogue
	Statue/Monument
	Beach
	Airport

Regional maps

	Freeway/Highway/Motorway (with junction)
	Freeway/Highway/Motorway (under construction)
	Divided Highway
	Main Road
	Secondary Road
	Minor Road
	Track
	Footpath
	International Boundary
	State/Province Boundary
	National Park/Reserve
	Marine Park
	Ferry Route
	Marshland/Swamp
	Glacier / Salt Lake
	Airport/Airfield
	Ancient Site
	Border Control
	Cable Car
	Castle/Castle Ruins
	Cave
	Chateau/Stately Home
	Church/Church Ruins
	Crater
	Lighthouse
	Mountain Peak
	Place of Interest
	Viewpoint

INDEX